The Evolutionary Bases
of Consumption

Marketing and Consumer Psychology Series
Curtis P. Haugtvedt, Ohio State University
Series Editor

Cele C. Otnes and Tina M. Lowrey • *Contemporary Consumption Rituals: A Research Anthology*

Gad Saad • *The Evolutionary Bases of Consumption*

For more information about books in this series, please contact Lawrence Erlbaum Associates at www.erlbaum.com

The Evolutionary Bases of Consumption

Gad Saad
Concordia University

LEA

LAWRENCE ERLBAUM ASSOCIATES, PUBLISHERS
2007   Mahwah, New Jersey   London

Lawrence Erlbaum Associates, Inc., Publishers
10 Industrial Avenue
Mahwah, New Jersey 07430
www.erlbaum.com

Cover design by Tomai Maridou

Library of Congress Cataloging-in-Publication Data

Saad, Gad.
The evolutionary bases of consumption / by Gad Saad.

p. cm.

Includes bibliographical references and index.
ISBN 0-8058-5149-6 (cloth : alk. paper)
ISBN 0-8058-5150-X (pbk. : alk. paper)
ISBN 1-4106-1630-4 (e-book : alk. paper)
1. Consumer behavior. 2. Consumption (Economics)—Psychological aspects. 3. Evolutionary psychology. 4. Consumers—Psychology. I. Title.

HF5415.32.S2 2007
339.4'701—dc22   2006030454
                                                              CIP

Books published by Lawrence Erlbaum Associates are printed on acid-free paper, and their bindings are chosen for strength and durability.

Printed in the United States of America
10 9 8 7 6 5 4 3 2 1

To Annie, my hokis

Contents

Series Foreword

Curtis Haugtvedt
Ohio State University

The goal of the Marketing and Consumer Psychology book series is to summarize and integrate existing theoretical and empirical research with the goal of stimulating new research and discussion. Gad Saad's book, *The Evolutionary Bases of Consumption*, is the newest addition to the series.

Understanding the fundamental basis of human preferences and behavior is of long-standing interest to social scientists, business practitioners, policymakers, and individual consumers. In recent years, research papers, discussions, conference sessions, and special conferences on the topic of evolution have grown in popularity.

In this book, Gad Saad argues succinctly that we gain new insights by using evolutionary perspectives as a general guide in our quest for understanding and predicting the consumption behavior of individuals and groups. Parts of this book will make a great deal of sense to practitioners, social scientists, and consumers. Parts of this book will likely be controversial and will lead to future debates and healthy discussion.

Preface

In the preface of her 1997 edited book titled *Human Nature,* Laura Betzig describes how many of the leading evolutionary psychologists were first exposed to the power of Darwinian theorizing. I have a similar story to tell. In my first semester of doctoral training at Cornell University, I took Advanced Social Psychology taught by Professor Dennis Regan. Unbeknownst to me, one of the assigned readings in that course would profoundly alter my professional career. Roughly halfway through the semester, I read *Homicide* by Martin Daly and Margo Wilson, wherein they provide a Darwinian account of criminal behavior (e.g., murders and sexual abuse). My epiphany had taken place. Though I was previously aware of Darwin's theories and had perhaps vaguely heard of sociobiology, I now realized that I had been exposed to a powerful framework for understanding human behavior.

In my doctoral dissertation, I investigated the adaptive stopping strategies that individuals use when deciding to terminate their information search and accordingly commit to a choice. In a sense, my doctoral work related to a central tenet of evolutionary theory, namely adaptability. Whereas adaptation in the context of natural selection is typically delimited to among organisms, adaptive behavior in this case occurs within organisms. Numerous evolutionists recognize that Darwinian processes function at both levels as evident in Donald T. Campbell's universal selection theory (Cziko, 1995, 2000; Heyes & Hull, 2001). Upon assuming my assistant professorship in 1994, I continued to work within the adaptive decision-making stream while solidifying my interest and expertise in evolutionary psychology and related Darwinian frameworks. I was well aware that my evolutionary focus might place me at the periphery of the consumer behavior discipline. It was one thing to be a behavioral decision theorist questioning the normative tenets of rational choice. After all, behavioral decision theorists have amassed an impressive research stream in their attacks on *Homo economicus*. Hence, my work within the adaptive decision-making literature was within a well-entrenched field. However, as an evolutionist and consumer researcher, I was treading on minimally charted territory. Though such a journey might be perilous, it affords exciting research opportunities. It is my hope that in writing this book, I can stimulate new ideas by demonstrating the relevance of evolutionary theory in understanding consumption phenomena. By exploring manners by which Darwinian processes have shaped our consuming minds, it hopefully allows us both to view familiar problems in new ways, and to identify new research streams. The current book is the culmination of my intellectual journey, which began close to 15 years ago as a young graduate student. I thank the reader for taking an interest in my ideas.

Acknowledgments

I am indebted to Professor Dennis Regan for having been the first to introduce me to the field of evolutionary psychology. Professor Jay Edward Russo, with whom I have maintained a close personal relationship long after my graduation from Cornell, possesses all of the great qualities of a mentor. Accordingly, I thank him for having provided me with the rigorous intellectual training that he did. Though he is not an evolutionist, he has always encouraged me to pursue my intellectual journey to wherever it may lead me. Professor Rajan Nataraajan, editor of *Psychology & Marketing*, deserves much credit for having recognized the relevance of evolutionary psychology to the marketing, consumer behavior, and advertising disciplines. As such, he provided me with a platform to publish some of my original papers in this field when many other editors were perhaps less receptive to the Darwinian paradigm. His support for evolutionary theorizing was such that he commissioned the first ever special issue in the marketing literature on the links between evolutionary theory and consumption (ably guest edited by Professor Donald Hantula). Professor Curt Haugtvedt, the editor of the current book series, has demonstrated unbridled enthusiasm for this project beginning with our first phone conversation. His academic pluralism has been instrumental in allowing this project to move forward. Anne Duffy, my representative at Lawrence Erlbaum, has facilitated the administrative issues inherent to seeing a scholarly book come to fruition. The diligent efforts of Sara T. Scudder and her Erlbaum colleagues during the production stage are duly noted. Research funds provided by Dean Jerry Tomberlin allowed me to hire a student assistant (Richard Sejean) for ad hoc requests (e.g., tracking down secondary sources). The Concordia library administration was kind enough to grant me expanded library privileges. I am appreciative of the four anonymous reviewers for their feedback.

For new paradigms to develop and prosper within an academic discipline typically requires a critical mass of supporters. Without the input and championing of these early adopters of a scientific innovation, it becomes onerous to diffuse the novel ideas. Accordingly, I thank my former student Professor Tripat Gill for having been a stimulating coauthor on many of my earliest papers in the field. That the pursuit of evolutionary theorizing in consumer behavior was a risky proposition for a young graduate student did not dissuade Tripat from joining my research program.

On a personal note, my companion Annie Ortchanian has provided me with all of the support that one can expect from a life partner. Whether listening to my tirades late into the night, putting up with my fluctuating stress level, or providing me with much needed assistantship, she has offered me her full and unconditional support. Her kindness and generosity know no limits. I owe much gratitude to my mother for having provided me with her love and succor throughout my studies and academic career. Finally, Amar (our Belgian sheepdog) deserves much credit for highlighting the power of symbiotic relationships, an important Darwinian mechanism for explaining interspecies altruism.

Introduction

My purpose in writing this book is simple. I hope to demonstrate that consumer behavior cannot be accurately understood, nor fully investigated without the necessary infusion of biological and Darwinian-based phenomena that have shaped our human nature. As consumers, we engage in a wide range of behaviors, most of which can ultimately be traced to one or more key Darwinian modules. We purchase products that are meant to make us attractive in the mating arena. We consume foods that appeal to our evolved gustatory preferences. We engage in gift-giving rituals that solidify family ties and reinforce bonds of friendship, both important Darwinian goals. We are drawn to alluring advertising cues (e.g., nubile and attractive women) because they correspond to evolutionarily relevant information. We succumb to "darker" consumption practices including pathological gambling, eating disorders, and pornographic addictions because of our biological heritage. From the latter examples, it should be apparent that my use of the term *consumer behavior* entails a much more exhaustive and encompassing set of behaviors than that which might typically be covered in the leading journals of the field. For example, human mating behavior is certainly subsumed within my definition of consumer behavior, as is the consumption of products of popular culture, including song lyrics, self-help books, movies, and television shows. As Holbrook (1987) has stated:

> In a sense, even if we ignore animals and plants, consumer research encompasses almost all human activities, regarded from the viewpoint of consummation. ... In other words, our lives comprise one constant and continual (though not always successful) quest for consummation. (p. 131)

It is in this all-encompassing sense that I refer to consumption practices throughout the current book. In his call for a grander definition of what constitutes consumption, Holbrook (1987) discusses macro- and micro-economics, psychology, anthropology, sociology, philosophy, and the humanities, as viable fields of inquiry within the consumption arena. Missing from his list of relevant disciplines are biology and evolutionary theory. A key objective of the current book is to highlight possible ways by which evolutionary-based frameworks can contribute to our understanding of consumption phenomena.

T. S. Kuhn (1970) proposed that radical scientific innovations occur in a discontinuous manner. In other words, to borrow the parlance of the Harvard paleontologist Stephen Jay Gould, radical scientific breakthroughs arise via punctuated equilibria rather than as a result of incrementalism within the established paradigm. The discontinuity, which gives rise to the radical scientific breakthrough, results in a paradigm shift wherein a novel worldview is created. I mention this epistemological point because the Darwinian revolution, which is well established in the natural sciences and gaining ground in the cognate social sciences, is missing in the consumer behavior discipline. As such, from the perspective of most consumer researchers, many of the points made herewith challenge the worldview espoused by the standard social science model (SSSM; see Tooby & Cosmides, 1992, for a description of the model). Does this imply that the infusion of Darwinian theory into our discipline will require a Kuhnian revolution? I do not think so, because evolutionary theory can in many instances complement the research streams of the majority of consumer scholars.

Chapter 1 introduces evolutionary psychology and contrasts it with the SSSM (Tooby & Cosmides, 1992). In doing so, it also provides a historical overview of the Darwinian-based movements leading up to the development of evolutionary psychology. Chapter 2 argues that the paucity of Darwinian-based theorizing within consumer behavior has profound implications regarding the levels of analysis and causation addressed by consumer scholars. All phenomena addressed by consumer researchers are done so at the proximate level. In other words, ultimate causation (i.e., adaptationist theorizing) is seldom if ever within the purview of the consumer scholar. The theories, models, and frameworks within the consumer behavior discipline espouse domain-independent, general-purpose mechanisms (e.g., classical conditioning) that evolutionists would challenge as unlikely to have ever evolved in such a form. I demonstrate these points by exploring specific areas that have historically been of interest to consumer researchers, including learning, motivation, culture, decision making, perception, attitudinal theories, emotion, and personality. Chapter 3 maps consumption phenomena along four key Darwinian

modules, namely the survival, reproduction, kin selection, and reciprocation modules. In other words, the key consumption habits that we engage
in are ultimately rooted in a few key innate Darwinian phenomena. Hence,
contrary to Abraham Maslow's intuitively appealing albeit empirically
unsubstantiated hierarchy of needs, the latter Darwinian modules are
rooted in universal empirical evidence spanning countless cultures and
eras. As such, Maslow's framework might be subsumed within the current
Darwinian framework, providing theoretical parsimony and consilience
in understanding consumption motives. In chapter 4, the premise that the
media is an all-powerful socialization agent is explored. As a specific case,
I explore the position that sex roles are shaped by our exposure to countless
media forms. I argue that these contents exist in their particular forms precisely because they are a manifestation of our innate human nature. Hence,
sex roles are not nearly as malleable as postulated by the tabula rasa tenet. I
then turn my attention to advertising content and demonstrate how evolutionary psychology can be used to understand the reason that ubiquitous
and universal advertising images exist in their particular forms. As a case
analysis, I explore from a Darwinian perspective the manner by which
women are depicted in advertising, and this is contrasted to the viewpoint
that advertising is dominated by patriarchal forces bent on exploiting
women. I then demonstrate how the local-versus-global strategic issue in
advertising might be tackled by using Darwinian-based theorizing to determine which advertising cues are likely universal versus those likely to
be culture-specific. Pursuing the theme developed in chapter 3 regarding
the mapping of consumption choices onto key Darwinian modules, I then
argue that many advertising slogans can be mapped onto the latter four
evolved modules. Finally, I conclude chapter 4 with a Darwinian explanation of the ubiquitous use of beauty as an advertising cue. Chapter 5 argues
that products of popular culture, including television shows, song lyrics,
soap operas, movies, self-help books, talk shows, literature, religion, and
art, exist in their particular forms because they are mirrors to our common
Darwinian heritage. I propose that the key themes in any of the latter forms
of popular culture are universal ones that transcend time and place and as
such can be mapped onto the key Darwinian modules. Chapter 6 explores
several specific instantiations of "dark-side" consumption, including the
obsessive interest in pornography, eating disorders, pathological gambling, and compulsive buying. I begin by highlighting how the majority of
such dark-side behaviors can be linked to the seven deadly sins, which
theologians have warned against since time immemorial. These deadly
sins are difficult to eradicate precisely because they are inextricably tied to
our Darwinian heritage, and hence provide an irresistible allure. Each of
the latter dark-side phenomena has a robust and universal sex-specific
morbidity suggesting a possible Darwinian etiology. In order to explore

why such maladaptive behaviors might arise, I utilize principles from various evolutionary-based fields including Darwinian medicine and Darwinian psychiatry. Finally, chapter 7 summarizes the benefits that might be achieved by incorporating evolutionary psychology within the theoretical bases of consumer behavior.

1

What Is Evolutionary Psychology?

In an important sense, there is no such thing as "evolutionary psychology" because there is no such thing as non-evolutionary psychology (after all, scientific psychologists cannot be "creationists"). Evolutionary psychology is likely to be a temporary discipline, which will exist only as long as it is needed. As psychologists of all stripes come to make explicit their currently implicit hypotheses about human nature, past selection pressures and environments of evolutionary adaptedness, evolutionary psychology will wither away as a distinct field and all psychology will be "evolutionary"—for precisely the same reason that all biology is evolutionary. Psychology is, after all, a branch of biology.

—Salmon and Symons (2003, p. 22, emphasis in original)

Historians of science have identified a list of radical scientific theories that have profoundly altered the manner by which we view the world (cf. Sulloway, 1996, for a survey of these). Four revolutionary thinkers who are ubiquitous on any such list are Copernicus, Newton, Einstein, and Darwin. Going against the prevailing theological orthodoxy, Copernicus demonstrated that the earth was not at the center of the universe. Newton developed his formulae of celestial mechanics, which could among other things, explain the orbital path of the moon around the earth. Einstein proposed a framework that challenged the manner in which we intuitively view the world. Through his theory of special relativity, he showed that both time elapsed and the length of an object are relative metrics (i.e., they are not invariant properties). Finally, Darwin's theories of natural and sexual selection explain the process that gives rise to the unimaginable biological diversity found in both the fauna and flora kingdoms. Each of the latter four theories has served as a building block within its field, be it in astrophysics, mechanics, theoretical physics, or biology. The success with which the natural sciences have been able to identify and develop such overarching frameworks has alas been lacking in the social sciences. One of the key contentions of this book is to demonstrate how Darwinian theory, specifically evolutionary psychology, can be used to unify the disparate frameworks within the field of consumer behavior.

Darwin's theory of natural selection (1859/1985) encompasses three steps, namely variation, inheritance, and selection. Random mutations result in variations within a species. If a particular mutation is beneficial to the survival of an organism, those possessing it will have a higher survival rate. Over an extended period of time and in light of the fact that the advantageous mutation is inheritable, it is selected for and subsequently becomes part of the organism's genetic endowment. In addition to natural selection, Darwin recognized that many morphological traits arise through another evolutionary mechanism, namely via sexual selection (Darwin, 1871). In such instances, traits evolve for either intrasexual combats or intersexual wooing. Hence, sexual selection operates via mate choice. Many of the original applications of evolutionary theory focused on explaining the evolution of morphological and phenotypic traits within a given species (e.g., the claw of a sand crab). That being said, Darwin himself was clear in arguing that his theories could just as easily be used to explain the evolution of behavioral dispositions. Despite his heed, the systematic application of Darwinian principles in understanding human behavior did not develop into a full-fledged field of inquiry until the recent founding of evolutionary psychology. The central tenets of evolutionary psychology are explained shortly, but prior to doing so, a brief historical exposé of some of the key Darwinian movements covering the past 80 years is provided.

HISTORICAL OVERVIEW LEADING UP
TO THE FOUNDING OF EVOLUTIONARY PSYCHOLOGY

Ethologists and behavioral ecologists were among the first scientists to systematically apply Darwinian principles to explain animal behavior. Konrad Lorenz, one of the cofounders of the field of ethology (behavioral biology), studied both aggression and parental imprinting as evolved behaviors. He went on to describe the phenomenon of fixed action patterns, namely instinctual behaviors that when begun are carried through to their completion (i.e., they cannot be aborted). Nikko Tinbergen, a student of Lorenz with whom he coshared a Nobel Prize in 1973 (along with Karl von Frisch), proposed that ethology addresses four levels of analyses. First, ethologists might be interested in causation, namely exploring the mechanisms that cause a behavior to take place. Second, they can explore ontogenetic issues, that is, the manner by which a species-specific behavior develops within a given individual of that species. Third, they might address the phylogenetic roots of a behavior, namely the manner by which the behavior has evolved.

Finally, they can explore the adaptive function that a particular behavior serves, that is, its survival value. Tinbergen coined his now famous acronym ABCDEF to capture these levels of analyses (Animal Behavior Causation Development Evolution Function). These four layers notwithstanding, in reality most ethologists have worked within the levels of causation and development (Alcock, 2001). Hence, though evolutionary theory serves as a backdrop for the ethologists' theorizing, they have not as often addressed the two layers of analyses most directly linked to the Darwinian framework, namely evolution and function.

Though ethologists apply a wide range of methodologies to test their theories, most often they observe behavior in a naturalistic environment. Behavioral ecologists on the other hand typically develop mathematical models of optimal behavior within a given ecological niche and subsequently test it empirically. For example, optimal foraging theory explains how animals choose their food acquisition strategies (cf. Krebs & Davies, 1987). Specifically, it is assumed that animals gauge the trade-offs between the costs and benefits of the available foraging or hunting strategies and accordingly choose the optimal one (i.e., the one that yields the best trade-off) given the particular environmental constraints. As such, the objective is to explain a particular behavior as an evolved response to a given ecological niche or environmental reality. Not surprisingly, given the focus on optimality, behavioral ecologists have frequently relied on the normative game theoretic approach as originally developed by Maynard Smith (1982). Not only do behavioral ecologists explore interspecies adaptations to local niches, but also they investigate intraspecies variations as adaptive solutions to local environments. This is perhaps one of the most notable differences between ethology and behavioral ecology, namely that the latter discipline much more so than the former focuses on intraspecific variations in behavior.

By the 1960s, despite the successes reaped from the Modern Synthesis achieved in the 1930s and the 1940s (integrating natural selection with Mendelian mechanisms of inheritance), Darwinian theory still faced several vexing problems. First, there were considerable controversies regarding the level at which natural selection operates. Does natural selection operate on the gene, the individual organism, the group, the population, or the species (see L. Keller, 1999, for multiple-level approaches to selection; see also Sober & Wilson, 1998)? Two related problems that ultimately were linked to the latter question dealt with altruistic behavior toward kin and perhaps more puzzling altruistic behavior between unrelated individuals. If individuals were selfish in their Darwinian pursuits, why would they ever engage in altruistic acts? Up until George Williams' (1966) eloquent albeit nonmathematical refutation of group selection, the standard argument proposed that although an altruistic act might be costly to the individual engaging in it, it was beneficial to the group. William Hamilton provided the definitive formal model demonstrating that natural selection operates at the gene level. Specifically, he defined the notion of inclusive fitness, which measures an individual's reproductive success in terms of not only the number of offspring produced by the individual but also those produced by his or her kin. Up until Hamilton's (1964) pioneering work, Darwinian fitness explicitly assumed that selection operated on the individual level, because the number of offspring produced by a given organism solely measured reproductive success. Hamilton's kin selection model operates at the gene level by arguing that an organism's inclusive fitness (i.e., ultimate Darwinian success) can be augmented by engaging in behaviors that promote its own reproductive fitness and those of its genetically related individuals (i.e., the crucial unit of selection is the gene). Simply put, his model considers three factors that are necessary to establish whether or not an altruistic act will be selected for. First, there are the benefits accrued to the altruist for engaging in the act. Second, by performing the act, the altruist incurs a set of associated costs. Third, the genetic relatedness between the altruist and the recipient of the act serves as a good predictor of the likelihood of engaging in the act. The measure of genetic relatedness, r, can be construed as the average number of genes shared by two individuals. Hamilton's model posits that an altruistic act between kin could be selected for as long as the benefits to the altruist multiplied by r is greater than the associated costs accrued to the altruist. Dawkins (1976, 1982) has provided extensive treatises in support of gene-level selection, of which kin selection is one such example.

Kin selection provides the mathematical and theoretical support for the old adage that "blood is thicker than water." That being said, what possible explanation other than group selection could explain altruistic acts between unrelated individuals? Trivers (1971) solved the problem with the development of his theory of reciprocal altruism. Imagine two unrelated individuals foraging for food during the Pleistocene era. Both individuals would have faced a recurring environment of caloric scarcity and caloric uncertainty that would have profoundly affected their survival likelihood. One means to reduce the dangers associated with such a harsh environment would have been to engage in a reciprocal arrangement of food sharing. This would have reduced the variance of daily caloric intake resulting in an increased chance of survival to all those engaging in this arrangement. Hence, what might at first appear as unselfish and altruistic behavior, beneficial to all group members, can easily be construed as self-serving in that engaging in such altruistic behavior improves one's chances of survival. Trivers' theory provides the conditions under which reciprocal altruism could be selected for, a topic to which I return in chapter 3.

By the mid-1970s, evolutionists had developed a wide arsenal for understanding animal behavior and had generated a substantial and varied literature of findings, all of which were commonly linked via their adherence to Darwinian-based theorizing. E. O. Wilson cataloged the extant literature in his mammoth book titled *Sociobiology* (1975). Sociobiology sought to apply Darwinian principles to explain the evolution of social behavior, of which both kin selection and reciprocal altruism are examples. Wilson's extraordinary feat lay in his ability to collect and analyze such a rich literature within the confines of a single book.

To recapitulate, the past eight decades have seen the proliferation of several disciplines that have each applied evolutionary-based theorizing in studying behavior. These include ethology, behavioral ecology, and sociobiology, all of which have historically focused to a much greater extent on animal behavior. Offshoots of the latter disciplines have sought to apply the Darwinian frameworks in investigating human behavior. These include human ethology (cf. Eibl-Eibesfeldt, 1989), human behavioral ecology (cf. Winterhalder & Smith, 2000), and human sociobiology (cf. Alcock, 2001, chap. 8; the last chapter in E. O. Wilson, 1975). Some scholars have amalgamated all of these approaches under the rubric of Darwinian anthropology (cf. Cartwright, 2000, p. 49). Though differences do exist between each of these approaches, the boundaries are not well delineated. By the early 1990s, the ground was fertile for the founding of evolutionary psychology, the latest discipline to contribute to the Darwinian revolution. The interested reader is referred to Laland and Brown (2002) for a comprehensive review and comparison of many of the key Darwinian-based movements.

WHAT IS EVOLUTIONARY PSYCHOLOGY?

Evolutionary psychology posits that the human mind has evolved via natural and sexual selection, a point that Darwin had originally alluded to. Hence, in the same way that our liver and kidneys have evolved to solve very specific survival problems, many of the affective, cognitive, and conative components defining the human experience have been forged by the same selection mechanisms. In the same manner that bodily organs are function-specific (e.g., the heart pumps blood), the human mind has evolved a set of domain-specific Darwinian modules, as adaptive solutions to recurrent survival problems. Some of these problems include gathering food, avoiding predators, finding and retaining mates, protecting and investing in kin, and building and maintaining friendships, coalitions, and social networks. Evolutionary psychologists fix the relevant time of adaptation to the Pleistocene era, also coined the Environment of Evolutionary Adaptedness (EEA; Tooby & Cosmides, 1992). Hence, cognitive mechanisms that universally manifest themselves in today's environment are in actuality cognitive adaptations to survival problems that *Homo sapiens* have faced in the evolutionarily relevant past. This approach is somewhat different from that taken by Darwinian anthropologists and human behavioral ecologists, for these explore adaptive behavior to current differences in ecological niches (cf. Cartwright, 2000, p. 49; Laland & Brown, 2002, pp. 132–145). In other words, whereas evolutionary psychologists construe current universal behaviors as adaptations to ancestral environments, other Darwinists explore current behaviors as adaptations to current environments. In reality, both approaches are perfectly in line with the Darwinian framework (Cartwright, 2000). We are indeed products of cumulative adaptations rooted in an evolutionary past while at the same time having evolved the behavioral plasticity that would allow us to adapt to changes in local environments. This is precisely one of the key distinctions between among-organism Darwinian selection and within-organism Darwinian selection (cf. Cziko, 2000).

Given that adaptations are by definition those that maximize fitness, does this imply that humans consciously engage in behaviors that maximize theirs? The differential response to this question defines one of the key differences between most human sociobiologists and evolutionary psychologists (Buss, 1995). In the same vein that classical economists view all purposeful behaviors as a manifestation of utility maximization, human sociobiologists often construe behaviors as conscious and deliberate fitness maximizing. The position espoused by evolutionary psychologists is well captured by David Buss (1995) wherein he states:

> Humans are living fossils—collections of mechanisms produced by prior selection pressures operating on a long and unbroken line of ancestors. Today we activate and execute these specific mechanisms, but we do not have some domain-general goal, either consciously or unconsciously, to maximize the replication of our genes relative to others. (p. 10)

For example, evolutionary psychologists recognize that many evolved behavioral and cognitive dispositions are maladaptive in today's environment precisely because these adaptations were relevant in an ancestral environment that might be radically different from the current one. The universal preference for fatty and sweet foods, for instance, is an adaptation to the ancestral environment, wherein caloric scarcity and caloric uncertainty were the norm. This gustatory preference coupled with unfettered gorging is maladaptive in today's plentiful environment. See Tooby and Cosmides (1990) for additional details regarding how current behaviors are manifestations of past adaptations.

Over the past 15 years, the evolutionary psychology framework with its focus on domain-specific Darwinian modules has been applied in numerous disparate areas. These include but are not limited to human mating, parent–child conflicts, gustatory preferences, landscape preferences, war and ethnic strife, sexual abuse, rape, homicide, gestational morning sickness, sibling rivalry, gift giving, language acquisition, fears, and phobias (cf. Barkow, Cosmides, & Tooby, 1992, for the seminal edited book describing many of these studies, and Buss, 2005, for the most recent handbook of the discipline). Despite its increased acceptance in a wide range of fields, evolutionary psychology continues to be ignored by most social scientists in part due to various erroneous epistemological criticisms and ideological-based concerns. Charges have included that the discipline espouses racist, sexist, and/or atheistic doctrines, supports genetic and/or behavioral determinism, posits unfalsifiable theories, generates fanciful post hoc just-so stories using a greedy form of ultra-adaptationist thinking (or Panglossianism according to the late Stephen Jay Gould), and holds a grossly reductionist view of human phenomena. Numerous evolutionists have expended considerable effort addressing each of these issues, a subset of which includes G. C. Williams (1966), Tooby and Cosmides (1989), Dawkins (1976, 1991), Segerstråle (2001), Pinker (2002), Andrews, Gangestad, and Matthews (2002), Ketelaar and Ellis (2000), Conway and Schaller (2002), Leger, Kamil, and French (2001), and Hagen (2005).

Given that over the past 100 years, many scholars have abdicated our biological and Darwinian heritage, what is their alternate framework for understanding human behavior? The answer lies in the all-encompassing standard social science model (SSSM; Tooby & Cosmides, 1992), which consists of several fields of inquiry, including many of the leading schools of thought in 20th-century American anthropology, sociology, and psychology, all of which espouse several points in common. First, it is argued that culture cannot be broken down into smaller units of analysis. It simply exists sui generis. Second, social phenomena must be explained using units of analyses at the social level. Hence, to try to explain a social phenomenon using the minds of those individuals comprising the group can lead to the onerous accusation of being a reductionist. Third, by rejecting biology as an explicative force in shaping human behavior, the SSSM effectively rejects the idea of a universal human nature. Fourth, human behavior is thought to be unconstrained in its malleability as it is assumed that humans are born with empty-slate or tabula rasa minds (cf. Pinker, 2002). Socialization forces (of which culture is one such example) subsequently shape each individual based on his or her idiosyncratic life experiences. In addition to these key divisions between the Darwinian-based evolutionary psychology framework and the SSSM, two other crucial differences define the schism between the two paradigms. First, much of the theorizing within the evolutionary psychology framework seeks to address the ultimate origins of a particular phenomenon (i.e., the adaptive roots) whereas the SSSM has almost completely focused on proximate mechanisms. Second, whereas evolutionary psychology posits that the human mind is comprised of domain-specific context-dependent modules, the SSSM argues that domain-general context-independent processes guide human behavior (Tooby & Cosmides, 1992). These two distinctions are expounded on in the ensuing two sections.

Proximate Versus Ultimate Explanations

Tinbergen's (1963) definition of the four levels at which ethological questions can be posed is a good starting point in explaining the difference between proximate-level and ultimate-level explanations. As previously mentioned, the four layers used to explain animal behavior are causation, development, evolution, and function. The first two levels constitute issues at the proximate level whereas the latter two are at the ultimate level. Specifically, proximate questions address *how* mechanisms operate and *what* factors influence the workings of such mechanisms. Ultimate questions seek to identify *why* a particular behavior, cognition, emotion, or morphological trait has evolved to its current form (in a Darwinian adaptive sense). A few examples should clarify this crucial distinction.

When a pregnant woman experiences pregnancy sickness, hormonal and physiological variables drive this dreadfully unpleasant experience. Physiologists and anatomists will typically address issues dealing with pregnancy sickness at the proximate level. For example, *how* do a woman's hormonal levels affect her propensity to suffer from pregnancy sickness? *What* are the triggers that will increase the likelihood of experiencing nausea associated with pregnancy sickness? All such questions address the inner workings of this medical condition; hence they focus on proximate issues. On the other hand, evolutionists would seek to understand the evolutionary roots of the condition. In other words, to the extent that this is a ubiquitous physiological reaction experienced by countless women spanning cultures and eras, it might confer some adaptive benefits. Profet (1992) has shown that pregnancy sickness is an adaptation to the possible ingestion of toxins (teratogens) during the critical parts of a child's formation. Specifically, the period during which pregnancy sickness typically lasts roughly corresponds to human organogenesis, namely the embryonic period when the key organs are forming. Hence, the evolved physiological reaction of vomiting is an adaptive response that expels consumed toxins that might otherwise harm the developing fetus. If one were to poll 1,000 physicians, few if any would likely be aware of the ultimate evolutionary origins of pregnancy sickness. If anything, medicine has often sought to alleviate symptoms that are otherwise adaptive and that actually confer great benefits to the sufferer. For example, women who experience pregnancy sickness are less likely to suffer a miscarriage compared to those pregnant women that do not experience this unpleasant period. In a similar vein, Nesse and Williams (1996) discuss findings showing that if mild symptoms associated with a cold infection are left untreated, the recovery period is quicker (see also Berlim & Abeche, 2001). The ultimate (i.e., Darwinian) explanation is quite simple. The human body has evolved a set of adaptive reactions when faced with a viral invasion, including fever (which induces sweating), coughing, and a running nose. Each of these responses expels a small viral load from the body. Hence, to the extent that the unpleasant symptoms are left untreated, cold sufferers recover more quickly. Needless to say, both academic medicine and commercial medicine (e.g., pharmaceutical companies) have focused almost exclusively on the proximate mechanisms associated with human diseases.

The aforementioned examples demonstrate the difference between proximate and ultimate explanations within the physiological realm. In the ensuing paragraphs, additional examples are provided from the behavioral realm, namely those most directly relevant to evolutionary psychology. There does not exist a culture wherein men have consistently been more sexually restrained and coy than their female counterparts, despite Margaret Mead's intrepid and persistent efforts to prove otherwise with her field expeditions among the Samoans (see Freeman, 1999, for a caustic attack on Mead's research). The academic literature is replete with proximate explanations to explain this ubiquitous sex difference in mating behavior. The most frequently espoused view is that sexual behavior is learned. For example, it is argued that the pink-dressed doll and the blue tractor truck offered to young girls and young boys respectively begins a process of socialization that will leave an indelible mark on the subsequent sex roles that these children will occupy as adults. Evolutionary psychology provides ultimate explanations for universal, persistent, and seemingly unshakeable sex differences in mating behavior (cf. Buss, 1994, for a thorough summary of some of the key findings; see Symons, 1979, for perhaps the original account of human sexuality from an evolutionary perspective).

A central tenet of evolutionary psychology is that sex differences should arise in those domains wherein men and women have faced different adaptive and survival problems. For example, men and women react in the same manner when infected by a cold virus. Evolutionarily speaking, this is because both sexes have faced this particular adaptive problem (viral infection) and have accordingly developed the same evolved physiological defenses. On the other hand, when it comes to reproductive behaviors, the two sexes face drastically different survival problems. Men produce hundreds of millions of spermatozoa per day whereas women ovulate at most 400 times between the onset of menarche and the start of menopause. Hence, an ovum is astoundingly more precious than sperm. This inequality in the importance of the male and female gametes drives the differential behaviors of the two sexes. From the perspective of reproductive fitness, a male benefits from engaging in numerous mating dalliances (can impregnate many women with easily reproduced gametes) whereas in light of the dearth of ova women must be extremely judicious in their mating choices. Furthermore, whereas men's contribution to parenting could be as small as a brief sexual encounter, women bear the costs of gestation and lactation, face the dangers of childbearing (associated with high mortality in the ancestral environment), and are exposed to increased environmental threats associated with reduced mobility when pregnant.

Trivers' (1972) parental investment hypothesis was the first to argue that the differential costs and benefits of mating should translate into clear differences in mating behavior. His hypothesis was even more sweeping in that it posited specific sex differences in mating behaviors *across* species. Specifically, he argued that in any given species, the sex that bears the greater parental costs is sexually choosier. In the majority of species including *Homo sapiens*, females lose more by investing in an "inferior" suitor; correspondingly, they are more sexually choosy. That being said, in rare species where males provide greater parental investment (typically occurs in species with external fertilization and/or incubation), sexual behaviors are exactly reversed. Males are coyer, choosier, and in many cases smaller than their female counterparts. Hence, sexual roles are not mysteriously imposed. Rather, there are ultimate forces (i.e., Darwinian roots) that guide sexual behaviors as well as the socialization forces that shape these.

Why are men so unforgiving of cuckoldry? One proximate explanation is that the greater testosterone level in men induces them to react more violently when faced with the infidelity of a spouse. Numerous additional proximate explanations exist, albeit none addresses the ultimate origins of this cross-culturally invariant reality of the male psyche. The ultimate explanation for men's intolerance of cuckoldry is simple. *Homo sapiens* did not evolve with the assurances of DNA paternity testing. The most egregious attack on a man's genetic interests would be to invest in the offspring of another man. Daly and Wilson (1988) provide compelling data demonstrating that male sexual jealousy and its ugly consequences (battery, spousal homicide) are triggered by suspicions of infidelity or realized infidelities (see also Daly, Wilson, & Weghorst, 1982). Hence, men have evolved behaviors (leaving a cheating spouse), cognitions (preference for nonpromiscuous long-term mates), and emotions (extreme sexual jealousy) as a means of combating the threats of paternity uncertainty. Note how both proximate and ultimate explanations coexist in explaining the phenomenon in question.

Countless legal, moral, and religious edicts covering a heterogeneous set of cultures and spanning several millennia of human culture are similar in their contents when stipulating codes of sexual conduct. It would be an extraordinary coincidence that all of these cultures evolved the same set of governing norms by chance. Evolutionary psychology provides an ultimate explanation for the generation of such cultural norms of conduct. It is insufficient to argue that a reality exists because of cultural learning. This is a tautological explanation. One must explain the genesis and the specific form of cultural learning. As Tooby and Cosmides (1992) explain, learning is to proponents of the SSSM what "protoplasm" (a mysterious life substance) was to past biologists (p. 122). They then add:

> "Learning" is a name given to the unknown agent imagined to cause a large and heterogeneous set of functional outcomes. This name was (and is) then used as an explanation for results that remained in genuine need for an explanation. (p. 123)

The ethologist Konrad Lorenz was well aware of the evolutionary constraints that are imposed on learning processes (Laland & Brown, 2002). For example, an animal that is exposed to various schedules of reinforcements will learn more quickly if the particular form of learning is congruent with the phylogenetic history of its species (cf. Cziko, 2000, pp. 142–144). This notion is congruent with that espoused by E. O. Wilson via his epigenetic rules, which drive gene-culture coevolution (cf. E. O. Wilson, 1998). Evolutionary theories provide ultimate explanations for the specific contents of cultural learning as well as the evolutionary constraints on learning processes. The evolutionary psychiatrist Randolph Nesse (1990) has stated, "The necessity for both proximate and evolutionary explanations is well accepted in biology, but it still elicits raised eyebrows elsewhere" (p. 265). By tackling phenomena at both the proximate and ultimate levels, consumer researchers will likely ameliorate their understanding of consumption phenomena.

By conducting a content analysis of various legal and moral codes, one can identify the ultimate Darwinian roots driving a particular rule of conduct. For example, Hammurabi's Code (named after the Babylonian ruler) consisting of 282 laws is the oldest known legal code dating to approximately 4,000 years ago, making it older than Mosaic law. Several of the laws deal with adultery, chastity, infertility, and incest in manners that are well in line with evolutionary psychology. A few of the relevant codes are listed next, as translated by King (1915a, 1915b):

128- If a man take a woman to wife, but have no intercourse with her, this woman is no wife to him.

129- If a man's wife be surprised (in flagrante delicto) with another man, both shall be tied and thrown into the water, but the husband may pardon his wife and the king his slaves.

130- If a man violate the wife (betrothed or child-wife) of another man, who has never known a man, and still lives in her father's house, and sleep with her and be surprised, this man shall be put to death, but the wife is blameless.

131- If a man bring a charge against one's wife, but she is not surprised with another man, she must take an oath and then may return to her house.

135- If a man be taken prisoner in war and there be no sustenance in his house and his wife go to another house and bear children; and if later her husband return and come to his home: then this wife shall return to her husband, but the children follow their father.

155- If a man betroth a girl to his son, and his son have intercourse with her, but he (the father) afterward defile her, and be surprised, then he shall be bound and cast into the water (drowned).

156- If a man betroth a girl to his son, but his son has not known her, and if then he defile her, he shall pay her half a gold mina, and compensate her for all that she brought out of her father's house. She may marry the man of her heart.

157- If any one be guilty of incest with his mother after his father, both shall be burned.

Code 128 recognizes that the reproductive act defines a human mating pair (Darwinian fitness). Code 129 explicitly states that cuckoldry is a capital offense (protection against paternity uncertainty). Code 130 recognizes that because chastity is a desired trait in women (insurance against paternity uncertainty), a man that "steals" this valuable insurance is punishable by death. Code 131 highlights the fact that proofs of cuckoldry are difficult to obtain unless the cheating spouse is caught in the act (paternity certainty is difficult to gauge). Code 135 explicitly states that a man should not have to invest in the offspring of another when it is clear that he is not the father. Code 157 recognizes the dangers of incestuous couplings (one of the reasons for the evolution of sex is to create a heterogeneous gene pool). Finally, Codes 155 and 156 stipulate different penalties on a father if he defiles his son's woman. The penalties are contingent on the chastity status of the woman. At first glance, it might appear paradoxical that the penalty is less severe if the woman is a virgin. This appears counterintuitive given the premium that men have historically placed on chastity. However, from a paternity certainty perspective, this makes perfect sense. Sleeping with a woman who has yet to take a man does not trigger any paternity uncertainty (as long as the woman does not sleep with another). However, if the son has already mated with the woman prior to her dalliance with the father, this creates the condition for paternity uncertainty (a much more serious threat from an evolutionary perspective), resulting in the harsher penalty.

Similar codes exist in countless societies and religions. For example, in Judaism, one's religion is passed via the mother precisely because one can never be certain as to who the father is. In Shariah law (Islamic religious code), very stiff penalties are dispensed to women adulterers (e.g., the recent and highly contentious case in Nigeria). *Crime passionel* is an accepted defense in many countries. Specifically, if a man catches his wife in flagrante delicto (i.e., in the act) and causes her injury or even death, he can be legally acquitted (cf. 19th-century France or current-day Brazil). This does not imply that such practices should be condoned or are justifiable from an evolutionary perspective. Rather, it suggests that to the extent that these patterns recur across eras and cultures, evolutionary psychologists seek to understand the ultimate roots of these behaviors. Dickemann (1979) has argued that many practices such as foot binding (in China), sequestering (e.g., in harems), and modest dress codes (under Shariah) are meant to ensure chastity, thus increasing a man's paternity certainty. Strassmann (1992, 1996) proposed that women's sequestration during their menses are quite similar cross-culturally and serve as honest signals of their reproductive states, thus augmenting men's paternity certainty. Other Draconian practices meant to control women's sexuality including the wearing of a chastity belt and the dreadful practices of infibulation and clitoridectomy can be found in numerous cultures. Each of the latter historical examples is rooted in a common Darwinian heritage, which by definition transcends time and place. The Spanish philosopher José Ortega y Gasset famously asserted that "man has no nature; what he has is history" (as quoted in Pinker, 2002, p. 24). He was incorrect. The history of our species is a manifestation of our human nature. Human history does not lie outside human nature; rather, it occurs in part because of it.

Domain-Specific Versus General-Purpose Modules

Tooby and Cosmides (1992) provide an exhaustive discussion of this defining difference between the two approaches. Evolutionary psychology views the mind as consisting of domain-specific context-dependent modules that have evolved to solve precise survival problems. The SSSM, on the other hand, sees the mind as an amalgamation of domain-general context-independent algorithms and mental processes. For example, according to behaviorism, all learning arises from associations between stimuli and the corresponding responses. These mechanisms are hypothesized to be operative in explaining learning processes across a slew of unrelated tasks and domains. Skinnerian conditioning not only can explain how an animal learns a given schedule of reinforcement for obtaining food but also can be used to explain how consumers are shaped into becoming loyal customers. Similarly, Pavlovian conditioning not only is operative in addressing how a dog learns to salivate at the sound of a bell but also is equally relevant in assessing how consumers learn to associate the consumption of Marlboro cigarettes with being rugged and masculine. Thus, according to most proponents of the SSSM, a given mental process is sufficiently general as to transcend contexts and tasks. The latter proponents do not provide an explanation for the genesis of a given general-purpose mechanism. This yields a contradiction. Proponents of the SSSM adhere to the tabula rasa tenet, namely that humans are born with an empty slate that is infinitely malleable. At the same time, they espouse theories that assume the a priori existence of general-purpose machinery.

Though behaviorism is perhaps the most often cited example of a general-purpose domain-independent theory, countless others exist within the SSSM realm. Cognitive psychologists rejected the antimentalism of behaviorism by specifically developing a research paradigm that sought to look inside the metaphorical black box. Viewing human behavior as nothing more than the mapping of stimuli to the appropriate responses was seen as too simplistic, especially when dealing with higher order purposive behavior. That said, the proximate mechanisms that cognitive psychologists developed also espoused mechanisms that were general-purpose and domain-independent. Early in the cognitive revolution, the human mind was construed as a serial Von Neumann information processor. This spawned the information-processing revolution so fully diffused within the consumer behavior literature (see the discussion in chap. 2). More recently, biologically inspired frameworks such as parallel-distributed models (e.g., connectionism) have usurped the cognitive limelight. According to this more recent view, learning is contained within the synaptic paths of an artificial neural network. As such, all learning is modeled as the reorganization of the weights assigned to the paths within a neural network. For each of the latter two cognitive movements, a given architectural and algorithmic process is conjured to explain a varied set of cognitive phenomena irrespective of the context. An architectural structure of the mind is adopted (e.g., serial vs. parallel processor) with subsequent theorizing proposing general-purpose domain-independent processes in line with the chosen structure.

One of the most pervasive of all general-purpose content-independent algorithmic modules is the *cost–benefit* framework. I conducted a keyword search of the term *cost–benefit* on ABI/INFORM (on October 29, 2003), which yielded 1,150 hits within peer-reviewed journals. A perusal of the titles and abstracts of the most recent 230 articles (i.e., 20% of the hits) revealed that the cost–benefit framework has been used in explaining a heterogeneous set of decisions. The cost–benefit framework was utilized to investigate how individuals choose a risky diet. It was also used to understand how individuals choose a decision rule to use (effort–accuracy) and how much information to acquire. The framework was also applied to investigate how individuals decide whether or not to be whistle-blowers, and whether or not they should engage in ethical decision making. It was employed to understand one's desire for inaction (maintaining the status quo) and one's proactive actions (e.g., complaining as a consumer). Finally, the cost–benefit framework has been used in exploring the decision to use a decision model, and has been applied in conducting a cost–benefit analysis of cost–benefit analyses. This epitomizes the domain-independent and general-purpose approach; namely, the cost–benefit framework becomes a master key, capable of explaining countless decisional processes in innumerable domains.

To recapitulate, evolutionary psychology views the mind as consisting of Darwinian modules that have each evolved to solve very specific survival problems. Accordingly, the process by which the mind adaptively solves one problem is not necessarily transferable to another domain (see Hirschfeld & Gelman, 1994, for examples of domain-specific theorizing across a wide range of cognitive tasks). For example, the cognitive tasks employed when identifying a prospective suitor are different from those used when avoiding predators. Evolutionists have accordingly defined four key Darwinian modules, namely the survival (e.g., preference for fatty and sweet foods), reproductive (attracting and retaining a mate), kin selection (investing in one's kin), and reciprocation (forming and building friendships and coalitions) modules (cf. McGuire & Troisi, 1998). The interested reader is referred to Samuels (2000) for a comparison of various views of the mind's modularity, including those espoused by Jerome Fodor and Noam Chomsky. He concludes that the modular view of the human mind as developed within evolutionary psychology appears very promising. In chapter 3, consumption choices specific to each of the four Darwinian modules are highlighted.

Some evolutionary-minded scholars have argued that the domain-specificity position has been oversold and have accordingly questioned the so-called massive modularity hypothesis (cf. Samuels, 1998). These scholars typically propose that although it is indeed true that domain-specific modules are integral to understanding the human mind, it is equally important to recognize the fact that domain-general mechanisms are likely to have evolved as part of our innate repertoire of mental modules (cf. MacDonald, 1991).

Chiappe and MacDonald (2005) have proposed that general intelligence is a good example of a domain-general module precisely because it permits one to solve novel problems that by definition do not have domain-specific modules dedicated to solve them. Interestingly, Kanazawa (2004a) has challenged the latter position by arguing that general intelligence can indeed be construed as a domain-specific adaptation. Notwithstanding the latter debate, the more general point is that both domain-specific and domain-general modules exist within the human mind. Survival problems that were recurrent in the EEA (cf. Tooby & Cosmides, 1992) have resulted in the evolution of domain-specific modules to solve such challenges. On the other hand, given that not all survival challenges are perfectly predictable and recurring (as to allow for a precise adaptive solution), natural selection should have also selected for domain-general modules. This is the case with our immune system, which has evolved to be flexible and adaptable in combating new pathogens. In other words, it has evolved adaptability (i.e., its Darwinian adaptation is to be adaptable) because it must deal with an uncertain future (cf. Cziko, 2000). If the immune system had been fully specified (i.e., with no degrees of freedom) in responding solely to a very specific set of pathogens, one can imagine that a rapidly mutating bacterium or virus could easily defeat the otherwise inflexible and rigid immune system. On the other hand, our gustatory preferences for fatty and sweet foods constitute a domain-specific adaptation precisely because they are a solution to the same and recurring selection pressures found in all relevant EEAs (i.e., caloric scarcity and caloric uncertainty). In other words, gustatory preferences are less adaptable (as evidenced by their maladaptive nature in the current environments of plenty). Accordingly, a parsimonious evolutionary-based theory of the mind must include both domain-general and domain-specific processing as integral components, with the brain using a meta-algorithm to decide when to use which type of processing.

CHAPTER SUMMARY

Natural and sexual selection explain, in an accurate, parsimonious, and consilient manner, the rich biological diversity that defines all living organisms. The Darwinian revolution has spawned numerous fields of inquiry, each interested in understanding the vast array of human behaviors. These include ethology, behavioral ecology, Darwinian anthropology, sociobiology, gene-culture coevolution modeling, memetics, and most recently, the founding of evolutionary psychology. Despite the vast diffusion of Darwinian theories across countless scientific domains, the social sciences have historically abdicated biology and evolutionary theory as relevant forces in shaping human behaviors and social phenomena. Instead, most social scientists adhere to the foundational tenets of the SSSM with its exclusive focus on culture, learning, socialization, domain-general mental mechanisms, and proximate issues. On the other hand, evolutionary psychology posits that the human mind is comprised of domain-specific modules that are adaptive solutions to challenges that *Homo sapiens* has recurringly faced in its environment of evolutionary adaptedness. As such, evolutionary psychology is typically concerned with ultimate causation rather than proximate phenomena.

Although the field of consumer behavior has amassed an impressive database of empirical findings, it has done so with minimal input from evolutionary-based theorists. However, a great majority of our consumption choices are manifestations of our innate human nature, which has been shaped by a long evolutionary process. Accordingly, evolutionary theory can enrich our discipline by proposing different ways for tackling existing phenomena, and/or identifying novel research streams that might have been difficult to isolate without the appropriate evolutionary lens.

In the next chapter, I explore many of the key areas of interest to consumer researchers (e.g., perception, decision making, attitudinal formation, and culture) and demonstrate how they all share two common elements, namely the focus on proximate phenomena and the espousing of domain-general mental mechanisms. I hope to show that the introduction of evolutionary theory into each of the key subareas of consumer research can complement the existing research traditions.

2

Consumer Research: Domain-General and Proximate-Level Theorizing

These days, to study any animal species while refusing to consider the evolved adaptive significance of their behavior would be considered pure folly. That is, of course, unless the species in question is Homo sapiens. *Graduate students training to study this particular primate species may never take a single course in evolutionary theory. ... These methodologically sophisticated students then embark on a career studying human aggression, cooperation, mating behavior, family relationships, or altruism with little or no understanding of the general evolutionary forces and principles that shaped the behaviors they are investigating.*

—Kenrick and Simpson (1997, p. 1, emphasis in original)

Of all multidisciplinary fields, perhaps none is more so than the consumer behavior discipline. The consumption context provides one of the most fertile forums within which the rich tapestry of human behaviors is fully displayed. Cognate disciplines within the social sciences that bear a direct influence on consumer behavior include economics, psychology, sociology, and anthropology. These can further be broken down into several subdisciplines of relevance to consumer behavior. For example, within psychology, relevant subdisciplines include behaviorism, cognitive psychology, developmental psychology, cross-cultural psychology, social psychology, and clinical psychology. Notably absent from any such list are Darwinian-based frameworks and fields, including human ethology, human behavioral ecology, human sociobiology, Darwinian anthropology, and evolutionary psychology. Recently, Wilkie and Moore (2003) provided a historical overview of marketing thought over the past 100 years as broken down into four distinct eras. The eras might have varied on how much focus was placed on the commodity, institutional, and functional approaches. Similarly, different eras might have paid greater or lesser attention to the economics, motivational, or information-processing (i.e., cognitive) approaches. However, what is common across all four eras is the absence of biology and evolutionary theory as relevant forces in understanding marketing and consumption phenomena. Given the increasing acceptance of evolutionary theory in both the natural and social sciences, this is perhaps surprising. As such, my goal in the current chapter is to propose ways by which evolutionary psychology might be useful to the consumer behavior discipline by exploring specific subdisciplines that have historically interested consumer scholars.

PROXIMATE MODELS UTILIZING DOMAIN-INDEPENDENT GENERAL-PURPOSE MECHANISMS

Many of the substantive areas explored by consumer scholars share two things in common. Phenomena are investigated at the proximate level via the espousing of domain-independent, general-purpose mechanisms (i.e., evolutionary-based domain-specificity is not explored). Recent reviews of the consumer psychology discipline by Tybout and Artz (1994), as well as of the consumer behavior field by Jacoby, Johar, and Morrin (1998), Simonson, Carmon, Dhar, Drolet, and Nowlis (2001), and Ekström (2003) did not identify any ultimate-based theories. Incidentally, when the term *domain-specific* is used in consumer behavior, it is used in the opposite manner than that implied in evolutionary psychology. In consumer behavior, affect or information processing are examples of domain-specific research. Note that the definition of domain-specificity in consumer behavior is in line with general-purpose domain-independent machinery. For example, the same affective process is thought to transcend across substantive domains just as a given information-processing mechanism can be applied across contexts. As previously mentioned, domain-specificity in evolutionary psychology refers to a specific adaptive mechanism within an evolutionarily relevant domain. Hence, sexual jealousy is a domain-specific adaptive emotion that is triggered within the context of the mating module.

In support of the points raised in the previous paragraph, I analyze several substantive areas of relevance to consumer scholars including learning, motivation, culture, decision making, perception, attitude formation and attitude change, emotions, and personality. I hope to show that the infusion of evolutionary theory can augment the explanatory power of our discipline, notwithstanding the substantial advances achieved by consumer scholars in each of the latter areas.

Learning

Consumer researchers studying learning have typically focused on the following types of proximate questions:

1. How does a consumer learn relevant information?
2. What are some factors that facilitate or hinder the consumer's ability to learn information?
3. How is consumer learning measured?

The models that have been proposed to address these issues have been general-purpose domain-independent mechanisms. Most evolutionists would propose that learning processes should correspond to adaptive solutions in domain-specific contexts (cf. Gallistel, 2000). Gallistel (1998) states:

> Traditional psychological and neurobiological theories of learning assume that the brain is a general-purpose problem solver. These theories, and the neurobiological concepts to which they give rise, emphasize associative processes as the foundation of all higher learning. This is biologically unprecedented. In other domains, biological structures arise as solutions to specific problems, and the characteristics of the problem to which they are a solution are strongly reflected in the structure of the mechanism. Adaptive specialization is the rule at every level of analysis in biology. Eyes are for seeing and ears are for hearing; there is no general purpose sensing organ or process. Why should there be a general purpose learning organ or process? (p. 56)

In consumer behavior, classical conditioning (a domain-general mechanism) has been used in innumerable settings because of the premise that learning is a general-purpose, domain-independent process. For example, it has been applied to explain consumers' responses to a sports event sponsor (Speed & Thompson, 2000). Feinberg (1986) proposed that individuals' conditioned reactions to credit cards were due to classical conditioning, a claim recently contested by Shimp and Moody (2000). It has also been applied to explore the manner by which consumers evaluate brand extensions (cf. Till & Priluck, 2000) and choose colors (Grossman & Wisenblit, 1999). Additionally, it was utilized in studying the effects of affect on attitude formation (Kim, Lim, & Bhargava, 1998), the manner by which attitudes toward the ad and brand are formed (Gresham & Shimp, 1985), and the separate effects of music and humor in advertising (cf. Gorn, 1982). Thus, the same general learning mechanism is viewed as easily transferable to a countless number of settings. The results from close to 20 years of research on the applications of classical conditioning in the consumption setting have been equivocal and in a few instances the effects were very weak (e.g., Gresham & Shimp, 1985). As previously mentioned, evolutionary psychologists argue that the brain could not have evolved to possess such general machinery that is not only transferable across countless human settings but also supposedly explains the mechanisms of learning across a wide range of species. Each species has a phylogenetic history that makes it more or less likely to learn certain associations. For example, a dog can quickly learn the aversive association between two stimuli when it uses its olfactory as compared to its auditory sense. This is because the instinctual preparedness of the dog to learn is tied to its species-specific environment and hence evolved genotype. By the same token, the phylogenetic history of *Homo sapiens* is rooted in a set of species-specific survival domains (e.g., avoid predators, find mate). Hence, the mechanism by which individuals learn to avoid predatory animals is unlikely to be the same as the one by which they learn the societal rules and norms governing proper conduct. Even if one were to accept classical conditioning (or operant conditioning for that matter) as the operative learning mechanism, how would this fit with the tabula rasa view of the human mind, which is typically espoused by behavioral learning theorists? In other words, where does the neural machinery used to implement this general-purpose mechanism originate from? Finally, what are the roots of a given unconditioned stimulus? If men react to sexual images in certain predictable ways, it is insufficient to propose that these images constitute the unconditioned stimulus. The ultimate issue that needs to be posed is why is the reaction to such images unconditioned. Socialization-based theorists argue that men's unconditioned responses to sexual imagery are learned, yielding a tautological reliance on learning as the explanatory mechanism.

The unconditioned stimuli that have been used in close to 20 years of consumer research have had one thing in common, namely their ability to elicit either a positive or negative reaction in those exposed to them. In some instances, the unconditioned stimulus was chosen as a function of whether or not it had informational content relevant to the product. For example, Kim et al. (1998) found that the use of a kitten as the unconditioned stimulus, which had no product beliefs associated with it, yielded an affect transfer (as compared to a more cognitive-based one). They also demonstrated that the number of times that the conditioned and unconditioned stimuli were paired together influenced whether an affective or cognitive transfer occurred. Other unconditioned stimuli that have been used include visual scenes (Grossman & Till, 1998), scenes of waterfalls and sunsets (Shimp, Stuart, & Engle, 1991; Stuart, Shimp, & Engle, 1987), as well as two runners and a race car (Kim, Allen, & Kardes, 1996, Experiment 1). Other than the visual sense, some scholars have used an auditory unconditioned stimulus, namely music (Bierly, McSweeney, & Vannieuwkerk, 1985; Gorn, 1982).

As mentioned earlier, an evolutionary perspective of classical conditioning would propose that which sense is used in establishing the paired association between the conditioned and unconditioned stimuli is highly important and is tied to a species' phylogenetic history. To the extent that *Homo sapiens* place greater reliance on their visual as compared to auditory sense, one might posit that ceteris paribus (e.g., holding the level of attitudinal valence constant), the number of repetitions required to yield maximal "learning" will be least for visual stimuli. Additionally, evolutionary psychology would posit that the efficacy of an unconditioned visual stimulus will be in part determined by whether it triggers a reaction that is directly linked to one or more of the key Darwinian modules. For example, when targeting men, the use of attractive female models as the unconditioned stimuli yields predictable effects. Unlike a man's reaction to a kitten or a scene with a waterfall, the trigger mechanism associated with sexual imagery has a Darwinian genesis (see chap. 3 for a discussion of human mating from an evolutionary perspective). Hence, the choice of which unconditioned stimulus to use for a given audience can be enhanced via an understanding of evolutionary theory. This could prove to be a fruitful area for future research.

Because marketing and consumer scholars focus on proximate phenomena, the latter issues are less likely to ever be addressed without the necessary evolutionary lens. It is important to reiterate that ultimate-based theorizing is not meant to supplant its proximate counterpart, be it in the context of classical conditioning and/or most other areas of inquiry. Exploring how competitive advertising affects an individual's ability to learn via classical conditioning is within the proximate purview. Understanding the genesis of universally experienced unconditioned stimuli (e.g., reaction to physically attractive endorsers) falls within the ultimate rubric. Hence, both approaches are necessary for a complete understanding of human behavior.

Operant conditioning is another example of a general-purpose domain-independent theory that has been used in consumer behavior. Its origins stem from the work of B. F. Skinner. In his theoretical conception, an organism learns via a schedule of reinforcement (positive and/or negative) guided by the environmental consequences of its behaviors. Interestingly, Skinner proposed that a Darwinian process of selection and retention drives the generation of behaviors that an organism attempts while navigating through its environment (cf. Cziko, 2000, p. 38). Hence, all organisms (including humans) are viewed as mechanistic robots void of higher order cognition and/or purposive behavior. Accordingly, as long as one could construct the proper schedule of reinforcement, behaviors can be shaped into desired courses of action. In their discussion of possible applications of behaviorism in marketing, Nord and Peter (1980, p. 36) state,

"We maintain that many marketing objectives can be (and in fact have been) accomplished ... by simply studying environmental conditions and manipulating them to influence consumer behavior." Hence, there is a natural and intuitive appeal in using this theoretical approach in marketing because it suggests that consumers' behaviors are within the control of marketers. As long as marketers could identify the optimal schedules of reinforcement and accordingly manipulate the relevant environments, consumers could be shaped to conform to the marketers' whims. Despite early interest in Skinnerian conditioning, consumer scholars appear to have lost interest in the framework (see Foxall, 1987, 1994; Peter & Nord, 1982, for a discussion of this form of conditioning in the consumer setting). A search on ABI/INFORM and a perusal through leading consumer behavior textbooks reveals the same set of dated references with very little infusion of newer work in the area. Why has operant conditioning not lived up to its promise? I propose that it is precisely because the theory is void of any domain-specificity (in the Darwinian sense). It is insufficient to argue that organisms seek rewards while wishing to avoid punishments. A possible area for future research would be to develop a theoretical framework capable of explaining why particular rewards are important, which rewards are universal, and under which contexts is a particular reward important or not. A valuable framework would seek to explain whether certain rewards are sex-specific, age-specific, and domain-specific. In other words, rewards and punishments (or motives, goals, or any other driver of purposive behavior) should be understood within the context of a species' phylogenetic history. The demotion of one's social status is likely a more drastic punishment to men than it is to women. The reward associated with access to multiple sexual partners is likely a stronger driver to men than it is to women. The fear of being ostracized from one's peer group is invariably stronger for teenagers as compared to newly wed couples. Numerous rewards and punishments that display universal patterns in their instantiations do so because they are associated to domain-specific Darwinian modules that guide purposive behavior. Operant conditioning has been instrumental in identifying consumption settings driven by "generalized" rewards (e.g., frequency and loyalty programs). The incorporation of a domain-specific calculus in understanding operant conditioning can hopefully expand the frontiers within this research stream.

Motivation

What motivates consumers to engage in the consumption acts that they do? A perusal through leading consumer behavior textbooks reveals that the most ubiquitous theory to address this issue is Maslow's hierarchy of needs. Maslow proposed that there are five sets of hierarchical needs that individuals strive to meet, namely physiological, safety, belongingness, esteem, and self-actualization needs. Accordingly, consumer motives are mapped onto one of the five hierarchical levels, as are the consumer products and services that cater to those needs. By joining the American military, one is addressing one' self-actualization needs (i.e., "Be all that you can be"). Similarly, by engaging in conspicuous consumption of fashion items, one is meeting his or her belongingness and possibly esteem needs. Despite its popularity and intuitive appeal, Maslow's theory has received little scientific support (cf. Berl, Williamson, & Powell, 1984; Soper, Milford, & Rosenthal, 1995, for a discussion of the theory within the marketing context).

Several other motivation theories have been applied in the consumer context, none of which provides an account of the ultimate causation that gave rise to the postulated elemental motives. Why do humans have needs for affiliation, for sensation seeking, for power, for superiority, for sex? Where do Murray's needs come from? What is the etiology behind Rokeach's instrumental and terminal needs? An evolutionary-informed perspective would propose that humans possess universal motives, goals, needs, and drives that can be mapped onto a set of key Darwinian modules, each of which serves as an integrative umbrella for a common set of adaptive problems. This same position has recently been independently espoused by Vyncke, Poels, and De Backer (2003) wherein they proposed that whereas Maslow's hierarchy of needs and Rokeach's values are both empirically and theoretically unjustified, a Darwinian perspective would posit coherent explanations of ultimate causation regarding universal human motives.

Culture

Of all environmental influences that have been explored within the consumption setting, culture is one that has been receiving increased attention (cf. Luna & Gupta, 2001; Maheswaran & Shavitt, 2000; McCort & Malhotra, 1993). Most research within marketing and consumer behavior that has explored the effects of culture has sought to identify cross-cultural differences as opposed to focusing on cross-cultural similarities that would be indicative of a universal human nature. A search on ABI/INFORM (December 24, 2003) using the search words *marketing* and *cross-cultural* yielded 434 hits. Table 2.1 provides a listing of some of these topics broken down into distinct categories, including marketing research, behavioral, attitudinal, specific consumption, environmental influences, cognitive, individual traits, marketing cues and programs, and product-related issues. Hence, although the marketing cross-cultural literature is replete with several hundred studies that have identified differences between cultures, little parsimony exists across the findings. One can generate thousands of additional cross-cultural differences along behavioral, conative, and cognitive variables. A more challenging task is to identify parsimonious theo-

TABLE 2.1
Selected Topics Investigated from a Cross-Cultural Perspective

social desirability bias, response styles (e.g., extreme responses), differences in response rates

Internet buying, Web site navigation, shopping, bargaining, purchasing from sponsors, complaining, green purchasing, gift giving, brand switching, variety seeking, adoption of innovations, and behavioral intention models

attitude toward time, advertising, political advertising, credit cards, energy conservation, consumerism, and aberrant consumer behaviors

consumption of chocolate, organic foods, alcohol, fish, prostitutes; status and luxury consumption

marital roles, spousal influence, family life cycle, children's influence, group influences, word-of-mouth effects, consumer socialization

satisfaction formation, brand equity creation, information processing, decision-making styles, framing effects, overconfidence in memory for brand information, tests of the elaboration likelihood model, size of consideration sets, processing of international advertising

optimum stimulation level, inner-age satisfaction, ethnocentrism, materialism, the Intergenerational (IGEN) scale, the List of Values, marketing ethics, consumer innovativeness/resistance

price as a marketing universal, use of price and warranty cues in product evaluations, acculturation and sensitivity to prices, universal symbols (left and right), color meanings and preferences, country-of-origin effect for products and services, content analyses of print ads, television ads, and music videos, reactions to English accents in audio stimulus, effects of alcohol warning labels, response to antismoking ads, perceived impact of thin models in advertising, direct-mail receptivity

store selection criteria, situational influences on shoppers, comparative service quality, supervisee trust and sales performance, personal selling interactions, domestic retail loyalty, fashion style

perceptions of product prestige, involvement with and use of products, brand extensions, brand identity impressions, perceptions of product complexity, familiarity, and compatibility, travel activity preferences, travel distance, self-congruity and product evaluation, risk reduction in holiday purchases, perceived risk during CD purchasing

retical frameworks that can help scholars predict when one should expect to find cross-cultural similarities versus cross-cultural differences. Evolutionary psychology can help achieve this unifying exercise. Beneath countless cross-cultural differences exists a common Darwinian heritage that binds people across cultures, time, and space.

Luna and Gupta (2001) recently argued that cross-cultural consumer behavior research is disjointed, for it lacks any coherent and organizing frameworks. They review the dichotomy that has been most often used in classifying cross-cultural research, namely the difference between the emic and etic approaches. The former postulates that cultures cannot be compared to one another but rather they must be investigated as independent and unique entities. This is the ideology espoused by cultural relativists beginning with Franz Boas and continuing with many contemporary and highly influential anthropologists such as Clifford Geertz. Luna and Gupta propose, "Emic researchers view culture as inseparable from the individual, as an inherent quality (Geertz, 1973)" (p. 48). Hence, the emic approach amounts to a cataloging of culture-specific findings, without integrating these into a coherent framework. To integrate such cultural phenomena under a unifying rubric would be antithetical to the emic approach. The etic approach on the other hand proposes that cultures can indeed be compared along specific universal cultural traits, which each culture possesses to a varying degree. Hence, in this case, by *universal* one is not referring to a universal human nature as would be espoused by evolutionary psychologists but rather to the fact that cultures can be assigned a quantifiable score on a given cultural trait. See Luna and Gupta (pp. 52–54) for a listing of consumer-related cross-cultural studies stemming from the emic and etic perspectives and Berry (1989) for a five-step approach for integrating the two perspectives.

The majority of cross-cultural psychologists espouse the etic approach, as do most of the marketing scholars who study the effects of culture on consumption phenomena. Perhaps the most frequently used taxonomy of cultural traits is that of Geert Hofstede, wherein he proposes that some of the key traits along which cultures vary include individualism–collectivism, masculinity–femininity, power distance, and uncertainty avoidance (cf. Hofstede, 1997). Consumer researchers have accordingly used one or more of the latter cultural traits in explaining a given cross-cultural difference. For example, Lee and Green (1991) incorporated a cross-cultural component to the Fishbein attitudinal model by demonstrating that collectivist societies (e.g., many of the cultures of the Far East) place a greater weight on group norms as compared to their individualistic counterparts. Working from within the dual-process models of persuasion (the heuristic systematic model and the elaboration likelihood model), Aaker and Maheswaran (1997) found that the extent to which a given type of information affects persuasion is influenced by the individualism–collectivism trait (e.g., consensus-based information is more diagnostic in collectivist societies). Pornpitakpan and Francis (2001) used three of Hofstede's cultural traits in exploring the differential persuasive effect of source expertise and argument strength for Thai (collectivists) and Canadians (individualists). Hence, despite the fact that scholars steeped in the etic approach are using universal cultural traits, they nonetheless focus on identifying cross-cultural differences along these.

A few scholars have explored marketing universals and cross-cultural similarities within the consumption setting (albeit not in the evolutionary sense). For example, LeBlanc and Herndon (2001) found that the number of alternatives in people's consideration sets were equal across two cultures (United States and Hong Kong). No theory was provided to explain the finding nor was any confound that could be driving this null effect controlled for. Liefeld, Wall, and Heslop (1999) found no differences in the information-processing styles (attribute vs. alternative-based) of individuals from three countries, although they did obtain cross-cultural differences in terms of the extent of use of extrinsic or intrinsic cues. Cohen (1996) argued that the notions of "right" and "left" hold the same universal symbolic meaning and as such might be used as standardized global symbols in advertising. Using an econometric approach, Clements and Chen (1996) found substantial similarities in aggregate consumption patterns across a wide range of countries (database varied from 32 to 43 countries depending on the analysis) for a set of standard product commodities (e.g., food, clothing, housing, durables, medicine, transport, recreation). The main difference across countries was the percentage of income spent on food expenditures, namely the richer the country, the lower the proportion of income spent on food expenditures. Key differences in aggregate economic measures (e.g., demand elasticity) were predominantly due to cross-country differences in income and prices and hence the authors concluded that consumer tastes appeared to be culturally invariant. Hence, in this case, the identification of cross-cultural similarities was based on a modeling of aggregate consumption data without providing a theoretical framework for explaining such similarities. Dawar and Parker (1994) cite several authors who have each concluded that there exists a paucity of research that has explored similarities across cultures. Accordingly, they sought to address this lacuna by seeking to identify specific marketing universals, which they define as phenomena that are culturally invariant but are specific to particular products and market segments. Furthermore, they proposed that such universals could be addressed at three distinct levels. First, a scholar could demonstrate the ubiquitous existence of a particular behavior across cultures. Second, one could show that the relative importance of a set of behaviors was culturally invariant. Third, the extent of the behavior (i.e., its absolute level) could be shown to be the same across cultures. They found that the use of four cues as signals of product quality, namely brand name, price, physical appearance, and retail reputation, adhered to the latter three criteria of a marketing universal. This research, though impressive in its ability to identify a set of empirical findings that were statistically the same across cultures, was atheoretical. What is the theory that guides this particular universal?

In their review of key trends in global consumer psychology, Maheswaran and Shavitt (2000) state that the most common objective of this research stream has been to generalize and validate existing models, in new cultural environments. Examples of such studies include those conducted by Durvasula, Andrews, Lysonski, and Netemeyer (1993), and Steenkamp and Burgess (2002). Despite the efforts of cross-cultural scholars to generalize existing models to cross-cultural settings, Maheswaran and Shavitt (2000) conclude, "The lack of frameworks that are robust across cultures has severely limited the development of theory-based empirical work" (p. 59). The lack of progress is likely due in part to the methodological oversight of not having established cross-cultural equivalence of the utilized procedures (see Hui & Triandis, 1985, for the four types of equivalence). That said, evolutionary psychology can provide a possible solution. The human mind is not comprised of general-purpose domain-general algorithms (e.g., the Fishbein attitudinal model, the elaboration likelihood model, or classical conditioning). As such, seeking to demonstrate that such frameworks are globally operative is bound to fail. Instead, one can identify domain-specific modules that have evolved via natural selection to solve specific survival problems and these in turn are likely to be ubiquitously found across all cultures.

To summarize, there are at least four approaches that have been taken within the cross-cultural consumer behavior research stream. First, emic-based scholars have sought to describe phenomena that are idiosyncratic to a particular culture. Second, etic-based researchers have typically used cultural traits (e.g., individualism–collectivism) as moderators of a given consumption phenomenon. Third, a small group of academics have attempted to identify cross-cultural similarities and marketing universals (not in the Darwinian sense). Finally, a fourth stream has sought to generalize cross-culturally existing models and frameworks. Evolutionary psychology can contribute to these research streams by identifying the contexts under which one might expect to identify cross-cultural differences versus commonalities. I turn to a fuller discussion of this issue in the next section.

Standardization Versus Adaptation. The importance of being able to predict when one should expect to find cross-cultural differences as opposed to universals manifests itself most clearly in the long-standing debate regarding the strategic decision of standardization versus adaptation. In his seminal paper, Levitt (1983) argued that advances in technology would facilitate globalization resulting in a homogenized global culture. As such, this would provide the ideal environment for the implementation of standardized strategies yielding substantial economies of scale. From this perspective, when cross-cultural similarities arise, they are attributed to environmental factors (technology and globalization). This environmental outlook is in contrast with evolutionary psychology, which proposes that cross-cultural similarities (e.g., in consumption patterns) are in part due to a common human nature (i.e., many similarities are innate).

Some scholars have challenged Levitt's assertion and have instead supported the adaptation approach (cf. Douglas & Wind, 1987; Kotler, 1986). In the past 20 years, numerous studies have addressed this debate within a wide range of strategic decisions, including brand strategy, marketing strategy, advertising, and market segmentation (cf. Agrawal, 1995; Hassan, Craft, & Kortam, 2003; J. F. Medina & Duffy, 1998; Shoham, 1995; Szymanski, Bharadwaj, & Varadarajan, 1993; van Mesdag, 2000). Ryans, Griffith, and White (2003) provided a recent overview of this vigorous debate (as relating to international marketing strategy). They concluded that despite close to 40 years of scholarly work and 80 years of staunch debating by practitioners, little insight has been gained due to the lack of relevant theoretical frameworks guiding the research programs. They add that much of the focus of the debate has been on the firm with little attention given to the homogeneity of consumers in the cross-cultural arena. They conclude the article by asking which theory might be relevant in addressing this important debate, given that it is fraught with both practical and theoretical implications. Evolutionary psychology might prove a promising framework in answering their call.

One topic of relevance to the standardization–adaptation debate is the field of comparative marketing (cf. Boddewyn, 1981; Iyer, 1997). Scholars within this tradition seek to identify similarities and differences between national marketing systems (e.g., distribution channels or political environments). The idea in this case is that the more similar the marketing systems and environments are between countries, the greater the likelihood that a standardized marketing approach will prove efficacious. The weakness of this research stream is the same as that which was identified earlier for both cross-cultural consumer behavior research and the standardization–adaptation issue. Parsimonious theoretical frameworks have yet to be proposed that can organize and integrate the findings, be it when similarities or differences are found. Hence, the literature has amounted to a cataloging of disjointed findings (e.g., the distribution channels in Japan are different from those in the United States; the political climates in France and England are equally stable). Furthermore, as was true for the standardization–adaptation debate, the comparative marketing approach has focused on macro variables as the units of comparison with lesser attention paid to the consumer.

Where does this leave us? The cross-cultural psychology, global consumer psychology, standardization–adaptation, and comparative marketing systems literatures have each arrived at the same conclusion. They have each generated a rich and valuable set of empirical albeit disconnected findings because they lack the theoretical frameworks that can help integrate the results and drive the research agendas. An infusion of Darwinian-based theorizing in the study of the global consumer does not imply that current approaches (e.g., the emic and etic perspectives) are irrelevant. Rather, a more pluralistic outlook might be adopted in order to achieve a full understanding of global consumption phenomena. Though he did not allude to evolutionary psychology, Garfein (1989) provided a good example of how a given phenomenon can be amenable to an investigation of both its universal and culture-specific manifestations. In the abstract of his article on the cross-cultural outlooks of prestige, he states, "While the need for prestige is universal, the manifestation and satisfaction of this need vary across cultures" (p. 24). Similarly, although the definition of what constitutes power in a given culture varies, women of all cultures prefer to mate with powerful men. Though culinary traditions are culture-specific, preferences for fatty and sweet foods are universal. Hence, which approach is taken, either an emic, etic, or evolutionary approach, depends on the phenomenon under investigation. One of the benefits of the evolutionary paradigm is that it can serve as a unifying framework from which the cross-cultural findings, be they differences or similarities, can be cataloged and organized. This is not to imply that all cross-cultural research can be integrated within the evolutionary framework. For example, the boycott of Israeli products by some Arab consumers is rooted in idiosyncratic historical and geopolitical forces; as such, its investigation is most amenable to an emic approach. Similarly, the extent of group conformity might be driven by a specific cultural trait that varies between two countries and this in turn might explain a given cross-cultural consumption difference (e.g., cross-cultural difference in adherence to fashion fads). Hence, in this case, an etic-based approach based on universal traits (cf. Schwartz, 1994) is appropriate. Not all cross-cultural similarities have a Darwinian etiology. For example, a given fashion fad (e.g., faded jeans) might diffuse around the world for reasons that have little to do with Darwinian theory. Similarly, not all cross-cultural differences can be explained by evolutionary theory (e.g., some culinary traditions). However, when the question of interest is either to identify cross-cultural similarities rooted in a common human nature, to understand the ultimate roots of a given cross-cultural difference, or to provide a framework for predicting when to expect cross-cultural differences versus similarities, then evolutionary psychology is an appropriate theoretical framework.

I conclude this section by providing a telling quote regarding the inextricable link between culture and biology. Boyd (1998) proclaimed, "Culture is part of biology, not an alternative to it; without innate domain-specific mental mechanisms, we could not acquire the culture we do, and without the input of culture, those mechanisms would not be switched on" (p. 4). Culture exists as an instantiation of our evolved human nature rather than as a separate phenomenon to be contrasted with biological principles.

Decision Making

Understanding how consumers acquire competing information and how they decide on a winning alternative are two of the leading questions within this research stream, both replete with clear practical and theoretical implications. There are at least four research streams that have sought to address these issues. The traditional economics perspective views all behaviors within the lens of utility maximization. Hence the choice of a product amounts to identifying that which maximizes one's utility (cf. Antonides, 1989, for some relevant seminal references). Similarly, information search will continue as long as the marginal benefits of obtaining the next piece of information exceed its marginal costs (cf. Stigler, 1961). Traditionally, the investigation of such issues is achieved via the development of normative mathematical models (cf. Hagerty & Aaker, 1984, for such an approach). This epistemological approach views behaviors against the backdrop of a set of axioms of rational choice (e.g., utility maximization, transitivity of preferences, procedural invariance, independence of irrelevant alternatives, and the regularity axiom). As such, the models that are developed within this research tradition adhere to axioms of behavior guiding *Homo economicus* (rational "economic" man) while forgoing its relevance to *Homo sapiens*. In other words, descriptive validity is sacrificed for predictive power and mathematical rigor. Humans did not evolve the cognitive capacity to engage in Bayesian updating. They do not have an innate ability to minimize purchase costs assuming that prices follow a Weibull distribution. The accumulated findings demonstrate that not only are humans reluctant and in most cases incapable to engage in such mental operations but also when they do so, they perform quite poorly. To the extent that classical economics views decision makers as nonadaptive and inflexible utility maximization agents, this cannot correspond with any notion of a sentient being that has evolved through natural selection. As discussed in chapter 1, the capacity for organisms to display adaptability and behavioral plasticity is a central and ubiquitous Darwinian trait. Notions of rationality as relevant for *Homo economicus* have little descriptive validity for *Homo sapiens* because these two species do not share a common phylogenetic history. Interestingly, W. S. Cooper (1987) argued that the currency of the classical economist, namely the all-pervasive util, can be subsumed within evolutionary theory by translating utility maximization into fitness maximization (in the Darwinian sense; see also Gandolfi, Gandolfi, & Barash, 2002). The schism between behavioral scientists and classical economists has accordingly manifested itself most clearly in the manner by which each field has addressed decision-making behavior. This leads to the second decision-making approach, namely behavioral decision theory (BDT), a discipline that I discuss next.

   The past 30 years have seen the blossoming of BDT, a field that has cataloged an impressive number of violations of axioms of rational choice. For illustrative purposes, a few seminal examples are discussed here. The transitivity axiom proposes that if A is preferred to B and B is preferred to C, then A must be preferred to C. Close to 35 years ago, Tversky (1969) demonstrated violations of this axiom. The axiom of procedural invariance posits that a given preference should be the same irrespective of how it is elicited. Grether and Plott (1979) showed that preferences between competing gambles could be reversed as a function of how these were elicited. Similarly, Tversky and Kahneman (1986) established the existence of the framing effect, namely that two isomorphic scenarios if framed differently would yield preference reversals. Slovic (1975) demonstrated that participants utilized systematic heuristics to choose between equally valued alternatives, when the axiom of utility maximization would posit that choices for such alternatives should be random (e.g., flipping a coin). Kahneman and Tversky's (1979) prospect theory proposed that an individual's risk proclivities are not invariant (as was assumed by classical economists) but rather are sensitive to various contextual factors (e.g., whether the individuals are facing gains or losses). Huber, Payne, and Puto (1982) ascertained that the introduction of an asymmetrically dominated alternative (i.e., one that is dominated on all attributes with regard to a competing alternative) into an existing consideration set increased the probability of choosing the dominant alternative, a violation of the regularity axiom. For summaries of this research stream, see Kahneman, Slovic, and Tversky (1982), Kahneman and Tversky (2000), and Gilovich, Griffin, and Kahneman (2002). By focusing almost exclusively on debunking axioms of rational choice, BDT has firmly established that we do not share the cognitive processes of *Homo economicus*. However, the lacuna within this research stream is that it has spent all of its intellectual capital informing us of what we are not rather than explaining why we would have evolved to be the way we are. Hence, BDT has yielded a rich body of proximate theories and findings without tackling the ultimate origins of such cognitive processes. Loewenstein (2001) made several suggestions meant to move the behavioral decision-making field forward. Though he alluded to evolutionary concepts (e.g., recognizing that the brain is modular and hence not comprised of general-purpose algorithms), he did not explicitly argue for an evolutionary-based approach to decision making. That said, Weber, Blais, and Betz (2002) proclaimed, "Goldstein and Weber (1997) document a transition from content-independent to content-specific theories in several areas of cognitive psychology, including memory, learning, and problem solving. *BDT is also starting to show a trend in that direction* [italics added]" (p. 267).

A third research stream within the decision-making literature has sought to identify moderators of search behavior (see Beatty & Smith, 1987, pp. 86–87, for a table summarizing studies of this sort). These include individual-level variables (e.g., personality traits or demographics), environment-based factors (e.g., store density or price variance for a given commodity), and situational factors (e.g., time pressure or mood). Most studies within this camp have been survey based and hence correlational in nature. To establish the directional relationship between product expertise and information search is different from demonstrating that the two variables are causally linked. This research stream has yielded some obvious findings in terms of the directional relationships between moderators of search and extent of search. For example, it is not surprising that time pressure results in a decrease in information search or that individuals scoring high on the need for cognition scale engage in greater search. The moderators of search that have yielded the most equivocal findings include many of the key demographic variables such as sex, education, socioeconomic status, and age. The failure to provide definitive directional relationships for some of the more important moderators of search (e.g., sex of an individual) stems from the faulty assumption that these relationships should hold across decisional domains. For example, scholars within this tradition seek a sex effect for the extent of search that one engages in, independent of the domain. There is no theoretical basis for expecting either sex to engage in greater or lesser search throughout all possible decisional domains. This mind-set has yielded a singular focus on domain-independent general-purpose theories throughout much of the social sciences. As mentioned repeatedly here, evolutionary psychology proposes that the human mind is equipped with domain-specific modules that have evolved to solve specific and recurring survival problems. Hence, depending on the evolutionarily relevant domain, one might expect either men or women to engage in greater information search. One telling example is within the context of human mate search. Which sex engages in greater information search prior to choosing a mate? Buss and Schmitt (1993) have shown that the temporal context of a relationship (i.e., short- vs. long-term) affects the behaviors of men and women in radically different manners. The costs of a suboptimal mating decision are the same for a woman independently of whether she engages in short-term or long-term mating. This is why the characteristics that women seek in an ideal mate are more correlated across both temporal contexts. On the other hand, men's preferences could be quite different depending on the temporal context of the relationship. A promiscuous woman is highly desirable as a short-term partner but highly undesirable as a long-term mate. Hence, the extent to which men and women will be choosy (as evidenced by how extensively they search for prospective partners) is intimately linked to this specific domain (i.e., mating). There are no theoretically sound reasons to explain why one sex should search more than the other across all decisional domains albeit consumer researchers have sought to catalog such findings (cf. Darley & Smith, 1995; Meyers-Levy & Maheswaran, 1991; Meyers-Levy & Sternthal, 1991).

The fourth approach to have addressed information search and information processing within the decision-making literature is rooted in the bounded-rationality tradition as originally espoused by Herb Simon (cf. Simon, 1982). Contrary to the classical economists' insistence that humans possess the ability and desire to engage in laborious and complex calculations in arriving at a choice, Simon argued that individuals are bounded by cognitive and environmental constraints. Hence, rather than seeking perfect information, individuals satisfice by applying heuristics that take into account the latter constraints. For example, individuals are unlikely to acquire all of the available information prior to making a choice as would be postulated by a normative rule. Rather, they use a heuristic that prunes through the information space such that more often than not it leads to a satisfactory outcome. In the context of consumer behavior, bounded rationality is well exemplified by the process-tracing information display board (IDB) work as summarized in Payne, Bettman, and Johnson (1993). In such an environment, there are many decision rules that an individual can use in arriving at a final choice, a few of which are discussed here. The normative rule, also known as the Weighted Additive (WADD) Rule, stipulates that all information (excluding the cutoffs) be used in choosing a winning alternative. Specifically, the decision maker calculates $\Sigma W_i \times A_i$ for each alternative, where W_i and A_i are respectively the weight and attribute value for attribute i, and accordingly chooses the one that yields the highest score. The Lexicographic Rule posits that the alternative that scores highest on the most important attribute is chosen. The Conjunctive Rule proposes that the winning alternative is the one that passes all of the aspired cutoffs. The Disjunctive Rule stipulates that the first alternative that passes a single cutoff is chosen. As such, the order in which the alternatives are evaluated is particularly important when using this rule. This demonstrates that for a given decision problem, individuals can arrive at different final choices as a function of which heuristics they use. This is in stark contrast to the classical economic viewpoint, which posits that there can be only one winning alternative for a given consumer because the process by which a choice is made is assumed invariant.

If a consumer can use any one of several decision rules in arriving at a final choice, what is the meta-process by which a decision rule is chosen (i.e., deciding how to decide)? Payne et al. (1993) demonstrated that this arises as a result of a trade-off between the accuracy of a heuristic and the cognitive cost of using it. For example, the Conjunctive Rule is more effortful to use as compared to the Lexicographic Rule; however, on average it yields more accurate outcomes by virtue of the fact that it uses a greater portion of the available information. Payne et al. add that the cost–accuracy trade-off is affected by two sets of environmental cues, namely task and context variables. Task variables refer to the generic structure of the task at hand, for example, the size of the IDB or the presence or absence of time pressure. Context variables are comprised of specific instantiations of the problem at hand such as whether the attribute weights are roughly equal or the similarity of the competing alternatives. Additionally, individual-level variables (e.g., an individual's need for cognition) and social characteristics (e.g., justifiability and accountability of a decision) affect which decision rule will be chosen. Payne et al. demonstrated that the choice of a decision rule is *contingent* on specific instantiations of the latter factors. The authors also identified *constructive* processes that occur online (i.e., during the decision) in reaction to specific data that decision makers might be exposed to. For example, if the range of attribute values for a given attribute is very small, it might be deleted from further consideration because the acquisition of information on that attribute will not be very diagnostic. Hence, whereas constructive processes are bottom-up (i.e., data driven), contingent decision making assumes that a decision rule is chosen from an existing repertoire of available strategies (top-down process). Both contingent and constructive processes are manifestations of adaptive behavior, quite distinct from the invariant calculations postulated by classical economists. How compatible is this paradigm with evolutionary theory? To the extent that it demonstrates within-organism adaptability, it is more congruent with a Darwinian outlook than is the classical economics approach. However, it remains a fundamentally proximate framework that proposes a general-purpose algorithm independent of the decisional domain (i.e., a trade-off between a heuristic's accuracy and its associated cognitive effort). In other words, true to the central tenet of the SSSM, the IDB process-tracing approach posits a domain-independent, general-purpose mechanism, without providing its genesis or ultimate roots. Why would humans have evolved the capacity to apply such a cognitive process independently of whether they are choosing between toothpastes, universities to attend, or prospective suitors? An evolutionary approach steeped in the logic of domain-specificity might propose that the decision rule that will be chosen is in part a function of the decisional domain. For example, a man choosing a prospective mate for a short-term mating opportunity might use the Lexicographic Rule with "physical attractiveness" as the most important attribute. On the other hand, he might apply the normative WADD Rule when seeking a long-term partner precisely because it is a compensatory strategy that utilizes all of the available information. In this case, the choice of which heuristic to use is intimately linked to a domain-specific module (i.e., mating) and accordingly is not driven by any of the contingency factors as identified by Payne et al.

It would appear that none of the four decision-making/information search approaches explicitly incorporates evolutionary theorizing within its purview. They posit domain-independent and general-purpose mechanisms that are operative across decisional settings. The classical economics approach posits axioms of rational choice based on *Homo economicus*. The behavioral decision theory paradigm catalogs violations of rational choice while maintaining a domain-independent focus on laws of probability as the benchmark of rationality (but see X. T. Wang, 1996, for an evolutionary-informed and domain-specific perspective of the framing effect). The "moderators of search" approach seeks to identify a directional relationship between a given moderator (e.g., income) and the extent of search without recognizing that such relationships cannot typically be posited across all decisional domains. Finally, the IDB process-tracing approach proposes that individuals engage in domain-independent accuracy-effort trade-offs, using the WADD Rule as the "rational" normative backdrop.

Does there exist a decision-making framework that specifically incorporates evolutionary theory within its theoretical purview? Gerd Gigerenzer and his colleagues have developed such a framework using the notion of ecological rationality (cf. Gigerenzer, 2000; Gigerenzer & Goldstein, 1996; Gigerenzer, Todd, & the ABC Research Group, 1999). Gigerenzer and Todd (1999) define ecological rationality as follows:

> Traditional definitions of rationality are concerned with maintaining internal order of beliefs and inferences, as we will see in the next section. But real organisms spend most of their time dealing with the external disorder of their environment, trying to make the decisions that will allow them to survive and reproduce (Tooby & Cosmides, 1998). To behave adaptively in the face of environmental challenges, organisms must be able to make inferences that are fast, frugal, and accurate. These real-world requirements lead to a new conception of what proper reasoning is: ecological rationality. (p. 18)

Note that inherent to the definition of ecological rationality is an exploration of the adaptive (i.e., Darwinian) reasons that an organism would have evolved a particular cognitive process. Hence, this new definition of rationality recognizes that cognitive processes should be domain-specific; namely, heuristics that have evolved to solve adaptive problems in one domain (e.g., identifying prospective allies) are unlikely to be relevant in other domains (e.g., providing parental investment). Gigerenzer and Todd make this exact point when they state:

> How is ecological rationality possible? That is, how *can* [italics in the original] fast and frugal heuristics work as well as they do, and escape the

trade-offs between different real-world criteria including speed and accuracy? The main reason for their success is that they make a trade-off on another dimension: that of generality versus specificity. While coherence criteria are very general—logical consistency, for instance can be applied to any domain—the correspondence criteria that measure a heuristic's performance against the real world require much more *domain-specific* [italics added] solutions. What works to make quick and accurate inferences in one domain may well not work in another. (p. 18)

Examples of domain-specific decision-making processes that adhere to ecological rationality include those dealing with mate search, parental investment, and predator avoidance (see Gigerenzer et al., 1999, for a wide range of such illustrations). The recognition heuristic as described by Goldstein and Gigerenzer (1999) is one such example. They demonstrated that if one simply chooses the stocks of recognizable firms (e.g., IBM, GE, and Bell), this trivially simple strategy performs as well as highly sophisticated investment models. They argued that from an evolutionary perspective, many survival problems involve a recognition task (e.g., visual and auditory recognition of friends and foes, recognition of toxic plants and dangerous predators). Accordingly, from an ecologically rational perspective, it is expected that individuals have the proclivity of using the recognition heuristic and that on average its use should yield accurate outcomes. Incidentally, neurologists have found that injuries to the temporal lobe (e.g., due to a stroke) can result in the loss of one's ability to recognize faces (a condition known as proposagnosia). Hence, there appears to be a specific region of the brain that is dedicated to the recognition of faces (a clear demonstration of modularity). Many marketing and consumption phenomena can be reformulated as examples of the recognition heuristic. For example, both the building of brand equity and the fostering of a country-of-origin effect effectively cater to individuals' proclivities to choose that which is recognizable. The incumbency advantage in politics is partly due to voters' propensity to choose a candidate who is well known and recognizable (Saad, 2003). Classical rationality and bounded rationality would interpret the latter behaviors in radically different manners. The former would argue that the chosen product or winning political candidate must be the one that corresponds to the consumer's or voter's highest utility. The latter perspective would state that the use of the recognition heuristic arises as a result of environmental and cognitive constraints.

Perception

Much of perception research in consumer behavior is driven by the information-processing view, which has traditionally been the dominant paradigm within cognitive psychology. The key focus within this research tradition is to provide proximate descriptions of the assumed linear and sequential stages of perceptual phenomena (e.g., exposure → attention → comprehension → learning). Additionally, variables that might affect an individual's information processing at one or more of the perceptual stages are typically explored. These include situation-specific, person-specific, product-specific, stimulus-specific, and environment-specific variables. A situational variable might be whether a consumer is currently on the market for a given advertised product. Accordingly, the likelihood that an individual will attend to a given perceptual stimulus is related to the extent that the advertised product is personally relevant at that particular moment. A person-specific variable might be a stable personality trait such as need for cognition, which is purported to affect the likelihood of attending to specific forms of stimuli more so than to others. That men are less likely to attend to feminine hygiene ads is an example of a product-specific variable. Stimulus-specific variables include salient characteristics of an advertised message such as its color, size, shape, contextual surroundings, and so on. Oftentimes, Gestalt principles are used to explain stimulus-specific phenomena. Finally, an environment-specific variable might be the extent of advertising clutter in a given medium resulting in stimulus/informational overload, which triggers mechanisms for achieving efficient perceptual filtering.

All of the latter issues and approaches have yielded important theoretical and practical advances in our understanding of perceptual phenomena. However, there has been little if any evolutionary-based and biologically grounded theorizing when consumer scholars have studied perceptual phenomena. Our five senses, which constitute the means by which we perceive and experience the world, exist in their given forms as a result of natural and sexual selection. Accordingly, our species-specific perceptual apparatus cannot be fully investigated without an understanding of the Darwinian forces that led to its evolution. For example, Kenrick et al. (2002) state:

> From an evolutionary perspective, cognitive processes involve adaptive selectivity: We attend to the information most relevant to important domain-specific goals. And our responses to that information are informed by heuristic decision-rules that, in ancestral environments, would have been functionally adaptive (i.e., facilitated reproductive success). (p. 348)

Dolphins and bats use species-specific sonar apparatuses that have evolved via natural selection. Sharks have the capacity to perceive the world around them using electric fields. Mole rats have done away with their sight and accordingly rely on their other senses, which are more adapted to their particular ecological niche. A dog's olfactory sense outperforms the most sophisticated man-made machines because natural selection has had millions of years to tinker with the dog's perceptual system. Thus, whereas perceptual phenomena across innumerable species are studied from an evolutionary perspective, Darwinian forces are largely ignored in explaining human perception when studied by consumer researchers (cf. Gibson, 1979, for a biologically and ecologically informed framework in studying visual perception).

An advertiser's first goal is to typically draw a consumer's attention to the message. Many of the perceptual cues that are used to achieve this goal function in universally predictable ways because they are evolutionarily relevant. The efficacy of using scantily clad young and beautiful women in drawing men's attention to ads is one such example. The snake, which serves as a fear-inducing cue not only to *Homo sapiens* but also to numerous other species, is another evolutionary relevant perceptual cue used by advertisers to draw a consumer's attention. DiMarzio, a guitar company, used a brightly colored snake in one of its most recent print ads. Although there might be semantic connections between this particular ad and snakes, the advertisers in question were likely aware that there exists a set of perceptual cues that humans are innately predisposed to attend to including beautiful endorsers and dangerous-looking snakes. Hence, our evolved perceptual apparatus guides the automaticity with which advertising cues are attended to. As Mealy, Daood, and Krage (1996) state, "We should not be surprised to find that the more ecologically and evolutionarily relevant a stimulus, the more automatic and specialized is its processing" (p. 119).

The manner by which men and women use perceptual cues to navigate through their environments seems to be linked to evolved physiological differences. Recently, Choi and Silverman (2002) have stated, "Differing concentrations of gonadal hormones early in development feminize or masculinize the organization of the brain, resulting in *perceptual biases* [italics added], and consequently, influencing how various environmental cues are used to solve spatial problems (Williams & Meck, 1991)" (p. 116). The problem that Choi and Silverman were tackling was the manner by which men and women navigate through the world, which can be extended to the consumer realm by exploring sex differences in browsing behavior. They demonstrated that testosterone was correlated to the use of a male-biased route-learning strategy (relying on cardinal directions such as north, west, east, and south and distances such as mileage) for men but not for women. They conclude that this seems to support the contention that there are evolutionary-based sex differences in spatial navigation that are influenced by sex-specific hormones (e.g., testosterone). See Silverman and Eals (1992) for an evolutionary explanation of sex differences in spatial abilities. On a related note, Silverman and Phillips (1993) found that women's spatial abilities were linked to their menstrual cycles whereas

Krug, Plihal, Fehm, and Born (2000) explored how various stimuli, varying in terms of their reproductive implications, would be perceptually attended to as a function of a woman's menstrual cycle. Such studies are unlikely to have been conducted if the researchers in question had not recognized that Darwinian forces have shaped our perceptual system. Countless phenomena would likely remain outside the purview of the researcher's perceptual field if one were to restrict one's epistemological lens to proximate mechanisms. Incidentally, not only have evolutionary forces shaped the manner by which individuals use perceptual cues to navigate through their environments but also they have affected the types of environments that are judged as most pleasing. For example, prospect-refuge theory (Orians & Heerwagen, 1992) posits that humans have an evolved preference for natural environments that permit for the scanning of hazards (e.g., presence of predators or belligerent conspecifics) from within a safe vantage point. Accordingly, man-made environments including architectural designs, urban plans, and retail atmospherics are likely to be judged as more or less appealing as a function of how congruent they are with evolved preferences for landscapes as postulated by prospect-refuge theory.

Countless other perceptual phenomena might have been missed had they not been tackled from an evolutionary perspective. For example, Gangestad and Thornhill (1998) asked women participants to rate the pleasantness of several T-shirts that had been worn by men for several days and hence were imbued with the men's idiosyncratic body odors. Gangestad and Thornhill found that the preferred smells corresponded to the men who were most symmetric. Given that facial and body symmetry is a marker of genetic quality, because greater symmetry implies lesser pathogenic infestation and/or lesser developmental problems (cf. Gangestad, Thornhill, & Yeo, 1994; Thornhill & Gangestad, 1993), this implies that women have a multisensorial system for identifying desirable suitors. In other words, women are able to perceptually navigate through the mating world using two senses that yield convergent validity. Incidentally, the link between preferred smells and symmetric men held true only for those women who were in the fertile stage of their menstrual cycle. This multisensorial perceptual system adept at identifying men of superior genetic quality is on heightened alert when the identification of such genes coincides with a woman's maximal fertility. This is congruent with a persistent finding in the evolutionary psychology literature, which suggests that at times women engage in mating behaviors that correspond to the shopping for superior genes (also known as the "sperm extraction" hypothesis).

Several scholars have explored the selective attention that individuals dedicate to threatening social cues (e.g., angry faces) as a function of their situation-specific mood (anxious or angry) or idiosyncratic physiological markers (e.g., level of testosterone). Hence, in this case, one's perceptual apparatus appears to be a preparatory mechanism for the ethologically universal response to either fight or flee (cf. Dimberg & Öhman, 1996; van Honk et al., 1999). On a related note, Mazurski, Bond, Siddle, and Lovibond (1996) found that men pay greater selective attention to angry male faces whereas women pay equal attention to angry faces of either sex. This would suggest that this perceptual bias might be linked to intrasexual male–male aggressive challenges (i.e., fight mode). How might such findings be applied in the consumer setting? First, it should be noted that the approach–avoidance mechanism, which consumer scholars have used, is an instantiation of the evolutionary-grounded fight–flight response. There are many settings wherein a consumer must determine whether to fight or flee. Take a hostile service encounter. Should the consumer walk away or be confrontational? Similarly, are there any social cues that the service provider can use in determining the optimal response? For example, I suspect that the social ranks of service providers and customers might yield differential behaviors that are best understood from an ethological perspective (e.g., physician with patient; Rolls Royce car salesperson with wealthy potential buyer vs. used-car salesperson with low-income potential buyer). In other words, displays of deference are likely conferred to high-status conspecifics in the consumption arena in roughly the same manner across cultures. In the same manner that basal emotions yield universal facial grimaces, status-related deference also contains universal nonverbal cues and signals (cf. Kowner & Wiseman, 2003, for a comparison of Japanese and American perceptions of status-linked behaviors). Understanding the intricacies of these naturally occurring dynamics would likely benefit from an infusion of the relevant Darwinian-based theorizing. Ethologists have developed a whole field of inquiry based on naturally occurring encounters between conspecifics. Consumer researchers might generate novel theories and research agendas by recognizing that the manner by which humans perceive social cues (e.g., facial grimaces and body language) is an integral element of the evolution of the human mind (see Salter, Grammer, & Rikowski, 2005, for an ethological study of nonverbal communication between male and female customers with dominant male bouncers outside of a discotheque). The specific subcomponent of the perceptual system that is dedicated to reading social cues is a manifestation of our evolved social intelligence.

One of the domains where our evolved perceptual apparatus manifests itself most clearly is in the mating domain. There exists a set of universal cues that are attended to in predictable manners because they carry important evolutionarily relevant information. One area where this is particularly clear is in the definition of the morphological cues that constitute beauty. Numerous socialization-based theorists have proposed that the definition of beauty is a social construction (cf. N. Wolf, 1991). In other words, that which is viewed as beautiful in one culture is radically different from that construed as such in another. A common example that is provided in support of this contention is the differences in the types of female bodies that are perceived as most alluring to men. The Rubenesque female models depicted in Renaissance paintings were more rotund than the models on today's haute couture catwalks. The women most likely to be viewed as beautiful in certain Central African regions are noticeably larger than the standards of female beauty as depicted in Hollywood. Socialization-based theorists argue that this is definitive proof of the vagaries of defining beauty. All of the latter body types tend to share one common evolutionarily relevant metric. They yield a waist-to-hip ratio (WHR) that is close to 0.70 (see Singh, 1993). Numerous evolutionists have established the fact that men possess a near-universal preference for women that adhere to the 0.70 ratio (cf. Singh, 1993; Singh & Luis, 1995; Streeter & McBurney, 2003). Despite challenges to this finding (cf. Freese & Meland, 2002; Tassinary & Hansen, 1998), there exists unequivocal support that WHR is at the very least an important evolved visual cue in judging attractiveness (cf. Furnham, Tan, & McManus, 1997). In other words, whereas the specific value that is preferred seems to be contingent on the particular ecological niche, WHR is an important perceptual cue when forming an attractiveness judgment. For example, environments that are defined by endemic caloric scarcity are more likely to yield higher preferred values of WHR (cf. Sugiyama, 2004; Westman & Marlowe, 1999). Thus, although there appears to be a near-universal preference for a female WHR of 0.70 given that this serves as a reliable cue of youth, health, and hence fecundity (see Singh, 2002a, for a summary), this preference is "adjustable" as a function of idiosyncratic ecological niches. This should serve as another example of the inherent plasticity that is espoused by evolutionary psychologists, a position that is antithetical to biological determinism.

What are some perceptual cues that women attend to when judging the physical attractiveness of men? Height appears to be one such visual cue. Male CEOs tend to be taller than the average height of men within the relevant population. On a related note, the winning candidate in American presidential elections in the past century has overwhelmingly been the taller one (see Dunbar, 1996, pp. 144–145, for a discussion of height in the political arena; see also Pinker, 1997, pp. 495–496). The latest victory of the shorter George W. Bush will certainly serve as a disconfirming datum. That said, those who watched the first presidential debate between Bush and Kerry in 2004 might have noticed that the two candidates were shown on the television screen as though they were of equal heights precisely to negate the height advantage of Kerry. Not only is evolutionary theory valuable in identifying the sex-specific perceptual cues that are deemed important within the mating domain (e.g., WHR and height) but also it can predict how men and women will react (either similarly or differently) across the various cognitive stages when exposed to beautiful individuals. For example, Maner et al. (2003) investigated the manner by which men and women perceptually attend to and cognitively encode, recognize, and recall images of beautiful people. The findings were consistent with sexual selection; namely, sex differences at each of the cognitive stages were linked in a domain-specific manner to the mating module. The obtained results are not congruent with a domain-general perceptual framework as might be postulated by the information-processing view. Rather, each evolutionarily relevant domain shapes the manner by which individuals attend to, encode, recognize, learn, and recall perceptual cues within that particular domain (cf. Springer & Berry, 1997, for an evolutionary-based ecological approach in studying social perception). There are countless other perceptual cues within the mating arena that are selectively attended to because of their evolutionarily relevant informational content. Many of these are further discussed in chapter 3 when describing consumption phenomena that fall within the rubric of the mating module and in chapter 5 when exploring the use of physically attractive endorsers in advertising.

To summarize, our perceptual apparatus is a product of natural and sexual selection. Hence, human perceptual processes are defined in a domain-specific manner such that the cues that might be relevant in a social domain when interacting with same-sex conspecifics are radically different from those relevant in the mating domain. I have provided several examples wherein the manner by which individuals attend to perceptual cues in the environment, be it in advertising, browsing behavior, retail atmospherics, service encounters, or countless other social domains (e.g., those relevant to mating) are guided by Darwinian forces. Hence, the information-processing view of perception, though valuable, is also limiting. Incorporating evolutionary-based theorizing might yield a fuller understanding of perceptual phenomena in the consumer setting.

Attitude Formation and Attitude Change

Two leading attitudinal theories in consumer behavior research have been the theory of reasoned action (cf. Ajzen & Fishbein, 1980), and the elaboration likelihood model (ELM; cf. Petty & Cacioppo, 1986). Although the latter two models have generated a substantial body of knowledge, a supratheory of how attitudes are formed and changed remains elusive. In part, this is due to the fact that the leading attitudinal frameworks operate at the proximate level while proposing general-purpose domain-general mechanisms. It is beyond the current scope to provide a detailed discussion of each of the key attitudinal models. However, I wish to briefly highlight how the infusion of evolutionary-based theorizing can complement and improve the explanatory power of the existing attitudinal frameworks. As an illustrative example, I restrict my discussion to the ELM. The ELM proposes that as a result of one or more proximate factors (e.g., one's motivation and ability to process information), individuals use either the central or peripheral routes to persuasion typically corresponding to conditions of high and low involvement respectively. Proximate factors that affect which route will be used include but are not limited to personality traits (e.g., need for cognition), personal relevance (e.g., whether one is currently on the market for the advertised product), and characteristics of the product (e.g., hedonic vs. utilitarian, consequential vs. inconsequential). One of the key tenets of the ELM is that a given persuasion variable (e.g., physical attractiveness) can assume one of several roles contingent on contextual factors (see Postulate 3 in Petty, Rucker, Bizer, & Cacioppo, 2004). These distinct roles include being a peripheral cue, functioning as an argument, serving as an inducement to elaborate, and generating biased elaboration (Petty & Wegener, 1999). Though ELM researchers have identified proximate conditions that determine which role might be operative in a given setting, an ultimate domain-specific account is missing. For certain classes of decisions (i.e., those that operate within evolutionarily important contexts), which role is triggered and accordingly the persuasion route that is subsequently pursued is a domain-specific process. The physical attractiveness of a celebrity endorser is typically construed as a peripheral cue when forming an attitude toward a technical product. On the other hand, physical attractiveness is an argument for most men when evaluating prospective mates. A woman who is seeking a short-term extramarital dalliance might place greater importance on the physical attractiveness of a prospective partner as compared to when evaluating suitors for marriage. Hence, the same piece of information (physical attractiveness) is either a peripheral cue or argument as a function of a domain-specific calculus (see Buss & Schmitt, 1993, for a description of sexual strategies theory). The image of a cute baby is typically categorized as a peripheral cue within the ELM framework. However, if an advertiser wishes to trigger feelings associated with parental investment, the image of a helpless and cuddly infant becomes an argument linked to an evolutionarily relevant domain (i.e., kin selection).

Many held attitudes exist in their particular forms because they are linked to a domain-specific adaptive problem. For example, Hayward and Rohwer (2004) administered a survey to both men and women in order to explore possible sex differences in their respective attitudes toward paternity testing. Congruent with the evolutionary prediction, which suggests that men have much to lose in being cuckolded, Hayward and Rohwer found that men were more in favor of paternity testing conducted at hospitals than were women. Hence, in this particular case, domain-general theorizing does not drive one's attitude toward a new product innovation; as such, neither the ELM nor the theory of reasoned action are relevant. Rather, both the likelihood of holding a positive attitude toward this innovation as well the likelihood of adopting it (e.g., purchasing a home-administered paternity test kit) are predicted by a domain-specific mechanism steeped in the Darwinian module of human mating.

Whereas existing attitudinal theories have elucidated the proximate mechanisms associated with attitudinal formation and change, ultimate-based theorizing adds explanatory power to existing theories. The extended Fishbein model incorporates one's desire to comply with group norms as an integral part of attitude formation. That said, not only is the desire to affiliate with a group an innate need but also its differential import across the life stages is evolutionarily determined as per the Darwinian-based life-history theory. For example, the abhorrence that most teenagers feel at being ostracized from their reference group is a universally recurring finding, leading global advertisers to utilize a group conformity appeal when seeking to shape teenagers' attitudes. As such, proximate and Darwinian-based attitudinal theories can complement one another in yielding a more complete and parsimonious meta-theory of attitudes.

Emotions

Emotions are triggered in many consumption settings including when viewing ads, consuming a service, or recalling a specific consumption experience. Thus, it is not surprising that numerous studies have explored emotions, feelings, and moods within the consumption context (the conceptual distinctions between the latter affective states is irrelevant here). That said, the focus has largely been on proximate issues. For example, Alice Isen has dedicated her career to exploring the effects of affect on countless tasks (e.g., problem solving, word association, and variety seeking) without providing an ultimate-based meta-theory to synthesize her research stream. Others have explored the conditions under which cognitive processes are more likely to supersede emotive-based ones (or vice versa). The theoretical assumption here is that there are two possible forms of processing, one of which will be triggered as a function of a slew of possible proximate variables. How might emotions be explored from an ultimate perspective? Not only are basal emotions found in the exact same forms universally but also the specific emotional triggers are consistent across cultures and eras. Hence, evolutionists have long argued that a complete understanding of emotions cannot take place without realizing that emotions are adaptive solutions to specific survival problems (cf. Nesse, 1990). On a related note, MacDonald (1995) has proposed, "The evolutionary basis of motivation is thus the evolution of affective systems underlying particular adaptive behaviors in the environment of evolutionary adaptedness" (p. 531). Individuals experience love, jealousy, anger, envy, guilt, and fear to name but a few evolutionarily relevant emotions because these guide adaptive behaviors in important Darwinian domains. Male sexual jealousy is an adaptive emotional response to thwart the threat of paternity uncertainty (see Buss, Larsen, Westen, & Semmelroth, 1992). Romantic love is in part an adaptive solution to the heavy biparental investment that is required to raise successfully one's offspring. Individuals have the biological preparedness to fear snakes but not rabbits. People are angered when cheated in social contracts and will accordingly retaliate to redress the inequity (e.g., a "cheated" consumer will boycott the offending firm). One's conscience and prospective sense of guilt serve to guide one's behavior across a wide range of evolutionarily important relationships including those with one's mate, kin, and close friends. Along those lines, Nesse (1990, p. 275) cites several evolutionists that have proposed that each of the four cells in a standard prisoner's dilemma triggers specific adaptive emotions. I suspect that one of the reasons that the prisoner's dilemma game has been so influential in studying dyadic behavior is because of its ability to trigger ecologically relevant emotions.

Loewenstein (1996) has argued that research in decision making has largely been dominated by an approach that relies on "cold" cognitive processes. In other words, irrespective of whether one operates within the normative camp of *Homo economicus* driven by axioms of rational choice, or within the behavioral decision theory camp, both share the near complete paucity of "hot" cognitions within their theoretical purview. Loewenstein proposes that a complete theory of decision making will require that we study issues such as hunger, lust, and anger among countless other hot cognitions (on a related note see Elster, 1998, regarding the incorporation of emotions into economic theories). Although this is a valuable suggestion, it falls short in that these hot cognitions are not rooted within an evolutionary framework (but see Ariely & Loewenstein, 2006, for an evolutionary-informed exploration of sexual arousal as a hot decision-making state). Humans experience hunger, lust, anger, guilt, envy, and jealousy in universally similar manners because each is rooted in a Darwinian etiology. Hence, to call for an infusion of hot cognitions naturally implies that such a process would be guided by the appropriate Darwinian meta-theory. Loewenstein's position is in line with the standard dual-process viewpoint espoused in consumer behavior regarding the emotion-versus-cognition dichotomy. However, as Nesse (1990) states, "Of particular interest is the possibility that the very 'irrationality' of these emotions may be essential to their adaptive functions. Love, anger, guilt, and anxiety can achieve their purposes only if they cannot be overriden by cognition" (p. 284). It is pointless to pit the two processes against each other for they have each evolved as adaptive solutions to specific evolutionary challenges.

Whereas the large majority of evolutionary psychologists have argued for the adaptive relevance of emotions at the phylogenetic level, Westen (1997) has provided a selectionist account of affective states at two distinct levels (i.e., at both the within- and between-organism levels). He proposes:

> Affects are a mechanism for the selective retention of mental and behavioural responses, including defences, compromise formations, and conscious coping strategies. Affects as motivators are as "biologically based" as the drives of classical theory, since they evolved as solutions to problems of adaptation, and the neural structures that mediate them are encoded in our DNA. (p. 542)

Hence, at the within-organism level, affective states are selected in a manner similar to that espoused by the Skinnerian selectionist behaviorist viewpoint whereas at the phylogenetic level key universal affective states are adaptive solutions to evolutionarily relevant challenges. This perspective on affective states is a more encompassing Darwinian account congruent with the universal selectionist position espoused by Cziko (1995, 2000).

How is any of this discussion relevant to consumer behavior? Emotional states serve both as antecedents and as outcomes of countless consumption phenomena. Love can be the precursor of gift giving such as when offering gifts to one's children or mate. Love can also be the outcome of the gift-giving ritual such as when couples fall in love following an elaborate courtship replete with gifts and other acts of generosity. Each of the universal emotions can just as easily be linked to a wide range of consumption choices. That said, I restrict my focus here to three interrelated emotions, namely jealousy, envy, and *Schadenfreude*. I begin with a brief discussion of sexual jealousy from an evolutionary perspective.

Buss et al. (1992) found that there are substantial sex differences with regard to the specific triggers that elicit romantic jealousy. Buss and his colleagues theorized that each sex would consider different scenarios of infidelity (emotional vs. sexual) as potentially threatening and accordingly one's felt romantic jealousy should closely correspond to these sex-specific and evolutionarily relevant threats. Whereas sexual infidelity serves as the greatest threat to a male's reproductive interests (i.e., triggers paternity uncertainty), emotional infidelity is viewed as the more serious attack on a woman's. From an evolutionary perspective, a woman's greatest threat is the loss of investment that she will incur if her partner leaves the union (e.g., loss of resources, protection, and aid with parental rearing). In other words, emotional infidelity is a more accurate predictor of a man's likelihood of leaving a union than would be a short-term extrapair copulation. Using both survey responses and multiple physiological measures to capture psychological stress, participants in the Buss et al. study imagined one of two scenarios of infidelity regarding their mates. The emotional-infidelity scenario described a loving bond whereas the sexual-infidelity scenario described a sexual liaison. The findings were supportive of the Darwinian-based predictions. Specifi-cally, the type of infidelity yielded the expected sex differences. This does not imply that men are thrilled at the thought of their partners forming an emotional bond with another man. Similarly, the findings do not suggest that women are unaffected by sexual infidelity for it certainly does cause great hurt when a man cheats on his long-term partner. However, an evo-lutionary-informed position predicts that these two forms of infidelity will be differentially experienced and felt by the two sexes (for additional readings regarding an evolutionary perspective on sexual jealousy, see Buss, 2000; Sesardic, 2003; but see DeSteno, Bartlett, Braverman, & Salovey, 2002, and C. R. Harris, 2003, for a challenge of the evolutionary account).

What of the deadly sin of envy? Is there an evolutionary account that can explain why we covet other people's lives, properties, mates, or posses-sions? Habimana and Massé (2000) measured individuals' felt envy using multiple items, covering a wide range of contexts (e.g., being popular, pos-sessing high intelligence, or having an attractive girlfriend or boyfriend). Though no sex differences were obtained with regard to the total amount of felt envy, they did find sex-specific triggers of envy. For example, the re-searchers state that women were much more likely to be envious of physical looks whereas men were particularly envious of traits that correspond with high status (e.g., having a prestigious profession). Though Habimana and Massé did not explore the reasons for these sex-based differences, an evolu-tionary explanation exists in support of the findings. Each sex should be en-vious of those items that might constitute threats if intrasexual rivals possessed these. A low-status man is unlikely to care if a romantic rival has beautiful lips, however he might indeed be threatened and hence envious if the rival is a wealthy industrialist. Similarly, a woman is much more likely to be envious of an exceptionally attractive woman who monopolizes men's gazes while perhaps caring less about and being less envious of an unattrac-tive yet brighter rival. I am currently testing many of these ideas in an ongo-ing project with Tripat Gill. On a related note, Jill Sundie has been exploring the emotion of *Schadenfreude* (personal communication with Jill Sundie, Feb-ruary 27, 2004). This is the emotional reaction that one experiences when they rejoice at the mishap of another. Though perhaps related in its etiology to envy and jealousy, it is a distinct emotional reaction. Numerous scholars have explored *Schadenfreude,* albeit none have done so from an evolutionary perspective. It is likely that an evolutionarily informed mental calculus influences the situations that trigger this emotion. For example, a male driver who is overtaken on the road by another aggressive male driver will experience a differential amount of *Schadenfreude* upon seeing that the aggressive driver has been stopped by a state trooper, as a function of whether the latter was driving a Lada or a Ferrari. The proverbial "keeping up with the Joneses," which leads to various forms of conspicuous consumption (see chap. 3), is in part driven by the latter emotional states. Furthermore, the sex-specific triggers of jealousy, envy, or *Schadenfreude* in the consumption arena should correspond to evolved dispositions tied to sexual signaling.

Personality

Many consumption habits seem inextricably linked to a consumer's personality. For example, individuals who score highly on a sensation-seeking scale are more likely to engage in consumption activities that carry great physical risk (e.g., bungee jumping). From a practical perspective, the ability to segment the consumer market along distinct personality types has intuitive appeal. Given both its theoretical and practical promise, how has personality research fared within the consumer behavior discipline? In his recent invited essay published in the *Journal of Consumer Research,* Baumgartner (2002) takes stock of personality research in consumer behavior and arrives at some dire conclusions. He states:

> Personality research has long been a fringe player in the study of consumer behavior. Little research is directly devoted to personality issues, and if consumer personality is investigated at all, it tends to be from the narrow perspective of developing yet another individual difference measure in an already crowded field of personality scales or considering the moderating effects of a given trait on some relationship of interest. (p. 286)

He adds, "The few articles that do deal with personality issues are focused on individual differences, and the field is balkanized and in a state of disarray" (p. 286). Baumgartner proposes that the "sorry state of personality research in the consumer context" (p. 286) is unwarranted in light of recent advances in personality research. He describes newer taxonomies for studying persons and their personalities (e.g., the McAdams three-tiered framework and Mowen's 3M model) as examples of innovative research streams in personality research that might rekindle consumer scholars' interest in this field. However, these new approaches possess some of the same weaknesses of earlier personality and motivation taxonomies (e.g., those espoused by Karen Horney, Alfred Adler, or Abraham Maslow) in that they do not provide ultimate-based explanations for the elemental needs, personality types, and motivations in question. The building blocks of any motivation theory or personality taxonomy have a Darwinian etiology. This is the position espoused by Buss (1991) and other evolutionary-minded psychologists in their description of evolutionary personality psychology, to which I turn next.

Buss (1991) has proposed that evolutionary theory is the meta-framework that is needed to organize and unify the field of personality research. He states:

> Evolutionary theory promises to circumvent the plethora of seemingly arbitrary personality theories by anchoring a theory of human nature in processes known to govern all life. There is no reason to believe that humans are exempt from the organizing forces of evolution by natural selection. Personality theories inconsistent with evolutionary theory stand little chance of being correct. (p. 461)

For example, Freud's Oedipal complex is a classic example of a developmental theory that is incongruent with foundational tenets of evolutionary theory. This is why it is incorrect. Similarly, Maslow's highest need, namely self-actualization, is based on his humanistic vision rather than on any empirical validation or veridical theoretical grounding. Buss highlights several distinct ways by which evolutionary theory could improve the plight of personality research (but see Cervone, 2000, for two important challenges facing evolutionary theorists wishing to apply a Darwinian-based approach in understanding personality). He argues that the Big Five model of personality has been repeatedly validated both cross-culturally and longitudinally because these key personality factors can be construed in part as solutions to adaptive problems that humans have had to solve in their phylogenetic history. This is in line with the position espoused by the famous depression scholar Aaron T. Beck, who has apparently "argued that personality is a collection of evolved behavioral strategies that facilitate the solving of adaptive problems" (Henriques, 2003, pp. 161–162). MacDonald (1998) poignantly echoed this point when he proposed the following:

> I conclude that an evolutionary perspective is able to make theoretical sense of much of the FFM [Five Factor Model] literature as well as provide personality psychology in general with a very broad theoretical foundation. A particular advantage is that an evolutionary perspective is able to provide a deductive basis for personality research. Sub-theories within the evolutionary framework, such as the theory of sex differences, parent–offspring conflict theory, and life history theory, are able to provide a predictive basis for personality psychology—predictive in the sense that the patterns actually found are embedded in a much wider theoretical framework that ultimately links psychology to the natural sciences. (p. 144)

Buss (1991) proposed that the debate regarding the stability of one's personality (i.e., enduring vs. situation-specific), which has raged within the personality literature for several decades, is resolved once framed as a manifestation of evolutionary interactionism. Finally, he summarizes several competing evolutionary-based explanations regarding the maintenance of heterogeneous personality types. Within the spirit of the position espoused by David Buss, Ashton, Paunonen, Helmes, and Jackson (1998) found a relationship between two of the Big Five personality factors (agreeableness and emotional stability) and one's disposition to engage in altruistic behaviors. In other words, the proclivity to engage in altruistic behaviors is in part determined by one's personality. Though the authors did not pronounce a position as to why interindividual variations in personality scores might occur (in an evolutionary sense), they were able to link the Big Five traits to two Darwinian modules (kin selection and reciprocal altruism). This is another example that invalidates the claim that evolutionary psychology is tantamount to espousing biological determinism. Though at the population level humans have evolved the predisposition for altruistic behaviors, the extent to which a given individual is predisposed to display such behaviors is in part determined by their unique personalities, these being in part shaped by the particular ecological niche that the individual occupies. More recently, Schmitt and Buss (2000) applied evolutionary personality psychology in understanding the manner by which individuals are described within the mating domain. For additional biologically inspired approaches to the study of personality at both the ultimate and proximate levels of analysis, the reader is referred to the special issue of the *Journal of Personality* edited by Buss (1990) and more recently to the work of Bouchard and Loehlin (2001). For a thorough review of the various approaches to the study of personality including the evolutionary perspective, see Revelle (1995).

Consumer segmentation is a foundational concept in the practice of marketing. Numerous variables can be used to segment a market, one of which is along personality types. An evolutionary-informed perspective on personality types can guide one's choice as to which traits are relevant in segmenting consumers within a given product category. For example, the sensation-seeking trait would appear relevant in segmenting the "extreme sports" market. That said, there exists universal evidence that men score considerably higher than women do on the sensation-seeking trait (cf. Rosenblitt, Soler, Johnson, & Quadagno, 2001), a finding congruent with evolutionary theory (as is discussed in chap. 3). Let us suppose that for an individual to engage in extreme sports requires that their sensation-seeking score be higher than a prescribed threshold. The service provider offering opportunities for engaging in extreme sports would be well advised to know that sex is a very good discriminating variable regarding those that fall above or below the postulated threshold. Furthermore, this sex effect will manifest itself in the same manner across cultures because the instantiation of this personality type is rooted in a Darwinian etiology.

Machiavellianism is a personality trait that has received considerable attention within the marketing literature. Oftentimes, the research objective has been to establish where salespeople, marketers, or business students fall on the Machiavellianism continuum as compared to some relevant groups. Business ethicists have sought to establish the link between Machiavellianism and one's ethical proclivities. Another research stream has attempted to draw links between Machiavellianism and demographic or personality traits (e.g., Type A personality). One demographic variable that has received considerable attention is sex, with the results yielding mixed and contradictory findings (i.e., males > females; females > males; and no sex differences). An evolutionary-based perspective recognizes that a main effect for sex should not be expected across domains. Instead, men and women display differential manipulative intent as a function of the particular domains in question, an issue further elaborated in the ensuing paragraph.

Over the past 25 years, a wide range of evolutionists stemming from various research streams have investigated Machiavellianism while providing plausible ultimate-based accounts of the existence of this trait. Why have humans evolved such large and complex brains capable of manipulative intent? One theory suggests that the evolution of an ever-more complex human mind was an adaptive solution to the increasing complexity of the social environment faced by our ancestors (see Byrne & Whiten, 1988, and relevant references therein). One finding in support of the latter hypothesis is the fact that in comparing across primates, there exists a positive correlation between social complexity and brain size (cf. Dunbar, 2003, for a review). This notion has led to the positing of the Machiavellian intelligence hypothesis (see Byrne & Whiten, 1988; Whiten & Byrne, 1997), which suggests that humans are in part endowed with large brains in order to navigate their complex social and hierarchical environments with the hope of achieving two concomitant goals. First, individuals seek to take advantage of their conspecifics (mates, kin, friends, or strangers) while trying to disguise their manipulative intent. Second, they seek to identify such intent in others given that they will be the targets and possibly the victims of such manipulation. In a sense, this is the classic evolutionary arms race that is found in various dyadic interactions, be it between predators and their prey, between men and women in the courtship dance, between hosts and pathogens, or in this case between two conspecifics seeking to outsmart one another. In the consumption and political settings, two groups of conspecifics might be salespeople and customers, and politicians and the electorate, respectively. Hence, an evolutionary-informed approach recognizes that Machiavellianism can be explored both as an enduring and as a situation-specific trait (cf. D. S. Wilson, Near, & Miller, 1996). The stripper that manages to wryly smile at her male customers in order to entice them to hire her for several expensive solo dances is equally Machiavellian as the man feigning a long-term interest in a prospective short-term mate. In other words, though it is indeed true that individuals vary along the Machiavellianism trait, this is perhaps not as important as the recognition of the situation-specific instantiations of this trait. By exploring the Darwinian etiology of this personality trait, new research opportunities are created beyond the proximate phenomena that have thus far been addressed in the literature.

Having identified the paucity of Darwinian-based theorizing in consumer behavior, in the next section I briefly highlight the wide range of disciplines that have adopted evolutionary theory within their theoretical purview.

APPLICATIONS OF EVOLUTIONARY PSYCHOLOGY IN OTHER DISCIPLINES

Of all scholars housed in business schools, game theorists and mathematical modelers are probably those who have made the greatest use of evolutionary principles. Typically, they utilize analytical tools that were originally developed by evolutionary-minded scholars such as Axelrod (1984), Axelrod and Hamilton (1981), and Maynard Smith (1982). Other disciplines within the business schools that have relied on Darwinian principles (albeit rarely) are organizational behavior and management. At the micro level, Colarelli (1998) proposed an evolutionary-based approach for designing appropriate psychological procedures and interventions in organizational settings. Darwinian theorizing has also been applied in understanding human resource management (Colarelli, 2003), sexual harassment in organizations (Studd & Gattiker, 1991), and organizational life (Nicholson, 1997, 1998). At the macro level, Hanna and Freeman (1977, 1989) used Darwinian-based frameworks in developing the now-burgeoning field of organizational ecology (an offshoot of population ecology). Most recently, Pierce and White (1999) have argued that the forms that organizations assume (e.g., the extent to which they are hierarchical) are driven by ecological realities that are assessed by individuals using their evolved domain-specific mental modules. For recent works on the links between Darwinian theory and organizational behavior, the reader is referred to the 2006 special issue in the *Journal of Organizational Behavior* on that topic.

How extensively have consumer researchers and behavioral marketing scholars utilized evolutionary psychology and other Darwinian-based frameworks? Using *evolutionary psychology, Darwinian, Darwinism,* and *sociobiology* as key search terms, Saad and Gill (2000) searched seven academic databases to establish the prevalence of evolutionary theorizing in various disciplines. They demonstrated that despite the increasing adoption of evolutionary theorizing in the social sciences, most marketing scholars have ignored the relevance of Darwinian theory in explaining consumption phenomena. Subsequently, they enumerated three ways by which evolutionary psychology could be applied in the marketing and consumer behavior disciplines. First, previous findings in the literature could be reanalyzed using a Darwinian lens. Evolutionary explanations of previously obtained findings need not necessarily supplant the heretofore-accepted explanations. However, they might provide an integrative framework to unify otherwise disparate findings and/or propose ultimate-based explanations to supplement the ubiquitous proximate theories (e.g., the sex-in-advertising literature affords an opportunity for this dual purpose). Second, they might provide ultimate-based explanations for existing aggregate consumption patterns (e.g., that men consume more pornography whereas women constitute the majority of cosmetic surgery patients). Third, an infusion of evolutionary theorizing into the consumer behavior and marketing disciplines might yield new hypotheses and research streams that would remain invisible if not tackled with an evolutionary lens (e.g., the links between menstrual cycle and specific consumption choices).

Few other researchers have applied Darwinian principles in consumer behavior and marketing. Lynn, Kampschroeder, and Perriera (1998) proposed speculative links between evolutionary psychology and consumer behavior. For example, they argued that the facial features of toys have become increasingly neotenous (possessing babylike features). In a recent issue of *Psychology & Marketing* dedicated to the links between evolutionary theory and consumption, Colarelli and Dettman (2003) provided several examples highlighting the relevance of evolutionary psychology in marketing. Donald Hantula, the guest editor of the latter special issue, has published several papers wherein he utilized a model from behavioral ecology to investigate online shopping behavior (cf. Rajala & Hantula, 2000). Finally, Saad (2006a) explored the Darwinian etiology behind a wide range of consumption phenomena in the special issue of *Managerial and Decision Economics* dedicated to the links between evolutionary psychology and management.

Saad and Gill (1999) categorized and tabulated the departmental affiliations of authors who have published in the premier journal dedicated to an evolutionary approach to human behavior (*Ethology and Sociobiology*, whose name was changed to *Evolution and Human Behavior*) covering 1979 through 1998 (see Table 2.2). Although the majority of those who publish in the premier consumer behavior journals are housed in marketing de-

TABLE 2.2
Departmental Affiliations of Authors in
Ethology and Sociobiology/Evolution and Human Behavior **(1979–1998)**

Discipline	*79–83*	*84–88*	*89–93*	*94–98*
Biological	**14**	**19**	**26**	**26**
Biology	10	6	16	20
Zoology[a]	2	12	8	6
Genetics	2	1	2	0
Psychological	**28**	**59**	**64**	**60**
Psychology	21	33	45	40
Psychiatry	5	20	2	14
Behavior Science[b]	2	6	17	6
Medical	**7**	**19**	**7**	**12**
Medicine[c]	1	5	1	6
Physiology	1	2	1	0
Pediatrics[d]	2	1	1	2
Neuropsych[e]	3	11	4	4
Environmental	**7**	**8**	**7**	**6**
Environment Studies/Science[f]	3	2	1	4
Ecology/ Ethology	4	6	6	2
Applied Sciences	**0**	**4**	**1**	**3**
Science/Tech[g]	0	3	1	1
Maths/Stats	0	1	0	2

(continued on next page)

TABLE 2.2 (continued)

Discipline	79–83	84–88	89–93	94–98
Social Sciences	**22**	**41**	**53**	**41**
Anthropology	13	23	34	23
Sociology[h]	6	3	9	9
Political Science	2	2	0	1
Education	0	4	3	1
Economics	0	0	2	2
Law	0	8	3	0
Management	0	0	1	1
Population Studies	0	1	1	4
History	1	0	0	0

[a]Includes the departments of zoology and primate studies.
[b]Includes the departments of behavior science, behavior studies, and human behavior and evolution program.
[c]Includes the departments of medicine, obstetrics, surgery, and gynecology.
[d]Includes the departments of pediatrics and child development.
[e]Includes the departments of neuropsychology, neurology, neuropsychiatry, and neurosurgery.
[f]Includes the departments of environmental studies, environmental science, and marine science.
[g]Includes the departments of chemistry, astrophysics, science and technology, and food and nutrition science.
[h]Includes the disciplines of sociology, social science, and social work.

partments, Table 2.2 lists close to 40 departmental affiliations. This is the epitome of interdisciplinary research as one might expect, given the ability of Darwinian theory to provide consilience across the various branches of learning (E. O. Wilson, 1998).

In addition to the "traditional" Darwinian-based fields such as evolutionary biology, ethology, sociobiology, behavioral ecology, evolutionary psychology, Darwinian anthropology, and zoology (e.g., primatology), there are several disciplines, including cognate social science fields, that have developed Darwinian-inspired specializations covering an extraordinarily wide range of fields (see Table 2.3 for a nonexhaustive subsample of these). Peterson and Somit (2001) provide a compendium of evolutionary-inspired works in a wide range of fields including economics, history, international relations, law, philosophy, politics, psychiatry, and sociology.

The list of disciplines that have adopted evolutionary psychology and related Darwinian frameworks extends well beyond that which I have discussed and/or listed in this section. Hence, disparate fields in both the social and natural sciences have recognized the relevance of evolutionary theory in understanding wide-ranging phenomena. Given that consumer behavior is an arena wherein our innate human nature manifests itself, our discipline might benefit from an infusion of evolutionary-based theorizing.

TABLE 2.3
Darwinian-Based Disciplines or Subdisciplines

Discipline	*Representative Sources*
Biopolitics/evolutionary politics	Masters, 1989; G. Schubert, 1989; Rubin, 2002
Bioeconomics	see articles in the *Journal of Bioeconomics*
Darwinian-based law	Gruter Institute; O. D. Jones & Goldsmith, 2005
Evolutionary game theory	Maynard Smith, 1982
Neuroeconomics	see works of Paul Zak and Colin Camerer; Sanfey, Rilling, Aronson, Nystrom, & Cohen, 2003
Evolutionary archaeology	Barton & Clark, 1997 (edited book)
Evolutionary architecture	Barton & Clark, 1997; Tsui, 1999
Biomimetics	Bar-Cohen, 2005
Evolutionary developmental psychology	Bjorklund & Pellegrini, 2002
Evolutionary social psychology	Simpson & Kenrick, 1997 (edited book)
Evolutionary cognitive neuroscience	See the lab of Stephen M. Platek (Drexel Univ.)
Darwinian ecology	Penn, 2003
Darwinian agriculture	Denison, Kiers, & West, 2003
Ecological economics	Jackson, 2002
Darwinian sociology	Sanderson, 2001; Lopreato & Crippen, 1999
Evolutionary anthropology	See articles in the journal of that name
Human behavioral ecology	Cronk, 1991; Winterhalder & Smith, 2000
Darwinian medicine	Nesse & Williams, 1996
Darwinian psychiatry	McGuire & Troisi, 1998
Evolutionary health promotion	Eaton, Strassman, et al., 2002; Eaton, Cordain, & Lindeberg, 2002
Genetic programming/ evolutionary computation	Koza, 1992
Neural Darwinism	Edelman, 1987
Darwinian gastronomy	Sherman & Billing, 1999
Literary Darwinism	Carroll, 2004; Gottschall & Wilson, 2006 (edited book)

(continued on next page)

TABLE 2.3 (continued)

Discipline	Representative Sources
Evolutionary Musicology	Wallin, Merker, & Brown, 2000 (edited book); Fitch, 2006
Evolutionary ethics/morality	Farber, 1998; Ruse, 1999; L. D. Katz, 2000 (edited book)
Evolutionary epistemology	Heyes & Hull, 2001 (edited book); Hull, 2001
Evolutionary aesthetics	Dissanayake, 1992
Darwinian creativity	Simonton, 1999
Memetic theory	Lynch, 1996; Blackmore, 1999; Aunger, 2002
Gene-culture coevolution	Boyd & Richerson, 1985; Richerson & Boyd, 2005

CHAPTER SUMMARY

As is true of most of the social sciences, to date consumer behavior has largely renunciated evolutionary forces from within the purview of its explanatory frameworks. This has led to a reliance on the environment in understanding consumption phenomena. Furthermore, consumer research typically addresses proximate issues via an exploration of domain-general mental mechanisms. I demonstrated this point by analyzing several substantive areas of interest to consumer researchers including learning, motivation, culture, decision making, perception, attitudes, emotions, and personality. Accordingly, I suggested ways by which evolutionary theorizing might be infused within each of the latter key areas as a means of complementing the existing research streams. We can achieve a more accurate and complete understanding of consumption phenomena by recognizing the Darwinian heritage that shapes much of our behaviors as consumers. Humans are inextricably shaped by both their biological heritage as well as their unique environments and life experiences; accordingly, our theoretical models should be congruent with this reality. It is important to reiterate that evolutionary theory will not dislodge proximate-based explorations; rather, both are needed for a complete understanding of consumption phenomena.

In the next chapter, I demonstrate that most of the key consumption phenomena can be subsumed within four key Darwinian modules, namely those associated with survival, mating, kin investment, and reciprocity.

Consumption and Darwinian Modules

Four ultimately caused behavior patterns or systems are thought to apply to Homo sapiens: the survival, reproductive, kin assistance, and reciprocation systems.

—McGuire and Troisi (1998, pp. 60–61)

My goal in this chapter is to demonstrate that countless consumption acts are specific instantiations of the four most elemental Darwinian modules that drive purposive behavior. Specifically, I highlight how many consumption phenomena can be subsumed within the reproductive, survival, kin selection, and reciprocation modules (see the table of contents of Buss, 2005, for a similar breakdown of key Darwinian systems). Hence, the current taxonomy was generated using ultimate-based theorizing and empirical findings across countless species (including humans). Other evolutionists have come up with slightly different classifications of ultimate goals. For example, Kenrick et al. (2002) list six such social goals, these being coalition formation, status, self-protection, mate choice, relationship maintenance, and parental care. That said, the latter six goals could be subsumed within the four elemental Darwinian modules discussed in the current chapter. I begin with the reproductive module.

THE REPRODUCTIVE MODULE

Of all decisions that individuals make within their lifetimes, few are as important as their choice of a mate. The mating decision can be construed as a consumption choice in that individuals can be viewed as "products" in the mating market (cf. Bernard, Adelman, & Schroeder, 1991; Hirschman, 1987). Within the latter market, people advertise themselves as viable products and they search for information about prospective partners (products). They form a mating intention and subsequently choose a winning suitor. They derogate competitors in a process akin to comparative advertising (see Schmitt & Buss, 1996, for an evolutionary account of mate derogation). They experience either postchoice satisfaction or dissatisfaction and will oftentimes succumb to cognitive dissonance having made a mating choice. Hence, all of the key consumption stages are operative within a mating choice. Perhaps because of the immediately obvious relevance of Darwinian theory to human mating, evolutionary psychologists have addressed this domain more than any other (see Symons, 1979, for one of the original treatises of human mating from an evolutionary perspective). Of all domains studied by evolutionary psychologists, none has yielded as many sex differences as the mating domain. Evolutionarily speaking, men and women have faced distinct problems within the mating domain. As such, their respective behaviors, emotions, preferences, and physiology within the sexual realm are in many instances distinct from one another precisely because they represent sex-specific adaptive solutions to recurring mating problems.

The most influential and parsimonious theoretical model that has been proposed to explain sex differences in mating behavior is the parental investment model (Trivers, 1972; see also Bjorklund & Shackelford, 1999; Feingold, 1992; Gangestad & Simpson, 2000; Kenrick, Sadalla, Groth, & Trost, 1990). As briefly addressed in chapter 1, the model states that within sexually reproducing species, the sex that provides the greater parental investment will be more sexually choosy and restrained. In other words, whenever the two sexes within a species provide a differential amount of parental investment, this should translate into differences in mating behavior including the mating characteristics sought in ideal suitors, and the proclivity to engage in short-term versus long-term mating. In most species (certainly the case with mammals), the female provides the greater parental investment resulting in females being more sexually coy, more discriminating, and physically smaller than their male counterparts (behavioral and physical dimorphism). In a few rare species, typically those where either fertilization or incubation occurs externally (e.g., birds or fish), males might provide greater parental investment (cf. the Jacanas and the Phalaropes for sex role reversals in avian species). As a result, in such species the pattern of dimorphism (i.e., which sex is bigger, less sexually choosy, etc.) is exactly reversed. In yet other species, both parents provide roughly equal parental investment, in which case one would not expect any dimorphism within such species (e.g., Emperor penguins). Upon laying the eggs, female Emperor penguins leave on long food-foraging voyages. The male penguins are left to incubate the eggs for several months, which exposes them to great survival challenges including the threats of starvation, predation, and exposure to the exceptionally harsh Antarctic climate. Thus, the pattern of behavioral and physical dimorphism (if any) across species is well captured by the parental investment hypothesis (see Eens & Pinxten, 2000, for additional mechanisms that might affect the instantiation of sex roles within a given species). For *Homo sapiens*, because females provide exceptionally higher parental investment, this yields a wide range of psychosexual behaviors that are sex-specific because they are adaptive solutions to sex-specific evolutionary problems. Evolutionists do not question the fact that human mating patterns could display substantial plasticity both within and between the sexes. This is the idea behind the strategic pluralism view of human mating as espoused by Gangestad and Simpson (2000). For example, though men have a stronger proclivity for short-term mating, this hardly implies that women are never interested in such opportunities. Urbaniak and Kilmann (2003) found that although women do appreciate and desire nice guys, physical attractiveness mattered a bit more for short-term mating contexts (see also Scheib, 2001). On a related note, Tombs and Silverman (2004) demonstrated the link between women's preferences for larger pupils in men and a corresponding preference for "bad boys." Many women who are desirous of bad boys are so for short-term dalliances. As such, it would make evolutionary sense that cues that signal sexual interest (e.g., pupil size) would be more likely to be attended to if one is interested in a short-term mating opportunity. Additional evidence of women's strategic interest in short-term dalliances is discussed in the ensuing paragraph. I should mention that strategic pluralism recognizes not only the existence of both within-sex and between-sex differences in mating behaviors but also the possibility of differential mating behaviors within the life stages of single individuals. Along those lines, Burnham et al. (2003) administered a salivary testosterone assay to students at the Harvard Business School. They found that men in committed relationships (i.e., either married, or unmarried but pair-bonded) had lower testosterone than did unmarried men. It is hypothesized that this is likely due to a trade-off between parental effort (even though a pair bond might not have children, I suppose) and mate search effort. In other words, the same man can experience a shift in his mating behaviors as a function of his parental status. Hence, an evolutionary theory of human mating does not suggest that individuals are biologically destined to pursue a single, deterministic, and invariant mating strategy.

Another influential theory within the human-mating literature is sexual strategies theory (Buss, 1998; Buss & Schmitt, 1993; Schmitt et al., 2003). It stipulates that the sexual behaviors and preferences of the two sexes are dependent on the temporal context of the relationship (see also Kenrick et al., 1990). Hence, short-term dalliances might yield radically different behaviors and preferences as compared to long-term pair bonds. Furthermore, the two sexes are differentially affected by the temporal context of the relationship precisely because the implied parental investment varies more so for men than it does for women. A woman experiences the same parental investment irrespective of the temporal context of the relationship; however, for a man, a short-term copulation might involve nothing more than a 5-minute encounter whereas a long-term relationship requires tremendous parental commitment. Not surprisingly, the attributes that men seek in an ideal partner can be diametrically opposed depending on the mating context. A promiscuous woman is potentially desired as a short-term partner but likely abhorred as a long-term mate. Some non-evolutionists have misinterpreted the key tenets espoused by these Darwinian-based theories of human mating. Specifically, they have misconstrued these as implying that men should seldom be interested in long-term pair bonding whereas women should rarely desire short-term mating opportunities. Both positions are erroneous as elucidated by sexual strategies theory. The phylogenetic history of *Homo sapiens* is such that the successful rearing of offspring (i.e., until sexual maturity) requires biparental investment. As such, it is indeed within men's evolved interest to provide long-term parental care. That said, the optimal strategy is to monopolize the reproductive resources of one or more women while seeking multiple short-term mating opportunities. On the other hand, a woman's optimal mating strategy is hardly prudish or Victorian and can be equally duplicitous as that pursued by men. Women seek to identify suitable suitors who would be willing to provide a long-term investment while shopping around for better genes (cf. R. Baker & Bellis, 1995).

Of what relevance are the latter Darwinian-based theories to consumer behavior? First, human mating can be construed as the ultimate consumption decision. Hence, one might apply evolutionary psychology to investigate how people advertise themselves as products in the mating market, how they search for information on prospective partners, and how they choose a final winning suitor. Second, one can explore sex differences in aggregate consumption patterns with regard to specific products that cater to the mating module. I begin by exploring the former, namely using evolutionary psychology to investigate mating as the ultimate consumption choice.

Human Mating as a Consumption Choice

Within the human-mating literature, the topic that has been most investigated is the mating characteristics sought by men and women. This has been addressed using a multitude of data collection procedures including surveys (cf. Buss, 1989; Kenrick, Groth, Trost, & Sadalla, 1993), content analyses of personal ads (cf. Campos, Otta, & Siqueira, 2002; Greenlees &

McGrew, 1994), demographic data (Kenrick & Keefe, 1992; South, 1991), and experiments (Townsend & Levy, 1990a, 1990b). Two universal and robust findings are that men place a greater premium on youth and beauty whereas women place greater importance on social status and ability to acquire, retain, and share resources. The reason for this pervasive sex difference is that mating preferences cater to sex-specific evolutionary problems. These findings hold true independent of era, cultural setting, sociopolitical context, economic reality, and geographical location (see Buss, 1994, for a thorough summary of relevant studies). Socialization-based scholars have sought to challenge the evolutionary explanations. For example, Alice Eagly (cf. Eagly, 1987) has repeatedly argued that sex differences in the characteristics sought by each sex is a reflection of the sex roles that have been historically assigned to the two sexes. As is true of most socialization-based arguments, this explains little because the ultimate reason for this particular and universal pattern of sex role assignments is due to our Darwinian-derived phylogenetic history. One popular socialization-based account argues that because women have been historically oppressed on all possible fronts (e.g., economically, politically, and socially), it is not surprising that they would seek to obtain resources via their mating choices. Buss (1994, pp. 45–47) discusses several studies that have refuted this explanation, coined the structural powerlessness hypothesis. An increase in a woman's educational, occupational, and economic status yields a corresponding increase in the socioeconomic status that she demands from potential suitors. Highly educated, independent, and wealthy women who certainly do not necessitate the financial assistance of any man nonetheless retain a persistent (if not stronger) attraction to high-status men. Evolutionarily speaking, women who mated with high-status males had a higher chance of successfully rearing offspring. As such, women have evolved a preference for men that either are socially dominant or have the potential of becoming so. Choosing males based on their ability to acquire, protect, and share resources is a ubiquitous female mating strategy across a diverse range of species (see Batten, 1992). It is important to note that women are not singularly attracted to men with resources; rather, they can be equally attracted to men who have yet to achieve status but are on a trajectory of social ascendancy. Accordingly, cues of intelligence, ambition, drive, and focus can be equally intoxicating to women. Unique talents that are socially valued, including those possessed by successful artists, singers, athletes, and actors, are typically desired by women. Ceteris paribus, professors, politicians, business executives, lawyers, and surgeons make for attractive long-term male partners. This point demonstrates that Darwinian principles are not deterministic. Although the Darwinian goal "seek status" is an evolved goal that men pursue assiduously, there are multiple paths that can be taken to achieve the goal. The unique environment, life experiences, and innate abilities of a given individual will determine whether the instantiation of pursuing this Darwinian goal will be to rob a bank, become a pop star, or receive board certification as a neurosurgeon. Note that the definition of status varies across cultures. For example, the number of livestock owned is the metric of choice among the Masai of Kenya whereas the size of one's bank account is one relevant status indicator in Western societies. Nonetheless, irrespective of the cross-cultural variations in the definition of status, wealth, and power, women have a universal preference for high-status, dominant, powerful, and wealthy men.

Why do men have a universal preference for youthful and beautiful women? Social constructivists propose that men have been taught these preferences (e.g., via media images); accordingly, it is argued that there is nothing innate about these. There are several problems with this account. First, socialization-based theorists have to explain why it is that men are socialized to have these preferences. By not providing the ultimate genesis of this socialization process, this explanation is at best incomplete. Second, these theorists must explain why this socialization process seems to have existed in this specific form across every known culture and era. To date, there does not exist a single culture that scholars have uncovered where the mating preferences of men have not been of this particular form (see Buss, 1994). Cultural artifacts and narratives across countless cultures extol women's beauty. Varied data sources—be they archival and historical records, anthropological studies, cross-cultural experiments and surveys, content analyses of cultural artifacts, narratives, and daily anecdotal evidence—all suggest that men desire attractive and youthful women. The evolutionary explanation is simple. Those men who had a singular interest in mating with elderly women did not pass on their mating preference (the same point applies to those women who solely desired low-status males). In an ensuing section, I demonstrate that in most product categories where the purchases are dominated by one of the two sexes (e.g., cosmetics), one can easily identify the link between the product category in question and sex-specific mating preferences. I next turn to a discussion of how a domain-specific calculus drives search behavior in the mating arena.

Information Search in Mate Selection. How do individuals search for information when seeking prospective mates? Frank (1988) argued that people engage in constant search with regard to both their current and prospective partners. However, given that search is effortful, one must utilize a stopping rule in deciding when sufficient information has been acquired to justify committing to a course of action (e.g., choosing or leaving a mate; rejecting unsuitable suitors, etc.). Optional stopping rules have been studied in a myriad of sequential sampling contexts, only one of which is in the context of human mating. Numerous approaches have been applied in the study of sequential mate search (cf. Dombrovsky & Perrin, 1994; Mazalov, Perrin, & Dombrovsky, 1996; Wiegmann, Mukhopadhyay, & Real, 1999). In the context of human mating, sequential sampling has typically been modeled as an alternative-based process. In other words, assuming that one has to choose between n prospective suitors, the iterative counter consists of deciding the size of the subset (i.e., the number of prospective mates) that will be evaluated prior to committing to a final choice. Hence, each acquired piece of information corresponds to one suitor (cf. G. F. Miller & Todd, 1998; Todd & Miller, 1999). On the other hand, in attribute-based sequential sampling models, the number of options (i.e., mates in the current context) is fixed at two whereas the number of attributes that can be acquired along the two alternatives is the iterative counter. Saad and Eba (2005) utilized such a sequential sampling approach to explore information search when individuals are choosing between two competing suitors. Additionally, in line with sexual strategies theory (cf. Buss & Schmitt, 1993), participants were randomly assigned to either a short-term mating or long-term mating context. The DSMAC process tracing computerized interface (Saad, 1998) was used to implement the experimental task. One of the features of the interface is that it allows individuals to acquire information either until they are ready to choose a winning suitor between the two competing alternatives or until they have acquired sufficient information to reject both suitors. This is particularly important given that when evaluating prospective mates, rejections are outcomes that occur quite frequently. Several noteworthy findings were obtained all supportive of the sex-based dimorphism as postulated by evolutionary principles of human mating. First, women were much more likely to reject both suitors as compared to men (main effect of sex). This is in line with parental investment theory, which predicts that women should be much more selective in their choice of suitors. When broken down by temporal context, women seeking short-term mating opportunities and men seeking such dalliances were overwhelmingly the most and least likely respectively to reject both suitors. In other words, women are substantially less interested in casual sex as compared to men, another result in line with evolutionary-based theories of human mating. Third, men acquired significantly more attributes prior to rejecting a pair of suitors as compared to women. Thus, not only are men less likely to reject suitors (because the costs of a suboptimal choice looms smaller for men), but also they require more convincing to arrive at such a decision (as evidenced by the greater amount of information acquired). Furthermore, women acquired the same amount of information prior to rejecting a pair of suitors irrespective of the temporal context. On the other hand, men seeking long-term mates acquired more information prior to rejecting mates as compared to their short-term counterparts. Given that women's parental costs are the same irrespective of the temporal context (but not men's), evolutionary-based theories of human mating would exactly predict that men's behaviors (but not women's) would be affected by the temporal context of the relationship.

In addition to providing additional support for several evolution-ary-based theories of human mating, the work by Saad and Eba highlights the weakness of information-processing theories that postulated a main effect of sex irrespective of the domain in question. For example, the selec-tivity hypothesis (cf. Meyers-Levy & Maheswaran, 1991; Meyers-Levy & Sternthal, 1991) proposes that women are comprehensive information pro-cessors whereas men are selective and hence rely on heuristics to prune the search space (irrespective of the domain). The logic behind the majority of gender role theories that are applied in the context of information process-ing is that sex-based differences arise because of role-specific socialization. Hence, that women are more comprehensive processors of information (across all domains) is due to their subordinate roles in patriarchal societ-ies, which forces them to be attuned to all relevant cues in the world around them (see Hupfer, 2002, pp. 3–4 for additional details). As such, ir-respective of whether purchasing toothpaste, making financial decisions, or identifying prospective suitors, women will supposedly process more information because they have learned this role via the pervasive influ-ences of the patriarchy. Evolutionary principles would posit that which sex will engage in greater information search is intimately linked to the do-main in question. Returning to the Saad and Eba work, they found that women acquired *less* information prior to rejecting prospective suitors. That women are *more selective* in the context of mate selection serves as a refutation of the central postulate of the socialization-based *selectivity* hy-pothesis (which posits the opposite effect).

On a related note, Putrevu (2001) reviewed sex and gender differences in information processing and the possible implications that these might yield in an advertising context. Though it was encouraging to see that bi-ological and evolutionary forces were acknowledged, the crux of the arti-cle revolved around two theories, both disconnected from biological and ultimate-based theorizing. Each theory espouses dichotomous forms of information processing (selective vs. comprehensive processing; item-specific vs. relational processing). The respective theories suggest that men are selective and item-specific processors whereas women are comprehensive and relational processors. Putrevu proposes that the item-specific-versus-relational-processing dichotomy is perhaps needed given that the selectivity hypothesis has received equivocal and mixed support in the literature. Domain-general theories that posit sex-specific forms of information processing across contexts are unlikely to yield strong empiricial support, because they assume a highly untenable evolutionary outcome. Evolutionary theory posits that sex-specific mental modules (i.e., forms of processing in this case) are adaptive solutions to sex-specific problems; as such, by definition these modules could not have evolved to transcend decisional domains.

Gift Giving as a Courtship Ritual.   Gift giving is an integral element of the courtship ritual across a wide range of species (e.g., insects and mammals). For example, in some insect species, females choose to mate with those males that offer them the most nutritious gifts. In several species of gazelles, the gift consists of permitting prospective females to graze on a territory that is protected by a dominant male. In perhaps the most "romantic" manifestation of courtship gift giving, the male praying mantis offers himself as a nuptial packet of calories to be devoured while mating with the exceptionally larger and more dangerous female suitor. In most species, the pattern of behavioral dimorphism between the two sexes with regard to gift giving is the same; namely, males woo the females with gifts. This pattern of gift giving defines the human courtship ritual, and this holds true across eras and cultures. It is no surprise that DeBeers (a company specializing in the sale of diamonds) has yet to find a culture where women are more likely than men to use diamond rings as a means to woo prospective suitors. A recent ranking by *Advertising Age* of the top advertising slogans of the 20th century placed DeBeers' "Diamonds are forever" as the top one (see http://www.adage.com/century/slogans.html). This slogan is timeless because it caters to an innate element of human mating, namely the fact that men have to typically engage in behaviors that signal long-term commitment (see Cronk & Dunham, 2003, for an evolutionary-based exploration of male signaling via the purchase of engagement rings). With that in mind, Saad and Gill (2003) utilized Darwinian-based theorizing in exploring the motives that drive young adults to offer gifts to their romantic partners. They compared the sexes along two sets of motives, namely tactical and situational ones. Tactical motives serve an ultimate purpose, such as displaying one's resources or seducing one's partner, whereas a specific occasion or norm (e.g., offering a birthday gift) drives situational motives. As hypothesized, they found that men were much more likely to have tactical reasons for offering gifts, whereas no sex differences were obtained for situational motives. Saad and Gill also explored whether men and women possess differential abilities in understanding the motives behind their partners' offerings. In other words, are men and women equally adept in reading these intersexual courtship signals? The findings demonstrated that whereas men navigate in ignorance, women are fully cognizant of the reasons that men offer them gifts. Specifically, men extrapolated their own motives onto women's; namely, they thought that the motives that drive their offerings are exactly those of women. In the current courtship context and as postulated by parental investment theory (Trivers, 1972), misreading interspecific signals carries different benefits and costs for each sex. Women who might carelessly mate with every suitor who offered them a token gift coupled with deceitful promises of eternal love and commitment, would sustain severe fitness costs (mating with an ill-suited or suboptimal male). On the other hand, if a nondiscriminating man were sufficiently "naïve" to succumb to similar advances by a multitude of women, this would yield substantial fitness benefits (i.e., opportunity to mate with numerous receptive females). As such, that women are better calibrated in navigating through the minefield of intersexual communication is a testament to the differential costs and benefits associated with not being able to do so. Hence, women's evolved superiority in reading these courtship signals is an adaptation to a sex-specific mating problem. Incidentally, it is perfectly within the purview of evolutionary psychology to accept the fact that women are in part socialized and taught how to read such signals. That said, evolutionists provide an ultimate explanation for a given socialization pattern. Specifically, to the extent that a given socialization standard transcends cultures and eras, its roots are likely Darwinian based.

The misreading of sexual signals does not merely arise in the context of gift giving. When reading intersexual facial expressions, such as an innocent smile and/or glance, men are much more likely to incorrectly attribute sexual interest on a woman's part (Abbey, 1982; Haselton, 2003; Haselton & Buss, 2000). This makes sense from an evolutionary perspective. Given men's greater desire for short-term mating opportunities, it is no surprise that their misinterpretations of intersexual signals would encourage approach behavior. Given the differential fitness costs and benefits associated with an accurate decoding of nonverbal communiqués, the differential abilities of each sex in deciphering the semiotics of these nonverbal cues is indeed expected. There are countless consumption-related contexts where this differential capacity to comprehend nonverbal signals is evident. In certain service settings, men's poorer abilities along this interpersonal domain are harvested to the service provider's benefit. Blatantly fake smiles by female strippers are irresistibly enticing to male patrons, so much so that men are willing to spend considerable sums of money (e.g., purchasing private dances) to foster and maintain the "interest" displayed by a Machiavellian female stripper. Sijuwade (1995) used a dramaturgical analysis to explore the latter fake interaction, which he coined "counterfeit intimacy." Alas, Sijuwade provides no compelling reason as to why the stripper's transparently fake acting (in the dramaturgical sense) is so convincing to her viewing audience. The scantily clad waitress who prowls the bars, clubs, and pool halls, smiling

suggestively at male customers in order to entice them to purchase exor-
bitantly expensive alcoholic shots, and to encourage them to offer her
large tips, is fully aware that men will likely succumb to this approach.
One seldom witnesses male strippers and scantily clad male waiters using such alluring tactics with much success. That this selling tactic would
be differentially successful when targeting male and female patrons is
due to each sex's evolved abilities (or lack thereof) in deciphering such
communication cues. Incidentally, men's greater proclivity to bestow
sexual meaning to unwarranted situations occurs in advertising as well.
For example, Mick and Politi (1989) found that men overattributed sexual meaning when viewing an ad depicting a couple at the beach sipping
vodka. Once again, this pattern of misreading signals is congruent with
evolutionary predictions.

To summarize, human mate choice can be construed as the ultimate of
all consumption acts. The attributes that we seek in others, the attributes
that we advertise in ourselves, the courtship rituals that we engage in, the
manner by which we derogate competitors, and the pattern of information
search prior to choosing a mate are driven by a domain-specific calculus
linked to the reproductive module. In other words, the consumption act of
choosing a mate cannot be properly investigated via the application of domain-general mechanisms. In the next section, I demonstrate that countless specific consumption purchases cater to the innate forces emanating
from the reproductive module.

Sex Differences in Aggregate Consumption Patterns

If one were to categorize all products as a function of whether they are predominantly purchased by one sex or are equally purchased by both sexes,
robust patterns would emerge. For example, men are much more likely to
seek the services of both male and female prostitutes, and are much more
likely to be consumers of hardcore pornography. Women constitute the
majority of consumers in the cosmetics industry. Countless conspicuous
consumption choices are mere sexual signals, meant to advertise one's self
to prospective mates. These sexual signals appeal to the evolved preferences of the opposite sex. For example, men are much more likely to purchase expensive sports cars as a signal of their resources and
corresponding high social status. In ethology, a lek refers to a specific area
where males of a given species engage in the conspicuous signaling of fit-
ness-related cues in the presence of a captive female audience. Accordingly, that men engage in the conspicuous display of status symbols is
merely lekking behavior (see Lycett & Dunbar, 2000, regarding men's use
of cellular phones as lekking signals when present at a bar). On the other
hand, women wear provocative clothes as a means of attracting the atten-

tion of prospective suitors. Hence, many sex-based differences in aggregate consumption patterns are manifestations of sex differences arising from the reproductive module. That being said, Darwinian sexual signaling need not be used solely to understand the heterosexual mating market. It can just as easily explain why homosexual men, as compared to heterosexual men, are much more likely to make consumption choices that highlight physical attributes. In exploring sex differences in aggregate consumption patterns, I explore toy preferences, appearance-enhancing products, and the consumption of risk in both the financial and physical domains. This is followed by the final topic to be covered within the mating module, namely an analysis of the evolutionary roots of conspicuous consumption.

Toy Preferences

I begin with a discussion of toy preferences because social constructivists have argued that the differential parental socialization associated with toys is of great import in shaping one's sex typing and gender identity. They propose that the proverbial "blue truck" and "pink doll" are at the root of our gendered identity. The surface validity of this position is tenuous while the empirical evidence is hardly supportive of it. I provide herewith a brief discussion of research that has challenged this claim.

Berenbaum and Hines (1992) explored the relationship between masculinizing androgens and a specific gendered manifestation, namely children's preferences for sex-typed toys (e.g., dolls or trucks). Their samples consisted of children suffering from congenital adrenal hyperplasia (CAH), an endocrinological disorder that causes young girls to have not only masculinized morphological traits but also masculinized behaviors. Girls afflicted with CAH displayed an increased (decreased) preference for boy-specific (girl-specific) toy preferences. This result held even though the socialization patterns of parents toward both the afflicted and unafflicted girls did not differ (i.e., the differences in toy preferences could not have been due to differential socialization).

Alexander (2003) reviewed a large number of studies that demonstrate a pervasive visual dimorphism within *Homo sapiens,* a summary of which I provide herewith. For example, she discusses how sex-specific differences in retinal development are congruent with evolved adaptive solutions to sex-specific problems, yielding pervasive sex-based differences, in the ability for facial recognition, in the capacity to accurately decode facial expressions, and for preferences for objects of motion. These sex-based differences manifest themselves in infants in the presocialization ontogenetic stage. In other words, they could not be attributed to socialization. Furthermore, the same pattern of sex differences has been found in other related species (e.g., vervet monkeys; see Alexander & Hines, 2002), rendering it difficult to argue that it is due to socialization forces. Finally, human infants exposed to sex-typed hormones typical of the opposite sex adopt play and toy preferences that are in line with the sex-typed hormones rather than with one's own biological sex. These sex differences are adaptive solutions to specific survival problems that arose in our phylogenetic history. Hence, sex-typed toy preferences (in terms of the objects and colors preferred) and types of play are not due to capricious forces of socialization. Rather, as stated throughout the current book, socialization forces typically proceed in directions that are congruent with evolved predispositions. Alexander's article is powerful in that it summarizes multiple streams of research that are all connected via biologically inspired Darwinian-based theorizing. This unifying theoretical rubric permits Alexander to unify a large stream of research into a coherent whole. For additional details regarding the evolutionary roots of sex-specific toy preferences, see Campbell (2002, chap. 1).Toy companies are fully aware that the design of toys should be congruent with sex-specific preferences (cf. Colarelli & Dettman, 2003). Given their desire to maximize profits, they develop products that are successful in exactly the same sex-specific manner across innumerable cultures. Hence, in the same manner that hardcore pornography and romance novels appeal differentially to the two sexes, toy preferences are equally rooted in innate sex-based differences. I next turn to a class of products that yields some of the most robust sex differences, namely appearance-enhancing products.

Appearance-Enhancing Products and Services

Cosmetic and Plastic Procedures. Women have 10 times as many plastic surgeries as compared to men (Kalb, 1999, as cited by Lauzen & Dozier, 2002). I accessed aggregate statistics on plastic procedures via the 1998 and 2001 National Clearinghouse of Plastic Surgery Statistics (American Society of Plastic Surgeons, see www.plasticsurgery.org), which are congruent with the data referred to by Kalb. Of 24 listed procedures for the 1998 projected figures, 22 were performed more frequently on women. The only two that were male-dominated were sex-specific procedures, namely breast reduction in men and male-pattern baldness. The total number of procedures performed on men and women were 99,031 and 946,784 respectively, corresponding to 9% and 91% of the total number of procedures. The 2001 figures were very similar. Of 19 surgical procedures, 16 were performed more frequently on women (20% and 80% of surgeries performed on men and women respectively). All of the 12 nonsurgical procedures were performed more frequently on women (11% and 89% performed on men and women respectively). The aggregate total number of procedures (i.e., surgical and nonsurgical) performed on men and women were 965,840 (13%) and 6,503,714 (87%) respectively. What can explain such a pervasive sex effect? Socialization theorists would propose that the previously learned social expectation that women be beautiful is so entrenched in the female psyche that there simply has not been sufficient time for these to be extinguished. Second-wave feminists would propose that despite the great strides that women have made in the social, economic, political, and educational spheres, they remain shackled by oppressive aesthetic expectations. Additionally, cultural relativists will point to numerous cultures were men are ostensibly more likely to adorn the outcomes of plastic surgeries (e.g., the Maori facial tatoos). Accordingly, this is meant to highlight the fact that there is nothing fixed about the sex specificity of aesthetic adornments and procedures. There are several problems with these explanations. First, in cultures where men are more likely to have cosmetic procedures performed on them, these are meant to cue a man's strength and his coming of age as a potential warrior, and accordingly in many instances serve to accentuate cues of dominance. The plastic and cosmetic procedures most likely to be performed on women are precisely those that accentuate cues of youth (e.g., procedures to lift the breasts and the buttocks, liposuction, Botox injections, antiwrinkle creams, and face-lifts). Given men's evolved preferences for young and beautiful women, the pattern of cosmetic procedures is congruent with these. A manifestation of the sex-specific nature of plastic surgeries was recently displayed on a reality-based television show. *The Swan*, which aired on the Fox network, had several women (not men) contestants competing in a beauty pageant following a set of transformational procedures including plastic surgeries.

Of all noninvasive procedures, antiacne creams and related remedies constitute one of the most lucrative markets. Most television shows, magazines, and other media targeted to adolescents, are replete with the requisite advertisements hailing the rewards of having healthy skin (being attractive and desired) and warning against the risks of having acne (being socially ostracized). Having clear, smooth, and unblemished skin is a universal marker of beauty precisely because the quality of one's skin serves as a reliable cue of youth and health. Given the universal importance of both mating and social acceptance to hormonally charged adolescents, it is not surprising that advertising messages regarding antiacne products are very similar cross-culturally. Hence, that acne elicits shame and that it does so differentially across the sexes (more so for women) can easily be explained within an evolutionary framework (see Kellett & Gawkrodger, 1999; Kellett & Gilbert, 2001; see Bloom, 2004, for an adaptive explanation regarding the onset of acne during adolescence).

High Heels, Haircuts, and Provocative Attire. E. O. Smith (1999) conducted an evolutionary analysis to explain the reason that women wear high heels, the key points of which I summarize in the ensuing few paragraphs. He began by providing a historical perspective of this particular fashion accoutrement. High heels and high platforms have at times been associated with high status in part due to the fact that men of short stature but of high status have sported them (e.g., King Louis XIV). Hence, in those instances when men have worn such footwear, it has typically been to mask a physical shortcoming that is an evolutionarily relevant physical cue of female mate choice. That said, why would women wear high and spiky heels? Rossi (1993, as cited in E. O. Smith, 1999) estimated that 80% of shoe purchases are for sexual attraction. Specifically, wearing high heels creates the visual illusion of lordosis (arching of the back when a female is in a sexually receptive position) and furthermore accentuates the body curves that are particularly appealing to men. Smith cites research showing that a 2-inch heel results in a 20° "lift" of the buttocks. Rossi (1981) states:

> High heels may well be the most potent aphrodisiac ever concocted. When worn by women, the high heel sensuously alters the whole anatomy—foot, leg, thigh, hips, pelvis, buttocks, breasts, etc. ... Men are perfectly frank in admitting that high heels stimulate their sexual appetite. They seldom fail to express their predilection for them, and women, consequently, assign to stilted shoes all the magic of a love potion. (as quoted in E. O. Smith, 1999, p. 269)

Smith adds, "These anatomical changes brought about as a consequence of wearing high heels have been recognized by authors and song writers for decades" (p. 269) This speaks to the key point of chapter 5, namely that the contents of popular culture are largely driven by our Darwinian heritage. It is no coincidence that women appearing in pornographic magazines and movies targeted at heterosexual men will often be shown wearing high heels. Similarly, female strippers are almost always wearing high heels despite the fact that their dance routines could be more safely and comfortably performed with less enticing foot attire. Finally, anecdotal evidence suggests that high heels are one of the most frequent accoutrements worn by women during the instantiation of bedroom fantasies. Thus, when Smith (1999, p. 271) questions which occasions might prompt women to wear high heels, one might expect that high heels are most likely to be worn in sexually laden contexts.

From a medical and public health perspective, it is important to note that women are willing to subjugate themselves to numerous physical ailments arising from the wearing of such unnatural footwear in order to appear attractive (E. O. Smith, 1999). For example, Smith (p. 267) estimates the economic costs arising from the wearing of high heels at $16 billion (e.g., time taken off work to recover from foot surgeries, medical costs, etc.). Smith adds that for a substantial number of podiatry-related injuries or conditions, women outnumber men by up to 40 to 1 with the suspected culprit in many instances being the wearing of high heels. Men and women are willing to go to great lengths to appeal to one another in the mating arena. These all-consuming efforts to cater to the evolved preferences of the opposite sex are pursued despite any deleterious consequences that might accrue, because they are thought necessary to secure an optimal mate.

Hinsz, Matz, and Patience (2001) explored the relationship between a woman's hair length and hair quality, and several predictors most of which could be linked to specific evolutionary-based predictions. The predictors included age, relationship status, reproductive status, subjective health, and physical complications (a more objective measure of health albeit it was measured as a binary variable). Hair length was negatively correlated with both age and health (physical complications). The exact same pattern was found for hair quality. The authors argue that the findings suggest that a woman's hair is likely used as an intersexual cue to signal reproductive fitness. In other words, younger women are more likely to have longer hair precisely because it stands to signal youth and health via its more lustrous qualities and fuller body. However, as a woman ages, her hair quality gets poorer (e.g., becomes thinner, duller, and more brittle); as such she is most likely to minimize the signal emanating from this cue (i.e., by cutting her hair shorter). Shampoo companies are aware of this relationship without necessarily knowing its Darwinian etiology. Shampoo and conditioning commercials promise fuller and shinier hair as depicted on young, healthy, and attractive female models. On a related note, gray hair seems to have radically different connotations when worn by men and women. Gray hair on a man is oftentimes described as elegant and distinguished, hardly the adjectives used to describe women with graying hair. Given the differential premium placed by the two sexes on youth as a desirable mate characteristic, it is perhaps not surprising that women are more likely to dye their graying hair. As such, it would seem that a woman's hair is indeed used as an ornamental intersexual cue in the mating arena (cf. Mesko & Bereczkei, 2004).

Not only do specific consumption purchases serve as sexual signals in the mating arena but also the likelihood of engaging in a particular form of signaling is tied to evolutionarily relevant physiological markers. For example, the likelihood of women wearing provocative attire at a bar and using appearance-enhancing products such as cosmetics is highly correlated to their ovulatory cycle (cf. Grammer, 1996; Grammer, Dittami, & Fischmann, 1993; E. Hill & Wenzl, 1981). Evolutionarily speaking, when women are maximally fertile, they are most likely to engage in self-advertisements in the mating arena. Incidentally, there are countless other behaviors replete with consumption implications that are linked to a woman's ovulatory cycle. For example, research has repeatedly shown that a woman's libido is linked to her menstrual cycle (cf. Pillsworth, Haselton, & Buss, 2004; Stanislaw & Rice, 1988). Accordingly, I propose that specific consumption choices, which are associated with beautification and that accordingly can serve as preparatory for an intimate encounter, might likely be correlated to a woman's ovulatory cycle. These might include getting haircuts, pedicures, and/or manicures, seeking epilatory services or products, or the wearing of high heels. Additionally, women might be more or less likely to be present in specific social settings such as studying at home or at the library, or going out to a bar or a café, as a function of their menstrual cycles. On a related note, there exists compelling evidence linking women's likelihood of engaging in personally risky activities to their menstrual cycles (Chavanne & Gallup, 1998).

The Myth Behind the Beauty Myth. In comparison to men, women display greater interest in countless appearance-enhancing products. As such, the fashion and cosmetics industries are predominantly geared to female consumers irrespective of cultural setting. According to some social constructivists, this is due to the patriarchy's backlash against women's emancipatory gains arising from second-wave feminism. In other words, that women care differentially more so about their appearance than do men is a recent reality constructed by the patriarchy to oppress women. This claim is the central tenet behind Naomi Wolf's 1991 best-selling book titled *The Beauty Myth*. Wolf states:

> We are in the midst of a violent backlash against feminism that uses images of female beauty as a political weapon against women's advancement: the beauty myth. It is the modern version of a social reflex that has been in force since the Industrial Revolution. As women released themselves from the feminine mystique of domesticity, the beauty myth took over its lost ground, expanding as it waned to carry on its work of social control.
>
> The contemporary backlash is so violent because the ideology of beauty is the last one remaining of the old feminine ideologies that still has the power to control those women whom second wave feminism would have otherwise made relatively uncontrollable: It has grown stronger to take over the work of social coercion that myths about motherhood, domesticity, chastity, and passivity, no longer can manage. It is seeking right now to undo psychologically and covertly all the good things that feminism did for women materially and overtly. (pp. 10–11)

Social constructivists have challenged the universal claim that women's self-concepts are more closely linked to their appearance, by attempting to identify a culture wherein it is the men that engage in a ritual of beautification. N. Wolf (1991) proposed that the Wodaabe people, who live in 18 African countries with a large concentration in Niger and Nigeria (Bovin, 2001), are an example of such a culture. A thorough understanding of the Woodabe invalidates Wolf's conclusion. First, no one questions the fact that men are concerned with their appearance. A growing number of men are choosing to have painful and expensive hair restoration surgeries as a means of improving their appearance. *Mr. Olympia* competitions pit the physiques of men against one another. In Greek mythology, Adonis is singled out for his exquisite beauty. The relevant question is whether there exists a culture whereby men are persistently less interested in female beauty as compared to the opposite pattern. To date, no such culture has been documented. Returning to the Wodaabe people, I summarize some of the key mating-related findings, most of which are obtained from Bovin. During Geerewol (or Jeerewol) dances (the festival wherein the male beautification pageant takes place), men from competing clans steal each other's women (Bovin, p. 52). Dancing at such events is viewed as a form of war. Bovin adds, "They [men] compete vigorously for women and the right to procreate, to reproduce themselves, and have many descendants. Fertility and having many children mean everything to the men" (p. 72). The male competitors are judged on their charisma, dance abilities, and physical stamina. As Bovin explains, men should be intelligent, speak well, and dance gracefully, tall men are preferred, and in many cases, exceptionally charming men (e.g., good singers) could compensate for their lack of beauty. Hence, from an evolutionary perspective, the Geerewol serves as a male lek wherein Wodaabe women can sample evolutionary-relevant information on the prospective suitors that extends beyond their mere beauty. Beautiful men (e.g., those having thick hair) are more likely to have multiple wives. Hence, the Geerewol is a form of male intrasexual rivalry whereby the ultimate prize is access to multiple young, attractive, and nubile women.

The young female judges also engage in appearance-enhancing procedures and are accordingly recognized for being beautiful. More generally, Woodabe girls are also expected to possess certain key aesthetic qualities. Girls should be shorter than their male counterparts. Bovin (2001) adds:

> A "round" girl is valued higher than a skinny girl (maybe because it is good to be round when you get pregnant and later have babies?). Morever, the ideal girl should have graceful movements and know how to kneel down respectfully when serving food to men, and she is expected to look down at the right moments. (p. 29)

Hence, in the Wodaabe tribe, men remain fully interested in the same cues that attract men in all other cultures (cues related to fertility). The winning male is provided with an opportunity to engage in multiple short-term mating opportunities with the female judges. It is recognized that this mate choice, which is in part based on beauty, is appropriate during the Geerewol whereas male marriage partners are much more likely to be chosen as a function of their wealth (amount of cattle that they own). Finally, Wodaabe men are allowed to marry up to four women and the ability to do so is typically a function of the man's wealth. Bovin explains that Wodaabe society is one of the only ones in the world where both men and women can have more than one partner. Despite this apparent culturally sanctioned sexual freedom, Bovin states, "Women (more than men) prefer to live in a monogamous marriage. Men prefer to have two or more wives, if their economic situation allows" (p. 42). Hence, once one explores the full gamut of Wodaabe mating customs, these are hardly congruent with Wolf's interpretation. The Wodaabe people do not display the sex role reversals that Wolf claims to have uncovered.

Incidentally, Bovin, who has spent extensive periods living among the Wodaabe people, summarizes some of the key metrics and customs associated with their aesthetics. One issue that she repeatedly mentions is the importance that symmetry holds to the Wodaabe. They use symmetry in judging the beauty of their tribe members (both men and women) and their cattle (e.g., symmetry of the horns), in evaluating art, and in applying facial cosmetics (Bovin, 2001). Given the evolutionary importance of symmetry as a cue of health (see relevant references in chap. 2), it is no surprise that the Wodaabe sense of aesthetics is so dominated by it (see Cárdenas & Harris, 2006, for the universal importance of symmetry in evaluating facial decorations and decorative nonfigurative images). Another common theme in Woodabe art according to Bovin is the hourglass form. This is congruent with evolutionary principles in that the hourglass female figure is a universal male preference as it serves as a reliable cue of fertility (cf. Singh, 1993).

That said, let us assume for a moment that the Geerewol ritual was solely beauty based. Does the identification of a ritualized event in a single culture falsify the otherwise ubiquitous finding that men are more concerned with female beauty as compared to the opposite pattern? This is perhaps the most common strategy for challenging evolutionary-based theories, namely seeking to identify a single instance that supposedly falsifies the whole Darwinian edifice. For example, the statement that *Homo sapiens* is a physically dimorphic species whereby males are roughly 15% larger than females, is thought falsified by identifying a female who is physically larger than some living or deceased male. Evolutionarily relevant phenomena typically operate at the population level. Hence, it is implicitly understood that many behavioral and morphological traits are defined by a distribution of values rather than a fixed point (this is one of the reasons why evolutionary theory is not deterministic in terms of its assignment of one value onto a whole class of individuals). Hence, this form of "falsification" is merely demonstrating that two distribution functions can overlap (e.g., the heaviest women weigh more than the lightest men) without recognizing that the two means are statistically different.

Risk-Related Consumption Phenomena

Financial Risk Taking.   In their meta-analysis of sex differences in risk taking, Byrnes and Miller (1999) found that on the aggregate (i.e., across contexts and tasks) women are more risk-aversive than are men. That said, specific domains do indeed moderate the strength of the sex effect. For example, men are substantially more risk seeking when it comes to physical activities (e.g., bungee jumping, parachuting, or hang gliding). Silverman (2003) conducted a meta-analysis of sex differences in delay gratification and found a small effect size; namely, women delay gratification more so than men do. There are several evolutionary-based explanations to explain men's greater proclivities for engaging in risky behaviors and their lesser abilities to delay gratification. Specifically, the patterns of intrasexual rivalry in *Homo sapiens* and the differential parental investment (Trivers, 1972) of the two sexes would precisely predict these two findings. Not surprisingly, findings consistent with the latter meta-analytic results have been obtained in several domains, one of which is in personal and institutional investment behaviors. Women are consistently found to be more risk-aversive when it comes to financial decision making (cf. Jianakoplos & Bernasek, 1998; Powell & Ansic, 1997). Olsen and Cox (2001) investigated sex differences in risk perceptions of professional investors. The findings were consistent in demonstrating that women investors were more risk-aversive across a slew of risk-related measures. Additionally, the authors cite numerous studies in a wide range of areas (e.g., personal financial investments, entrepreneurship, and experimental economic experiments) that all yield the latter sex effect regarding risk proclivities. Graham, Stendardi, Myers, and Graham (2002) focused on gender differences within the investment domain. They cited numerous studies all pointing to a consistent and pervasive sex effect; namely, women are less risky as compared to men across a wide range of investment domains. Graham et al. add, "Few studies have focused on the underlying factors that may lead to gender differences in investment strategies" (p. 17). In their quest to address this lacuna, they utilized the selectivity hypothesis (see Meyers-Levy, 1989; Meyers-Levy & Maheswaran, 1991; Meyers-Levy & Sternthal, 1991), which suggests that men are more selective processors of information (i.e., make greater use of simplifying heuristics) whereas women are more comprehensive and deliberate processors. In the investment domain, Graham et al. argue that because men use simplifying heuristics when processing information, this translates to their focusing on the most important cue, namely investment returns, yielding more risk-seeking behavior (because risk information is ignored). On the other hand, given that women are more comprehensive in their information processing, they will acquire a more complete set of investment information (e.g., investment returns and their associated risk), resulting in more risk-aversive and judicious investment behavior. This explanation relies on an erroneous theoretical position. Specifically, the selectivity hypothesis posits a domain-general effect, namely that men are more selective in their information processing throughout all possible decisional domains. There is no ultimate-based mechanism that could have evolved to generate such an indiscriminate pattern of sex-specific processing. As such, there are numerous empirical falsifications of the selectivity hypothesis, one of which is the study by Saad and Eba (2005) discussed earlier. The greater risk-seeking behavior of men in the investment domain is merely one of many instantiations where men engage in riskier behaviors.

Risk taking in the financial domain is not restricted to investment decisions. The attitudes that men and women hold toward money and the means they seek to acquire it yield the expected sex-specific patterns. Furnham (1999) explored the attitudes and behaviors of young individuals toward money. Of relevance here, he found that girls were more conservative with their money (e.g., greater proclivity to save). Socialization is proposed as the explicative force responsible for the findings. For example, Furnham states, "Certainly it seems as children get older and have an increased understanding of their social world they may be more prone to develop the gender-linked stereotypical behaviours acceptable in their society" (p. 693). Betz, O'Connell, and Shepard (1989) explored sex differences in the likelihood of engaging in several forms of unethical behavior. In each of five scenarios, men were much more likely to engage in unethical behavior. Furthermore, in describing the key career objectives by age 40, men were much more motivated by money, power, and hierarchical ascendancy than were women. As in Furnham's study, the explanation for these findings rested on gender socialization. The genesis of these gender roles and their universality were not addressed in either study. Finally, Collins (2000) conducted a review of articles published in the *Journal of Business Ethics* that have addressed sex differences in ethical proclivities. Forty-seven studies were included in the analysis, 32 of which yielded that men were less ethical than women with the remaining 15 studies yielding no sex differences. To the extent that ethical breaches are a form of risk taking, the robust male effect is expected from an evolutionary perspective.

Weber et al. (2002) recently developed a comprehensive risk scale from a domain-specific and hence evolutionary-congruent perspective. Rather than assuming that one's tolerance for risk is a stable and enduring trait, they sought to establish that one's risk propensities vary as a function of the domain in question (e.g., financial vs. social risk). Furthermore, they explored gender differences along each of five domains imbued with potential risk (financial, health/safety, social, recreational, and ethical). The findings were strongly supportive of an evolutionary perspective; namely, risk propensities were indeed domain-specific with women displaying greater risk aversiveness in four of the five domains (social risk yielded no sex differences). Others have previously argued that one's risk proclivities cannot be captured by a single invariant metric, most famously perhaps by Kahneman and Tversky (1979) in their formulation of prospect theory. For example, prospect theory posits that depending on whether one is in the gains or losses region of the utility function will determine the risk tolerance that will be assumed. That said, the latter tenet is purported to hold true irrespective of the domain in question. In other words, prospect theory remains a domain-general theory, albeit it is more descriptively valid in comparison to the relevant axioms of rational choice. A domain-specific perspective of risk proposes that evolutionarily relevant selection pressures that arose as adaptive solutions to domain-specific survival problems have shaped risk proclivities. Hence, one cannot speak of a domain-general risk proclivity any more than one can speak of a domain-general addictive personality (see chap. 6).

Physical Risk Taking.   Queenstown, on the South Island of New Zealand, is reputed to be one of the thrill-seeking centers in the world. Adrenaline aficionados visit Queenstown from around the world to partake in a wide assortment of extreme sports including to bungee-jump off the first commercialized site dedicated to this extreme sport. There now exists a subculture of sports enthusiasts who participate in a wide range of extremely dangerous activities including base jumping, skydiving, extreme snowboarding, steep skiing, sky surfing, big-wave surfing, and "buildering" (or urban climbing as made famous by Alain Robert, the so-called French Spiderman). Other activities of perhaps lesser danger include wakeboarding and hang gliding. ESPN, the cable sports network, has been instrumental in developing the X Games, an Olympic-style event dedicated to extreme sports. Of relevance here is the issue of whether sex differences exist in terms of the participation rate in the various extreme activities. The data suggest a universal male effect. Such behaviors are overwhelmingly skewed toward male participation (cf. Schrader & Wann, 1999) with men also serving as the innovators within any given novel extreme activity. Most social constructivists propose that this is due to a gendered social construction, yielding a hegemonic definition of masculinity as instituted by the patriarchy. In other words, that men are more likely to engage in such activities across every culture and era (e.g., countless cultures have rites of passage for males linked to acts of courage and bravery) is due to socialization forces.

The Greek fraternity and sorority system constitutes an important social forum for undergraduates at American universities. Pledgees have to go through an elaborate rite of passage prior to being accepted into their chosen Greek group. Whereas many such rites are inocuous, others fall under the more problematic rubric of hazing. Examples of hazing rituals include binge drinking leading to alcohol poisoning, excessive water consumption leading to drowning, acts of sexual victimization, forced criminality (e.g., having to steal), and acts of humiliation (e.g., urinating on a pledgee). Propelled by the universal need to belong, many pledges have lost their lives during the hazing ritual. That said, of 60 reported hazing deaths, 57 of the victims were men (Nuwer, 1999). As is true in numerous cultures that have explicit rites of masculinity, extreme forms of physical hazing are restricted to men. As is further discussed in the ensuing passages, this serves as an honest signal (Zahavi & Zahavi, 1997) of a man's fearlessness, and commitment to the group, both of which are attributes of evolutionary import for males to possess.

Hirschberger, Florian, Mikulinger, Goldenberg, and Pyszczynski (2002) explored the proclivity of men and women to engage in risky activities as a function of whether or not they were cued about the salience of death and mortality. In two studies, men but not women were more likely to engage in risky actions when the salience of death was cued. At first sight, this seems counterintuitive in that, if one is primed about the possibility of death, this should reduce the likelihood of engaging in death-defying actions. Hirschberger et al. applied a logic based on terror management theory to explain this otherwise paradoxical result. For example, they state:

> People may often be more invested in symbolic defenses against the meaning of death than in biological self-preservation itself and, that for men, behaviors that are life-endangering or that involve physical risks may constitute an important symbolic death repressing mechanism. Consequently, men may opt to defend the symbolic structures that regulate their fear of personal death rather than protect their actual existence in the long run. (p. 134)

This explanation is reminiscent of the psychoanalytic writings of the Freudian era (e.g., Freud's logic regarding the death instinct). I propose herewith an evolutionary-based explanation of the latter finding based on honest signaling (Zahavi, 1975; Zahavi & Zahavi, 1997). As mentioned earlier, males in countless cultures and epochs have engaged in rites of passage that are meant to signal exceptional courage and bravery. For example, the N'Gol ritual in Papua New Guinea (in Wanur, Pentecost, and Vanuatu) involves young males jumping off exceptionally high platforms with vines tied to their ankles. The vines are adjusted according to the jumper's weight, as is the length of the rope such that the complete unfolding of the rope occurs a few inches from full impact between the head of the jumper and the ground floor. Because of the extreme dangers associated with this rite of passage (which is incidentally the precusor to commercialized bungee jumping), it serves as an honest signal of the advertised traits (i.e., extreme courage). A rite of passage that would not push the human limits would permit "cheaters" (i.e., those who are not maximally brave and courageous) to successfully complete the task. Returning to the Hirschberger et al. finding, Zahavian signaling would predict that the more death defying a risk-taking activity is, the more likely will men engage in it. That some women are irresistibly drawn to men in uniform (policemen, firemen, soldiers, and sailors) is precisely due to the honest signal that such attires entail regarding the extreme bravery and courage that are required as prerequisites for these occupations. Hence, the arguments that men engage in risky behaviors because it is part of their worldview, that they are socialized to be risk takers, that they are pursuing a death instinct, or that they are symbolically repressing death explain little if anything. Death-defying activities are honest signals of a man's valor, a trait that has been highly sought by human females throughout the phylogenetic history of our species (see the next section on conspicuous consumption for additional details regarding Zahavian signaling). In their study of skydiving, Celsi, Rose, and Leigh (1993) proclaimed, "Of course, situations that are too easily mastered retain little interest to skydivers. ... Many high-risk performers quickly learn to prefer contexts that test their abilities and sometimes the limits of their control" (p. 16). This is congruent with the death-defying finding of Hirschberger et al.; namely, exposing one's self to extreme physical risks provides the risk taker with a Zahavian-based signaling premium.

Consumer scholars have largely ignored the universal finding that males are overwhelmingly more likely to participate in high-risk physical activities. For example, in their exploration of skydiving motives, Celsi et al. (1993) did not report the sex breakdown of their sample. I recently contacted the lead author (Richard Celsi) to inquire about this point. He advised me that a majority of the sample were males (he thought around 70%). In their study of high-risk sports, Shoham, Rose, and Kahle (1998) stated, "Overall, hedonic research has qualitatively described the experience of, and motivations for, engaging in risky sports among participants but has neither predicted nor examined who might participate in risky sports among the general population" (p. 307). Contrary to the latter quote, there is ample cross-cultural evidence that young, single males are the most likely participants. Shoham et al. focused on age as the key demographic variable. They found that younger people were more favorably disposed toward risky sports. The authors proposed that other demographic variables should be explored in the future and they suggested family status as one prospective example. Sex was not proposed as a potentially relevant demographic variable, despite the fact that their own sample (Study 2), consisting of enrollees in risky sports, was comprised of 78.1% and 84.1% of males and singles respectively. Shoham, Rose, and Kahle (2000) reported that 81.9% and 64.7% of their sample of risky-sport participants was comprised of males and singles respectively. Furthermore, they found that men scored higher than did women on thrill and adventure seeking (which the authors state was the only significant demographic variable for this particular scale). The authors concluded the following with regard to the male effect:

> Our sample included younger, male-dominant individuals. We believe that this bias reflects the demographic composition of practitioners in Israel. However, the generalizability of the findings to older, more balanced gender samples is open to question. There is a need for further studies with more heterogeneous samples in Israel and in other nations. (p. 249)

In other words, they are proposing that the male effect is likely due to a cultural or situational idiosyncrasy. The amassed cross-cultural findings on this issue suggest otherwise.

Consumer scholars who have conducted research in this area have typically adhered to the central tenets of the SSSM (i.e., focusing on proximate motives, domain-general theories, and socialization). For example, Celsi et al. (1993) proposed that participation in the latter activities is due to *dramatic enculturation* (e.g., via media images). They state:

> We begin our enculturation to a dramatic worldview at the time we hear our first story. But it is largely through the mass media that our affective and cognitive expectations are shaped, as dramatic story lines form the content of cartoons, comics, music, novels, film, and television. However, it is not only through the arts that the dramatic worldview is conveyed, but through most social exchange, including written and oral history, legend, play, the news, sporting events, and religion (Barnard, 1968). (p. 3)

The latter premise is central to the SSSM worldview, namely that we are born with empty minds, which are subsequently shaped by the media and/or other socialization agents. In chapters 4 and 5, I demonstrate that the contents of both the media and cultural products exist in their particular forms because they are an instantiation of our human nature rather than being the socialization agents by which our behaviors are shaped. As previously mentioned, high-risk rites of passage exist in specific forms (e.g, male dominated) in countless cultures and spanning several millennia.

Hence, to explain that the genesis of such behaviors is due to dramatic en-culturation (Celsi et al., 1993) or the bureaucratic malaise that people apparently face in their daily lives (Shoham et al., 1998) does not recognize the universality and temporal invariance of the effect. Shoham et al. (2000) empirically tested many of the proximate motives that were originally discussed by Celsi et al. (1993). For example, they explored four needs thought to affect the frequency of participating in risky sports, namely the need for identity construction, efficacy, camaraderie, and experience, and found that camaraderie was the sole significant predictor. Finally, Shoham et al. (1998) used expectancy value theory to explain individuals' participation in extreme sports, which they construe as an instantiation of hedonic consumption. The latter theory postulates a domain-general algorithm, as evidenced by the fact that the authors proclaim that it has been successfully applied in a myriad of contexts including weight loss, marijuana use, media use, voting behavior, and the purchase of products and services. In the current setting, Shoham et al. (1998) found that adventure seeking and thrill seeking were positively correlated with liking of risky sports. Hence, of the proximate phenomena that have been investigated, few have received empirical support and/or yielded surprising findings. By exploring the Darwinian etiology behind high-risk activities, which lies at the root of such pursuits, new research opportunities will likely be identified.

To summarize this section, I have argued that consumption acts that involve financial and/or physical risk taking yield a universal male effect because of Darwinian reasons. In the next section, I turn to an evolutionary-based explanation of conspicuous consumption.

The Evolutionary Roots of Conspicuous Consumption

Thorstein Veblen (1899) coined the term *conspicuous consumption* in referring to purchases and leisure activities that are meant to signal one's membership in a privileged social class. Though several scholars had written about this issue prior to Veblen's *Theory of the Leisure Class*, the phenomenon has become inextricably linked to his name. Despite the apparent ubiquity of this consumption practice, numerous scholars have concluded that the phenomenon has received minimal attention within both the economics and consumer behavior traditions:

> The concept of social comparison, or "relative consumption", as it is known within the field, has been widely neglected. (Chao & Schor, 1998, p. 108)

> However, despite the pervasiveness of the concept of conspicuous consumption, empirical research and theoretical models on the nature and influence of conspicuous consumption have been relatively scarce. (O'Cass & Frost, 2002, p. 70)

> Historically, conspicuous consumption was seen by economists as a relatively trivial phenomenon, of little importance and of interest only as a *curiosum* [italics in original] within economics. For many years, mainstream economists continued to believe that the macroeconomic consequences of such behavior were overstated, and of little or no real concern. Analysis and discussion was remarkable largely by its absence. (Mason, 2000, p. 131)

One possible reason that little research has been conducted on the motives behind conspicuous consumption is because most people are unwilling to admit to their true motives when they engage in this particular behavior (Mason, 1981, p. 125). That said, despite the difficulties in eliciting such latent motives, Veblen had a good grasp of the phenomenon albeit he did not provide a Darwinian-based account of it. Veblen understood that at the individual level conspicuous consumption needed to be wasteful while also recognizing that this was regrettable at the societal level. Inherent to his position is an implicit assumption that individuals should at times act selflessly for the benefit of the group, which is reminiscent of antiquated notions of group selectionism.

An ultimate explanation for the wasteful nature of conspicuous consumption was achieved only recently. The evolutionary roots of this behavior lie in the dual forces of sexual selection and Zahavian signaling (cf. G. F. Miller, 1999b) as exemplified by the peacock's tail. Despite the sexual selection pressures for the peacock to evolve its elaborate tail, it carries a huge burden in that its survival is compromised because the ornate tail affects its likelihood to escape predators (for detailed discussions of sexual selection, see Cronin, 1991; Darwin, 1871; G. F. Miller, 1998). This same phenomenon can be observed in many species whereby sexual selection pressures have yielded exceptionally elaborate albeit costly (in a survival sense) ornamentation. How could a sexually selected trait evolve when it places the organism in question at such a survival disadvantage? In 1975, Amotz Zahavi resolved this conundrum by proposing the handicap principle, which at first was viewed contentiously but has since achieved wide acceptance as a Darwinian phenomenon (see Zahavi & Zahavi, 1997, for an excellent summary). Zahavi argued that to the extent that a trait serves as a signal of an organism's fitness, it should be one that is difficult to imitate or fake. In other words, "cheaters" might wish to advertise that they possess the signal when in reality they do not. These poseurs can be stopped from engaging in such duplicitous practices, if the signal is so costly to possess that only those that are truly fit could ever hope to possess it. This creates a barrier to entry that is so formidable as to ensure that elaborate ornamentation constitutes an honest signal. Some winner-take-all markets (Frank & Cook, 1995) can be viewed as extreme examples of the handicap principle. Everyone would be better off if the signals were not so costly, however the one who wins the sexual signaling game reaps all of the rewards (cf. van Kempen, 2003, p. 173). Thus, a positional arms race for status symbols results in outrageously high prices for products that cannot in any way be imitated and/or that others cannot afford to buy when competing for status. In other words, the Bentley is tantamount to the "nonimitable" peacock tail (see G. F. Miller, 1999b, for an excellent discussion of the Darwinian forces that shape consumption waste). Hence, in order to ensure that a status signal is honest, that which appears wasteful at the societal level needs to be so at the individual level.

Though the handicap principle is relevant in explaining the purchase of exceptionally exclusive and expensive products, Veblen effects (paying a price premium to signal status) arise with products across the price spectrum. For example, Chao and Schor (1998) explored the relationship between how visible a cosmetics product is and the importance assigned to price in purchasing the product. It was hypothesized and found that the more visible and conspicuous the product was, the lesser weight price carried. In other words, the greater the extent of social signaling that was communicated via the product, the less the price–quality relationship mattered. This suggests that in those instances when a product carries high social signaling value, one is willing to pay a price premium to communicate the signal. There are countless other consumption choices that are predominantly driven by a need to signal one's social status. Individuals spend more money decorating living rooms as compared to bedrooms, car manufacturers place the insignia of expensive car options (e.g., antilock, four-wheel drive) on a car's frame, and clothes designers increasingly use logos to signal apparel quality, because of the same need to signal social status (Chao & Schor, 1998).

An understanding of the innate motives that drive individuals' needs to conspicuously consume has clear pricing and product-positioning implications. A luxury brand that prices a product line in a manner that is affordable to the masses is engaging in a risky strategic endeavor, for such a "democratization" of the brand will oftentimes yield deleterious effects on sales. Recently, Mercedes introduced its C series. By attempting to increase its prospective market, Mercedes runs the very likely risk of alienating the conspicuous consumers who purchase this brand precisely because it has historically been a costly signal that is difficult to emulate. In other words, the utility derived in paying more for a luxury brand is the price premium that must be paid to send the honest signal. Parker pens have historically been positioned as prestigious and exclusive. Several years ago, the company introduced an "affordable" product, which resulted in sluggish sales. Demand went up only when the company increased the price of the product, hence violating one of the most basic economic assumptions regarding the structural relationship between demand and price. Economists typically "fix" such violations by redefining the utility of a luxury product. For example, products that yield Veblen effects are assigned a signaling utility as part of their overall utilities. In other instances, economists have developed mathematical models to predict the conditions under which Veblen effects might take place (cf. Bagwell & Bernheim, 1996). The ultimate origins of the phenomenon in question (i.e., the reason that people engage in conspicuous consumption) are ignored within this research stream.

The Taj Mahal, the pyramids of Giza, Stonehenge, and the Inca and Mayan monuments constitute architectural wonders. Millions of tourists each year marvel at these magnificent products of human ingenuity. Does there exist a common force that can explain the commissioning and building of such monumental architecture spanning four continents and several millennia? Neiman (1998) proposes an explanation based on the handicap principle (i.e., Zahavian signaling). Specifically, it is argued that extravagant architecture occurs as a means for rulers to send honest signals to both their competitors and subjects regarding their all-encompassing power. It is precisely because such architecture is "wasteful" that it serves as an honest signal. Aranyosi (1999) contrasted the latter Zahavi-inspired model to another Darwinian-based model (the bet-hedging model) in exploring the geographical distribution of megalithic monuments in Ireland. It is noteworthy to highlight Aranyosi's exclusive reliance on Darwinian principles in explaining this particular architectural phenomenon. Incidentally, both archaeology and architecture have developed Darwinian-based subdisciplines, namely evolutionary archaeology and evolutionary architecture. For example, Tsui (1999) has proposed that the field of architecture needs to incorporate evolutionary-based principles within the discipline. Specifically, he argues that the natural world is replete with innumerable examples of evolved structures (e.g., a snail shell or a termite tower) that are adaptive solutions to recurring environmental challenges. Tsui proposes that these evolved structural properties, which arose as a result of a long evolutionary process, should be incorporated within the architect's toolbox of knowledge. This would permit for the creation of architectural structures that are much more in line with our evolved aesthetic preferences as compared to the "functional" buildings of the 1960s and 1970s.

In most instances, the naturally occurring structures that Tsui refers to have evolved because they solve an adaptive problem linked to survival. However, there exists an exception to the latter statement wherein the evolved structure is driven not by natural selection but rather by sexual selection guided by female mate choice. The male bowerbird found in several countries in Oceania builds a bower (not to be confused with a nest) with the expressed goal of impressing females. Specifically, female mate choice within this lekking species is based on a male's ability to create a nest that has artistic and aesthetic appeal. Interestingly, one of the cues that females look for is the symmetry of the bower, a cue that has widespread appeal when instantiated as a morphological trait across a wide range of species. Hence, the bowerbird's phylogenetic history has affected not only its morphological phenotype but also the structures that it has evolved to construct as part of its mating rituals. This is the idea behind Richard Dawkins' notion of the extended phenotype (Dawkins, 1982), namely that forces of natural and sexual selection will oftentimes manifest themselves beyond an organism's own phenotype. In the same manner that the bower constitutes an integral element of the bowerbird's extended phenotype, countless human products can be construed as elements of the *extended phenotype* of *Homo sapiens* (see G. F. Miller, 2000). Architectural monuments of gargantuan proportions, Ferraris, and products of culture can be viewed as instantiations of our extended phenotypes. In the consumer behavior literature, Belk (1988) has developed the notion of the *extended self*; namely, he has argued that material possessions will oftentimes be imbued with personal meaning that become inextricably linked to an individual's sense of self. However, he does not provide any ultimate-based explanations as to why certain self-defining items seem to be used in universally recurrent manners. In their recent review of the material possession literature, Kleine and Baker (2004) addressed universal patterns of sex differences. They relied on the socialization-based dichotomy regarding men's desire to seek autonomy versus women's desire to seek affiliation in explaining the prevailing sex differences. I propose that the extended self is a specific instantiation of the extended-phenotype concept. Viewed from an evolutionary perspective, men are more likely to incorporate high-status cars as integral elements of their extended selves precisely because one of the instantiations of their extended phenotype is to signal social ascendancy. Hence, material possessions have little to do with the autonomy-versus-affiliation dichotomy and much to do with the manner by which the sexes utilize evolutionary-relevant cues in defining themselves.

Despite the Darwinian etiology behind various facets of conspicuous consumption, marketing scholars have operated at the proximate level when investigating this ubiquitous phenomenon. In their recent review of prestige-seeking consumption, Vigneron and Johnson (1999) sought to integrate multiple disciplines that have each explored conspicuous consumption, including marketing, consumer behavior, social and clinical psychology, anthropology, and sociology. Only one of the cited articles appeared to have adopted a biological perspective. The authors cite research suggesting that individuals succumb to the bandwagon and snob effects because it is a means by which they can improve their self-concepts. Similarly, the importance that people ascribe to belonging to reference groups (referent power) is proposed as an explanatory mechanism driving prestige-seeking behaviors. These proximate issues are relevant and worthy of exploration. That said, an ultimate-based account of why individuals' self-concepts are tied to their social status, or why individuals have an innate desire to signal belongingness via the luxury items that they purchase, would add explanatory power to existing research streams while proposing new possible avenues.

Conspicuous Consumption in Religious Settings. The innate need for individuals to compete in a positional race for status is so alluring that theologians, well versed in human frailties, have enacted religious edicts that seek to tamper this tendency. This desperate quest to signal status manifests itself even on religious occasions covering the gamut of human emotions (e.g., funerals, bar mitzvahs, and weddings). Referring to conspicuous consumption at Jewish services, Spero (1988) states:

> Plagued also by a need to convince others, and themselves, that they have "made it" in America, many individuals believe that such evidence is affirmed in acquisitions and showy demonstrations of material trappings, and by their ability to live and entertain lavishly.

> Still others are driven by a need to keep pace publicly with their neighbors and friends or by a desire to live up to expected and fashionable community standards; to do otherwise would render them conspicuously "poor." These pressures, however, can eventuate in protracted debt and strain for many families unable to afford these $30–40,000 outlays. Many have mortgaged their future years for a mere five hours of hoped-for acceptance. The Rabbis, ever-mindful of man's social insecurities, responsibly warned that even the purchase of actual mizvah [sic] objects should not exceed one-fifth of one's personal savings, let alone the incurring of heavy debt for celebrations. (pp. 103–104)

This quest to signal social status does not solely manifest itself on joyous occasions, for even in the most solemn of settings, namely funerals, the pressure to engage in a positional race for status is exceptionally difficult to eradicate:

> For example, where formerly the wealthy brought food to mourners in baskets of silver and gold and served drinks in crystal-like glasses, the Rabbis decreed that henceforth food brought to a house of mourning be delivered in plain, twigged baskets, and that drinks served there be poured into plain, colored glasses. They did so in order that the poor, possessing modest utensils only, would not be so embarrassed that they would eschew bringing food altogether. …

> In fact, the Talmud insightfully remarks that, until that time, the high costs of funerals created greater anguish among some poor families than did the actual death of their relative. (Spero, 1988, p. 107)

In at least one synagogue that I am aware of, although this likely holds true in many others, high holidays involve a ritual that has little to do with religious piety and more to do with human vanity. Prior to engaging in a particular religious act (e.g., opening the curtain that hides the Torah from the eyes of the worshipers), the rabbi, the cantor, or some other elder will call for a public auction wherein attendees bid for the honor of performing the action or ritual. Typically, the same group of wealthy men seeks to outdo one another in their respective attempts to engage in maximally altruistic acts (i.e., donating sums of money to the congregation). Are they merely being altruistic with no ulterior motives but rather for the sheer act of being kind and generous? Are they engaging in a behavior that is beneficial to the group akin to the group selectionist argument that has been proposed by Kevin Macdonald in describing the within-group affiliational outlook of the Jewish people? If that were the case, then the auctioneers can achieve the same goal by donating the money privately. Holding the auction publicly in front of the whole community triggers a form of competitive altruism (or nonreciprocal altruism) that is perhaps a manifestation of the handicap principle. In most instances, only those who can truly afford to participate in the auction do so, thus serving as a costly signal for those who seek to reap the social benefits of appearing altruistic yet cannot truly afford to take part in the exercise. Because all attendees find out who the winning auctioneers were, this public signal serves to further enhance the reputation and social standing of these. This is incongruent with the second-highest level of *Tzedakah* (righteous and just giving) as espoused by Maimonides, one of the greatest of all Jewish philosophers, namely that neither a recipient nor a giver should know one another's identity. Note that close to 900 years ago, Maimonides had the foresight to recognize that individuals can engage in altruistic and charitable acts for selfish reasons.

Conspicuous consumption during the commission of a rite of passage (e.g., weddings) is hardly restricted to Jewish functions. It is found across a wide variety of cultures separated by time and space. For example, using econometric modeling, Bloch, Rao, and Desai (2004) demonstrated that wedding festivities in Indian villages (as organized and paid by the bride's parents) are meant to serve as cues of social status. In most instances, the financial burden that the bride's family must assume is substantial; as such, the authors propose that this cultural practice might be construed as wasteful consumption. As previously mentioned, conspicuous consumption when analyzed through a Darwinian and Zahavian lens has to be wasteful; otherwise, the signal is not an honest one. Hence, the ultimate explanation for such wasteful cultural practices lies within the rubric of evolved social strategies.In chapter 5, I revisit religion while focusing on the various evolutionary-based research streams that have investigated this human universal (i.e., possessing a religious narrative).

The Universality and Innateness of Conspicuous Consumption.
Some scholars have argued that the need to signal one's status is moderated by demographic variables including social class. For example, Chao and Schor (1998) explored whether certain demographic subgroups were more likely to engage in conspicuous signaling via the cosmetics that they purchased. They found that education, race, income, and the urban–rural distinction were relevant moderators such that more educated, wealthier, White women, and urban dwellings yielded greater levels of status consumption. However, these findings simply demonstrate that this particular status symbol (i.e., cosmetics) is more likely to be used by specific demographic groups. Chao and Schor interpreted their findings as being supportive of the premise that educational attainment socializes individuals to care increasingly about status (but see Frank, 1985, and van Kempen, 2003, for discussions of why status consumption might be negatively correlated with socioeconomic class). This is another manifestation of the focus on identifying socialization agents as drivers of behaviors (see Chao & Schor, 1998, pp 113–114), without recognizing that some behaviors constitute integral elements of our Darwinian heritage.

O'Cass and Frost (2002, p. 75) cite research suggesting that the signaling of self-image is a higher level need (as per Maslow's hierarchy of needs). Self-image encompasses numerous dimensions, some of which might indeed cater to higher level needs. However, one component of self-image, namely one's social status (perceived or real), caters to an innate Darwinian goal that is at times as important as satiating one's hunger. Individuals of all social strata seek to signal their social standings including those at the lowest end of the spectrum. For example, Tommy Hilfiger, whose clothes have found a niche among ghetto youths, has proposed that in many instances these kids would prefer owning a Rolex rather than a house (see the quote in O'Cass & Frost, 2002, p. 81). On a related note, Belk (1988) declares, "Even third-world countries are often attracted to and indulge in aspects of conspicuous consumption before they have secured adequate food, clothing and shelter" (as quoted in O'Cass & Frost, 2002, p. 81). Maslow's hierarchy assumes a strict hierarchical ordering of needs, goals, and motives. In other words, the theory proposes that higher level needs are pursued, only after lower level ones have been met. van Kempen (2003, see pp. 165–167) proposes that this could not be a veridical theory because it cannot explain why the poor spend money on status products when they are deprived of their most basic needs. An evolutionary account recognizes that seeking status is a Darwinian drive that can at times be as important and primordial as many of the other first-level needs identified by Maslow. van Kempen (2003) correctly states:

Contrary to what one would expect on the basis of Maslow's needs pyramid, status considerations can be so powerful that they *override even the most basic needs, such as hunger. Supportive evidence is to be found across space and time* [italics added]. (p. 166).

Van Kempen (2003) studied poor individuals' use of fake status signals in developing nations. This once again speaks to the ubiquitous fact that status signaling is hardly restricted to the upper classes in developed countries. In this particular context, poor individuals are unable to procure "honest" cues of wealth, in which case they simply engage in deceptive signaling. M. Cooper (2001) states:

> A recent police checkpoint in the posh Vitacura neighbourhood [*Santiago de Chile*] found that a high percentage of drivers ticketed for using their cell phones while in motion were using toy—even wooden—replicas. Other middle-class motorists bake with their windows closed pretending they have air conditioning. Workers at the ritzy Jumbo supermarket complain that, on Saturday mornings, the dressed-to-kill clientele fill their carts high with delicacies, parade them in front of the Joneses, and then discretely [*sic*] abandon them before having to pay. (as quoted in van Kempen, 2003, p. 157)

That said, deceptive signaling is certainly not restricted to inhabitants of lesser developed countries. Canal Street in New York City is a testament to the insatiable desire of American consumers to purchase fake products that nonetheless signal high status. The demand for counterfeit products is indeed a universal phenomenon as evidenced by data, which estimated that the global market for such products in the 1980s was valued at U.S. $60 billion (Mason, 2000, p. 128).

van Kempen (2003, p. 172) has argued that fake products are more likely to be found in developing countries because it is easier to fool relevant others in those countries given that these might have never been exposed to the real product. On the other hand, he proposes that consumers in developed countries would have a much easier time detecting fakes. Furthermore, van Kempen (pp. 172–173) discusses how deceptive signaling is more likely to occur in large urban areas where there is greater anonymity and accordingly where an individual's occupational prestige and social standing is not public knowledge. Note that these points can easily be reframed from a Zahavian perspective; namely, that which might be construed as an "honest" signal varies as a function of the ability of members within a given ecological niche to detect mimicry. Countless nonvenomous species have evolved aposematic colors that mimic those of their venomous counterparts. The relevant predators have to evolve the ability to differentiate between the fake and genuine warning signals. The evolutionary arms race between "fakers" and their prospective predators is similar in spirit to the issues raised by van Kempen regarding the situational parameters likely to promote deceptive product signaling.

In most consumer behavior textbooks, two key proximate issues that are discussed regarding social class are how to measure the construct (e.g., subjectively vs. objectively) as well as describing the specific consumption patterns inherent to each social class. However, there are numerous evolutionary-based universal phenomena related to social class that manifest themselves in roughly similar manners across cultures. For example, that all cultures display hierarchical structures (even supposedly cultures that are egalitarian) and that they each use symbols and cues to signal their social ranks is indeed a human universal (cf. D. E. Brown, 1991, and relevant references therein). Hence, social class is merely one of several possible ways to assort people along a social hierarchy. Furthermore, there are consumption patterns specific to particular classes that occur in very similar ways irrespective of cultural setting. The nouveau riche syndrome is a manifestation of conspicuous consumption wherein new members of a social class engage in behaviors that serve as signals of their newly obtained status. Hence, a substantial proportion of one's disposable income might accordingly be spent on ornate signals of power including expensive cars, ostentatious homes, elaborate durable goods, and other consumption choices that reaffirm one's social standing. The Darwinian urge to engage in this form of social and sexual signaling can result in personal bankruptcies when pursued to its morbid extremes. There is ample anecdotal evidence suggesting that those who rapidly acquire an exorbitant amount of money can just as quickly lose their amassed wealth (e.g., shortsighted athletes, musicians, actors, and lottery winners). The television shows *MTV Cribs* or VH1's *The Fabulous Life of*, which chronicle the ostentatious assets of celebrities, highlight the evolved need to reaffirm one's status within some socially relevant group. This nouveau riche syndrome is not restricted to American society. Rather, it occurs in predictably the same manner across countless cultures that are otherwise quite distinct.

Mason (2000, p. 127) has suggested that advertisers create status wants. This is true only insofar as advertisers might confer status onto a *specific* object or product (e.g., via a process of classical conditioning). However, advertisers do not create the need to signal status. In other words, the need to attain and subsequently to signal one's social status is an innate Darwinian drive (cf. van Kempen, 2003, pp. 165–167) whereas the specific cues that are used to signal status might indeed vary across cultures and eras. For example, globalization can create homogeneity of cues that are considered appropriate for displaying status. Hence, Western advertisers might indeed have influenced consumers from other cultures to agree that Gucci, Prada, and Rolex are the appropriate consumption cues of status. This "cultural imperialism" is so only insofar as advertisers are setting the relevant cues for displaying status. However, the need to seek and display status is a human universal that is outside of the advertiser's reach. Note that advertisers need not be the sole determinants of the specific cues that signal status. Oftentimes, these are situationally determined such as occurred during the New York blizzard of 1888. As a result of the historic storm, there was a severe shortage of milk resulting in an upsurge in its price. Men began to purchase glasses of milk in bars precisely because this served as a cue of their social status. Hence, whereas the cues of status are bound by cultures, social classes (e.g., upper and middle classes might respectively use yachts and cars as status cues), eras, and situations, the quest to signal one's status is a universal and Darwinian-driven phenomenon.

The universality and innateness of conspicuous consumption makes it somewhat difficult to legislate against. Beginning with the premise that conspicuous consumption is an economically wasteful endeavor given that it leads to a positional zero-sum game, Mason (2000) reviewed policy measures that might attenuate its supposed deleterious effects. One such attempt proposed that individuals' social ethics might be altered in a manner that lessened their proclivity to pursue "selfish" self-interests such as engaging in conspicuous consumption (Hirsch, 1976). This form of social engineering could not succeed for three distinct reasons. First, it triggers a classic example of the Tragedy of the Commons; namely, though it might be superior if all members of the system were to adhere to the established rules, there are selfish incentives to "cheat" while at the same time hoping that all others do not. Because this incentive structure holds true for all participants, the collusion quickly breaks down. Second, the inherent logic driving this proposal is reminiscent of the largely discredited group selectionist arguments in evolutionary biology, which posits that an organism might act altruistically and selflessly for the good of the group/species despite the individual costs that it might bear. Third, Hirsch's proposal assumes that an innate drive (i.e., seeking social status) can indeed be suppressed via a program of social conditioning. Status seeking is a human universal that is prevalent in countless cultures across varied eras. Even societies that claim to be classless are hardly so on closer inspection (e.g., communism requires the existence of the Proletariat and the party elites). Frank (1985) recognized that such a system would fail and accordingly proposed that rather than trying to eradicate the desire for engaging in the behavior, policymakers should seek to "punish" the behavior once it occurs. Specifically, he argued that a consumption tax should be levied against "wasteful" consumption signaling. Along those lines, Mason (2000) discusses the Excise Tax of 1990, meant to levy a consumption tax on five products, namely furs, automobiles, boats, planes, and jewelry. Note that all are highly visible products that serve as clear signals of ostentatious wealth. Additionally, Mason proposes several other economic policies to curb conspicuous consumption. For example, he argues (p. 129) that the systematic increase of a product's availability (e.g., eliminating exclusive distribution agreements) would reduce the likelihood of it being used as a status cue. This is a cat-and-mouse game because eradicating one status symbol merely ensures that several others will come along to take its place. Mason concludes, "Attempts to introduce greater elements of management and control into status-driven economic activity, whether demand led or supply led, have, to date, met with little success" (p. 128). This is so because the need to show off one's status is innate; hence, it is doggedly difficult to attenuate and likely impossible to eradicate. Therefore, I propose that conspicuous waste is very difficult to legislate precisely because it serves a very important Zahavian function. If anything, the insatiable desire of consumers to engage in conspicuous showing off seems to be growing despite any legislative attempts to curb this behavior. Mason concludes, "In the United States, data showed that, by 1996, luxury, status-linked spending was rising four times faster than spending overall, and similar, if less emphatic, rises were recorded elsewhere" (p. 129). As seen in the preceding discussion, most scholars associate conspicuous consumption with the "selfish" need to show off one's resources via a public display of expensive products. That said, even apparently philanthropic actions (e.g., generous donations) are in many instances nothing short of an extravagant form of Zahavian signaling. I turn to this form of conspicuous consumption in the next section.

Philanthropy: Costly Signaling via Nonreciprocal Altruism. Several authors have independently argued that individuals' needs for showing off their social status could be funneled in ways that might yield greater societal benefits. For example, Congleton (1989) suggested that conspicuous consumption could be beneficial at the macro level if used for philanthropic purposes (e.g., charity events). In other words, wealthy industrialists who spend $1 million on a showy charity event would be instantiating their need to signal their social status in a socially beneficial manner. Though it is indeed true that the latter $1 million generates greater positive externalities than had the money been spent on a custom-made Rolls Royce, this is unlikely to be due to selfless altruism. Rather, it is a likely manifestation of costly altruistic signaling in a Zahavian sense. Competitive altruism wherein several altruists compete for the "honor" of providing an incredibly costly act of altruism without expecting anything in return (i.e., nonreciprocal or unconditional altruism) is an honest signal precisely because it serves as a handicap (cf. G. Roberts, 1998). Trigg (2001, p. 103) has argued that in the post-Depression era, it became socially unacceptable for the wealthy to engage in the ostentatious showing off of their riches. Accordingly, he proposed that more socially acceptable mechanisms of signaling were subsequently used, such as offering charitable donations. From a Darwinian perspective, both conspicuous consumption (of the "selfish" kind) and showy "altruistic" donations cater to the same innate drive and achieve the exact same goal, namely the signaling of one's social standing to the world. On a related note, Grosvenor (2002) explored possible links between evolutionary psychology and the ideological principles of the Intellectual Left. His quest was uncommon given that antagonists of the evolutionary psychology movement have most often drawn illusory links between evolutionary psychology and the Conservative Right (see Segerstråle, 2001, for a discussion of these attacks). Grosvenor prescribes that:

> In particular, the left should try to connect social status to altruistic behavior, rather than to the "conspicuous consumption" identified by the economist Thornstein Veblen in *Theory of the Leisure Class* (1899), and satirized by Tom Wolfe in *Bonfire of the Vanities* (1987) [italics in original]. (p. 443)

Individuals need not wait for the Left to teach them to funnel their selfish pursuits into more lofty social goals. Individuals already engage in this behavior in innumerable settings precisely because both behaviors are examples of selfish Zahavian signaling. The interested reader is referred to Gintis, Smith, and Bowles (2001), and Lotem, Fishman, and Stone (2002) for game-theoretic approaches exploring conditions that might promote the maintenance of such costly signaling. See E. A. Smith and Bliege Bird (2005) for a summary of the literature on costly signaling as manifested via various forms of prosocial and altruistic behaviors.

Competitive altruism manifests itself in a personally relevant setting, namely when benefactors compete for the right to offer large donations to business schools. I perused through an exhaustive list of American business schools to determine the number of schools that were named typically in honor of a financial benefactor (accessed at http://www.usnews.com/usnews/edu/grad/directory/dir-mba/dirmbaindex_brief.php on March 21, 2004). Of the top 25 business schools, only 7 were not named (Harvard, Stanford, Columbia, Chicago, Michigan, Yale, and Carnegie-Mellon). Of the next tier of 25 business schools, only 5 were unnamed (University of Illinois at Urbana-Champaign, UC–Davis, University of Washington, UC–Irvine, and University of Wisconsin–Madison). Hence, of the top 50 business schools in the United States, 76% are named. Of the remaining 313 listed schools, only 92 were named (i.e., 29% of the schools that are not in the top 50). Given that it is more "expensive" to have one's name associated with an elite business school, this form of altruism can be construed as competitive in that benefactors are willing to pay a substantial premium to have their signals bear greater social weight. One might argue that given that wealthy alumni are more likely to originate from top schools, the latter pattern merely reflects that affiliation-based donations are more likely to arise in those samples that will yield wealthy individuals. That notwithstanding, if "pure" altruism were the key motive behind these donations, one might suppose that this money would yield greater social value in reducing the gap between elite institutions and their poorer counterparts. As Mason (2000) states, "Personally financed foundations and charitable trusts, carrying the name of the benefactor, have always been seen by the wealthy as ideal vehicles for consolidating and displaying social rank" (p. 128).

Prior to tackling the survival module, I provide a brief summary of the reproductive module covered thus far. Our behaviors within the mating market are rooted in our evolved sexuality. Our evolved mating minds drive the attributes that we solicit in prospective mates, and those that we advertise about ourselves. Countless consumption acts are forms of sexual signaling including both selfish and philanthropic forms of conspicuous consumption. Given that the reproductive module invokes important sex-specific differences in mating behaviors, it is not surprising that most of the discussion thus far has focused on sex differences across various consumption acts. That said, evolutionary theory is not restricted to the cataloging of sex differences. In the ensuing section, I focus on one specific aspect of the survival module, namely food-related behaviors, many of which do not yield sex-based differences because the relevant adaptive problems were oftentimes similar for both sexes.

THE SURVIVAL MODULE

For most organisms, one of the most recurring and enduring challenges is meeting the caloric requirements that are requisite for survival. Accordingly, it is no surprise that a substantial amount of research in behavioral ecology has focused on optimal foraging models, namely the manner by which organisms expend energy in order to obtain the caloric intake necessary for survival. The threat of starvation, due to both caloric scarcity and caloric uncertainty, has been a ubiquitous force in defining our species' phylogenetic history. Accordingly, evolutionary psychologists have identified several phenomena that are adaptations to this specific survival problem. For example, the gustatory preferences of most individuals display a strong penchant for fatty and sweet foods. The ultimate-based explanation is that these foods are preferred because they are laden with calories, thus addressing the survival problem of caloric scarcity and uncertainty. Few individuals would prefer to eat steamed carrots rather than a barbecued steak. Similarly, most people have a pronounced preference for sweet cakes as compared to dried prunes. In the environment of evolutionary adaptedness (EEA), holding such gustatory preferences and gorging on fatty and sweet foods when these were at hand would have been highly adaptive (cf. Burnham & Phelan, 2000). The EEA did not come equipped with food storage facilities; hence gorging would have served as a proxy behavior for the hoarding of otherwise perishable foods. Note that the latter gustatory preferences, which were highly adaptive given our phylogenetic history defined by caloric uncertainty and scarcity, yield maladaptive outcomes in today's environment. Not only do most people no longer face an endemic threat from caloric uncertainty and scarcity but also the calories that are expended to obtain the sources of food have been greatly reduced. Hence, for most individuals in today's environment of plenty, the only uncertainty associated with food acquisition is the length of the queue at the checkout counter. Similarly, the calories expended are those needed to "forage" at our local grocery store. As such, our gustatory preferences are vestiges of an evolutionary past (the Pleistocene era) that is not aligned with today's reality. This misalignment has led to the record morbidity rates of certain chronic and debilitating diseases that have afflicted the Westernized world (e.g., diabetes, certain diet-related cancers, and heart disease). This point reaffirms the fact that our behaviors do not necessarily yield fitness-maximizing outcomes, and as such identifying such behaviors does not translate into a refutation of evolutionary principles. This discussion of our evolved gustatory preferences highlights another important point regarding the synergy that can be achieved if a given phenomenon is studied from both proximate and ultimate perspectives. Cultural relativists are likely to focus on cross-cultural differences in culinary habits and traditions. For example, Hinduism forbids the consumption of beef whereas Islam and Judaism alike have a prohibition against the consumption of pork. In addition to being influenced by religious edicts, culinary traditions are shaped by geographical and climactic factors (e.g., greater use of spices in warmer climates). Countless other historical events are at the root of the culinary traditions of a given culture (e.g., consumption of dairy products as a function of whether a culture is agriculturist or nomadic). That said, underneath this rich panoply of culinary differences, there exists a universal preference for fatty and sweet foods. A scholar's research interests will determine whether a proximate or ultimate-based approach is appropriate. That said, both perspectives are needed for a complete understanding of the gustatory preferences and culinary habits of *Homo sapiens*. It is important to note that evolutionary theory cannot provide an explanation for idiosyncratic food preferences at the individual's level. In other words, evolutionary psychologists cannot explain why a given individual prefers chocolate ice cream more so than cheesecake, or why another enjoys roasted lamb more than grilled hamburgers. Given their focus on population-level universals, evolutionary psychologists can safely state that irrespective of individuals' instantiated preferences, they will prefer fatty and sweet foods more so than "healthy" alternatives. The multibillion dollar diet industry is a testament to that reality. Numerous other food-related behaviors and preferences have Darwinian-based etiologies. For example, Nisbett and Kanouse (1969) found a positive correlation between situational hunger and the amount of food bought at a grocery store. From a Darwinian perspective, this makes perfect sense. Situational hunger triggers physiological signals that promote the ravenous hoarding of calories. Hence, that the "hoarding" of products at a supermarket is more likely to occur the hungrier we are, is a manifestation of our evolved behavioral and physiological triggers when facing hunger.

There are countless other physiological and psychological phenomena that fall under the rubric of the survival module. For example, the evolved capacity of the human body to achieve homeostasis (equilibrium) along several internal gauges is one other such example. Parker and Tavassoli (2000) explored the manner by which consumers seek to achieve psychological and physiological homeostasis via specific consumption choices. They provide cross-cultural differences in the aggregate consumption of specific products (e.g., alcohol and coffee) and argue that this is in part predicted by a country's climate and latitude (correlates of ambient temperature and amount of sunlight). Similarly, they propose that certain personality predispositions (e.g., risk taking, variety seeking, and sensation seeking) are also likely affected by a country's climate. This work is certainly promising in that it incorporates a universal physiological mechanism (achieving homeostasis) as an explicative factor within the consumption arena. However, it does not contextualize this research within an evolutionary framework. That humans have the innate physiological need to achieve homeostasis has to be rooted within the greater evolutionary context. For example, that individuals adjust the manner by which they seek homeostasis as a function of local niches falls within the Darwinian-based behavioral ecology research agenda. An evolutionary perspective would permit one to categorize those variables requiring homeostasis, as either adaptable to local niches or invariant to such variations and hence being universally specified. A brief example highlights this point. Parker and Tavassoli discuss how variety seeking can be construed as a means of achieving homeostasis as a function of one's optimal stimulation level. Subsequently, they provide an environmental variable (a country's latitude), which is purported to have predictable effects on individuals' optimal stimulation levels. Note that variety seeking in mating can also be construed as an attempt to meet one's optimal stimulation level, albeit in this case there are universal and consistent sex-specific differences in the desired optimal stimulation levels (men desire greater sexual variety as per the Coolidge effect). Hence, whereas local niches affect coffee consumption, they minimally (if at all) alter certain mating-related consumption. The appropriate Darwinian lens can help in predicting which consumption acts are locally influenced versus those that are globally invariant.

Sherman and Hash (2001) conducted a content analysis of food recipes originating from 36 highly heterogeneous countries. As specified by the authors, the chosen countries were diverse on numerous relevant metrics including both geographic and linguistic diversity (e.g., the countries spanned six continents and represented 16 of the 19 most important linguistic groups in the world). There were two key objectives to the study. First, Sherman and Hash explored whether the use of spices varied as a function of whether a dish was meat or vegetable based. Second, they explored whether the use of spices varied as a function of a country's average ambient temperature. They used the antimicrobial hypothesis, which suggests that spices destroy foodborne microbes, to make two key predictions. First, vegetable dishes should contain fewer spices than meat dishes; and second, the use of spices should be positively correlated with a country's ambient temperature (which is correlated with a country's latitude as per the work of Parker & Tavassoli, 2000). In other words, they are proposing that environmental conditions specific to a local niche shape a country's culinary traditions. Thus, gastronomy is a cultural product that in part evolves as an adaptive solution to the prevalence of foodborne pathogens, parasites, and microbes in a given niche (see Wrangham & Conklin-Brittain, 2003, for a discussion of cooking as an interaction between cultural and biological evolution; see also S. H. Katz, 1990). The findings were strongly supportive of their Darwinian-based predictions. Incidentally, the "meat dish versus vegetable dish" analyses were conducted within countries, further attesting to the robustness of the findings (because they control for intercountry differences such as the availability of spices). Taken together, the study by Parker and Tavassoli coupled with that by Sherman and Hash demonstrates the value of using both proximate and ultimate approaches in tackling a phenomenon. Whereas Parker and Tavassoli established aggregate differences in consumption patterns as a function of a country's latitude, Sherman and Hash provide an evolutionary (i.e., ultimate) explanation for such differences.

There are countless additional food-related behaviors that are driven by evolutionary forces. For example, Fessler (2003) summarizes a wide range of studies that have explored the link between a woman's caloric intake (as influenced by a satiety point) and her menstrual cycle. He finds that a preponderance of studies have documented a decrease in food consumption at the maximally fertile point of a woman's cycle. Accordingly, he proposes an adaptive explanation for this mechanism (which incidentally occurs across a wide range of species). Specifically, the decrease in caloric consumption is a manifestation of a female's shifting focus from one adaptive goal (hoarding calories) to another (finding a mate). In support of this ultimate explanation, Fessler discusses findings that have shown that females across several species are more likely to move about their environment when maximally fertile (i.e., in search of prospective mates). Hence, a woman's appetite appears to be linked to her menstrual cycle in ways that are congruent with a trade-off between her varying adaptive pursuits (mating vs. caloric hoarding). As mentioned throughout the current book, numerous other behaviors are linked to a woman's menstrual cycle in ways that can be explained only via an evolutionary lens (e.g., likelihood of exposing one's self to danger, initiating sexual activity, likelihood of wearing provocative attire).

To reiterate, though I have exclusively focused on food-related behaviors, many additional consumption acts fall within the survival module. For example, those products associated with physiological and safety needs within Maslow's hierarchy can be subsumed within the survival module. I next turn to the third of the four key Darwinian modules, namely kin selection.

THE KIN SELECTION MODULE

I begin with a brief overview of family research within the consumer behavior discipline. One pattern that emerges from the latter literature is that despite important progress that has been achieved in this area, consumer scholars have investigated family issues while largely ignoring the Darwinian mechanisms that influence family dynamics. With that in mind, I then discuss evolutionary-based research that has explored the effects of kin selection on human behavior. In demonstrating the relevance of evolutionary forces in shaping family dynamics, I hope to highlight new research opportunities for consumer scholars interested in family research. I conclude with a discussion of a Darwinian-based approach for understanding the influence of birth order within the consumption arena.

Family Research in Consumer Behavior

Family research in consumer behavior reached its zenith in the 1970s and 1980s. The past 15 years have been witness to a steady decline of published works in this important area. As explained in the recent and comprehensive review of the field by Commuri and Gentry (2000), family researchers have tended to focus on a few central issues. Some of these include the influence of the family life cycle on consumption, the relative influence that husbands, wives, and children wield in consumption choices, and the influence of roles (e.g., role overload and/or gender roles) in family decision making. In evaluating this research stream, Commuri and Gentry state:

> One of the factors that has limited the breadth of research questions that have been asked by scholars in the field is a *lack of integration* [italics added] of all the relevant issues into a template that would then offer a road map for future research streams and agenda in the field (Tallman, 1993). (p. 1)

Biologists and other evolutionary-minded scholars who study family dynamics in innumerable species (including *Homo sapiens*) recognize the evolutionary forces that have shaped these. As such, evolutionary theory is the integrative framework that drives their research agendas when investigating kin-related dynamics. I propose that evolutionary psychology can equally help in integrating family research (in consumer behavior) under a common theoretical rubric.

Consumer scholars who have conducted family research have operated solely at the proximate level as such opportunities exist for expanding the research stream into the ultimate realm. It is important to reiterate that proximate and ultimate approaches do not compete in a zero-sum game for paradigmatic influence. Rather, a more complete understanding of family forces in the consumption arena would require that both approaches be used. Proximate questions are certainly important when conducting family research. For example, understanding how the greater participation of women in the labor market affects family consumption processes is an important proximate issue. Identifying which jointly consumed purchases children initiate has clear practical and theoretical implications at the proximate level. Tracking the longitudinal changes that have occurred to the traditional family life cycle stages (e.g., increases in single parenting in the United States) is yet another relevant proximate phenomenon. However, underneath all of these culturally and temporally specific phenomena exists a set of family-related ones that are universally defined. Sibling competition, sibling cooperation, parental investment, parental roles in sexually reproducing species, family structures, and other kin-related phenomena occur in their particular forms in a given species because of Darwinian forces (see the next section).

Returning to the exhaustive review of family research conducted by Commuri and Gentry (2000), most of the suggestions for future research stem from one or more of the central tenets of the SSSM. For example, when discussing the paucity of research on sibling influence, they state, "To our knowledge, sibling influence on purchase decisions has not been studied within consumer research, despite the obvious modeling by younger children of their especially same-sex older siblings" (p. 5). Hence, sibling relationships are viewed as an instance where the effects of socialization could further be studied (despite the authors' recognition that socialization processes have been extensively investigated in the familial context). Evolutionists recognize that one universal element of sibling relationships is the inherent rivalry that arises while competing for parental investment. This rivalry, which can manifest itself in numerous consumption settings (e.g., toy purchases or college tuition), has a Darwinian etiology, and as such is found across cultures. It is not surprising from an evolutionary perspective when Commuri and Gentry conclude that greater differences have been found when families are contrasted on their respective ideologies as opposed to their country origins. Family units have variables along which they minimally vary because many family dynamics are to a large extent evolutionary based (see Emlen, 1995, for an evolutionary account of the family unit). When discussing research on cross-cultural family decision making, they propose that the extent to which the patriarchy dominates within a given culture has been used as the relevant cross-cultural moderator. Regarding sex-specific research, they state, "There is a need to *deconstruct such gendered approaches* [italics added] to research on families so that we may pave the way for gender-neutral research" (p. 16). Many sex-specific parental phenomena have a Darwinian etiology, and as such can be neither deconstructed nor analyzed as an instantiation of patriarchal influence. For example, one of the most robust human universals is that men provide lesser parental investment to their offspring (see Eibl-Eibesfeldt, 1989, for a cross-cultural summary), a phenomenon rooted in parental investment theory (Trivers, 1972). Finally, the Durkheimian tenet that culture cannot be understood by studying the individuals comprising it is adhered to, albeit the supraorganism in this case is the family unit Commuri and Gentry propose, "In other words, the first step to overcoming the complexity of family decision making is to give up the individual and become concerned with only the family as the unit of analysis" (p. 16). Families are made up of distinct individuals, not automata operating under the control of a supraunit. Hence, it is difficult to extract much meaning from the Durkheimian position that supraorganisms (families, groups, or cultures) can be studied without a focus on the individuals comprising them. Parent–child relationships are fraught with evolution-ary-based investments and at times conflicts (e.g., gestational diabetes) as are sibling relationships. Consumer scholars might identify new research opportunities by recognizing the evolutionary role that each distinct individual holds within the context of the family unit.

To conclude, family research in the consumer behavior literature has been driven by many of the central tenets of the SSSM. It has displayed an exclusive focus on proximate issues and socialization forces, and at times has supported objectives such as achieving "gender neutrality" via the deconstruction of the supposed patriarchically imposed gender-specific familial roles. In the next section, I turn to a discussion of studies that have explored kin relationships from an evolutionary perspective. In many instances, it is unlikely that the investigated topics would have been identified had the researchers in question not utilized the Darwinian framework.

Evolutionary Account of Kin Relationships

Of all Darwinian-based theories, few have had as profound an effect as Hamilton's (1964) kin selection theory. As mentioned in chapter 1, Hamilton provided a framework that elucidated, across a large number of species, otherwise "paradoxically" altruistic behaviors between kin. Viewed from the pre-Hamiltonian perspective that organisms pursue their own selfish interests, altruistic acts that bore great costs to the altruist seemed paradoxical. However, once an organism is construed as maximizing its inclusive fitness (i.e., via both its own gene propagation and that of its kin), such selfless acts make complete sense. One can increase their inclusive fitness by reproducing (also known as direct fitness), by investing in their siblings, by loving their parents, and by caring for all others that are within their consanguinity (also known as indirect fitness). Humans engage in innumerable behaviors that adhere to kin selection theory. This reality transcends culture, era, political and economic systems, and geographical setting. People around the world love their own children more than their neighbors' children, and protect their siblings and parents more so than random strangers.

In the human context, there have been numerous validations of kin selection theory. A consistent finding is that the genetic relatedness between an altruist and the prospective recipient of the altruistic act affects both the likelihood and extent of engaging in the act. For example, Zvoch (1999) compared the investments in children's education in both stepfamilies (one of the two parents is a stepparent) and genetic families (biological parents). Using data from the U.S. National Education Longitudinal Survey, Zvoch found that stepfamilies were less likely to invest in the higher education of their children as compared to those from genetic families. Specifically, not only did stepfamilies delay the time at which they began saving for the educational expenses of their children but also they saved less money for such a purpose. Additionally, stepfamilies stated that they would allocate fewer funds toward the financial support of their children's first year of higher education. Even after controlling for potential covariates such as a child's scholastic abilities, a family's socioeconomic status, and the number of family members who receive parental resources, the latter findings persisted (albeit the effects were diminished). Case, Lin, and McLanahan (2001) compared the educational attainment of step-siblings with those of biological siblings within a given family. In other words, given that the analysis was within families, it could establish whether parental investment is discriminating in a manner that conforms to inclusive fitness theory. They found that the presence of a stepmother was detrimental to the educational attainment of nonbirth children (i.e., foster, adoptive, and step). Specifically, nonbiological children received on average 1 lesser year of education than their biological counterparts.

Saad and Gill (2003) used inclusive fitness theory to investigate the allocation of gift-giving expenditures across a wide range of gift recipients. They found that the allocation of gift expenditures was positively correlated with the genetic relatedness between giver and recipient. Additionally, individuals spent more on biological siblings as compared to that spent on step-siblings, and more on biological parents as compared to that spent on stepparents. On a related note, several researchers have recently demonstrated a pattern of grandparental investment (including gift giving), which has been coined grandparental solicitude. Specifically, grandparents are very discriminating in terms of the amount of investment that they provide to their grandchildren as a function of the paternity uncertainty inherent to a given relationship (cf. Euler & Weitzel, 1996). The greater the paternal uncertainty, the lesser the investment. Hence, maternal grandmothers provide the greatest investments because their genetic link is assured whereas paternal grandfathers offer the least investment because they face two sources of paternal uncertainty. It is difficult to envision an alternate explanation for this effect other than that provided by evolutionary theory. Furthermore, the effect is unlikely to have been uncovered were the problem not approached from an evolutionary perspective. Webster (2003) demonstrated that both the degree and uncertainty of genetic relatedness affect prosocial behavior within families. Incidentally, patterns of familial investments adhere to kin selection even when the altruist is deceased. For example, M. S. Smith, Kish, and Crawford (1987) found that bequeathed wills were affected by the genetic relatedness between the deceased and the beneficiaries. On a related note, patterns of bereavement are congruent with kin selection theory (cf. Segal & Ream, 1998, and references therein).

Using inclusive fitness theory, E. M. Hill, Grabel, and McCurren (2003) proposed a mathematical model to explain patterns of family caregiving (a form of kin investment). The three variables that were included in the model were genetic relatedness between the caregiver and recipient, the reproductive value of the prospective care recipient, and the likely inclusive fitness benefits to be reaped by the care recipient. Using hypothetical scenarios, the authors utilized a multiattribute model comprised of the latter three variables to predict whether a family member would be likely to receive care, and which of several competing prospective recipients might receive such care (assuming that the giver has limited resources to provide the care). On a related note, Burnstein, Crandall, and Kitayama (1994) showed that the likelihood of providing help was correlated to genetic relatedness (between giver and recipient) and this relationship was more pronounced in life-threatening situations. In other words, genetic relatedness might not explain altruistic acts in banal settings but it certainly does guide one's actions when responding to threatening contexts. It is important to reiterate that individuals are not consciously aware that their behaviors correspond to the kin selection calculus. However, evolutionary forces shape our behavioral predispositions with maximal opacity.

Jankowiak and Diderich (2000) compared the affiliation that individuals experience toward their siblings and half-siblings in the context of a Mormon polygynous community (one man cohabits with multiple wives). The authors reasoned that because Mormon communities are founded on the religious doctrine that genetic differences of children within a household should be depreciated, this would serve as a strong test of inclusive fitness theory. In other words, the socialization processes in this case are meant to attenuate the evolved kin selection calculus. Additionally, given that both siblings and half-siblings are raised in the same home, the physical proximity and extent of contact between the offspring is controlled for. If Mormons end up discriminating between their full and half-siblings, this would be yet another datum in support of kin selection. This is what Jankowiak and Diderich found; namely, that across three metrics of solidarity (functional, affectual, and associational), there was a pronounced preference for full siblings over half-siblings. On a related note, kin selection has been used to model game-theoretic behaviors between siblings (Bergstrom, 1995).

In perhaps the most morbid manifestation of inclusive fitness theory, Daly and Wilson (1988) have shown that patterns of child abuse fully conform to its precepts. Specifically, the greatest risk factor for the occurrence of child abuse (be it sexually, physically, emotionally, or via neglect) is the presence of a stepparent. Sexual abuse is overwhelmingly more likely if a stepfather is present in the family. Similarly, as is true of the infamous Cinderella fable, the possibility of various other forms of abuse increases with the presence of a stepmother (see Daly & Wilson, 1999).

Kin selection manifests itself in countless other settings including in the commercial, political, and linguistic arenas. Nepotism, irrespective of whether it occurs in family-run businesses, organizations, or governments (e.g., dictatorial regimes), is an instantiation of kin selection. John F. Kennedy was reputed to trust only his brother Robert. Vanhanen (1999) used kin selection theory to study the relationship between ethnic conflict and ethnic nepotism. He reasoned that to the extent that one is more likely to be genetically linked to their ethnic groups (many metrics of ethnicity are valid here), one should expect that the greater the ethnic heterogeneity within a given state, the more likely ethnic conflict is to occur (e.g., current-day Iraq). Using data from 183 states, Vanhanen found strong support for his kin-based hypotheses regarding the link between ethnic nepotism and ethnic conflict. Linguistic markers highlight the importance of kin selection as an evolved Darwinian module. In the African American vernacular, the terms *brother* and *sister* refer to members of one's affiliational group. A more recent term within Black slang is *cuz* (i.e., cousin), which is another marker of consanguinity. Older individuals will oftentimes address young individuals as *son* even though they are clearly not their parents. Some young African American males now use the appellation *son* in a rank-related manner when addressing members of their age cohort. Members of the same fraternity or sorority are Greek brothers and sisters. D. Jones (2003a, 2003b) has demonstrated that linguistic markers associated with kin contain certain universal elements that are congruent with evolutionary predictions. In other words, he has argued that the specific contents of languages (as relating in this case to classification according to kin, rank, and group membership) reflect evolutionary principles (e.g., kin selection). Thus, not only have we evolved a domain-specific module to learn language (cf. Pinker, 1994) but also the specific contents of language contain elements that are indicative of the evolutionary importance of certain key Darwinian modules.

Without the use of an evolutionary-based framework, many kin-based findings would be impossible to explain. For example, over 100 years ago, the anthropologist Westermarck had noted a sexual repulsion between children that were raised together even when these were not biologically related (Westermarck, 1891). There are several cultures wherein the rearing of non-kin-related children together is an integral part of an institutionalized cultural practice (see A. P. Wolf, 1993, for a good summary). One such instance is a marital practice in Taiwan/China whereby a bride-to-be is sent from a very young age to live with the groom-to-be and his family. Marriages arising from such arrangements are more likely to be unstable, and yield greater marital sexual dysfunction (cf. A. P. Wolf, 1995). Shepher (1971) has demonstrated the same sexual disinterest between young people that were raised together within the communal kibbutzim of Israel. At first glance, this seems to violate evolutionary theory in that there are no apparent biological reasons that would justify shutting off the sexual attraction between two unrelated individuals. However, these cross-culturally consistent findings make sense when one realizes that humans do not have a sensorial kin recognition system. Rather, the genetic dangers associated with incestuous relationships are avoided by simply adhering to the production rule "if raised together, shut off sexual attraction." In most instances, this leads to accurate outcomes in that children raised together are almost always related. However, in those cases when this is not true, the production rule "misfires." This example demonstrates that Darwinian mechanisms are typically epigenetic rules (see E. O. Wilson, 1998) in that they are contingently instantiated as a function of specific environmental inputs.

To summarize, parent–child and parent–parent interactions, sibling love and sibling rivalry, patterns of investment in one's nuclear and extended family, and countless other forms of kin-related behaviors are rooted in evolved Darwinian mechanisms. To the extent that consumption is one arena wherein many family dynamics manifest themselves, consumer scholars are likely to identify new lines of inquiry by incorporating biological and/or evolutionary-based theorizing within their existing family research agendas. In the ensuing section, I discuss a recent application of Darwinian-based theorizing within the family context, namely understanding birth order in the consumption arena. Readers interested in additional readings on evolutionary-based approaches in understanding family dynamics are referred to Emlen (1997), H. Keller (2000), Geary and Flinn (2001), and Floyd and Haynes (2005).

Darwinian Perspective on Birth Order Effects in the Consumption Setting

In countless species (e.g., mammals and avian species), one of the first survival problems that a newborn organism faces is finding ways to maximize the parental investment that will be bestowed on it. In doing so, the newborn typically faces substantial competition from its siblings with regard to the limited parental resources that are available for sharing. In many species, sibling rivalry at this early ontogenetic stage takes the form of siblicide (i.e., the killing of one's siblings). The pattern of sibling violence is such that younger offspring are most likely to be the victims of sibling violence. Hence, birth order appears to be a considerable variable in shaping behavioral adaptations across a wide range of species. In the human context, this does not appear to be the evolved strategy for handling sibling competition for parental resources. That being said, much of the research that has explored birth order within *Homo sapiens* has done so with little recognition of the Darwinian forces that might shape the adaptations to this early environmental challenge. Specifically, the majority of birth order theories have been nurture-based explanations void of ultimate-based theorizing (cf. Zajonc & Mullally, 1997, for a recent example), yielding in many instances contradictory and equivocal findings (see reviews by Ernst & Angst, 1983; Schooler, 1972; Stewart & Stewart, 1995). Similarly, the few studies that have explicitly explored the effects of birth order in the consumption and marketing arena have yielded disappointing results (see Claxton, 1995, 1999; Zemanek, Claxton, & Zemanek, 2000).

Sulloway (1995) conducted a meta-analysis of the birth order literature using the Big Five personality traits and evolutionary psychology as the integrative frameworks. The Big Five personality traits, which capture a significant proportion of the variance across personality profiles (as gauged via factor analysis), are openness to experience, extraversion, neuroticism, conscientiousness, and agreeableness. Sulloway's evolutionary theorizing was based on the Darwinian niche-partitioning hypothesis, which proposes that there are two separate sources of selection pressures that have been exerted with regard to the manner by which offspring respond to their birth order. As mentioned earlier, there are the inherent dangers of sibling rivalry; however, additionally patterns of parental investment are such that they tend to favor the eldest child whenever such a parental bias manifests itself. This is in part due to the greater contribution that a typical firstborn would have yielded to the parents' inclusive fitness in the environment of evolutionary adaptedness, where childhood mortality rates have been estimated at 50%. Daly and Wilson (1988) tested this proposition (i.e., preferential treatment of firstborns) using the extreme case of infanticide. They used historical records of 60 preindustrial societies that practiced infanticide as an adaptive response to the scarcity of resources needed to raise multiple children. In none of the studied societies were older children the victims of infanticide. Sulloway (1996, 2001) proposed that the latter selection pressures (i.e., sibling rivalry for parental investment and preferential treatment of firstborns by parents) would have yielded adaptive responses on the part of offspring in light of the birth order that they were born into. Older siblings typically seek to defend their preferred status by being biased toward the status quo and by associating with authority (because the source of authority is responsible for their favored status). For example, firstborns are likely to adopt the "I am a good boy/girl" strategy as a means of adhering to their parents' expectations. As each new child is born, it seeks to identify a unique niche (i.e., not occupied by its siblings) from which it will attempt to elicit maximal parental investment. As such, as one moves down the birth order, children must inherently be more "adaptable" in that not only do they have to identify a unique niche among fewer available niches but also they must negotiate older, larger, and physically stronger siblings. Sulloway (1995) showed that the meta-analytic findings of birth order effects along the Big Five traits were congruent with his Darwinian-based theorizing. Of relevance to the current discussion, he found that the largest meta-analytic effect was for openness to experience where laterborns scored higher than did firstborns. Specifically, laterborns displayed greater receptivity of novel ideas, and were more rebellious and less conventional, whereas firstborns preferred the status quo, were more traditional, displayed greater conformity, and manifested greater identification with their parents.

In his book titled *Born to Rebel*, Sulloway (1996) conducted an exhaustive empirical test of the "openness" birth order effect by exploring the receptivity of the most radical scientific innovations (e.g., Darwin's theory of natural selection) and social revolutions (e.g., the Protestant Reformation) as a function of one's birth order. Specifically, he theorized that if his hypothesis is correct, he should find that radical scientific innovations should be more likely to be supported by laterborns as compared to their firstborn counterparts. This is precisely what he found; namely, of the 28 most radical scientific innovations (as determined by an independent group of scholars), 23 were more likely (in a statistical sense) to have been supported by laterborns. Confirming findings were also obtained when Sulloway explored radical societal revolutions. Numerous social scientists have since tested Sulloway's theory in various settings (see Saad, Gill, & Nataraajan, 2005, for a listing of some of these). On the aggregate, the evidence seems to support Sulloway's contentions.

Of what relevance is the latter discussion of birth order and openness to new experiences to consumer behavior? Saad et al. (2005) recently answered this question by applying Sulloway's work in the consumption arena. Specifically, they reasoned that one's reception and adoption of product innovations and one's proclivity to be a conforming consumer (e.g., following fads) might be linked to their birth order in a manner that is consistent with Sulloway's findings. Using established psychometric scales to measure product innovativeness and consumer conformity, Saad et al. obtained findings supportive of Sulloway's theory. This raises several possible practical implications. For example, to the extent that many of the characteristics defining the innovators in the adoption curve are correlated with birth order, this would suggest that birth order might be used as a reliable predictor of one's membership in the various adopter categories.

To conclude, family-related phenomena manifest themselves in countless distinct ways within the consumption setting. Evolutionary theory can complement existing research agendas in family research by exploring the Darwinian etiology behind universal patterns of familial dynamics. The infusion of Darwinian theory might reverse the declining interest in family research by consumer scholars while tackling the lack of integration within this subdiscipline. In the ensuing section, I turn to the fourth and final Darwinian module covered in this chapter, namely the reciprocation module, and accordingly I discuss specific instantiations of consumption phenomena that fall within its rubric.

THE RECIPROCATION MODULE

Numerous social behaviors can be subsumed under the reciprocation Darwinian module. The acts of forming and maintaining friendships and coalitions, and the associated universal need to belong to an identifiable group are means by which individuals promote their chances of forging reciprocal-based relationships. The notion that individuals engage in altruistic acts with nonkin, expecting that such acts will be reciprocated at some later time, is the most common evolutionary-based interpretation of altruism (i.e., the theory of reciprocal altruism as originally developed by Trivers, 1971). As briefly discussed earlier in this chapter, evolutionists have uncovered various other forms of altruism that are not predicated on expectations of reciprocity. These alternate forms of altruistic behaviors (competitive and nonreciprocal altruism) are meant to serve as costly and hence honest signals of one's fitness, status, reputation, or other evolutionarily relevant metric. Altruists that engage in this form of costly signaling stand to benefit in numerous ways, one of which is via indirect reciprocity (see E. A. Smith & Bliege Bird, 2005, for a summary of key references regarding this form of reciprocity). Specifically, indirect reciprocity occurs when nonrecipients of the altruistic acts that have nonetheless viewed (or been made aware of) the acts increase their likelihood of forging reciprocal-based relationships with the altruists. In other words, the altruists can expect to forge new reciprocal-based arrangements as a result of an enhancement of their respective reputations. Viewed from this perspective, socially responsible firms that engage in philanthropic acts stand to reap the benefits associated with indirect reciprocity (on a related note, see Salamon & Deutsch, 2006, for an evolutionary account of organizational citizenship behaviors). Thus, evolutionists recognize that altruism has evolved to be dispensed strategically. This point is well captured by E. A. Smith and Bliege Bird (2000) in their study of collective turtle hunting by Meriam males of Torres Strait (Australia), a display of public generosity that serves as a costly Zahavian signal. They state:

> Generosity—the phenomenon of sharing food outside the immediate family, giving gifts, hosting public events, helping neighbors in need, all at some cost to ones' self—seems to be a cross-culturally ubiquitous feature of social life. But generosity is not universally nor unconditionally extended. Instead, it appears to be strategic: the contexts in which such acts occur, as well as the characteristics of donors and recipients, seem to be highly constrained and patterned. Some of this variability may be adaptive and hence explicable using theory from evolutionary ecology. (pp. 253–254)

Although there are innumerable behaviors that can be linked to the reciprocation module, I restrict the discussion to four key areas, namely gift giving as a means of forging and maintaining social bonds, consumption meant to signal group membership, identifying violators in social contracts, and cross-cultural norms of friendship. In each of the latter four cases, I draw explicit links to the consumption arena. I begin with a universal behavior studied by countless anthropologists in widely varying cultures, namely the practice of gift giving.

Gift Giving as a Means of Creating and/or Solidifying Bonds

The economic repercussions of the gift-giving ritual are enormous. Retail sales are profoundly affected by gift purchases offered on a few central occasions (e.g., birthdays, Christmas, Valentine's Day, Mother's Day, and Father's Day). That consumers are easily convinced to participate in marketer-influenced events is a testament to our innate drive to engage in reciprocal exchanges. Specifically, gift giving is one of the consumption behaviors that best exemplifies the reciprocation module. Of all instances where gift giving occurs, few involve a unidirectional flow of resources such as when parents invest in their children. Most gift-giving occasions entail very clear expectations of reciprocity. Many close friends have a tradition of inviting each other to restaurants on their respective birthdays. From a strict utility maximization perspective, the end result (once each friend has invited the other) leaves each individual no better off than had the reciprocal ritual not been entered into. The same principle applies across a wide range of occasions where gifts of roughly equal value are exchanged between parties. In some instances, the exchange occurs on the same day (exchanging Christmas gifts with one's closest friend at a dinner party) whereas on other occasions, the reciprocal exchange occurs on two separate occasions (e.g., birthday exchanges between close friends). Incidentally, ritualized and ceremonial exchanges of gifts of equal value occur not only between two individuals but also between two groups of individuals (cf. Bell, 1991, and references therein). Numerous cultural traditions replete with important consumption implications serve the primary goal of reaffirming the bonds of friendship as forged through reciprocal arrangements. Several rituals associated with Western marriages are precisely meant to solidify these bonds of reciprocity. These include bridal showers wherein a bride is literally showered with gifts, the bachelor and bachelorette parties, baby showers, godparenting, and finally the naming of the complete wedding party (best man, matron of honor, groomsmen, and bridesmaids). Needless to say, there are specific gift-giving rituals associated with each of these relationships, all of which serve to reinforce the bonds of reciprocity.

Much of the research on gift giving within the consumer behavior discipline has focused on proximate issues while largely overlooking the evolutionary origins of this universal behavior (for overviews of the gift-giving literature, see Laroche, Saad, Browne, Cleveland, & Kim, 2000; Saad & Gill, 2003). For example, cultural relativists have uncovered numerous variables along which gift-giving practices vary across cultures. Should one open a gift in front of the giver or wait until they are alone? How much effort should go toward choosing an appropriate gift wrap? How expensive and elaborate should the gift be? Given one's social rank within a given group, is it appropriate to pick up the tab at a restaurant or will this be construed as an affront to the dominant individual? All of the latter issues and countless others dealing with gift giving are indeed culturally determined. Perhaps of greater importance is that gift giving is found in all cultures irrespective of the culture-specific instantiations of some of the rituals involved. Gift giving is a human universal because it is a means by which evolutionary adaptive friendships and coalitions are formed, maintained, and solidified.

In their evolutionary-based study of gift giving, Saad and Gill (2003) found that individuals would spend the most money on their mates, followed by their closest kin (genetic relatedness of 0.50), and third on their closest friends. Other recipients including stepfamily members, and kin members with a genetic relatedness of 0.25 or lesser, received less generous gifts as compared to those offered to close friends. There are two noteworthy issues implicit in the latter findings. First, that close friends would be treated more generously than would various groups of family members speaks to the importance of gift giving as a ritual to cement friendships. Second, the strict ordering of gift-giving expenditures to various recipients might serve as a good proxy of the importance of the various Darwinian modules that are triggered during the gift-giving ritual (i.e., reproductive, kin selection, and reciprocation modules).

To reiterate, gift giving is a means by which one forges alliances, friendships, and coalitions; hence, it is certainly not surprising that humans have an innate proclivity for coalitional thinking (e.g., categorizing people as in-group vs. out-group members). Accordingly, humans engage in countless behaviors meant to advertise one's membership within a particular group. I turn to this issue next.

Consumption Behaviors Meant to Signal Group Membership

Many consumption choices are made with the intention of signaling one's membership in a particular group. For example, individuals wear university memorabilia to demonstrate their educational allegiances. Consumers wear clothes consistent with their age cohorts, social class, ethnic backgrounds, and professional affiliations. This is part of our innate desire to signal membership within some relevant in-group, namely to belong to an established group (cf. Baumeister & Leary, 1995). Evolutionarily speaking, those within a group are more likely to engage in reciprocal arrangements with one another (cf. D. Jones, 2000, for a discussion of group nepotism). As such, there are numerous cultural practices that are meant to solidify in-group behavior, one of which is via consumption choices that reaffirm our group memberships.

The fashion industry can be construed as an exercise of group conformity and group identification. In other words, the innate and evolutionarily relevant need to belong manifests itself in the context of the fashion industry by having millions of consumers engage in behaviors that ensure that they repeatedly belong to the "fashionable" group (see the first quote in Table 3.1). The fashion industry has usurped our innate need to belong and fashioned it in a manner that is maximally profitable. Specifically, the overt cues of belongingness are labile such that to continue to belong to the "fashionable" group, one must continuously buy the ever-changing attires, accoutrements, and accessories (see the second, third, and fourth quotes in Table 3.1). In light of the latter perspective, the fifth quote by Santayana in Table 3.1 suggests that he did not recognize the signaling benefits that are derived to those that adopt the

TABLE 3.1
Fashion Quotes Manifesting Darwinian Roots

Quote	Source
"When people are free to do as they please, they usually imitate each other."	Eric Hoffer
"Fashion is made to become unfashionable."	Coco Chanel
"Fashion is a form of ugliness so intolerable that we have to alter it every six months."	Oscar Wilde
"Every generation laughs at the old fashions but follows religiously the new."	Henry David Thoreau
"Fashion is something barbarous, for it produces innovation without reason and imitation without benefit."	George Santayana
"Fashion, for the most part, is nothing but the ostentation of riches."	John Locke
"Change of fashion is the tax levied by the industry of the poor on the vanity of the rich."	Sebastien-Roch Nicolas De Chamfort

Note. Quotes taken from various Internet quotation Web sites such as http://www.randomterrain.com/quotes/fashion.html on September 22, 2004.

latest trends and fashions. Finally, though it might have been veridical to view fashion trends as the ostentation of the privileged classes at the time that Locke and De Chamfort proclaimed their respective positions (see Quotes 6 and 7 in Table 3.1), popular fashion trends are now democratized to the masses. As such, consumers originating from any of the social classes can now signal their sense of belongingness (to their relevant reference group) via the fashion trends that they adopt. Some of Everett Rogers' seminal writings on the diffusion of innovations are Darwinian in spirit albeit he did not explicitly recognize them as such. For example, in discussing fashion innovations, he stated:

> Undoubtedly one of the important motivations for almost any individual to adopt an innovation is the desire to gain social status. For certain innovations, such as new clothing fashions, the social prestige that the innovations convey to its wearer is almost the sole benefit that the adopter receives. In fact, when many other members of a system have also adopted the same fashion, the innovation (such as longer skirts or designer jeans) may lose much of its social value to the adopters. This gradual loss of status given on the part of a particular clothing innovation provides a continual pressure for yet newer fashions. (Rogers, 1983, as quoted by Vigneron & Johnson, 1999, p. 5, footnote 10)

The latter mechanism is an instantiation of the relationship between snob and bandwagon demand (see Vigneron & Johnson, 1999, pp. 6–7, footnotes 13 and 15, for relevant references). From an evolutionary perspective, the dynamics driving the fashion industry and the corresponding snob and bandwagon effects are similar in spirit to those between pathogens and hosts locked in a classic evolutionary arms race. As soon as the fashion laggards have "inoculated" themselves against the new virus (i.e., by adopting the latest fashion trend), the innovators have "mutated" onto a new fashion trend. At a more macro level, this particular set of dynamics can easily be used to explain the adoption of new symbols of high culture. As objects of elite culture diffuse onto the masses and hence no longer serve as accurate indicators of one's social standing, new symbols must be found that delimit membership into the various strata. Art movements might be construed as an instantiation of the latter phenomenon. Art connoisseurs create a new trend (e.g., museum curators), which sets in motion the evolutionary arms race meant to clearly delimit the in-group and out-group members. The "wasteful" efforts needed to consistently maintain one's membership within the desired elite cultural group are a manifestation of the handicap principle in this particular case (see also G. F. Miller, 2000, for additional details).

There are innumerable cultural practices that are meant to signal one's belongingness to a group, many of which are instantiated in the consumption arena. Hagen and Bryant (2003) have proposed that both music and dance have evolved as a means of signaling the cohesiveness of a coalitional group (see W. M. Brown et al., 2005, for an alternate evolutionary account of dance, namely the relationship between dance ability and phenotypic quality). Specifically, elaborate songs and dances serve as accurate signals of a group's coalitional quality because these require time and effort to be collectively mastered. The All-Blacks (the New Zealand men's national rugby team) is famed for performing a Maori tribal song and dance prior to each of its games. It is meant to reaffirm the cohesion of the group prior to engaging in a sports battle (although it was originally performed prior to an actual battle). National anthems, folkloric songs, dances, attires, and even dialects and linguistic affectations serve to signal one's ethnicity, religion, tribal heritage, nationality, or social class. That said, such signaling practices also function to signal one's membership in dyadic relationships. Talismans and amulets containing the numbers 220 and 284 were worn in antiquity with the precise goal of celebrating and solidifying bonds of reciprocity between two close friends. The latter two numbers are the first pair of amicable numbers, which are numerologically speaking "mystically" joined. Two numbers A and B are said to be amicable if all of the positive divisors of A sum up to B and vice versa. Thus, the cultural practice of wearing medallions containing these two numbers signaled the importance of bonds of reciprocity and friendship as far back as the biblical era and ancient Greece. In today's street parlance, this unbreachable union between two loyal friends or group members is captured by the phrase "having your back." Members in street gangs wear conspicuous accoutrements to signal their group memberships. This is vividly captured in the dress attire of the Crips and Bloods via the wearing of either red or blue colors (see, e.g., the 1989 movie *Colors* with Robert Duvall and Sean Penn for a dramatic depiction of this street reality).

The innate propensity of the human mind to engage in coalitional and affiliational thinking manifests itself in both the participaton in and the viewing of sports events. Neave and Wolfson (2003) found that levels of salivary testosterone in male soccer players were higher when playing at home as compared to when playing away. Furthermore, testosterone levels were moderated by how staunch a rival team was (the greater the rivalry, the higher the testosterone). Hence, derby matches (soccer matches played between two teams from the same city such as Manchester United vs. Manchester City) are more likely to yield this effect. Neave and Wolfson proposed that this effect is a manifestation of the adaptive territoriality defense that is displayed in a variety of species. Incredibly, testosterone levels vary not only in those participating in the competitive matches but also in those viewing them. Bernhardt, Dabbs, Fielden, and Lutter (1998) found that spectators' testosterone levels changed as a function of whether their favored team was losing or winning. In other words, a physiological marker associated with the outcome of intrasexual competition was in this case experienced vicariously by the spectators. Close to 30 years ago, Cialdini et al. (1976) had described a related phenomenon known as basking in reflected glory. Specifically, they found that college students were more likely to wear university attire (e.g., T-shirt with university insignia) following a victory of their football team. It is no surprise that sports merchandising sales are closely correlated with recurringly victorious teams and prominent athletes. This is a manifestation of humans' innate desire to affiliate with dominant groups. Affiliational behaviors and favorable attitudes toward "winning" groups occur not only in the public sphere (e.g., as explored by Cialdini et al.) but also in private settings. For example, Boen, Vanbeselaere, and Feys (2002) found that Web site traffic for Belgian and Dutch soccer teams was correlated to whether a team had won or lost its last game. Specifically, wins and losses were associated with increased and decreased Web site visits respectively. This was construed as private forms of the established phenomena of basking in reflected glory and cutting off reflected failure. In other words, people have a tendency to associate themselves with winners and disassociate from losers in both the public and private spheres. Boen et al. provide several proximate explanations regarding these tendencies (e.g., self-presentation and social identity). However, the ultimate reasons for these universal behaviors are missing, providing consumer scholars with an opportunity to establish new lines of inquiry.

To recapitulate, belonging to a group is an imperative drive for countless social animals including *Homo sapiens*. As such, humans have developed innumerable ways to demonstrate their group allegiances, many of these instantiated in the consumption arena. Though belonging to a group provides numerous adaptive advantages, it also raises several challenges that require corresponding solutions if such a social arrangement is to remain stable. In the ensuing section, I discuss one of the key challenges inherent to bonds of reciprocity and in-group membership, namely ensuring that those individuals who might wish to benefit from such ties while providing less than an equitable investment in return are duly identified.

Identifying the Nonreciprocators

Evolutionists have proposed that several necessary conditions need to be present in order for reciprocal altruism to have evolved as a viable strategy. First, there must be an opportunity for repeated interactions because a one-shot encounter would not permit for reciprocity to occur. Second, there must be a set of mechanisms that permits individuals to keep track of those who have honored or cheated on their reciprocal obligations. Otherwise, even if repeat interactions were to occur, cheaters would bear no consequences for their duplicity. Leda Cosmides has been at the forefront of a research stream that has sought to identify a domain-specific module specifically meant to identify such cheaters. In implementing her research program, Cosmides has relied on the Wason Selection Task to demonstrate the existence of a domain-specific calculus within the social domain. The Wason Selection Task is a logic problem whereby participants are asked to determine whether the conditional statement "if p, then q" is veridical. Four cards are shown (p, not p, q, and not q) and the participants are asked to turn the cards that would either support or refute the conditional statement. When the problem is posed as an abstract problem of logic, individuals have a very hard time solving it. However, if the rule "if p, then q" is instantiated using a specific conditional social contract (e.g., "if an individual is drinking alcohol, then he or she must be at least 18 years old"), the rate of solving the problem increases drastically (cf. Cosmides, 1989; Cosmides & Tooby, 1992). This violates a central theorem of rational choice, namely procedural invariance. Specifically, if two problems are isomorphic (i.e., logically equivalent), they should yield the same response irrespective of the format in which they are presented. Cosmides and her colleagues have argued that the differential ability to solve the Wason Selection Task is indicative of a domain-specific module that is explicitly meant to scan for cheating in social contracts. Though several scholars have challenged the veracity of the latter interpretation, the accumulated evidence is strongly supportive of the domain-specific interpretation (see Fiddick, Cosmides, & Tooby, 2000, for a full account of the debate).

Additional support for the existence of a domain-specific cheater detection module has come from the finding that individuals have a differential ability to recognize the faces of cheaters from those of noncheaters. For example, Mealy, Daood, and Krage (1996) found that individuals who had been experimentally labeled as cheaters (via a brief description next to their facial picture) were more likely to be subsequently recognized as compared to those identified as noncheaters. In the latter study, the labeling did not correspond to any overt reality (i.e., the classification did not actually correspond to established cheaters or noncheaters). Suppose that participants are now shown facial pictures of known cheaters and noncheaters without providing an explicit identification of their "cheating/noncheating" status. The facial pictures shown correspond to individuals who had participated in an earlier prisoner's dilemma game such that their actual "cheating status" is based on realized behavior (i.e., their status as cooperators or defectors is based on overt behavior). Do people have the differential ability to recognize the cheaters when they are unaware who is or is not a cheater? Yamagishi, Tanida, Mashima, Shimoma, and

Kanazawa (2003) obtained findings that strongly suggest that facial cues exist that serve to expose cheaters. Yamagishi et al. state that their experimental design did not permit them to determine whether the cues in question correspond to emotional grimaces resulting from having defected (e.g., a guilty expression) or whether there exist stable morphological facial features that identify cheaters. If the overt facial cues responsible for exposing cheaters are situationally determined, this would support the notion of an evolutionary arms race between deceivers and their prospective dupes. Selection pressures would have existed for both parties to evolve adaptive solutions to achieve their respective goals (to deceive or to identify deception). Viewed from this perspective, Machiavellian intelligence is in part the evolved ability to do well in both roles (deceiving others while detecting deception in others). Taken to its morbid extreme, sociopaths are capable of "silencing" all physiological signals that might expose their deeds (e.g., they are known to reliably pass polygraph tests).

Several scholars have tested the existence of the cheater detection module (and related processes) in specific commercial settings (cf. W. M. Brown & Moore, 2000; M. G. Evans & Chang, 1998). That said, consumer and marketing scholars might wish to explore the opportunities that this research stream affords in understanding repeat interactions (e.g., between loyal customers and their preferred firms). Along those lines, relationship marketing has recently been recognized as an instantiation of the Darwinian-based module regulating reciprocal relationships (cf. Palmer, 2000).

Although the formation of coalitions and friendships is a universal reality, the speed at which such bonds are created and dissolved, along with the strength of the established ties, appears to vary cross-culturally. In the ensuing section, I propose that this cross-cultural difference is in part shaped by the ability to monitor cheating in social contracts within a given cultural context.

Cross-Cultural Differences in the Definition of Friendship

Some sociologists have argued that the extent of geographic and socioeconomic mobility affects how ephemeral friendships will be in a given culture. For example, most Americans form and dissolve friendships more rapidly as compared to Bedouins. MBA graduates might live in numerous cities across the four corners of the United States by the time that they retire. Similarly, an American born into a lower-class family can easily move up several notches within the social strata within a reasonably short time period. On the other hand, Bedouins live in a cultural environment with substantially lesser mobility. Hence, the ties of friendship in such environments are typically more deeply rooted and possibly longer lasting. A behavioral ecologist might propose here that the latter cross-cultural differences are manifestations of adaptability; namely, a change in the ecological niche (i.e., greater socioeconomic and geographic mobility) has led to a set of new cultural norms in the instantiation of friendships.

How does the latter manifest itself in the consumption setting and more generally in the culture of commerce? Watch a group of North American friends as they are about to split the bill at a restaurant based on what they have consumed and you would have identified a direct implication of the aforementioned cross-cultural difference in the definition of friendship. In Middle Eastern culture, it is terribly impolite and in bad taste to tally such accounts between friends. Along those lines, there exists a term in Arabic, nonexistent in either English or French, that specifically condemns an individual who seeks to remind you that they have performed a beneficent, generous, or kind act toward you (*Tarbeeh jmilé*). Typically there is an exaggerated ritualized "fight" between the various friends to decide who will have the honor of paying the total bill. This mechanism works only because it is expected that on average all regular members of the group will end up paying roughly the same number of times. In other words, given the stability of the network of friends and in light of the public nature of the payment, it is extremely difficult for anyone to cheat and violate the norms of reciprocity.

The cross-cultural difference in the importance placed on commercial contracts is another manifestation of this general phenomenon. In the Middle East, it has typically been viewed as offensive to require that a long and tedious legal contract be drawn. The Middle Easterner interprets this as implying that his or her word is not to be trusted. In other words, it is an attack on one's honor to require anything other than a handshake. This system would not work in North America because the anonymity that is afforded by our society would protect the cheaters from being caught. However, traditional Middle Eastern social networks make it next to impossible for anyone to violate their word. One might be able to recant on the agreement reached via a handshake once before their reputation is irreparably damaged. In the EEA, social interactions would have been predominantly restricted to those within one's band consisting of up to 150 individuals (cf. Dunbar, 2003; R. A. Hill & Dunbar, 2003; and references therein). As such, the ability to cheat was less, with the associated fitness costs of detection being high (e.g., ostracized from the group). In a sense, many Middle Eastern social networks approximate more closely the latter phylogenetic reality as compared to the anonymity provided by an urban mega-metropolis. On the other hand, the Californian culture of litigation stems in part from the transient nature of its populace. Millions of Americans and newly arrived immigrants have historically sought fortune and fame in California. Furthermore, the pressures to engage in ostentatious

121

signals of wealth are maximal in California in part because of the ripple effect stemming from the entertainment industry. This has yielded a dangerous mix of factors, namely social anonymity (given the large population), geographic and socioeconomic mobility, and societal pressures to engage in conspicuous consumption (even if the means are not available). Accordingly, legal contracts are prevalent even in many banal social interactions.

To recapitulate, cross-cultural differences both in the definition of friendship and in some of the consumption rituals associated with friendship (e.g., picking up the bill at a restaurant) are in part due to the differential ability to monitor reciprocity within a given cultural setting. This yields profound implications in other forums such as the extent to which legal documents guide both commercial and social interactions in a given culture. Note that this plausible ecological explanation for the latter cross-cultural differences fully recognizes the importance of the environment. However, rather than solely cataloging cross-cultural differences, an evolutionary-based approach (in this case based on the behavioral ecological tenet of adaptiveness) provides a mechanism for understanding such differences. This is not to imply that all cross-cultural differences have a Darwinian explanation; rather, it simply recognizes that idiosyncratic forms of cultural evolution typically occur in a manner that are congruent with evolutionary forces (see Boyd & Richerson, 1985, for the definitive treatise on gene-culture coevolution models).

To summarize, the reciprocation module is at the root of many consumption acts. Rituals of gift giving, to both kin and close nonkin, are a testament of the importance of ties of reciprocity. Numerous products are purchased with the explicit intent of signaling one's membership in a given group. Firms that "cheat" in their product or service delivery are only too aware of the great costs associated with having to deal with dissatisfied customers, who are much more likely to gossip about their negative experiences as compared to satisfied consumers. This is in part due to our evolved proclivity to detect, identify, and ostracize cheaters. As such, relationship marketing is congruent with evolutionary principles in that it recognizes the importance of equitable ties in repeat interactions. Finally, cross-cultural differences in the manner by which bonds of friendship and reciprocity are instantiated is in part due to the differential ability to detect and subsequently punish violations of reciprocal norms in a given cultural milieu.

CHAPTER SUMMARY

The majority of consumer scholars have historically relied on Maslow's hierarchy of needs as the integrative theory of consumer motives. However, the latter theory, though possessing much intuitive appeal, has been challenged on both theoretical and empirical grounds. Evolutionists have identified four key Darwinian modules that drive much of our purposive behaviors. These are the reproductive, survival, kin selection, and reciprocity modules. In this chapter, I have demonstrated that many of our most important consumption acts can be subsumed within one of the latter four modules. For example, various facets of conspicuous consumption are instances of sexual signaling, an integral element of the mating ritual. Our evolved gustatory preference for sweet and fatty foods is an adaptation that falls under the survival module. Gift giving and other forms of investment to kin and close friends can respectively be subsumed within the kin selection and reciprocity modules. There are advantages to such a classification system. The four Darwinian modules provide evolutionary-based ultimate motives that have been found to drive purposive behaviors across cultures and innumerable species. Hence, the theoretical and empirical base of this meta-framework of consumption motives would be founded on a veridical, consilient, and highly integrative framework.

In the next chapter, I turn to an exploration of media and advertising contents. Do media and advertising images shape our otherwise empty minds or are such images merely a reflection of our innate human nature? Social constructivists support the former option in light of their belief that we are born with empty and infinitely malleable minds. My goal in chapter 4 is to demonstrate that the causal link should be reversed. In other words, the images that we are exposed to as consumers exist in their particular forms because they are congruent with our evolved aesthetic preferences. Although advertisers and marketers are likely unable to articulate the Darwinian reasons that make certain images universally efficacious, they cannot extricate themselves from their own Darwinian heritage. Hence, they provide us with images of masculinity and femininity that are in line with our evolved mating preferences.

4

Advertising Content and Media Effects: Mirrors of Human Nature

Analyses of gender portrayals have found predominantly stereotypic portrayals of dominant males and nurturant females within the contexts of advertisements (print and television), magazine fiction, newspapers, child-oriented print media, textbooks, literature, film, and popular music.

—Garst and Bodenhausen (1997, p. 552)

The assertion that "culture" explains human variation will be taken seriously when there are reports of women war parties raiding villages to capture men as husbands, or of parents cloistering their sons but not their daughters to protect their sons' virtue, or when cultural distributions for preferences concerning physical attractiveness, earning power, relative age, and so on show as many cultures with bias in one direction as in the other.

—Tooby and Cosmides (1989, as quoted in Ridley, 1993, p. 267)

Proponents of the SSSM propose that the mediums of popular culture teach us what it means to be male or female (as per the first chapter-opening quote). Additionally, these mediums apparently socialize us about all other facets of our sexuality including whom we should find attractive and the manner by which we should interact with members of the opposite sex. These viewpoints are inherent to the tabula rasa premise, namely that we are born with empty minds (i.e., void of any innate or evolutionarily defined proclivities) with various subsequent socialization forces shaping us into the individuals that we become. In the ensuing two chapters, I propose a different perspective; namely, I posit that universal themes as found in cultural products exist in their particular forms because they are reflections of our innate human nature (as per the second chapter-opening quote). In the current chapter, I focus on advertising and related media effects, with a specific focus on sexual imagery (e.g., the depiction of women in advertising). In chapter 5, I extend the analysis to numerous other products of popular culture (e.g., movie themes and song lyrics).

The current chapter is structured as follows. I begin with a discussion of the social constructivist perspective, which suggests that masculinity and femininity are arbitrarily defined. I then provide an evolutionary-informed rebuttal to this position. In the second section, I analyze the literature that has explored the use of sexual imagery in advertising, most of which adheres to a central tenet of the SSSM, namely that sexuality is socially constructed. I demonstrate that such sexual imagery occurs in the same form across eras and cultures because it is an instantiation of our evolved sexuality. Finally, in the third section of the chapter, I highlight how evolutionary psychology can elucidate the local-versus-global issue, perhaps the central strategic decision faced by international advertisers. Additionally, I explore the Darwinian roots of some advertising slogans, as well as highlighting the evolutionary relevance of the ubiquitous use of physical attractiveness as an advertising cue.

MASCULINITY AND FEMININITY
FROM A SOCIAL CONSTRUCTIVIST PERSPECTIVE

Sexuality is socially constructed, that is, it is a learned set of behaviors accompanied by cognitive interpretations of these behaviors. Sexuality, then is less a product of *biology* [italics added] than of the socialization processes specific to a given culture at a particular point in time (Fracher & Kimmel, 1995). The most significant element of this construction is gender. (Rohlinger, 2002, p. 62)

Gender informs sexuality; sexuality confirms gender. (Fracher & Kimmel, 1995, as quoted in Rohlinger, 2002, p. 62)

One is not born a woman, one becomes one. (Simone de Beauvoir)

The preceding three quotes capture the foundational assumption behind the research that has explored the marketing of sexuality from a socialization perspective. Rather than arguing that the universality of sex role portrayals across cultures, eras, and mediums might suggest that these are innately shaped via a process of natural and sexual selection, social constructivists posit that advertisers and other media moguls teach us about sexuality (see Reichert & Lambiase, 2006, for an expansive exploration of sexuality across multiple mediums albeit from a largely nonevolutionary perspective). I begin with a review of an illustrative sample of studies that have explored the depiction of women in various mediums from the social constructivist perspective.

Depiction of Femininity

Ganahl, Prinsen, and Netzley (2003) explored gender representations in prime-time commercials. These representations are thought to influence the formation of sexist beliefs because it is argued that television is crucially important in defining gender identity. Hence, rather than theorizing that some instantiations of human nature are depicted on television, it is proposed that television creates our shared sense of "reality." Ganahl et al. found that women were more likely to be depicted as younger than their true demographic distribution. This is interpreted as indicative of the pervasive gender bias, which suggests that whereas men gain power with age, women lose theirs as they age. To the extent that men seek beauty and youth in women whereas women seek socially dominant men in their prospective ideal partners, this pattern of changing sexual power is expected. On average, age enhances many of the key attributes that women seek in men whereas the opposite holds true for those that men seek in women. This finding is rooted in evolved mating preferences.

Signorielli, McLeod, and Healy (1994) investigated gender stereotypes in MTV advertisements with MTV being viewed as an influential socialization agent. In other words, it was assumed that the contents on MTV (be it the music videos or advertisements) are those that socialize the audience members into the socially ascribed gender roles. The key findings were that women had more beautiful bodies (e.g., more fit), were more physically appealing, wore more revealing clothes, and were gazed at more frequently. Additionally, they were more likely to be depicted in ads selling appearance-enhancing products and to be the targets of such ads. On a related note, Ogletree, Williams, Raffeld, Mason, and Fricke (1990, as cited by Fouts & Burggraf, 1999) found that 86% of appearance-improving television ads were targeted at young women. This is meant to demonstrate that women are taught to care about their physical appearance via the advertisements that they watch. Evolutionary forces operating within the mating module drive the differential importance that women place on their appearance (cf. Buss, 1994). As such, an evolutionary perspective would suggest that MTV advertisements exist in their particular forms because they are reflective of our innate sexuality.

Krassas, Blauwkamp, and Wesselink (2001) sought to explore sexism via the manner by which women were depicted in *Cosmopolitan* and *Playboy*. They found that *Playboy* contained a greater number of sexually explicit pictures than did *Cosmopolitan*. Additionally, women in *Playboy* were less likely to be standing and more likely to be shown in suggestive positions. Whereas 70.9% of women were depicted as sex objects in *Playboy*, only 2.7% of men were shown as such. This is perhaps not surprising given that *Playboy* is a pornographic magazine targeting heterosexual men. *Playboy* contains more sexual depictions of women than *Architectural Digest, Scientific American,* or *Dog Fancy*. Similarly, pornographic magazines targeting gay men contain a greater number of sexual images of men. The contents of pornographic magazines exist in their particular forms in order to appeal to the aesthetic tastes of specific target markets, not to subjugate anyone. Krassas et al. discuss the fact that women are faced with paradoxical messages regarding their sexuality, namely of seeking self-sufficiency and independence while locating a man and subsequently providing him with sexual satisfaction. These two goals are not paradoxical once one recognizes that they are not mutually exclusive. Women can be independent and successful scientists, lawyers, diplomats, and surgeons while wishing to be sexually desirable.

Schlenker, Caron, and Halteman (1998) conducted a content analysis of the articles in *Seventeen*, a magazine targeted to adolescent girls and young women. The analysis covered a 50-year period (1945–1995), which spans several feminist movements. One of the goals of the study was to determine whether the various feminist movements had had an effect on the magazine's editorial topics. Appearance-related articles had the largest proportion of pages covered irrespective of the particular era. From an evolutionary perspective, this is an expected finding. As previously seen, aesthetic cues of beauty and youth are implicit to men's evolved mating preferences. Hence, though feminism should seek a world of social, political, and economic equality of the sexes, it cannot alter innate mating preferences. The assumption of mutual exclusiveness between a woman's interest in her appearance and her other pursuits is flawed. This presumes a zero-sum game between the various pursuits that a woman engages in. There is nothing incongruous about a woman becoming a scientist, diplomat, cop, lawyer, surgeon, or head of a country while maintaining an interest in her appearance. The problem arises when appearance-related evaluations are used in inappropriate settings. For example, in most professional settings, one's appearance is irrelevant to one's performance and hence it rightly should be illegal to use this cue as a basis of promotion or demotion. However, to expect that men will cease to be interested in women's appearance, and to equally expect that liberation implies that young teenage girls will cease to be interested in articles dealing with universal themes of romance, beauty, and gossip is ill-founded. Such expectations implicitly reject the possibility that evolutionary forces shape mating preferences. This point is captured by Salmon and Symons (2003):

> Most people assume that among humans—and humans alone—the determinants of attractiveness are arbitrary or capricious rather than reliable cues of mate value. This follows from the more general assumption that among humans the perception of attractiveness is completely or largely

"culturally constructed"—which simply means that humans acquire their standards of attractiveness by imitating those of other people. We will argue that the probability of this common assumption being correct is essentially zero. (p. 32)

A foundational marketing principle posits that marketers should provide products that cater to their customers' interests and needs. In the context of creating a magazine that appeals to the broadest group of young women, magazine editors are aware of the stories that have universal appeal to this particular segment. Similarly, *Sports Illustrated* contains images of male athleticism because the targeted readership values this particular trait. The mass media is in the business of creating cultural products that have the largest mass appeal. Accordingly, though some young men and women have a greater interest in differential equations as compared to basketball or cosmetics, they are in the minority.

Beginning with the premise that children spend 25% of their waking hours watching TV, Fouts and Burggraf (1999) argued that this medium subsequently shapes their sense of reality (via modeling and vicarious reinforcements). Using this socialization perspective, the authors explored the depiction of women on television sitcoms along with the forms of verbal reinforcements that women received on such shows. The first notable finding was that young women were overrepresented on situational sitcoms as compared to their prevalence within the general population. This is meant to demonstrate ageism, which promotes a focus on youth-oriented images. It would be equivalent to argue that the lack of women in pornography targeting gay men is a manifestation of sexism. The studied sitcoms are targeted to young people; hence it is not surprising that these would be overrepresented. This is the central tenet to target marketing and consumer segmentation. The same erroneous logic applies to the second reported finding by Fouts and Burggraf, namely that underweight and overweight women are overrepresented and underrepresented respectively on television sitcoms. It is unclear why cultural products should be perfectly representative of a given set of demographic variables. For example, most male action heroes have bodies that do not represent the body of the average male. A third finding was that male characters, more so than their female counterparts, made positive comments regarding women's bodies. The authors conclude: "The message for female viewers of situation comedies appears to be that males are expected to pay attention to women's bodies and make comments regarding their bodies more than do females" (p. 478). Hence, according to the socialization perspective, if men had not been taught via media conditioning to pay attention to women's bodies, they might have focused their sexual attention elsewhere. Furthermore, given that minds are assumed to be created empty of innate predispositions, that men might be attracted to women's bodies and that they might hold certain ubiquitous aesthetic preferences can only imply that these were taught to them (in this case via television).

Harrison (2003) proposed that the definition of female beauty, which includes the thin and medium-busted ideals, is learned via the mainstream media through cultivation theory. Despite the caveat that no causal relationships should be inferred from her study, Harrison found that women's but not men's idealization of the female body (i.e., which type is most beautiful) was influenced by television. To explain the null effect for men, she argues that men's preferences might be shaped by other media products including erotica, pornography, or the *Man Show* (male-oriented television show), more so than by mainstream television. In other words, if a null effect is found for a particular cultural product, it implies that some other medium must be the relevant socialization agent.

The latter studies constitute a small albeit representative sample of the SSSM-based research stream that argues that femininity is socially constructed. Scholars emanating from the SSSM tradition propose with equal aplomb that masculinity is defined via the same vehicles of social construction (e.g., media images, etc.). I turn to a representative sample of such studies in the ensuing section.

Depiction of Masculinity

Vigorito and Curry (1998) argued that masculinity is marketed through the images that are shown in popular magazines. They proposed that stereotypical images are created via media-driven symbolic interactions resulting in a hegemonic definition of masculinity. The ultimate cause, genesis, or universality of this definition of masculinity is never addressed. This definition of masculinity exists in its particular form because of evolutionary reasons. For example, that men would be predominantly depicted in prestigious occupational roles reflects the fact that women seek men with status; accordingly, men engage in behaviors that will confer status. Similarly, that lower-class males are targeted with ads that demonstrate physical dominance (rather than occupational dominance) is a manifestation of the fact that conspecifics at various levels of the social hierarchy use varying means to strive for status. Men of lower classes are more likely to seek physical dominance whereas high-status males seek occupational dominance. Finally, that women are targeted with ads depicting nurturing men does not imply that men and women are being targeted using contradictory messages of masculinity; rather, both the status seeker and the nurturer are evolutionarily relevant roles for males to occupy. Universal mating preferences (cf. Buss, 1994) suggest that women seek men that not only have resources (high status) but also are willing to share them (nurturance).

Rohlinger (2002) conducted a content analysis of *GQ* and *Men's Health* to investigate the depiction of male bodies. The implicit assumption is that if one were to uncover evidence of male objectification, this would highlight that sexist imagery need not be restricted to the female form. Rohlinger proposes that some marketers have begun using a dual marketing approach, namely utilizing the same "ambiguous" message to target both homosexual and heterosexual men. The content analysis revealed that the "unknown sexuality type" male model was the most frequently shown in the context of the erotic male. Given the substantial focus on the gay market in both of these media outlets, this result does not point to changing societal values toward the ascribed roles of men (as suggested by Rohlinger). Rather, it reinforces the evolutionary fact that men, irrespective of their sexual orientation, are drawn to visual stimuli and aesthetic cues.

Leit, Pope, and Gray (2000) conducted an analysis of *Playgirl* centerfolds covering the period 1973 to 1997. They found that the models have become increasingly more muscular, suggesting that the ideal body type of male beauty is changing. The findings are construed as a manifestation of the malleability and socially constructed nature of aesthetic preferences. In providing one possible cause for this change in male beauty, the authors state that "women have rapidly achieved parity with men in many aspects of life, including even military roles, leaving men with only their bodies as a distinguishing source of masculinity" (p. 92). The authors are suggesting that men arrive at the collective conclusion that they are losing "power" to emancipated women and that accordingly to regain some of their "lost" masculine identity, they collude to provide new images of hypermasculinity (i.e., greater musculature). Notwithstanding the lack of face validity of the latter explanation, evolutionary theory demonstrates unequivocally that intrasexual strife is the dominant form of competition and rivalry. A more plausible possibility is that because a large proportion of *Playgirl* readers are homosexual men (cf. Symons, 1979), the changing images of male beauty depicted in the magazine reflect the ever-increasing dominance of gay male consumers. The authors allude to this point when they state:

> It might be argued that female *Playgirl* readers are not representative of women as a whole. Similarly, it seems likely that a certain number of homosexual men purchase *Playgirl,* and that these readers may have influenced the evolution of the centerfolds' dimensions. Although these possibilities cannot be excluded, there are no compelling reasons to assume that *Playgirl* deviates consistently from general male and female preferences for how the ideal male body should look. (p. 92)

The empirical findings as rooted in evolutionary theory suggest that heterosexual women and homosexual men do not place equal importance on the physicality of prospective suitors; nor do they hold the same preferences with regard to the ideal standards of male beauty.

Pope, Olivardia, Gruber, and Borowiecki (1999) conducted an informal analysis (i.e., no statistical tests reported) of the changing musculature of male action toys. They found that the toys were depicted with ever-larger muscles, which they suggested might serve as a causative agent of muscle dysmorphia as well as the subsequent use of anabolic steroids. Fantasy toys depict an exaggerated form of male physical power, in the same manner that Batman, Superman, and the Incredible Hulk possess powers that extend beyond the human realm. Accordingly, why should the musculature of these fantasy figures adhere to real-life norms? Why should an action toy's morphological traits (e.g., size of the biceps) be accurate representations of human traits? That said, if one supports the tabula rasa view of the human mind (with its infinite capacity of malleability), then it becomes feasible to propose that the depiction of masculinity in action toys might lead to muscle dysmorphia.

On a related note, Harrison and Cantor (1997) suggest that within some microcultures (e.g., certain athletic groups), males have begun to develop strong concerns for their body weights. This does not suggest that eating disorders will eventually become equally distributed across the two sexes nor does it imply that the cause for the disorder is the same for both men and women. In the case of men, to the extent that an eating disorder is to be found, it has little to do with aesthetic motives. Many young males seek to augment their muscle mass not as a means of attracting women but as an intrasexual strategy of intimidation. For example, within the American male prison culture, achieving an ominous-looking physique is not meant to attract women. In other words, the same phenomenon is not at work when contrasting young men and women in terms of their respective objectives of achieving great muscle mass and extreme thinness. The latter sex-specific self-presentational goals are rooted in a Darwinian etiology; as such, they occur in these particular sex-specific forms irrespective of culture or era.

Knight and Giuliano (2001) used gender schema theory, which argues that men and women are taught their respective sex roles, to explain why male athleticism is valued more than its female counterpart. This socialization is then assumed to create all types of "sexist" realities in the sports industry, including the greater coverage of male sports on television, the greater exposure of male athletes on the cover of *Sports Illustrated,* and the greater success of male professional sports leagues. One socialization agent that is purported to promote such sexist attitudes is the media as manifested by the sexist attitudes of sport announcers who focus on male athleticism while restricting their attention to female athletes' physical appearance. Knight and Giuliano conducted an experiment to test these assertions empirically. They found that a description of an athlete based on his or her physical attractiveness as opposed to his or her athleticism yielded a significant effect for the female athlete only (i.e., null effect for the male athlete). The sex of the respondents did not moderate the effect. Hence, it would seem that the sexist attitudes are not restricted to male sports announcers but also manifest themselves with male and female college students. Anna Kournikova, the beautiful Russian tennis player, is perhaps the most famous individual on the women's ATP tour, despite having yet to win one singles tournament. Notwithstanding her less than illustrious athletic record, she is one of the most sought-after endorsers on the women's tour. Advertisers recognize that young and beautiful women constitute alluring and attention-grabbing images, and as such they are more likely to seek Anna Kournikova as an endorser rather than Billy Jean King. By the same token, countless cultures contain rites of passage of masculinity that are meant to celebrate and recognize physical acuity, athleticism, bravery, and courage because these are sex-specific attributes that are relevant in the mating arena. Hence, that athleticism and beauty are differentially appreciated in men and women (in the same universal sex-specific manner) suggests that this is not due to the socializing forces of the media.

Starting with the assumption that television is the most influential and powerful of all socialization agents (via the process of modeling and vicarious reinforcement), Fouts and Vaughan (2002) explored the depiction of, and reaction to, overweight male characters. They found that heavier male characters were underrepresented compared to the rates of heavy males in the population. This mismatch was not as substantial as that for heavy females, leading the authors to conclude that it is more acceptable for males to be heavier. Additionally, it was found that female characters did not make negative references with respect to the weight of heavy male characters in contrast to the opposite effect having been found in previous research. Finally, that heavy males made self-deprecating comments that were followed by audience laughter led the authors to conclude that this form of vicarious conditioning teaches men that it is appropriate to make fun of themselves in social settings. The tabula rasa premise is central to each of the latter findings. Specifically, individuals are assumed to be passive receptacles of socialization forces, which in this case is delivered to them via television. An evolutionary perspective recognizes that each of the findings is congruent with the universal fact that appearance (in this case, one's weight) is differentially important to the two sexes. As such, television is a medium by which an evolutionary-based reality is depicted rather than being a dispenser of a socially constructed reality to otherwise empty minds.

Garst and Bodenhausen (1997) sought to determine males' perceptions of three types of male models whose masculinity had been manipulated along three levels of androgyny and two levels of youth (young or old model). It was hypothesized that participants' scores on a Gender Attitude Inventory (conservative or not) would predict their perceptions of the various possible depictions of masculinity. Implicit to this study was the assumption that the media shapes one's score on the latter gender attitude metric. The strength of the findings and related theorizing is captured well by the following quote:

> Since less traditional men's representations of men are rather wide, including both traditional and nontraditional elements, less traditional men are susceptible to images that make more traditional elements of their attitudes salient. The salience of less traditional images, on the other hand, fails to induce change. This lack of influence may occur because the media representations are not sufficiently different from less traditional men's preexisting attitudes or even that less traditional men are less sensitive to nontraditional masculine images that are largely unsupported, if not discouraged, by strong cultural norms. (p. 567)

In the same manner that many academic feminists and social constructivists cannot reconcile that emancipated women could be neurosurgeons, CEOs, or diplomats while caring about their appearance, the same logical error occurs when discussing masculinity. For example, Garst and Bodenhausen (1997) state:

> In contemporary society, messages about appropriate standards for male behavior are mixed at best. Some socializing influences emphasize the importance of traditionally masculine, agentic qualities, while others emphasize the desirability of developing the communal side of the male psyche. It is thus quite plausible that for many men, attitudes about appropriate male behavior are based on somewhat conflicting ideas and prescriptions. For this reason, these attitudes may be susceptible to momentary influences that emphasize either more traditional or less traditional images of masculinity. (p. 553)

Many social constructivists seem to possess an all-or-nothing mentality when it comes to the definition of sex roles. A woman can either care for her appearance or be a career woman. She can either be a stay-at-home mother or be intelligent and enlightened. Similarly, men are either brutish agentic beasts or nurturing and sensitive beings. The reality is that men and women have the potential to possess many qualities and pursue many paths. This is not indicatory of the malleability of the human mind as espoused by the empty-slate premise; rather, it is a recognition that natural and sexual selection have produced individuals possessing both sex-specific proclivities and potentialities while allowing for great behavioral plasticity.

In this section, I have summarized a representative sample of SSSM-based studies that have sought to identify mediums (e.g., magazines, toys, and television) that supposedly socialize individuals into accepting hegemonic definitions of masculinity. Social constructivists propose that these sex-specific stereotypical depictions are particularly influential when targeted at children. I provide a summary of such studies in the next section.

Depiction of Masculinity and Femininity in Children's Mediums

Murnen, Smolak, Mills, and Good (2003) used objectification theory to investigate how young children react to idealized images of both sexes. In developing their experimental stimuli, Murnen et al. state that it was much easier to obtain sexually objectified pictures of female celebrities as compared to similar pictures for their male counterparts. Rather than exploring the ultimate genesis of this universal reality, it was implicitly attributed to the workings of the patriarchy. The differential frequency of objectified images of men and women in the media supposedly serves as the cultivating force that attacks women's sense of self-worth. In support of this "causal" link, Murnen et al. found that young girls yielded a lower Body Esteem Score (BES) as compared to young boys and they seemed more vulnerable to ideal images of women (thin and sexy depictions) than were boys to ideal images of men (muscularity). From an evolutionary perspective, one's sense of self should be congruent with the sex-specific attributes that are deemed important in the mating arena. As such, television images depict, rather than create, the universal finding that appearance is a more relevant metric of comparison for women.

Hargreaves and Tiggemann (2003) proposed that persistent exposure to "thin-ideal" images of women would cause young boys to rate appearance as more important in a prospective mate. Hence, media images are purported to guide male mate choice in addition to affecting women's self-worth. The power of the media is seemingly unlimited in its capacity to shape individuals' minds. Such a postulated causal link would have to explain why current cultures that are not exposed to media images or cultures in the premedia age (covering most of human history) seem to always yield males interested in female beauty as a desirable attribute. As would be predicted from an evolutionary perspective on human mating, the relevant results of the Hargreaves and Tiggemann experiment yielded null effects for the total sample.

L. Evans and Davies (2000) conducted a content analysis of elementary school textbooks to gauge the manner by which masculinity is depicted. The working assumption is that such depictions socialize children with regard to the proper expression of gender, with these "arbi-

trary" gender role assignments leading to pervasive sexism. According
to this logic, that most boys around the world prefer participating in athletic competitions rather than creating flower arrangements is in part due
to the fact that boys are seldom shown (e.g., in textbooks) engaging in
such "feminine" activities. This has led to the enactment of laws requiring schools to depict the two sexes in equitable (ergo indistinguishable)
manners. It is argued that such protection is needed because supposedly
individuals can develop into productive members of society only if exposed to such equitable portrayals (e.g., both sexes being equally represented and each sex possessing both masculine and feminine traits as to
eradicate any possibility for sex-based stereotypes). In their content analysis, Evans and Davies found that male characters in elementary school
textbooks displayed a greater frequency of masculine traits (aggressive,
argumentative, and competitive) whereas female characters exhibited a
greater frequency of feminine traits (affectionate, emotionally expressive, passive, and tender). The authors were surprised that despite the
best legal and pedagogic efforts, the two sexes are still being portrayed in
"stereotypical" manners in elementary textbooks (albeit males more so
than females). Accordingly, Evans and Davies conclude that the "hidden
curriculum" (i.e., the exploitation and derogation of women) continues
unabated to this day. Evolutionary theory would posit an alternate explanation. Many personality traits (e.g., aggression, nurturance, and risk
taking) yield the same sex differences irrespective of culture or era.
Hence, children's textbooks provide an accurate depiction of a universal
and temporally invariant reality (regarding sex-specific traits) rather
than being the promulgators of stereotypical gender roles.

Clark, Guilmain, Saucier, and Tavarez (2003) conducted a content analysis of female characters in award-winning children's picture books covering
the period between the 1930s to the 1960s. The latter period was broken
down into four eras to gauge whether gender stereotyping was a function of
specific temporal contexts. Fifteen personality traits that are typically associated with either masculinity or femininity were used to code the depicted
characters. Of 60 relevant scores (15 traits in each of four eras), I calculated
that 33 were in the stereotypical direction, 17 yielded a null effect, and 10
were in a direction that was reversed to the stereotypical expectation. Based
on my analysis, only one trait ("nurturant") yielded stereotypical depictions
across the four eras. In other words, irrespective of eras, female characters
were always depicted as more nurturing than their male counterparts. Accordingly, that the two sexes are not indistinguishable in the personality
traits that are ascribed to them is taken as a manifestation of sexism. The recurring ideological belief throughout this research stream is that in order for
the two sexes to be equal under the law, they must be indistinguishable in all
of their representations, failure of which will maintain the sexist and oppres-

sive institutions of the status quo. Given that gender stereotyping is thought to be a learned set of beliefs (i.e., its etiology is environmental), the authors propose several environmental agents that might have affected the prevalence of sexist beliefs. Included in this list were the Great Depression, McCarthyism, and the liberalism of the 1960s. Thus, despite universally recurring definitions of masculinity and femininity, most social constructivists reject the possibility that these might have a Darwinian etiology. To concede this point would be antithetical to one of the central tenets of the SSSM, namely that the human mind starts off as an empty slate.

Ward (2003) conducted a review of the influence that the entertainment media have on the sexual socialization of youths. First, she found that women were portrayed in more sexual ways across all possible mediums. Second, the key theme in magazines targeting young women revolved around ways by which they can attract men. Additionally, Ward concluded that the ubiquitous depiction of men as emotionally inferior in mediums of popular culture is problematic for *women*. She states:

> This depiction of young women as sex therapists and as communication teachers rather than as friends and partners is problematic for it advocates the subordination of self for others and encourages young women to suppress their own concerns and insecurities. (p. 356)

Hence, even in instances when men are shown as inferior along a given dimension (emotional acuity), this is construed as an obstacle to women's emancipation. Other learned "sexist stereotypes" that Ward identified included that men's sexuality is more urgent and insatiable, that women are taught to show sexual restraint, and that women should please their men by being beautiful and sexually available. According to Ward, that women are taught to be both sexually alluring and sexually restrained creates a form of semantic schizophrenia. This is reminiscent of the theory of schizophrenia as originally espoused by Gregory Bateson, famed husband of Margaret Mead. He proposed that schizophrenia occurs when children are exposed to their parents' contradictory and mixed language. Ward is forthcoming about the paucity of evidence in support of the oft-repeated tenet that the media is a powerful sexual socializer. She concludes, "While results are typically in the affirmative, the effects produced are seldom direct or sweeping, and null and counterintuitive outcomes have been reported" (p. 366). Ward adds, "Because no causal model specifically addresses the media's role as a sexual socializer, research in this area has been either atheoretical, or has drawn support from one of three theoretical models" (p. 360). The latter three models, namely cultivation theory, cognitive social learning theory, or priming theory, do not provide an ultimate-based account of why socialization forces exist in their particular forms. Another noncausal model discussed by Ward is the media practice model. According to Ward, the latter model posits that how a person reacts to media images is a function of sociocultural variables such as their gender or race, developing identity, neighbors, family, friends, peers, and religious worldviews. Therefore, one's biological sex is deemed unimportant when it comes to issues of sexuality.

To recapitulate, the key premise of this socialization-based research stream is that children are born with empty minds (i.e., no innate sex typing). The tabula rasa is subsequently filled with an onslaught of stereotypical material that teaches children all of the sex-specific schemata, preferences, attitudes, emotions, and behaviors associated with being male or female. These sexist materials are depicted in toys, cartoons, textbooks, fables, television, movies, comic books, and advertisements to name but a few sources. The stereotypes are subsequently reinforced by role models including parents, teachers, and religious figures. Hence, according to social constructivists it is not surprising that little boys and girls are so intensely sex-typed, given the onslaught of sexist materials that their infinitely malleable brains are exposed to, beginning at the earliest stages of cognitive development. As such, most proponents of the SSSM reject the possibility that sex differences might innately exist as a result of an evolutionary process.

In the fourth and final section dealing with the social construction of sexuality, I discuss studies that propose that the manner by which men and women interact with one another is a social construction.

Depiction of the Dynamics Between Men and Women

Lauzen and Dozier (2002) studied the pattern of appearance-related comments during the 1999–2000 prime-time television season. They found that male characters behaved differentially depending on whether they were interacting with males or females. Specifically, male characters offered more compliments to females and directed more insults at males. On the other hand, female characters were egalitarian in their distribution of appearance-related comments. Additionally, female characters received close to twice as many appearance-related comments as compared to their male counterparts. The assumption here is that television teaches the two sexes how to interact with one another. As such, social constructivists repudiate the possibility that sex dynamics as depicted on television might be a reflection of an evolved human nature. Does there exist a culture where heterosexual men are more likely to target appearance-related compliments to other men? Does there exist a culture where women are more likely to compliment men about their looks than vice versa? To date, no such cultures have been uncovered. Lauzen and Dozier found that the inclusion of female writers *increased* the number of appearance comments in television shows. These findings were construed as being indicative of the pernicious forces of socialization, namely that not only do women continue to view their worth as tied to beauty but also female writers participate in the maintenance of the sexist double-standard beauty myths.

Franzoi (2001) sought to demonstrate that *benevolent sexism* as opposed to *hostile sexism* drives a woman's esteem of her body. Franzoi proposed that although the former form of sexism "characterizes the 'fairer sex' as wonderful, pure creatures whose love makes men whole, it also conceives of women as being weaker than men and in need of their protection" (p. 177). It is further argued that benevolent sexism is a more effective tool for dominating women because it is not as direct in its approach as compared to its more virulent counterpart (i.e., hostile sexism). Franzoi adds, "In essence, the idealization of traditional feminine qualities in BS [benevolent sexism] can seduce women into accepting male dominance" (p. 178). She proposes that the respective preferences of men and women for immature and mature facial traits in the opposite sex highlight the inherent dominance-based preferences in defining heterosexual attractiveness, which it is argued are congruous with benevolent sexism. Evolutionary psychology posits that facial preferences are solutions to sex-specific adaptive problems rather than being instruments of sexist oppression. Women seek men who have strong testosterone markers (e.g., strong jaw) whereas men are drawn to neotenous features (referred to as "immature" by Franzoi) because these serve as accurate markers of estrogen. Finally, Franzoi found that women who scored high on benevolent sexism (i.e., give credence to this belief system) used more cosmetics when preparing for a romantic date and also held more favorable attitudes toward sexual attractiveness (one of the purported components of female body esteem). Thus, according to Franzoi, once a woman has recognized the importance of her appearance as a sexual cue, she has succumbed to benevolent sexism (see Scott, 2005, for a debunking of this argument). As previously mentioned, the differential importance that men place on physical appearance is a sex-specific adaptive solution within the mating arena. Accordingly, evolutionary forces, not benevolent sexism, have shaped women's proclivities to utilize their appearance as an intersexual mating cue.

Viki, Abrams, and Hutchison (2003) chastised the so-called "romantic" man, for he apparently engages in a two-pronged attack on women by being both benevolently sexist (e.g., complimenting politely a woman's looks) and paternalistically chivalrous (e.g., opening doors). That a man would claim that he needs a woman to be happy is indicative of his being guilty of benevolent sexism (Glick et al., 2000, as cited by Viki et al.). Apparently, despite the fact that benevolent sexism and paternalistic chivalry yield positive behaviors (on the part of men toward women), these "tools of domination" are to be condemned given that they restrict women's freedom and autonomy by imposing sex-specific expectations on them. Viki et al. administered a scale that measures paternalistic chivalry with the expectation of identifying sex differences along this measure (men being expected to score higher). One of the items read as follows: "During a date, a man should protect the woman if she is being harassed by other men." A man in agreement with the latter statement would be coded as displaying paternalistic chivalry. The researchers found that one's sex was not related to the extent of paternalistic chivalry. In explaining this finding, Viki et al. cite research that has suggested that "oppressed groups sometimes endorse the system-justifying ideologies of dominant groups in a manner that perpetuates their own expression" (p. 536). In other words, women and men agree on what constitutes chivalrous behavior but in the case of women, this is because they are passively allowing themselves to be dominated. This study is representative of the ideological-based research stream that construes most sex differences as instantiations of sexism.

Thus far, I have discussed several research streams that have each proposed that much of our sexuality is a social construction shaped by a slew of socialization forces. In the next section, I turn to an evolutionary-based account of these issues.

EVOLUTIONARY ACCOUNT
OF MASCULINITY AND FEMININITY

One of the key gender-based differences to have been documented by social constructivists is the agentic–communal dichotomy, which purports that men and women are socialized to be agentic and communal respectively. Hupfer (2002) contends that despite the standard ascription of agentic and communal characteristics to males and females respectively, advertisers frequently violate the implications of these role pairings. In other words, advertisers oftentimes use communal ads when targeting men and agentic ads when targeting women. Hupfer suggests that in large part this is due to the fact that gender-based theories are erroneous because of their singular focus on gender rather than biological sex as the explicative force. As Hupfer poignantly states, "In an era of emerging feminism, a vision of androgyny and sex-role adaptability had strong appeal" (p. 2). Hence, according to this worldview, little regarding one's sex is innate (other than perhaps one's genitalia). Apparently, even universal sex-specific traits are thought to be malleable by one's gender. This ideological stance generated gender-based information-processing theories including the selectivity hypothesis, gender schema theory, and self-schema theory (see Hupfer for relevant references). Hupfer concludes that studies that have utilized sex role self-concept as the relevant moderator have found that biological sex is a superior predictor as compared to gender. She adds that gender schema theory is largely discredited and that scholars have concluded that biological sex and gender are extremely linked, with gender yielding very little in terms of additional explanatory power. These conclusions are fully in line with evolutionary theory given its recognition that gender roles exist in their particular forms because of evolutionary forces.

Lueptow, Garovich, and Lueptow (1995) cite numerous cross-cultural and longitudinal studies demonstrating that despite the changes that have taken place with regard to socialized sex roles (e.g., as has occurred via the second-wave feminist movement), gender stereotypes have remained resilient to change. In the majority of instances where changes have taken place, there has been an *increase* in sex typing. Additionally, the latter authors provide empirical evidence from their own longitudinal surveys covering the period 1974 to 1991 yielding the same conclusions. More recently, Lueptow, Garovich-Szabo, and Lueptow (2001) have replicated the latter conclusions while covering a slightly longer time period namely 1974 through 1997. Lueptow et al. (1995) state the following regarding the sociocultural explanation dealing with gender stereotypes:

> *A more likely explanation is that the gender stereotypes reflect the perceptions of real personality differences between women and men, based to some undetermined degree on innate differences between the sexes* [italics in original]. The stability in gender stereotypes and personality traits over several decades observed in this and in previous research, which has occurred in the face of changing sex roles, is analogous to the stability of personality traits across different cultures that anthropologists treat as "human universals" and that are taken as reflections of innate dispositions (Brown, 1991). (pp. 526–527)

Sex-typed personality traits and other supposed gender stereotypes occur in the same form across cultures and eras. Hence, socialization-based theorists that espouse the traditional sociocultural explanation need to explain why such a pattern is universal and temporally invariant. Incidentally, evolutionists are accepting of the fact that sex-typed personality traits can in part be learned. However, the genesis of this particular socialization process rests on evolutionarily relevant forces. In other words, the relevant issue is not to try to tease out whether something is innate or learned; rather, it is to explain the ultimate causes of both innate dispositions and the patterns of socialization that accentuate and reinforce these.

Countless scholars emanating from a wide range of disciplines have demonstrated that innate biological differences exist between the two sexes (see Blum, 1998; Geary, 1998). Even sociology, a discipline that has historically served as a bastion of the gender-is-a-social-construction position, has yielded academics that have questioned the rejection of biology as a relevant force in explaining sex differences. For example, Udry (2000) demonstrated that gender-specific socialization is constrained within biological bounds. He showed that pregnant women's prenatal levels of a specific androgen (sex hormone–binding globulin or SHBG) during the second trimester of their pregnancies are highly correlated to their daughters' gendered behaviors as measured several decades later. As Udry explains, SHBG is a masculinizing agent that is particularly operative during the second trimester of a pregnancy because this is the period when the fetal brain is getting sex-typed. Udry found that women who had been exposed to high levels of SHBG and hence had significantly more masculinized behavioral patterns maintained such behaviors despite the pronounced feminine-based socialization efforts of the parents. Udry's work has profound implications with regard to the gender-is-a-social-construction position as espoused by most social constructivists. His findings suggest that not only do prenatal androgens typically operate in a sexually dimorphic manner but also socialization efforts support or even accentuate these evolved biological processes. In other words, gendered behaviors are not controlled by the whims of the patriarchy or by other arbitrary social forces. Rather, key elements of gendered behaviors are universally valid with subsequent socialization efforts (e.g., via parenting) serving as supportive of evolved gendered predispositions.

The worldview that sexuality and other sex-typed behaviors are arbitrarily learned has had deleterious effects beyond the walls of the academe. At the height of the social constructivist movement, John Money of Johns Hopkins University was recommending that male infants who were either born with "inadequate" male genitalia (e.g., micropenises) or had had their genitalia damaged during circumcisions, be surgically transformed into girls. The rationale for this recommendation was the tenet that infants are born without any sex typing and are "gendered" by subsequent socialization forces. Accordingly, if an infant were surgically reassigned to another sex prior to a crucial ontogenetic stage, Money reassured parents that they would grow up to be fully functional, happy, and well-adjusted individuals. His most famous patient (David Reimer) recently committed suicide following a lifetime of misery and pain. John Money's position was that although he possessed exceptionally convincing clinical data to support his theoretical claims, he could not divulge these because of confidentiality concerns.

To reiterate, understanding the genesis of masculinity, femininity, and other facets of sexuality is not merely an intellectual debate between evolutionists and social constructivists that is otherwise void of practical implications. On the contrary, a veridical understanding of human nature, of which our sexuality is an inherent element, is crucial in innumerable areas of human import. In the remainder of the current chapter, I focus on advertising images, one of the key culprits of sexist socialization according to social constructivists. I argue that such images exist in their particular forms because of Darwinian reasons rooted in our evolved mating minds.

DEPICTION OF SEXUALITY IN ADVERTISING

The advertising industry is an integral element of any capitalist and consumer-oriented economy. That said, it remains unclear whether its net effects are beneficial or harmful to society. Though advertising provides consumers with the requisite information needed to make informed decisions, critics have argued that it creates capricious and artificial needs and wants. Furthermore, advertising is accused of providing unrealistic images of sexy, beautiful, and young women, yielding societal problems such as anorexia nervosa, bulimia, and poor self-esteem. Gender feminists assert that because historically speaking the patriarchy has dominated Madison Avenue, it is not surprising that advertising images have depicted women in humiliating ways. I propose that although it might be veridical that advertising has deleterious effects on specific consumer segments (e.g., the self-esteem of some young women), advertisers are merely catering to our evolved Darwinian preferences. Advertisers are not in the business of oppression and subjugation. They simply use those images and themes that sell given their profit-making pursuits. In many instances, the maximally efficacious images and semiotics are those that cater to our evolved Darwinian preferences (see Cary, 2000; Grammer, 1998; Saad, 2004). Hence, I posit that the use of sex in advertising and the ubiquitous depiction of women in advertising as young, attractive and sexually alluring are due to evolutionary reasons.

Use of Sexual Imagery and the Depiction of Women in Advertising

Advertising scholars have generated an impressive body of knowledge that has addressed copy variables. When should fear appeals be used and what is the optimal amount of fear that should be induced? When is it appropriate to use humorous ads? Is it efficacious to use a celebrity endorser and if so which one should be chosen? When is it beneficial to make use of comparative advertising? What are the merits of one-sided versus two-sided advertisements? How many colors should be used in a print ad? What should the background music be in a television advertisement? Should an ad utilize an emotional or rational appeal? Should the execution of the ad consist of a slice-of-life portrayal of the product or is it better to employ scientific testimonials? Of all copy decisions, perhaps the one that is most frequently made across cultures is the use of sex as an integral part of the advertising message. Given the direct relevance of sexuality to reproductive fitness, I predominantly focus on this particular advertising copy decision.

In his review of the literature, Reichert (2002) points to the fact that studies on sex-in-advertising effects have almost solely focused on the effects of provocatively dressed women. That said, in those instances when the effects of both scantily clad men and women were explored, scholars have typically found the opposite-sex effect. Specifically, sexual representations of women are more efficacious when targeting men (cf. M. Y. Jones, Stanaland, & Gelb, 1998; LaTour & Henthorne, 1993) whereas sexual representations of men are more effectual when targeting women (cf. Reidenbach & McCleary, 1983; Simpson, Horton, & Brown, 1996). One of two theoretical approaches is typically used when studying sex-in-advertising effects, namely the information-processing perspective and the hierarchy-of-effects model (Reichert, 2002). Irrespective of the dependent measure that is explored (e.g., ad recall or attitude toward the ad) the focus has been on proximate mechanisms without exploring the ultimate genesis of many universal findings. Reichert states that "research that addresses the meaning in sexual ads will move the body of research beyond researchers' heavy emphasis on processing effects" (p. 268) and that "it is unfortunate that understanding of such a ubiquitous appeal as sex in advertising has not progressed further than the work reported in this article" (p. 269). The manner by which advertising scholars might respond to Reichert's call is by incorporating evolutionary psychology as an explicative framework when exploring sex-in-advertising issues. Irrespective of one's focus, sexuality cannot be fully investigated without an incorporation of the Darwinian forces that have shaped our innate mating modules. That there exists a set of ubiquitous findings in the literature that seem to transcend temporal contexts and cultural settings is a testament to its Darwinian etiology.

The American writer Norman Mailer is reputed to have stated, "There's a subterranean impetus towards pornography so powerful that half the business world is juiced by the sort of half sex that one finds in advertisements." Reichert (2002) declares:

> Sex in advertising, the use of sexual information in mediated promotional messages, has maintained a presence since advertising's beginning. Early on, wood carvings and illustrations of attractive women (often unclothed from the waist up) adorned posters, signs, and ads for saloons, tonics, and tobacco. (p. 241)

In his extensive review of sexual content in advertising, along with its effects and functions, Reichert makes it clear though that women are much more likely to be shown as decorative models and that "nearly all research has addressed the effects of scantily clad women on processing and evaluative responses" (pp. 264–265). Hence, the dictum "sex sells" typically implies a very specific sex effect. Specifically, women are overwhelmingly more likely to be shown in alluring and decorative roles across widely divergent cultures and commercial settings, of which a review of relevant studies is provided next.

Furnham and Mak (1999) reviewed content-analytic studies that have explored sex role stereotyping in advertising. The reviewed studies spanned 25 years, 11 countries (the United States, Mexico, Australia, Denmark, France, Great Britain, Italy, Portugal, Hong Kong, Indonesia, and Kenya), and five continents. The authors found universal patterns of sex-based stereotyping. For example, they state that "some of the sex differences seem impervious to change such as the fact that, on average, female central characters nearly always seem to be considerably younger than their male counterparts" (p. 434). Furthermore, in the preponderance of relevant studies (9 out of 11), women were more likely to be visually portrayed. More recently, Saad (2004) also reviewed content-analytic studies that had explored the depiction of women in advertising. The studies spanned a large heterogeneous set of cultures and several temporal periods. Some studies covered a single culture within a given time period (e.g., Lin, 1998; Neto & Pinto, 1998). A second type of content-analytic research covered a single culture longitudinally (e.g., Ferguson, Kreshel, & Tinkham, 1990; First, 1998; Reichert, Lambiase, Morgan, Carstarphen, & Zavoina, 1999). Finally, a third genre involved cross-cultural comparisons within a given time period (cf. Ford, Voli, Honeycutt, & Casey, 1998; Fullerton & Kendrick, 2000; Maynard & Taylor, 1999; Wee, Choong, & Tambyah, 1995). The latter three types of studies covered a wide range of cultures including Portugal, Israel, Malaysia, Singapore, Japan, the United States, and the Hispanic American culture. Irrespective of culture or temporal context, one finding was unequivocally robust; namely, women are always shown as younger and as more attractive than men, as alluring sexual beings, and in various other decorative roles. Cheng (1997) found that ads in China were more likely to show women in decorative roles. Neto and Pinto (1998) concluded that women were portrayed as younger than men in Portuguese ads and that this held true for other studies conducted in various cultures. Sverdrup and Stø (1992) cite several studies from Scandinavia demonstrating the typical findings, namely that women are likely to be shown as younger and in decorative roles (see p. 373). Boddewyn (1991, p. 26) lists a slew of countries that have been found to contain sexist advertising (consisting of sexy ads, sexist ads, objectification of women, and violence against women). The countries listed include Argentina, Austria, Bahrain,

Brazil, Chile, India, Indonesia, Ireland, Italy, Kenya, Lebanon, New Zealand, Norway, Peru, Philippines, Portugal, Singapore, Spain, Sweden, Switzerland, Trinidad & Tobago, and the United States. Hence, South America, Europe, Oceania, Africa, the Caribbean region, the Middle East, and the Far East are covered. As such, the totality of cross-cultural studies point to the same conclusion, namely that women, much more so than men, are depicted as young, beautiful, and sexually alluring.

Researchers have sought to link the "gender" of a nation with the prevalence of sex-based stereotyping in advertising. The implicit logic here is that these stereotypical depictions are culturally determined and hence are not only malleable but also can be eradicated. It is typically recognized that sex stereotyping is indeed universal and that it does occur in similar forms across cultures, however the argument is that its strength varies cross-culturally (cf. Odekerken-Schröder, De Wulf, & Hofstee, 2002). True to the SSSM, scholars engaged in this line of research prefer to focus on slight cross-cultural differences in the extent of sex stereotyping rather than understanding the ultimate origins of cross-cultural similarities in the instantiations of sex stereotyping. For example, Milner and Collins (2000) used Hofstede's Masculinity Index, which measures how delineated the sex roles are within a society, to explore differences in the portrayals of sex roles in television ads in Japan, Russia, Sweden, and the United States. The findings were very weak with the sole significant result being that more feminine countries (e.g., Sweden) had a greater number of relationships shown in the ads as compared to masculine countries. One of the only ubiquitous findings across all four countries was that women were portrayed as younger than men (see Milner & Collins, p. 76, Table 10). This finding seems to replicate in every cultural setting. Odekerken-Schröder et al. also investigated the link between the prevalence of gender stereotyping in advertising and a country's score on masculinity and obtained equally disappointing results. Of seven posited hypotheses, only two received support demonstrating that on the aggregate the gender of a country is minimally (if at all) related to the level of gender stereotyping in print advertising. The two countries studied in this case were the United Kingdom (masculine society) and the Netherlands (feminine society). In the UK and Dutch ads, the percentages of female characters that were young (18–35 years old) were 93.5% and 96.6% respectively, once again demonstrating the ubiquity of young women in advertising.

Not only are women more likely across all cultures to be depicted in decorative roles but also it appears that this reality is impervious to temporal contexts. Ford, LaTour, and Clarke (2004) cite research demonstrating that although sex role portrayals have improved, the "stereotype" that women are sex objects and that women are concerned with physical attractiveness has not been eradicated. MacKay and Covell (1997) argue that despite the fact that the portrayals of women have improved in advertising (e.g., in terms of the roles that they occupy), there has been an *increase* in the portrayal of women as alluring sex objects. Ferguson et al. (1990) showed that even in a bastion of feminism such as *Ms.* magazine, the portrayal of women as alluring sex objects had *increased* over the three studied time periods, as had the number of ads for personal-appearance products. MacKay and Covell (1997) state, "Whereas advertisers have begun to recognize the changing status of women, the increase of women's portrayal as sex objects indicates that stereotypes and sexual objectification continue (Sullivan & O'Connor, 1988; Timson, 1995)" (p. 575). First (1998) compared Israeli ads of 1979 and 1994 and found that women are still being represented as sex objects and in an *increasingly* provocative manner. Kang (1997) compared the portrayal of women in magazine ads from 1979 and 1991. She concluded that on the aggregate no changes in women's portrayals had taken place. Of 17 coded variables, "body display" (captures how revealing the clothes are) was 1 of only 4 variables that yielded a difference between the two time periods. Specifically, there had been an *increase* in such depictions. Kerin, Lundstrom, and Sciglimpaglia (1979) concluded that the use of women in decorative roles (e.g., as sex objects) had *increased* in the past decade (i.e., during the 1970s). This is particularly telling given that the study was published in 1979, namely when the feminist movement should have had its most trenchant effects.

Many scholars have argued that the reluctance of advertisers to eradicate the latter stereotypical depictions is clear proof of the pervasive sexism that permeates through the advertising industry. Putrevu (2001) provides a telling rebuttal to this position:

> However, despite such improvements in assertiveness, the traditional gender stereotypes seem to still apply (at least to some extent) in the world of mass media and advertising. ... One explanation for such stereo typical portrayals is that advertisers have been extremely insensitive to the changes in the socio-cultural landscape. However, this explanation seems somewhat naïve since advertisers are unlikely to spend billions of dollars in such a foolish manner. In today's competitive environment, the placement of advertisements in broadcast and print media is carefully planned with close attention to the characteristics of the audience. Hence, a more plausible explanation for such stereotyping is that despite the rapid increase in the female participation in the labor market, gender identities have not been so quick to change. In fact, the sex differences in psychological makeup seem to be larger in developed countries. (p. 9)

Thus, there appears to be unequivocal support that irrespective of cultural setting or temporal context, women are much more likely to be depicted in decorative roles. Furthermore, the decorative cues are roughly

the same across cultures. In the last section of this chapter, I provide an evolutionary explanation for some of these recurring findings (e.g., the premium on beauty). Alas, the currently accepted wisdom regarding this
issue stems from a combination of social constructivism (cf. Mayne, 2000),
feminism (cf. B. Stern, 1993), and postmodernism (cf. Elliott, Jones,
Benfield, & Barlow, 1995). In the following section, I discuss research that
has sought to identify variables that best predict one's reaction to sexual
imagery in advertising. Adverse reactions to such imagery appear less
driven by one's sex and more so by the extent to which one has been
inculcated with the feminist viewpoint.

Variables That Moderate Reactions to Sex in Advertising

Several variables have been found to affect one's reactions to sex in advertising, none perhaps as obvious as a consumer's sex. As would be expected
from an evolutionary perspective, there is unequivocal evidence that men
are more accepting of sexual stimuli in advertising and in many instances
are quite predisposed to it. For example, Reichert (2002, p. 262) cites research wherein a positive relationship between nudity/explicitness and
evaluations was found for males whereas the relationship was curvilinear
for females. In other words, whereas for men, more nudity is always preferred, this is not veridical for women. Sverdrup and Stø (1992, see Table
III, p. 383) reported that men are much more pleased than are women
about the fact that women are portrayed as sex objects. Cultural values and
belief systems also affect reactions to sexist advertising. All other things
equal, one might expect that with increased egalitarian attitudes toward
the sexes, the less the frequency of sexist ads, and the less tolerated such
ads will be. This is what Ford, LaTour, Honeycutt, and Joseph (1994) found
in their comparison of women from Thailand and New Zealand. Specifically, Thai women were less critical of their portrayals in advertising given
that they originate from a less egalitarian society. In a more recent study,
Ford et al. (2004) sought to study reactions toward stereotypical advertising in India, China, Singapore, and the United States. Hofstede's cultural
traits were used as a means of predicting such reactions. Their conclusion
was that there are cross-cultural differences in terms of the acceptance of
sexist portrayals in advertising. Accordingly, from a managerial perspective, the authors suggest the need to be aware of culture-specific movements (e.g., the rise of feminism in Japan) to ensure that advertising
messages do not yield boycotts or other forms of backlash against the offending companies. Additional variables that have been found to affect
one's reaction to sex in advertising and/or the portrayal of women in advertising include liberalism (Whipple & Courtney, 1985) and sexual liberalism (Mittal & Lassar, 2000). Mittal and Lassar did not obtain any sex

differences in terms of participants' reactions to ads with high sexual content. In other words, contrary to the expectation that women might inherently be more opposed to such an execution strategy, the researchers found that sexual liberalism was a relevant moderator but not an individual's sex. Finally, Kerin et al. (1979) proposed that the types of products advertised likely moderate one's reactions to sexual ads.

Are most women disturbed by the depiction of females in advertising? In a review of the literature conducted 25 years ago, Kerin et al. (1979) had concluded that this was hardly the case. They stated, "Based on proprietary research evidence apparently held by advertisers, and some academic research (35), it appears that stereotypic role portrayals are not offensive, and perhaps favored by a sufficiently large group of women to warrant it" (p. 39). More recently, Orth and Holancova (2004) gauged women's reactions to various role depictions in advertising. They created ads containing two characters, one of which was in a position of power over the other. Additionally, they manipulated the sex of both characters yielding four possible dyads. Accordingly, they explored how both men and women react to such sex role portrayals in advertisements. Interestingly, women's least favorable scores (in terms of attitudes toward both the ad and brand) corresponded to those ads highlighting women in roles superior to those of men.

Ford, LaTour, and Lundstrom (1991) explored women's reactions to the depiction of female roles in advertising. These reactions included both attitudinal and purchase intention measures. They found that women's negative attitudes were as strong if not stronger as compared to the equivalent ones that had been collected in 1977. Subsequently, the authors sought to determine which variables (e.g., age, household occupational status, family income, etc.) were correlated to the scores on each of the collected measures. By far, the most relevant correlate was a woman's score on Arnott's female autonomy scale followed by a woman's education. Hence, it appears that feminist socialization drives the backlash against the advertising industry. The majority of women are neither offended nor disturbed by the contents of advertising.

To recapitulate, there is very little (if any) direct evidence that one's sex is a strong predictor of one's adverse reactions to sexual imagery in advertising. Notwithstanding this fact, numerous social constructivists have expended their intellectual capital on seeking to establish the ill effects of advertising (e.g., in harming women's self-concepts). I briefly discuss this research stream in the next section.

Condemnation of Advertising

In order to alter the existing advertising landscape, one must demonstrate that it yields pernicious effects on various groups of individuals (cf.

www.about-face.org). Accordingly, advertising has been accused of causing a wide range of social ills. It is apparently responsible for causing men to be attracted to young and beautiful women. Furthermore, that women use "shallow and artificial" aesthetic cues in defining their self-concepts is claimed to be due to advertising. For example, Cohan (2001) states, "Much of the pressure to feel attractive and thin is, in the first instance, a situation—a set of values constructed by the advertising industry itself" (p. 333). Hence, an integral component of intersexual dynamics (i.e., the importance of women's physical beauty), which transcends cultural settings and eras, is apparently due to advertising. Cohan (pp. 327–328) discusses several social ills that seemingly result from having women depicted as perfect sexual objects in advertisements. Women become disillusioned because they cannot attain a sense of outer beauty and perfection; subsequently, they lose the desire to pursue "inner beauty." Men become depressed because the women in their lives are not as beautiful and as desirable as those shown in advertising. Additionally, rape and other types of violence are presumed to be in part caused by these images, despite the fact that Cohan recognizes that violence against women has always existed (as such, advertising could hardly be a causative agent). MacKay and Covell (1997) proposed that viewing images of women as sexual objects in advertisements results in negative attitudes that are supportive of aggression toward women (e.g., rape) and attitudes that are nonsupportive of movements of equality (e.g., feminism). Cohan has added that to extol women for their sexuality violates a central tenet of Kantian deontology, namely viewing women as a means to an end—in this case, seeking to have sex with them. Hence, according to Cohan, that men pursue women for sexual goals is an ethical breach. It has even been implied that because heroin consumption had increased among the youth during the heroin chic period as depicted in the fashion industry, the latter fashion trend (which was widely shown in various advertising outlets) might have caused the worsening heroin epidemic (Cohan, 2001, p. 330). Stephens, Hill, and Hanson (1994) proposed that advertisers are responsible for producing a "beauty myth" for women to adhere to, yielding several deleterious effects including poor self-esteem and severe eating disorders (e.g., anorexia nervosa, bulimia, excessive dieting). Building on the condemnation of advertisers, Martin and Gentry (1997) posit that young girls are shackled by such unattainable aesthetic standards.

Many content-analytic studies that have explored advertising have accordingly done so from a condemnation perspective. First (1998) described three issues that are typically addressed in content-analytic studies that explore the representation of minorities in advertising. Researchers explore how present minorities are in advertising, the manner by which they are depicted in terms of their status and roles, and the extent and manner in which they are interacting with the majority group. All three types of analyses are "adversarial" in nature; namely, the goal is to identify how the minority group is demeaned. This singular focus on identifying oppression can at times yield baffling results such as when First found that in Israeli advertisements men were more likely to be depicted as taller than women. Within *Homo sapiens*, the differential heights of the two sexes, which is a manifestation of our species' physical dimorphism, is construed as stereotypical (ergo sexist) rather than a biological fact. Additionally, First concludes that despite the fact that men and women are now shown in occupational roles of equal rank and status (in comparing Israeli ads across a 15-year span), "but the symbolic representation of women still demonstrated their inferiority" (p. 1075). This is in line with the prevalent feminist position that even in those instances when sexism appears absent, it lurks in the background. As Ferguson et al. (1990) state, "Thus, to suggest that meaning lies in objective content camouflages the institutional depth of sexism in culture and society" (p. 42).

In their quest to demonstrate sexism in advertising, most content analyses typically cast a wide net in terms of the coded variables. Some of the variables include the posture of the characters, whether they are touching the product or not, whether they are shown inside or outside the house, their occupational roles, their age, their height, and who is looking at whom (see Goffman, 1979, for a seminal example of this genre). For example, Bartsch, Burnett, Diller, and Rankin-Williams (2000) found that women were underrepresented in ads for nondomestic products, men were underrepresented for ads for domestic products, and there was an increase in female voice-overs, albeit women are less frequently used as voice-overs as compared to men. Ganahl et al. (2003) found that women were much more likely to be shown in ads for health and beauty/pharmacy products whereas men were more likely to be shown in auto/supplies ads. These findings are very much in line with those obtained by Neto and Pinto (1998); namely, women were more frequently shown in advertisements for body products and this held true for studies in other cultures, and men were more likely to be shown in advertisements for autos/sports cars. Hence, by coding a sufficiently large number of variables, any given content analysis will invariably yield one or more sex-based differences (e.g., men are depicted as taller; women are more likely to be depicted inside the house, etc.), which are subsequently construed as sexist.

Given that advertising supposedly constructs sexuality and gender, creates the pervasive beauty myth, promotes the rape culture, and condones the exploitation and subjugation of women, what are some strategies for alleviating the problem? I turn to some of the proposed suggestions in the ensuing section.

Prescriptive Strategies to Address "Sexist" Advertising

Cohan (2001) has suggested that because advertising is supposedly the most influential of all socialization agents (p. 325), advertisers are ethically bound to provide socially responsible content. That said, he explicitly recognized that sex in advertising has been used since time immemorial (p. 326). In order to explain the historically consistent use of sex in advertising, he provides a circular argument. He states:

> Also, utility may argue that the advertising industry merely mirrors the way society holds itself. That is, the culture has fostered or sowed the type of climate it wants, advertising simply feeds off of that—just as the contents of movies, TV, novels, and other media is often fueled by the way society already carries on. (p. 329)

What creates culture? Advertising. What creates advertising? Culture. What generates the particular advertising images? Socialization forces. What creates the particular forms of socialization? Advertising. The explicative infinite loops are set in motion.

In proposing ways that advertisers can improve the ethics of their practice, Cohan (2001) suggests:

> An advertisement for some fashion accessory or cosmetic might show a middle-aged, overweight model, immaculately groomed (wearing the advertised cosmetic or accessory) in a packed elevator; the picture can show that a handsome man next to her is making a pass, obviously being charmed by her, and he is ignoring a knockout gorgeous women on the other side, who has a perfect figure but lacks the immaculate grooming that goes with the product being advertised. (p. 331)

The latter prescription is neither an accurate depiction of male–female dynamics nor of men's evolved mating preferences. Along those lines, MacKay and Covell (1997) state, "Not surprisingly we have been unable to find any advertisements in which an older woman is presented as a sex object" (p. 581). Whereas most social constructivists would construe this as a manifestation of ageism, evolutionists posit that advertisers provide those images that are maximally effective in light of our evolved sexuality.

Some scholars have suggested yet stricter guidelines regarding advertisers' permissible practices. For example, Boddewyn (1991) proposed that advertisements should not even show men ogling at women. Hence, an innate sexual reaction is no longer allowable for it serves to further objectify women. Sverdrup and Stø (1992) provide a description of the regulatory and legal bodies that have been instituted in Norway to combat sexist advertising. Many of the cited examples demonstrate the dangers of having a "thought police" ruling on what constitutes offensive material. Wyckham (1993) states that one of the Canadian guidelines for nonsexist advertising is that advertising practices should refrain from exploiting sexuality. According to such a standard, any message that highlights sexuality could be construed as being exploitative. Is this a truly feasible and realistic benchmark of sexual equality? The suppression of sexual images that recognize evolved mating preferences does not seem congruous with the ideals of a free society. This is reminiscent of the issues raised by Kors and Silverglate (1998) regarding the thought police on American campuses.

Gulas and McKeage (2000) demonstrated that whereas advertising images of financially successful men and women had a negative effect on male viewers' self-worth, those depicting physically attractive members of both sexes did not yield any such effects on men's egos. An evolutionary perspective would posit such an effect given that for men, financial status is significantly more important than physical attractiveness in terms of both intrasexual rivalry and intersexual courtship displays. If one were to apply here the same standards as those meant to regulate other forms of harmful advertising, images that affect men's self-worth should equally be abolished or regulated (e.g., images of successful and powerful men). In a similar vein, images of tall men, ubiquitously found in the advertising, television, movie, and fashion industries, should also be construed as sexist (toward men) in that they do not conform to the normal distribution of men's heights in the population. Many shorter men might find it demeaning that these "constructed" images of male beauty exclude them from the "hegemonic definition of masculinity." On a related note, the prevalence of bald leading actors is less than that which occurs in society. Hence, Hollywood is equally guilty of "constructing" images that are demeaning to men with receding hairlines. An evolutionary perspective recognizes that the advertising and entertainment industries are not involved in any conspiratorial agenda. They provide images that conform to the evolved preferences of both men and women (e.g., young women and tall men). Signorielli et al. (1994) conclude:

> While we cannot say there is a causal relationship between commercial content and social problems like rape, eating disorders, and discrimination in the workplace, MTV commercials in no way contribute to a reduction of misconceptions about women and women's roles in society. As a popular maxim states, "If you're not part of the solution, you're part of the problems." (p. 100)

Thus, advertising is to be blamed even when it is conceded that it does not cause any of the standard social ills of which it is accused.

In the remainder of the current chapter, I demonstrate how an evolutionary-informed perspective can yield benefits to both the practitioners as well as theoreticians of advertising. I begin by illustrating how the strategic decision of developing either local or global advertising messages is best addressed via the use of evolutionary psychology. Specifically, a Darwinian outlook can help identify those advertising cues that are culturally specific (e.g., use of specific colors and/or type of humor) versus those that are culturally invariant (e.g., facial and body symmetry of attractive endorsers and/or the greater use of women in decorative roles).

STANDARDIZATION VERSUS ADAPTATION OF ADVERTISING MESSAGE

An ongoing debate among advertising academics and practitioners alike has been deciding on the relative efficacy of the standardization versus adaptation of an advertising message. Despite numerous studies that have addressed this important topic, little consensus has been achieved (cf. G. Harris & Attour, 2003). Agrawal (1995) conducted an analysis of this debate covering the past 40 years and concluded that whereas practitioners have oscillated between the two strategic options with a penchant toward standardization, academics have been for the most part proponents of adaptation as the optimal strategy. Agrawal quotes several practitioners, beginning with David L. Brown in 1923, the manager of advertising at Goodyear Tire and Rubber Company at that time, who seemed inherently aware that beneath numerous cross-cultural differences exists a common base of cross-cultural similarities that would render the standardization approach highly appropriate. For example, Norman B. Leo (advertising executive) stated the following in 1964:

> Because advertising, effective advertising, is an appeal to human fundamental needs, desires, and motivations, it is an appeal to basic human nature. People the world over have the same basic need for food, clothing, and shelter, the same ambitions, the same egotism, and the same temptations. The setting changes, the climate, the culture, the idiom, but *the basic human nature is the same everywhere* [italics added]. And so, the traditional advertising appeals of economy, comfort, advancement, and social approval are equally applicable in all markets. (as quoted in Agrawal, 1995, p. 30)

Other practitioners cited by Agrawal included Murray L. Barnes, vice president of Pan American Airways, who proposed that because motives are universal, they could be kindled by universal appeals. Perhaps the most telling of all quotes in support of the standardization approach was attributed to Pepsi-Cola wherein the company proposed that:

> In developing our international marketing strategy, we believe in the basic psychological truth that there are greater differences within

groups than between groups. It is the sameness in all human beings in which we believe we must base our selling appeals. (Boote, 1983, as quoted in Agrawal, 1995, p. 41)

In light of the apparent support of practitioners for the standardization approach, why have academics been such staunch supporters of the adaptation camp? Given marketing scholars' singular focus on the environment as the key explicative force in shaping marketing phenomena, culture is construed as an environmental variable that generates cross-cultural differences (i.e., human universals are largely ignored). Agrawal cites several scholars who have proposed a myriad of variables that are thought to affect the standardization-versus-adaptation decision (see also Mueller, 1991; Papavassiliou & Stathakopoulos, 1997; van Raaij, 1997). These include product-specific factors (e.g., type of product or service, stage in the product life cycle), existing marketing conditions (e.g., distribution channels), the strategic intent of advertisers, the physical and legal environments, macroeconomic indicators (e.g., economic and industrial development), competitive forces, and consumer-specific factors (e.g., demographics, psychographics). Because the majority of comparative studies have been much more likely to yield cross-cultural or cross-national differences, this has reaffirmed the academicians' penchant for adaptation as the appropriate strategy (cf. Shoham, 1996).

Several years ago, I attended a presentation given by an advertising executive who had been involved in developing the Pepsi campaign within the Quebec market. At the time, Quebec was one of the sole markets where Pepsi held a larger market share than did Coke. The executive had in part attributed the resounding success of Pepsi to the fact that it was using an adapted strategy (e.g., its use of a famous French-Canadian humorist as a celebrity endorser). This undoubtedly allowed the French-Canadian consumers to develop a greater bond with the Pepsi brand as opposed to Coke, who was apparently making greater use of a standardized approach. Given the distinct cultural traditions of French-Canadians, a localized approach was more likely to resonate with these consumers as compared to one developed in Atlanta (headquarters of Coke). Numerous additional examples exist within the international marketing sphere in support of the benefits of a culture-specific approach. Where does this leave us with regard to the relative efficacy of the two strategic approaches? Agrawal (1995) states that:

While the practical approach of standardization may contradict the theoretical findings pointing to adaptation, the practical approach can actually be made more effective if theory can determine *when* and to *what extent* [italics in original] standardization should be used. The conflict be-

tween the practitioner and the academician has come about because of
[*sic*] inability of academics to provide practitioners with practical frameworks for decision making. Although some academics have attempted to
provide decision models (Britt, 1974; Sheth, 1978), more needs to be done
to resolve this issue. (p. 45)

Evolutionary psychology can help in answering the latter call. Those
advertising cues that are directly guided or influenced by our Darwinian
heritage can be transported cross-culturally using a standardized approach. For example, the manner in which men react to sexual stimuli has
been shown to be a human universal. This does not imply that all cultures
are equally accepting of sexual imagery. Darwinian forces are oftentimes
constrained by societal norms and laws (e.g., sexual imagery is forbidden
in Saudi Arabia). That said, in those cultural environments where sexual
imagery is permitted, advertisers can reliably predict the directionality of
the sex differences in terms of both the reactions to such stimuli, and the
forms that such imagery will take. Advertising messages that appeal to parental duties and family bonds are likely transportable to all cultures. That
people judge symmetric individuals as more beautiful than asymmetric
ones has been shown to be a universal aesthetic cue. On the other hand,
countless other copy decisions are culture-bound and accordingly will require that they be adapted to specific environments (e.g., forms of humor,
celebrity endorsers, cultural icons, and language idioms). Accordingly, the
decision of standardizing versus adapting an advertising message can be
facilitated by recognizing which cues are culture-specific (i.e., within the
purview of cultural relativism) and which are universal (i.e., within the
domain of evolutionary psychology). Though some consumer researchers
have explored both global and culture-specific elements of an advertising
strategy (e.g., the investigation of humorous ads by Alden, Hoyer, & Lee,
1993), none has proposed a meta-framework for cataloging whether a
given cue is within the local or global realm. The conundrum that has
plagued the local-versus-global issue can be elucidated using evolutionary psychology, for it recognizes those instances when cross-cultural differences versus cross-cultural similarities dominate. On a related note,
Luna and Gupta (2001, p. 61) argued that the effects of advertising on cultural values are mixed and contradictory. Though advertising influences
some values, others remain impervious to change. Evolutionary psychology can integrate these seemingly contradictory findings under one common umbrella. A cultural value that is deemed a human universal is
unlikely to be influenced by advertising because its genesis lies in our Darwinian heritage. For example, advertisements cannot eradicate men's
evolved reactions to young and beautiful women. On the other hand, the
extent to which a culture adheres to green marketing practices is a value

that is influenced by socialization, of which advertising would be one such example. Viewed from this perspective, one can understand why some aspects of sexist advertising have decreased whereas other forms have remained unchanged and at times have increased in terms of their incidence. For example, that women are now omnipresent in the labor market should be shown in advertising. That women fulfill a multiplicity of roles beyond the traditional roles of mother and homemaker should be reflected in advertising narratives and images. However, that advertising depicts young and beautiful women in decorative roles caters to aspects of our universal human nature. Understanding which cultural values are malleable by advertising versus those that are impervious to it is conceptually equivalent to identifying which advertising cues are appropriate for a local versus global approach.

ADVERTISING SLOGANS AND DARWINIAN MODULES

Successful advertising campaigns will oftentimes yield highly memorable advertising slogans (e.g., Wendy's "Where's the beef?" campaign). That said, can the same successful slogan be transported cross-culturally (i.e., global approach) or is it almost always the case that slogans are bound to a specific cultural context (i.e., local approach)? I propose that the thematic contents of many advertising slogans can be mapped onto one of the four key Darwinian modules as described in chapter 3. These universal themes can be successfully transported cross-culturally because they cater to innate modules that are operative irrespective of time and place. As such, a content analysis of advertising slogans provides a rich source of data for testing evolutionary-based predictions. That said, although the thematic contents of some slogans might be universal, this does not absolve the advertiser from having to mind idiosyncratic linguistic structures and idioms when transporting the universal themes to disparate cultural settings. Table 4.1 lists advertising slogans that were mapped onto the various Darwinian modules. In many cases, the slogan caters to a very specific evolved behavior or preference.

In her discussion of advertisements containing claims meant to cater to men and women's agentic and communal traits, Hupfer (2002, pp. 7–8) provides various excerpts that fit well within the four key Darwinian modules. The first three listed next cater to the kin selection module whereas the fourth speaks to an evolved mating preference:

> "After I picked up hepatitis A on vacation, I felt terrible. When I learned I could spread it to my family, I felt even worse." —American Liver Foundation

TABLE 4.1
Advertising Slogans and Darwinian Modules

Reproductive Module

"Health is vital. Start with healthy looking skin." —Vichy skin care

"Keep that school girl complexion." —Palmolive Soap

"When monogamy becomes monotony." —Ashley Madison

"Enjoy your nature." —Moose Light

"Everyman man's a girl-watcher, and every girl wants to be a girl girl-watchers watch." —Diet Pepsi

Survival Module

"Obey your thirst." —Sprite

"Milk, it does a body good." —California Milk Processor Board

"Quenching thirst everywhere." —Coke

"Here's health." —Pepsi

"Guinness is good for you." —Guinness

"Don't leave home without it." —American Express

"There are a million and one excuses for not wearing a safety belt. Some are real killers." —American Safety Council

"Designed to save lives." —Bridgestone

Kin Selection

"If you have a son 10 years old, you'd better start worrying. Help unsell the war." —Sane

"Dreams are for passing on to your children, not to the IRS." —MetLife

"Choosy mothers choose Jif." —Jif peanut butter

"Now your kids don't have to miss Monday night football because they're studying for an exam." —Sony

"Mr. Bubble gets you so clean your mother won't know you." —Mr. Bubble

"Look Ma, no cavities." —Crest toothpaste

"Moms depend on Kool-Aid like kids depend on moms." —Kool-Aid

Reciprocation

"… Give me Frito corn chips and I'll be your friend… " —Frito-Lay (excerpt from jingle)

"We love to see you smile." —McDonald's

"You're going to like us." —TWA

"I love what you do for me—Toyota!" —Toyota

"You give us 22 minutes, we'll give you the world." —WINS Radio

"Like a good neighbor, State Farm is there." —State Farm Insurance

"Life would be simpler if the only person you had to look after was you. But would it really be living? Your family means everything to you." —Trimark's Mutual Fund

"The biggest reasons for buying a new Malibu are the little ones." —Chevrolet Malibu

"Power and control are the ultimate aphrodisiacs. Choose your passengers carefully." —Eagle Talon

When speaking of the universality of some advertising slogans, I am referring to thematic contents rather than to specific linguistic instantiations, which are culturally bound. Thus, a Darwinian perspective permits advertisers to establish whether a given message will have universal appeal as a function of whether this appeal constitutes a human universal. In the next section, I explore an advertising cue that is ubiquitously used in innumerable cultures, namely the use of physically attractive endorsers. I argue that the universal focus on beauty in advertising lies in the evolutionary-relevant information that such a cue conveys.

PHYSICAL ATTRACTIVENESS IN ADVERTISING: A DARWINIAN PERSPECTIVE

Despite several cross-cultural maxims that dissuade individuals from caring about physical attractiveness in forming a judgment about another (see Langlois et al., 2000, for a discussion of three of these maxims), most of us succumb to the allure of good looks. Physical attractiveness is relevant in countless social domains. For example, it is an important mate selection cue (albeit differentially so for the two sexes). Not only does physical attractiveness affect the types of personal attributions that we ascribe to individuals but also it drives the manner by which we behave toward them. This effect is so robust and ubiquitous that it has been coined the "what-is-beautiful-is-good effect" (see Eagly, Ashmore, Makhijani, & Longo, 1991, for a meta-analysis of this effect). In the advertising context, several studies have established the importance of the physical attractiveness of an endorser. For example, M. J. Baker and Churchill (1977) demonstrated that the physical attractiveness of endorsers affects positively the evaluation of an advertisement. Despite the importance of physical attractiveness as an advertising cue, advertisers should not be frivolous in their use of attractive endorsers as this can backfire if this copy decision is not implemented in a realistic manner (cf. Bower, 2001).

One might intuitively expect good looks to play a role in advertising given that so many advertising appeals are image based. That said, the effects of physical attractiveness extend to countless domains including those where one would otherwise expect one's looks to be an irrelevant or peripheral cue at best. For example, Saad (2003) summarized some of the cues that the electorate pays attention to when forming an impression of competing political candidates. Contrary to the commonsensical expectation that people would ignore candidates' physical cues because these are unrelated to substantive issues, factors that correspond to "looking like a leader" and to "being presidential looking" are quite influential. For example, Pinker (1997, pp. 495–496) highlights the fact that in the great majority of recent U.S. presidential races, the taller candidate had won (20 of 24 at the time that he wrote his book). J. Schubert and Curran (2001) investigated the effects of four facial features of politicians on their subsequent likelihood of electoral victory. The facial features captured how attractive, healthy, and dominant the candidates were. In addition, a fourth feature gauged how neotenous (childlike features such as large eyes or a small nose) the candidates' facial features were. A key result was that facial dominance significantly impacted a candidate's likelihood of winning the election. Economists have even managed to demonstrate that the looks and heights of employees have an effect on their salaries (even though in most instances such cues are irrelevant to one's job performance). Facial symmetry, facial dominance, neotenous features, height, and other key physical markers are noticed because they carry evolutionarily relevant information.

Socialization-based theorists propose that beauty is a social construction on two separate levels. First, that beauty is assigned such importance is thought due to our culture's shallow and superficial ethos. Second, the specific instantiation of what constitutes beauty is supposedly culturally specific and temporally bound. Accordingly, social constructivists have highlighted the heterogeneity of culture-specific beauty markers. In the marketing context (e.g., physical attractiveness of endorsers in advertising), most scholars adhere to the tenet that beauty is a social construction (e.g., Englis, Solomon, & Ashmore, 1994; Fay & Price, 1994). Typically, the beauty markers used in support of the latter position are not evolutionarily relevant. Hence, that Englis et al. identified six female archetypes (e.g., the sex kitten and the girl next door) depicted across several media says nothing about the universality of the relevant beauty cues. The beauty-as-a-social-construction position is similar in spirit as arguing that the fact that there are cross-cultural differences in gastronomic traditions implies that the digestive system is socially constructed. Similarly, this would be akin to suggesting that in light of the exceptional morphological differences between the various dog breeds (e.g., the miniature poodle and the Great Dane), they must constitute different species. The key issue is to identify the evolutionarily relevant metrics in describing the particular phenomenon in question. When it comes to physical attractiveness, numerous scholars have established the fact that there are universal standards of beauty (cf. Langlois et al., 2000; Rhodes et al., 2001). This holds true irrespective of the race of those making the beauty evaluations, the race of those being evaluated, and the amount of exposure to Western media (see Buss, 1999, pp. 141–142, for a synopsis of the relevant research). In their recent review of the evolutionary-based literature on facial attractiveness, Fink and Penton-Voak (2002) state:

> An obsession with beauty is not unique to modern Western culture but can be found around the world in almost all societies that have been studied. Several studies have shown that members of different ethnic groups share common attractiveness standards, suggesting that the constituents of beauty are neither arbitrary nor culture bound. Beauty and sexual attractiveness seem to be almost interchangeable concepts, and people of different social classes, ages, and sexes tend to rate human faces similarly. (pp. 154–155)

Furthermore, the importance of beauty is not due to socialization. For example, Langlois, Roggman, and Reiser-Danner (1990) demonstrated that human infants (as young as 6 months old) gazed longer at facial images that were more beautiful (i.e., more symmetric). Ontogenetically speaking, the infants were too young to have been socialized into preferring more beautiful faces, thus pointing to an innate aesthetic response.

Why should humans have evolved a ubiquitous universal preference for beauty and what are the exact cues that correspond to beautiful faces? Physical attractiveness corresponds to faces that are symmetric and that have "averaged" traits. There are several evolutionary arguments to explain the adaptive relevance of these visual cues. For example, symmetry is a good marker for the lack of both developmental injuries and pathogenic infestation, and is a reliable cue of youth (cf. Etcoff, 1999; Gangestad et al., 1994; Grammer & Thornhill, 1994; Rhodes, Roberts, & Simmons, 1999). Thus, we are drawn to attractive faces because this in part serves as a reliable cue of health and youth. The neuronal reaction to attractive faces was recently investigated by Aharon et al. (2001). They explored the rewarding properties of viewing attractive faces using both overt behaviors (the effort expended to maintain a beautiful face on a screen) and via functional magnetic resonance imaging (fMRI) of several regions of the brain. They found that young heterosexual males had patterns of neuronal activation that would suggest that attractive faces are rewarding. They suggest that the findings dispel the myth that beauty is socially constructed. The Aharon et al. findings highlight the potential of the nascent field of neuromarketing in developing new research streams. Advertising messages that contain sexual stimuli (e.g., scantily clad physically attractive endorsers) will likely elicit neural activation patterns that are in line with evolutionary theory. Hence, irrespective of whether one collects traditional paper-and-pencil measures or cutting-edge fMRI data, the findings will consistently point to the same evolutionary-based reality. Individuals are innately drawn to beautiful faces, a fact that has been recognized by advertisers since time immemorial.

Gangestad and Buss (1993) have shown that cross-cultural differences in the importance assigned to symmetry are affected by the prevalence of pathogens in a given ecological niche. Specifically, the greater the prevalence of pathogens, the more importance placed on symmetry. This makes evolutionary sense and is in line with the behavioral ecological approach. Though individuals have a universal preference for averaged and symmetric faces, the perceptual "dial" is adjusted according to how much informational diagnosticity will be reaped from this cue. Hence, an arbitrary and ephemeral socialization process does not drive this cross-cultural difference. Rather, to the extent that symmetry is an evolutionarily relevant cue, its importance will adaptively vary cross-culturally as a function of the idiosyncratic ecological parameters relevant to this visual cue. The advertising implications are numerous. For example, cross-cultural differences in the efficacy of using physically attractive endorsers should be in line with the varying premium that is placed on beauty across cultures (as guided by the latter ecological parameter).

Women's preferences for certain types of male facial features (e.g., degree of masculinization) are correlated with their menstrual cycles (cf. Johnston, Hagel, Franklin, Fink, & Grammer, 2001; Penton-Voak & Perrett, 2000). Several evolutionists have proposed that women might prefer more masculine faces when maximally fertile precisely because they are more likely to attend to phenotypic cues that signal genetic quality. Interestingly, Koehler, Rhodes, and Simmons (2002) did not find a relationship between women's preferences for male facial symmetry and likelihood of conception. The totality of findings seems to suggest that women's visual apparatuses respond differentially to sex-based cues in a manner that adheres to evolutionary-based predictions. The advertising implications abound. The same woman will likely react differentially to a given advertisement featuring a handsome male endorser as a function of where she is in her menstrual cycle. On a related note, whether the facial features of a male endorser are construed as peripheral cues or arguments (within the context of the elaboration likelihood model) are likely driven by a woman's ovulatory cycle.

The social constructionist position regarding beauty provides hope in that it proposes that the characteristics that define physical attractiveness are arbitrary, capricious, and hence malleable. This is reminiscent of the infamous quote attributed to Charles Revson, the former chairman of Revlon who pontificated, "In our factory, we make lipstick. In our advertising, we sell hope." Along those lines, Dove has recently launched a campaign to promote the idea that there are no universal standards of beauty. At their www.campaignforrealbeauty.com Web site (accessed on November 26, 2004), the company states:

> For too long, beauty has been defined by narrow, stifling stereotypes. You've told us it's time to change all that. We agree. Because we believe real beauty comes in many shapes, sizes and ages. It is why we started the Campaign for Real Beauty. And why we hope you'll take part. Welcome.

Visitors to the Web site are instructed to vote on the attractiveness of various women who might not otherwise conform to the standard norms of beauty. Five such images included an older woman with gray hair, a young woman with a substantial number of freckles and blemishes, an older woman with conspicuous facial wrinkles, a young woman with a small chest, and finally a young woman who was rotund. The dichotomous choices available to Web visitors for each of the latter five images were as follows: *gray or gorgeous; ugly spots or beauty spots; wrinkled or wonderful; half-empty or half-full*; and finally *oversized or outstanding*. Across the five binary choices (272,917 respondents at that point), the "stifling stereotype" option was chosen by 21.3% of the respondents (ranged from 16.8% to 25% across the five choices). Although these results demonstrate one's need for self-affirmation, they are not representative of men's evolved aesthetic preferences. That said, from Dove's perspective, the empty-slate premise regarding the social construction of beauty is a more profitable position to espouse, for it allows it to sell hope to its client base.

To summarize, the ubiquitous use of beautiful people in advertising is due to the evolutionary-relevant markers associated with this visual cue. Though advertisers might not be able to explain the Darwinian phenomena associated with images of sex and beauty, they are fully aware of their universal impact. As such, the SSSM position that advertisers are part and parcel of the social construction of beauty is demonstrably false (see Scott, 2005, for an exhaustive debunking of the oft-repeated opinion that beauty is a patriarchal tool of oppression).

CHAPTER SUMMARY

Media and advertising images contain universally recurring themes. Depictions of masculinity and femininity are not due to socialization forces and/or to the whims of the patriarchy. Rather sex-specific semiotics and images are rooted in universal sex-specific mating preferences. Whereas many advertising images are influenced by societal changes (e.g., the depiction of women in a wider range of roles), others are impervious to temporal or cultural context (e.g., the greater representation of women in decorative roles). The ability to recognize which advertising cues might be culture-specific versus those that are universal (i.e., local vs. global advertising approach) is greatly enhanced by the use of evolutionary psychology as the organizing framework. I concluded the chapter by demonstrating two specific applications of evolutionary theory in advertising. First, I argued that many advertising slogans cater to one of the four key Darwinian modules; as such, the thematic contents of such slogans are likely to have universal appeal. Second, I provided a Darwinian account to explain the importance of physical attractiveness as a ubiquitous advertising cue.

Whereas in the current chapter I have restricted the analysis mainly to advertising images and related media effects, in the next chapter I extend the argument to additional products of popular culture. Specifically, I propose that cultural products (e.g., song lyrics, soap opera themes, art images, and self-help topics) oftentimes contain certain universal elements because they are instantiations of our human nature. Hence, I question the social constructivist position that culture shapes our otherwise empty minds. Rather, our minds, which have evolved via a process of natural and sexual selection, create cultural products that are manifestations of our Darwinian heritage.

5

The Darwinian Roots
of Cultural Products

*It is a truism that sexuality is constructed rhetorically in the myriad of popular cul-
tural media. Movies and television, music videos, and magazines define sexual attractiveness. They delimit the when, where, how, and with whom of sexual behavior.
They tell us how we should look and how we should act in order to attain sexual satisfaction or satisfy our partners. They tell us how important sex is to our lives.*

—Krassas et al. (2001, p. 751)

*The chief function of popular literature, confession magazines, motion pictures,
and radio and television dramas may be to represent the "universe of experience"
(to use Dewey's term) which corresponds to the universe of love's discourse.*

—Horton (1957, footnote 12, p. 577)

The two opening quotes provide a diametrically opposite view regarding
popular culture. The first quote captures the central viewpoint as espoused by SSSM-based theorists of popular culture. Specifically, it is assumed that humans are born with empty minds, which are subsequently
filled with content via a multitude of socialization agents. One very important source of socialization according to these SSSM scholars is the collective material that is generated via mediums of popular culture. The second
quote is in line with the position that I take in this chapter; namely, I argue
that products of popular culture exist in their particular forms because
they are mirrors of our human nature. In making my case, I analyze several
products of popular culture including soap operas, song lyrics, music videos, movies, television talk shows, and self-help books. I demonstrate that
there exist universal themes within these cultural products that fully accord with key Darwinian principles.

Popular culture pervades our daily lives. Driving down the highway, one is besieged with numerous billboards that constitute an integral part of the modern landscape of urban life. These billboards contain countless images of popular culture, be it ads promoting the latest movie releases and music albums, the upcoming television shows on Must-See TV, the necessary products for achieving a desired lifestyle, or many other accoutrements of modernity. Turning on the car radio, one is exposed to the latest hip-hop songs with the requisite raunchy lyrics. Flipping through the repertoire of television stations, one is likely to come across music videos, all roughly containing the same theme, namely young men displaying cues of wealth and power while surrounded by innumerable young and attractive women. A visit to the nonfiction section of a bookstore will likely yield countless self-help books promising improved health, more passionate sex, better-looking bodies, stronger relationships, superior job prospects, a more confident sense of self, and countless other promissory goals.

Anthropologists and archaeologists alike specialize in the study of existing and extinct cultures. In the current context, how would an anthropologist tackle the exploration of popular culture? Are there theories that can explicate the forces that generate specific instantiations of popular culture? As mentioned earlier, E. O. Wilson (1998) has cogently argued that all human endeavors are best understood when united under the common rubric of Darwinian theory. Hence, the arts, the humanities, the social and natural sciences, and religion are not mutually exclusive spheres of human activity; rather, they are all products of the human mind, which has evolved via the process of natural and sexual selection. Viewed from this perspective, popular culture is an arena where our Darwinian heritage is advertised to the masses. The songs that we listen to, the movies that we watch, the books that we read, the art that we appreciate, the religious narratives that we share, and other products of culture that constitute our consummation experiences, can all be content analyzed using a Darwinian lens.

In the current chapter, I demonstrate that the socialization-based approach, rooted in the blank-slate premise, has held a virtual monopoly on the various disciplines that study products of popular culture. I do so by providing a summary of representative SSSM-based studies across a wide area of cultural products. I argue that cultural products contain key universal elements that serve as mirrors to a common evolved human nature. Prior to delving into the various types of cultural products (e.g., song lyrics or soap opera themes), I provide a brief summary of other evolutionary-based approaches for studying culture.

EVOLUTIONARY PERSPECTIVE ON CULTURE

Most evolutionary-inspired cultural theorists seek to identify the adaptive value of a particular cultural form. For example, they might ask, what is the adaptive and functional value of creating art (e.g., Dissanayake, 1992)? Geoffrey Miller, an evolutionary psychologist currently housed at the University of New Mexico, has proposed a radically different position albeit he is also seeking to explain the existence of cultural products from an evolutionary perspective. He argues that cultural products are merely sexual signals in the mating market (cf. G. F. Miller, 1999a, 2000). In other words, it is not the particular cultural form that has adaptive value; rather, the generation of such cultural products is a means by which humans advertise their desirability as mates. To the extent that for *Homo sapiens* sexual selection operates via female choice, it would accordingly be expected that the great majority of producers of cultural products would be males at the prime of their reproductive potential. This is what Miller found across a wide range of cultural domains including music, art, and literature (see G. F. Miller, 1999a). Miller provides a Zahavian explanation in support of his cultural model; namely, he argues that much of culture can be considered "wasteful" if only because of the time that is typically required to master and subsequently to contribute to a particular cultural domain. Specifically, the handicap principle (see Zahavi & Zahavi, 1997) suggests that wasteful and costly signals have evolved precisely because they serve as honest cues in the mating arena. Hence, the troubadour, rock star, painter, comedian, and musical conductor are simply showing off their elaborate ornamentation as a means of tickling the fancy of prospective mates. However, rather than using morphological traits as the relevant signals (e.g., the peacock's tail), they are utilizing their proclivity to entertain human minds as the honest cues.

I fully concur with Miller's assertions regarding the role that sexual selection plays in explaining why cultural products exist and in identifying who the majority of cultural producers are (males at the zenith of their reproductive potential). That said, I wish to extend his analysis by adding one important element to the Darwinian-based analysis of culture. I contend that the particular contents of a cultural product (i.e., song lyrics, movie themes, soap opera story lines, etc.) are oftentimes manifestations of our evolved human nature. Several Darwinian-inspired scholars have developed research programs that are congruent with this position (e.g., Joseph Carroll's application of Darwinian theory in exploring literary content; see later in this chapter). Hence, I propose that there are several distinct levels at which Darwinian theory can be applied, all of which can help elucidate a given set of cultural phenomena. First, one can explore the adaptive value of a cultural form. For example, cultural norms typically evolve in a manner that is congruent with adaptive solutions to survival problems. Second, cultural products can be viewed as elaborate forms of sexual signaling. Third, one can identify universal contents of cultural products as a means of shedding light on our evolved human nature. There are several additional approaches for studying culture from an evolutionary perspective (e.g., gene–culture coevolution models). Perhaps the most intriguing of these is memetic theory in that it explicitly recognizes that cultural evolution can pursue trajectories that are not necessarily adaptive in the biological sense. I provide a brief description of this framework in the ensuing section.

MEMETIC THEORY

Most evolutionists would agree that to fully understand human nature requires that one studies both biological and cultural evolution. That said, not only is it difficult to truly tease one from the other (hence the interactionism position espoused by most evolutionists) but also it is clear that both evolutionary tracks have shaped the human condition. In other words, cultural learning and its subsequent transmission to group members is an adaptive feature of human evolution. As Henrich and Gil-White (2001) state:

> Cultural transmission is adaptive because it saves learners the costs of individual learning. Once some cultural transmission capacities exist, natural selection favors improved learning efficiencies, such as abilities to identify and preferentially copy models who are likely to possess better-than-average information. (p. 168)

The standard approach for studying the dual evolutionary paths is via the mathematical and simulation-based techniques of researchers steeped in gene-culture coevolution modeling (cf. Boyd & Richerson, 1985). It is beyond the scope of the current discussion to delve into a detailed analysis of gene–culture coevolution models. That said, one of the main criticisms of this approach has been that it provides highly mathematical formalisms with minimal real-world empirical validation. Similar drawbacks have been levied against other formalized modeling approaches for studying human phenomena (e.g., analytic game theory). Descriptive validity is sacrificed for analytic rigor.

Memetic theory is a second evolutionary-based approach for studying the diffusion of cultural content. Dawkins (1976) coined the term *meme* to represent the elemental substrate of cultural evolution (equivalent to the gene in biological evolution). Though he certainly was not the first to describe a Darwinian-based process for the selection and transmission of ideas and beliefs, his name is forevermore associated with having popularized the concept (i.e., he has successfully transmitted and diffused his *meme* meme). Several authors have since contributed to the popularization of memetic theory (cf. Aunger, 2000, 2002; Blackmore, 1999; Brodie, 1996; Dennett, 1991, 1995; Lynch, 1996).

Heath, Bell, and Sternberg (2001) applied memetic theory to explore which types of rumors stand the greatest likelihood of being diffused. They argued that urban legends and rumors (as memes) are selected via a process of emotional selection; namely, memes that trigger evolutionarily relevant emotions are those most likely to diffuse. In their case, they explored a specific adaptive emotion, namely memes that trigger disgust, although one can easily extend their work to other adaptive emotions such as fear and anger (the interested reader should refer to Paul Rozin's work on the evolutionary origins of disgust). It is interesting to note that Heath et al. discuss memetic selection as a form of "runaway selection for emotional content," which I assume is a play on words of the classic Darwin-based runaway sexual selection (R. A. Fisher, 1930). Although they focused on the emotional selection of memes, they also discussed memes that might be selected and diffused because of their informational content or entertainment value. Heath et al.'s work is congruent with the point made by Kenrick et al. (2002) wherein they argued that the diffusion rates of rumors/urban legends are a function of whether or not these are intimately linked to evolutionary/adaptive issues. Hence, ceteris paribus, a consumer rumor that deals with a product that is contaminated with employees' urine and feces is more likely to be selected for diffusion, and will likely diffuse more quickly, than a rumor that associates a company with an onerous group (e.g., the Aryan Nation). This fact has nothing to do with the credibility or believability of the information, which is the typical proximate-based focus of scholars that study the diffusion of rumors. Rather, a memetic and Darwinian-inspired perspective asserts that certain packets of information are juicier to share because of the informational relevance of their contents (in an adaptive sense). That fact notwithstanding, memetic theory explicitly recognizes that successful memes need not yield adaptive advantage in the genetic sense (see Blackmore, 1999, for a detailed discussion of this point).

Memetic theory has yet to be applied to any significant extent in the business disciplines. Paul Marsden wrote a doctoral dissertation on the topic and has founded a consulting company that applies memetic theory in the marketing and advertising context. He has published several practitioner-oriented papers on the topic (cf. Marsden, 1998, 2002) albeit without any empirical testing of the memetic framework (see also R. Williams, 2000, 2002). Cohan (2001, p. 326) discusses Dawkins' memes as an example of how advertising messages spread throughout a social network. Pech

(2003) considers the use of memetics in the management of business innovations. One specific area of business innovations that has received a Darwinian-inspired treatment is new-product development. Massey (1999) contrasted Darwinian natural selection with a Lamarckian process as viable metaphors for both the creation of new products and their subsequent evolution. He proposed that natural selection is an irrelevant metaphor in explaining any of the new-product development processes given that it is a "blind" mechanism that generates variants randomly. On the other hand, Massey argues that product evolution is driven by the striving to meet consumer needs and hence is congruent with Lamarckian evolution, which recognizes that organisms acquire and pass on their traits because of their conscious striving. Simonton (1999) claims that creativity is an inherently Darwinian process given the manner by which ideas are generated and subsequently selected. Viewed from this perspective, truly novel product ideas might be modeled as arising from a Darwinian process. For example, discontinuous innovations that are exceptionally creative and novel products might have arisen as "random mutations" rather than specific solutions to an identified consumer need. In this case, the innovation would indeed be better aligned with a Darwinian as opposed to a Lamarckian process. On a related note, genetic programming (see Koza, 1992), an algorithmic technique that utilizes key Darwinian mechanisms and concepts such as mutation, sexual recombination, and fitness scores, might be used to identify novel and "optimal" product profiles rather than relying on predefined profiles as typically occurs in conjoint analysis. In other words, the generation of new-product profiles can inherently be modeled using a Darwinian-inspired algorithmic technique.

Having provided a brief discussion of various evolutionary-inspired approaches for studying culture, I next turn to the key goal of this chapter, namely demonstrating that cultural products contain certain universal elements that are indicative of our evolved biological heritage. Hence, successful cultural products (i.e., those that we are most likely to consume) are typically those that are congruent with our innate human nature.

CONTENT ANALYSIS
OF SPECIFIC CULTURAL PRODUCTS

In the same manner that fossilized and skeletal remains permit evolutionary-minded scholars to identify the phylogenetic trajectory of a given species, cultural products can serve as affective, conative, and cognitive "fossils" of *Homo sapiens*. Hence, by analyzing the contents of cultural forms and accordingly identifying key universal elements, evolutionary behavioral scientists have a direct window to our evolved human nature. I begin with an exploration of themes covered on television shows.

Television Themes

According to proponents of the SSSM, television socializes us into the beings that we are. Hence, television teaches men to be attracted to young and beautiful women. It also teaches women to be drawn to tall and powerful men. More generally, it arbitrarily ascribes sexist and stereotypical gender roles to the two sexes. In many instances, neither the genesis nor the universality of the particular socialization processes is addressed. When these issues are tackled, it is typically linked to a patriarchal agenda. An evolutionary perspective proposes a different outlook. The cultural products that are generated for television consumption are done so within the bounds of our human nature. In other words, to the extent that certain television themes are universally pervasive, this would suggest that these might be a manifestation of one or more elements defining our evolved nature. The ABC sitcom *8 Rules for Dating My Teenage Daughter,* which originally starred the late John Ritter, highlights this point clearly. A central and recurring premise of the show is the paternal worries experienced by John Ritter as he tries to protect the virtue of his young and beautiful teenage daughter. Does there exist a culture where parents are more protective of the sexual access to their sons while being fully permissive of their daughters' mating behaviors? Would viewers have been equally receptive of a show entitled *8 Rules for Dating My Teenage Son,* wherein prospective female mates are seeking elaborate strategies for mating with the son while the parents are vigilantly protecting access to him? Such a show is unlikely to be produced because it is contrary to one of the most elemental tenets of human mating (i.e., parental investment hypothesis). The history of television is replete with examples that highlight this point, a few of which I review next.

The critically acclaimed show *The Mind of the Married Man,* which began airing on HBO in 2002, revolves around a central issue of male sexuality. The show chronicles the lives of several married male friends as they navigate through their marriages and handle extramarital temptations in radically different ways. One of the male characters is a habitual philanderer equipped with minimal moral restraint. A second character is diametrically opposed in that he is never shown succumbing to temptation. The third and main character falls somewhere between the former two in terms of his ability to remain faithful to his wife. He is a frequent patron at a massage parlor wherein he steadfastly refuses offers by his regular masseuse of a "happy ending" (euphemism for sexual release). However, on one particular occasion, he does succumb to her advances and accordingly engages in an extramarital dalliance. He fantasizes about having sex with his assistant, her roommate, and his optometrist. He visits a clinician to find out why he desires to have sex with so many women while being fully in love with his wife. Evolutionists would propose that the central themes of the latter show are demonstrative of key elements of male sexuality. Men in committed relationships do struggle with temptations arising from the Coolidge effect. They do at times succumb to temptation. They do frequently fantasize about unencumbered short-term mating while being fully capable of separating such an act from their desire to remain with their wives. Different men do react in varied ways to their marriage vows of fidelity, dispelling the notion that to highlight the evolutionary roots of male philandering implies biological determinism. Hence, the show's central themes serve as accurate depictions of the complexities of human mating as viewed from a male lens. Would the exact same themes prove ecologically valid if the show were entitled *The Mind of the Married Woman*? Most television producers irrespective of their sex would likely know that female sexuality is not interchangeable with its male counterpart. This does not mean that women do not desire short-term mating (the recently terminated *Sex and the City* attests to this reality) or that women do not face their own extramarital temptations (as per *The Bridges of Madison County* with Meryl Streep and Clint Eastwood). However, a television show that would have women consistently ogling at coworkers while consumed by an incessant desire for no-strings matings would not be an accurate depiction of most women's sexual interests.

Beginning with the resounding success of *Survivor*, the past 4 years have been witness to a proliferation of reality-based television shows. Such shows are appealing to television executives in that they incur minimal production costs while having the potential to attract an exceptionally large viewing audience. Of all forms of reality-based shows, some of the most popular have been those that deal with dating. A plethora of reality-based television dating shows has been developed over the past few years including *Elimidate, Shipmates, Blind Date, Dating Story, Fifth Wheel, Rendez-View,* and *Change of Heart*. The latter shows can be thematically construed as descendants and variants of *the Dating Game* and *Love Connection*. There are two separate issues that can be addressed from an evolutionary perspective. First, one can explore why such shows seem to have universal appeal. Our voyeuristic fascination with such shows is rooted in our evolved interest in gossip, especially when dealing with the universally important mating market. Second, one can conduct a content analysis of the dynamics contained within the shows to test specific Darwinian-based components of human mate selection. I recently taped close to 50 hours of dating shows with this exact intent. Though I have yet to conduct a formal analysis of the data, several patterns seem to consistently occur. For example, male and female contestants are much more likely to focus on physical attractiveness and occupation respectively when judging their dates. Additionally, women appear exceptionally more selective and judicious in their mating choices. For example, on *Blind Date* contestants publicly proclaim their levels of interest in going on a second date subsequent to having gone on a public first date. Not only does the rejection rate of women seem much higher than that of men but also the incompatibility of the two partners seems to carry little informational value for men. A disastrous first date seems to minimally dissuade men from wishing to go out on a second date. Should the final analyses yield the latter findings, these would be congruent with evolutionary-based predictions of human mating.

Perhaps the most popular situational comedy of the 1990s was *Seinfeld*. One of the reasons that the show has struck a universal chord with the viewing audience is that it accurately captures, albeit in a humorous manner, many of the social predicaments and situations that most of us encounter in our daily lives. In one of the *Seinfeld* episodes, Elaine becomes very attracted to Jerry once she finds out that he has a lot of money (as signaled by his having purchased a Cadillac for his parents). She begins to flirt with him in an outlandish manner, for Jerry's recently disclosed financial status is truly intoxicating to her. On another show, Elaine is dating a medical intern who is about to graduate. Upon becoming a physician, he terminates the relationship, causing Elaine great distress for it shatters her dream of dating a doctor. He explains to her that one of the clear perks of becoming a physician is the expectation that male doctors will "trade up" in the mating market. Incidentally, this is congruent with the findings obtained by Townsend (1987), who found that male medical students had an increase in transient mating opportunities as a function of their rising social status. On the other hand, a similar increase in social status for female medical students did not yield the same mating benefits. Specifically, women recognized that as their social status rose, they had fewer desirable men to choose from (i.e., those that were of an equal or higher social status). Hence, contrary to the structural powerlessness hypothesis, which suggests that women seek men of high status because they are disenfranchised, the focus on a man's status increases with a woman's increase in her social status (see Buss, 1994, pp. 45–47; Ellis, 1992). It should be noted that on *Seinfeld*, Elaine is portrayed as the smartest of the characters and the sole one with a "serious" professional career to speak of. Hence, despite the fact that she is an intelligent and accomplished woman, she maintains a singular interest in dating men of high status.

One of the most memorable *Seinfeld* episodes dealt with masturbation, a seldom-addressed topic on television. The four main characters (three males and one female) lay a wager regarding who could remain the longest "master of their domain" (a euphemism for resisting masturbatory urges, which has now seeped its way into the lexicon of popular culture). The amount to be contributed by each of the four characters was different as a function of the participants' sex. In other words, there was an explicit recognition that it would be substantially easier for Elaine to remain master of her domain as there indeed exist innate sex differences that regulate the frequency that members of each sex will masturbate (see R. Baker, 1996, for an adaptive explanation for male masturbation). Interestingly, the catalyzing masturbatory stimulus was radically different for the various characters in ways congruent with evolutionary predictions. Whereas some of the male characters used visual stimuli (e.g., the attractive and scantily clad female neighbor who was conspicuously exercising) to inspire them, Elaine fantasized about becoming the wife of John F. Kennedy Jr. (a high-status suitor) as a precursor to her masturbatory activities. Not only do men and women make differential use of visual stimuli as an integral element of their sexual fantasies, but also their focus on short-term versus long-term mating occurs in predictable manners (see Ellis & Symons, 1990, for an evolutionary explanation of sex differences in sexual fantasies).

Larry David, one of the cocreators of *Seinfeld,* has recently developed the HBO series *Curb Your Enthusiasm.* On one of the episodes, the audience finds out that when Larry had gotten married, he and his wife had agreed that his 10th-year wedding anniversary gift was that he could sleep with another woman. A nonnegotiable condition imposed by his wife was that he could sleep only once with his chosen woman. There are several evolutionarily relevant points in the latter scenario. First, the Coolidge effect (differential desire of men for greater sexual variety) is implicit in the gift. Second, the evolved threat of paternity uncertainty ensures that such a gift is substantially less likely to be offered by a man to his wife. Cross-cultural patterns in the dissolution of long-term pair bonding suggests that men are much less forgiving of adultery whereas women can potentially forgive such a transgression especially if the affair is a short-term dalliance (i.e., void of emotional or resource-based investments on the man's part). Because the greatest threat to a woman's mating interests is the possibility that her mate will abandon her, a short-term sexual affair void of investment can actually be less threatening than a yet-to-be consummated affair fraught with emotional ties (see Buss et al., 1992). Thus, screenwriters (both men and women) manifest their evolved sexual minds via the television story lines that they create. Note that to provide an evolutionary-inspired explanation for the latter story line does not imply that one condones or justifies the behavior in question.

Robert Trivers has proposed that self-deception (cf. Trivers, 1985) has evolved in part to permit individuals to successfully implement their Machiavellian design. In other words, to the extent that individuals have evolved the capacity to detect cues that signal dishonesty, duplicity, or manipulative intent, self-deception ensures that such cues are maximally latent in the prospective deceiver. This point was poignantly captured in the *Seinfeld* episode wherein George (played by Jason Alexander), the duplicitous and Machiavellian character on the show, is trying to teach Jerry how to be a good liar. In a sagelike manner, George dispenses the following advice: "Jerry, just remember, it's not a lie if you believe it" (Leifer, Mehlman, & Ackerman, 1995). Hence, the latter advice if properly implemented reduces the likelihood of deceivers sending cues that expose their lies (e.g., if a liar's conscience were to suddenly manifest itself), thus ensuring that recipients of the lie are less likely to detect it. The endless capacity for individuals to engage in self-deception is at the root of the highly successful television reality shows *American Idol* and *WB Superstars USA*. The central premise of both shows is for a panel of judges to identify the top singer from an open cast of thousands of prospective applicants, most of whom are objectively void of any auditory talent. That so many people can engage in such blatant self-deception is in of itself a telling point. There is a twist to the story. Whereas *American Idol* truly does seek to identify the most talented singer, *WB Superstars USA* was designed as an elaborate hoax. Unbeknownst to the participants, the judges eliminate all promising singers and retain only those who are truly abysmal and yet display supreme self-confidence. The participants are not allowed to see each other's performance until late in the competition in order to protect the integrity of the hoax (i.e., remove all suspicions). This last fact demonstrates that participants would quickly become suspicious if they were to view the exceptionally poor singing talent displayed by their competitors. Hence, it is not that these participants are "auditorily challenged" and therefore cannot distinguish between good and bad singers. Rather, they are fully capable of recognizing disastrous voices except the one emanating from their own vocal chords.

In addition to the contents of television shows being congruent with evolutionary principles, which television shows are watched at a given moment in time appears linked to physiological variables steeped in our Darwinian heritage. As previously mentioned, a woman's menstrual cycle has been shown to affect numerous behaviors and preferences, all of which accord with central Darwinian expectations. For example, how provocatively a woman dresses, her sexual and caloric appetite, her shifting preference for various male facial features, and the likelihood of her engaging in personally risky behaviors are all linked to her ovulatory cycle. Could television viewing also be related to menstrual cycle? Weaver and Laird (1995) found that women's preference for either sitcoms or dramas was in line with their menstrual cycles as were their moods (e.g., feeling irritable) and sense of self (e.g., feeling beautiful). Accordingly, the authors argue that the choice of which television genre to watch at a given point in time serves as a means by which women can manage their moods. This is certainly a viable proximate explanation albeit the ultimate cause has a Darwinian etiology.

Having provided a broad overview of the evolutionary roots behind several television themes, I next turn to two very specific types of television shows, namely soap operas and talk shows. Accordingly, I demonstrate that the key topics covered on such shows are those of greatest evolutionary import.

Soap Operas

Throughout the world, one of the most popular and watched forms of television programming is the soap opera. Why is this form so transportable across national and cultural boundaries? I propose that there are two related reasons. First, soap operas cater to our evolved penchant for gossip. Second, the main story lines in soap operas are universal because they map onto key Darwinian modules. To the extent that people enjoy gossiping they do so regarding matters that carry evolutionarily relevant implications (cuckoldry, paternity uncertainty, sexual jealousy, sibling rivalry, etc.). Hence, soap operas are a good means by which our insatiable desire to gossip about evolutionarily important information is instantiated albeit in a vicarious manner.

Riegel (1996) highlights the importance of three distinct levels of gossip inherent to the soap opera genre. First, the story lines within soap operas are instantiated via extensive gossiping as carried out by the characters. Thus, unlike other forms of popular entertainment whereby dramatic impact is implemented via elaborate action scenes (e.g., the formulaic Hollywood summer blockbuster), soap operas deliver drama in part via a focus on gossiping. Second, viewers of soap operas engage in extensive gossiping with one another regarding the story lines. Third, there exist several platforms of popular media including soap opera magazines such as *Soap Opera Digest* and *Soap Opera Weekly* and newspaper columns whose raison d'être is to gossip about the story lines and the characters within. Riegel's work is clever in identifying the latter three levels of gossip, and in highlighting the importance of gossip as an integral element of human interactions. For example, she quotes Max Gluckman, who had remarked that gossip was the second most frequent activity (after work) that people engaged in during their waking hours. Lacking in Riegel's work is a discussion of the evolutionary and adaptive roots of gossip (cf. Dunbar, 1996; McAndrew & Milenkovic, 2002, for such accounts). Viewed from this perspective, the cross-cultural success of soap operas and television shows that focus on celebrity gossip (e.g., shows on the *E!* network, *Entertainment Tonight*, and *Celebrity Justice*) are utilizing our innate proclivity to be interested in gossip. That the gossip revolves around fictional characters and/or celebrities who are otherwise strangers to us is irrelevant. The desire to partake in the exchange of social information is simply too irresistible. On a related note, H. Davis and McLeod (2003) demonstrated that sensational news from around the world and spanning several eras consists of topics that are collapsed onto a set of recurring themes that would have all been relevant in the environment of evolutionary adaptedness. They performed a content analysis of sensational front-page newspaper stories originating from several continents including North America (the United States and Canada), Europe (England, France, and Germany), Asia (Bangladesh), Oceania (Australia), and Africa (Mauritius). The covered period was from 1700 to 2001. Some of the key themes included issues that dealt with sexuality (courtships, rape), families (child abuse, status of a family), survival (e.g., predatory attack resulting in injury or death, food contamination), and altruism (e.g., a heroic action). Davis and McLeod situate their findings within the research stream that has explored the evolutionary roots of gossip. Specifically, sensational news contains universal and recurring themes because they serve as a proxy form of gossip, namely a means by which one can acquire information that is evolutionarily relevant (see also Shoemaker, 1996, for an adaptive explanation regarding people's desire to follow the news). To support their claim, they cite several studies that have demonstrated that the themes covered in gossip tend to be cross-culturally invariant. Along those lines, McAndrew and Milenkovic (2002) applied evolutionary psychology in exploring various facets of gossip. They found that tabloid stories that elicited the greatest interest in people corresponded to those of celebrities of the same age and sex. Furthermore, they found that the pattern of informational exchange (i.e., gossip) was such that it served to enhance one's status (see also Scalise Sugiyama, 1996, for a discussion of the adaptive value of engaging in biased storytelling). Specifically, people are desirous to share negative information (e.g., dishonesty or promiscuity) about potential rivals while sharing positive information (e.g., obtaining an academic award or being the recipient of a substantial inheritance) about allies and coalitional members. Furthermore, individuals generally prefer to gossip about same-sex sources and about topics that are evolutionarily relevant in a sex-specific manner. For example, men were more interested to hear about the gambling problems and sexual inadequacies of other men whereas women manifested a more pronounced interest in hearing about the sexual promiscuity of other women. This seems to suggest that such information can potentially be used to derogate prospective intrasexual rivals (cf. Schmitt & Buss, 1996). The old adage that one chooses their friends but not their family would suggest that it is potentially more valuable (in a strategic sense) to exchange information about friends. The findings seemed to support the latter contention; namely, in all but two instances (receiving a large inheritance and being stricken with leukemia), people preferred to gossip about friends. In the latter two cases, people preferred to engage in gossip about these issues if it involves family members. This makes sense given that a large inheritance into the family and a life-threatening illness to a kin member trigger the kin selection module in obvious ways.

It would thus appear that the need to gossip about evolutionarily relevant topics drives the audience's insatiable appetite for soap operas. Accordingly, what are the key themes covered in soap operas? Matelski (1988) provided an analysis of the contents of soap operas including the key story lines, themes, and characters on such shows. First, she demonstrated that the key plots on soap operas are invariant irrespective of the era in question. For example, she states, "Clearly, it can be said that soap opera plots in the eighties still revolve around issues of love, family, health and security—much like the storylines [*sic*] in early radio daytime drama" (p. 11). Based on the reported findings of her content analysis of soap operas covering the 2-year period 1983–1985, I calculated the top 10 themes in terms of their occurrence. These were in decreasing order: secret, job, crime, deception, illness/injury, romance, parenthood, money, jealous lover, and investigation. Four of the latter topics, namely secret, crime, deception, and investigation, do not contain any specific information regarding the contents within these themes. If one were to conduct such an analysis, the findings would likely show that the topics map onto the key Darwinian modules that drive purposive human behavior. For example, a withheld secret might be that a character has slept with a friend's mate. A deceptive strategy might be a female character who has cuckolded her husband and hence has created the conditions for paternity uncertainty. A depicted crime might consist of a domestic-violence story line that was triggered by the infidelity of a spouse. Finally, an investigation story line might involve the hiring of a private investigator to follow a spouse suspected of infidelity. The six other topics for which we have sufficient information to surmise their contents all deal with domain-specific issues including mating (romance and jealous lover), social ascendancy (job and money), health (illness/injury and death), and kin (parenthood). Hence, the topics used to capture the attention of millions of viewers on a daily basis are those that are linked to the key Darwinian modules.

Krauss, Curran, and Ferleger (1983) contrasted the abilities of American and Japanese individuals to decipher the expressive contents displayed by characters on both American and Japanese soap operas. Both groups yielded highly correlated scores in terms of their understanding of the nonverbal expressions. In other words, even when the audio and semantic components were filtered out, both groups yielded similar attributions regarding the expressed emotions. The authors conclude that this suggests that there is a universal element to the deciphering of nonverbal communication. Incidentally, the authors state, "Despite the fact that their contents are typically Japanese, Japanese soap operas (or 'home dramas' as they are called there) are strikingly similar to their American counterparts" (p. 498). Thus, it would appear that not only do American and Japanese soap operas exhibit similar expressive displays but also other contents such as the story lines covered are highly similar. This is indicative of the universality of the key themes that people find enthralling when viewing this particular television genre.

Greenberg and Woods (1999) provided a descriptive account of the key topics and the typical characters found on soaps. For example, there is the philandering powerful man, which accords with the evolutionary fact that powerful males have greater access to mating opportunities. Whenever couples are shown, it is almost always the case that the man is older. This accords with the universal finding that men and women prefer to mate with younger and older mates respectively. Though in many instances the paternity of a child was known, there were numerous story lines focused on paternity uncertainty. This issue is an integral element in the evolution of human mating; hence, it is not surprising that it is frequently addressed in soap operas. Confirming this point, Olson (1994) states, "In fact, soap opera plots often include such identified themes as unwed motherhood and *deception about the paternity of children* [italics added]" (p. 842). Greenberg and Woods recognized that the two sexes have inherently different reactions to sexual themes albeit they did not provide an ultimate explanation for such differences. They state:

> It is unlikely that women and men have similar responses to the same content, or even similar motivations in experiencing that content. Those differences have yet to be made manifest in the research literature, and this summary suggests both the importance and the means of initiating such efforts. Efforts to date, for example, have not explored how sex is being used in these stories—is it for pleasure, for manipulation, for power? Surely, these elements need to be analyzed as we probe to understand responses to this genre of television, a daily favorite for millions of viewers. (p. 256)

I propose that the manner in which sex is used within the story lines of soap operas is demonstrative of the evolved sexualities of the two sexes. Thus, a complete analysis of the sexual contents of soap operas (or any other cultural product) requires that the Darwinian etiology behind our mating preferences and proclivities be recognized.

Harrington and Bielby (1991) provided an interpretive analysis of three 1980s fictional soap opera romances. They sought to determine whether the manner by which such romances were shown on television corresponded to so-called changes in the dynamics of relationships. First, it is noteworthy to point out the central focus that these SSSM-based scholars place on environmental factors (e.g., the growing participation of women in the labor market) in studying this particular phenomenon.

When it comes to the dynamics of mating, although there are issues that are bound to temporal realities, there exists a set of invariant mating variables that are steeped deep within our Darwinian heritage. Harrington and Bielby ask, "Why has the old idea, the traditional love mythology, remained despite change in the nature of commitment?" (p. 141). They continue, "We suggest further that although in reality the structure of women's roles, including responsibilities and opportunities, has expanded considerably, the dynamics of negotiating intimate male–female relationships have changed very little" (p. 142). An evolutionary perspective is capable of delimiting those components within human mating that are amenable to change versus those that are likely invariant to temporal vagaries. The authors alluded to the differential power that men continue to exert in society as an explanation for why soap operas continue to depict "traditional" relationship dynamics. That said, they did recognize that many soap opera writers are women as are the majority of viewers. It would seem difficult to see how the differential power of males could be the means by which the depiction of traditional relationships are maintained when in this particular medium, women are by and large the dominant force in shaping the final product.

In the same manner that romance novels, which are read predominantly by women, serve as a window to women's evolved mating preferences, the same can be said of soap operas. For example, the depiction of men on soap operas should correspond to the sex-specific idealized definition of masculinity as relevant to women. C. T. Williams (1994, citing a 1987 interview with the soap opera writer Bill Asher) states,"Women want strong men because [they want] fantasy" and "soap opera is a woman's medium. … You have to write men larger than life … so they don't come off weak" (p. 128). Another relevant quote cited by Williams includes the following:

> The hero must be part villain or else he won't be much of a challenge to a strong woman. … And the flat truth is that you don't get much of a challenge for a heroine from a sensitive, understanding, right-thinking "modern" man who is part therapist, part best friend, and thoroughly tamed from the start. You don't get much of a challenge for her from a neurotic wimp or a good-natured gentleman-saint who never reveals a core of steel. (Krentz, 1992 as quoted in C. T. Williams, 1994, p. 128)

It is claimed that the latter quote is veridical because the heroine (in soap operas or romance novels) is adventurous. I would argue that all other things equal, this preference for strong men holds true for most women. In the same manner that the male hero is referred to as the alpha male (ethological term) in the romance industry (Krentz, 1992, as cited in C. T. Williams, 1994, p. 128), similar attributes define the soap opera hero. For example, Mary Jo Putney (romance writer) stated, "A romance can survive a bland or even a bitchy heroine, but it cannot succeed with a weak hero" (Putney, 1992, as quoted in C. T. Williams, 1994, p. 132, note 3). These attributes of an idealized form of masculinity speak to women's evolved mating preferences given that soap operas are watched predominantly by women and in light of the fact that in many instances the characters are developed by women writers.

To recapitulate, soap operas entertain the universal masses because they employ story lines that transcend cultures and epochs. In other words, the success of soap operas rests in their ability to cater to our evolved need to gossip about topics of Darwinian import, which ostensibly is the recipe used by talk shows, a cultural form to which I turn to next.

Talk Shows

Other than soap operas, one of the most popular formats for daytime television has been the ubiquitous talk show. These include past or current shows hosted by Phil Donahue, Sally Jessie Raphael, Geraldo Rivera, Ricky Lake, Montel Williams, Jerry Springer, Jenny Jones, Maury Povich, Oprah Winfrey, and Dr. Phil. Audience members seem to have a ravenous appetite for the ever-growing litany of talk shows. That said, little academic research has been conducted on this television genre (Brinson & Winn, 1997). What might explain the success of such shows? I propose that these shows enthrall a large viewing audience because they address evolutionarily relevant issues that are linked to innate Darwinian modules. Most themes on these shows (notwithstanding the larger range of topics covered on shows such as *Oprah, Dr. Phil*, and the *Phil Donahue Show*) address sexual infidelity, family strife, food addictions, and friendship betrayals. Note that the latter four topics map onto the four key Darwinian modules, namely reproduction, kin selection, survival, and reciprocation. A frequent theme on the *Maury Povich Show* deals with DNA paternity tests. Such a show premise generates intense drama for it relates to one of the central issues in human sexuality, namely the ever-present dangers of cuckoldry. That we now have the technology to immediately alleviate ancestral and evolutionarily relevant fears of cuckoldry, which natural selection took millions of years to provide partial solutions to (e.g., male sexual jealousy), is a story line that makes for good ratings. Brinson and Winn (1997) ask, "Lastly, why are such large numbers of viewers attracted to these programs?" (p. 36). The answer lies in the evolutionarily relevant topics addressed on such shows.

Brinson and Winn (1997) sought to explore the depiction of interpersonal arguments on televised talk shows. They conducted a content analysis of 40 talk shows and found that there were no differences between the two sexes when it came to behaviors during interpersonal conflicts (e.g., interruptions, finger pointing, etc.). The authors state, "It is possible that television may be very effective at communicating information and educating audiences. ... Television teaches us which values/attitudes/beliefs are appropriate for whom" (p. 29). Hence, the social dynamics that might be depicted on such shows are not viewed as indicative of innate predispositions. They discuss research showing that television shows typically portray men and women in sex-typed behaviors. In other words, that men and women are shown behaving in "stereotypically" masculine and feminine ways respectively is implicitly taken as proof of the pervasive sex role socialization that occurs on television. This position is reasonable only if one assumes that the two sexes are born with equally empty minds and accordingly any sex-based differences that arise must be due to socialization agents. However, it is important to understand why sex-typed behaviors manifest themselves in the exact same manners irrespective of cultural and temporal setting. Thus that no sex differences were found was construed as surprising because a social constructivist perspective purports that the two sexes are socialized to behave differentially when engaged in interpersonal conflicts. One other notable finding was that of the three possible dyads (i.e., male–male, female–male, female–female), the mixed-sex dyad was the most frequent one depicting interpersonal conflicts. This was taken as supportive of another socialization-based tenet, namely that intersexual conflicts drive the dynamics between men and women. The authors state:

> Further, the fact that women and men were more likely to be arguing with each other, rather than with members of their own sex, perpetuates a growing stereotype that women and men don't, or can't, get along with each other. ... Although they manifest similar conflict behaviors, the fact that women and men are more likely to be arguing with each other focuses on the contention between the two sexes. Simply put, daytime talk shows represent another battlefield in the war between the sexes. (pp. 35–36)

Evolutionary psychologists hold a different perspective regarding the pattern of conflicts in the context of sexual dynamics. Specifically, they recognize that rather than being intersexual (e.g., men oppressing women), the majority of conflicts are intrasexual (e.g., male–male conflicts). This point was put forth by Buss (1994) when he proposed that:

> Feminist theory sometimes portrays men as being united with all other men in their common purpose of oppressing women. But the evolution of human mating suggests that this scenario cannot be true, because men and women compete primarily against members of their own sex. (p. 214)

Hence, although in the context of television talk shows it might appear that intersexual conflicts dominate, the more general reality is that intrasexual strife is a more common phenomenon in understanding sexual dynamics.

Greenberg, Sherry, Busselle, Hnilo, and Smith (1997) content-analyzed 10 episodes of each of the top 11 daytime talk shows of 1994–1995 (as per the Nielsen ratings). Two of the goals of the research were to explore the types of relationships that are displayed and the key themes and issues that are discussed on such shows. I calculated that of the 1,229 relationships displayed in Table 2 of their article (p. 418), 403 consisted of lovers, former lovers, or married persons, 360 of nonromantic friends and acquaintances, and finally 466 of parent, child, or sibling. In other words, 33%, 29%, and 38% of the displayed relationships appear to map onto the reproductive, reciprocation, and kin selection modules. In terms of topics addressed (as listed on p. 419, Table 3), the most frequent ones were those dealing with parenting (48%), marriage (37%), dating (37%), sexual activity (36%), reconciliation (26%), alienation (23%), physical health (25%), criminal acts (24%), abuse (23%), appearance (22%), and sexual infidelity (21%). The percentages refer to the proportion of times that a particular topic was addressed within the context of all talk shows that were content-analyzed. To reiterate, captivating themes on talk shows are precisely those that deal with matters of greatest evolutionary import.

S. W. Smith et al. (1999) analyzed the titles of television talk shows to explore, among other issues, which types of relationships are most depicted and the types of individual attributes used to describe the guests. They conclude, "The titles of television talk shows and their content frequently focus on personal relationships such as family, friendship, and romantic relationships" (p. 177). Specifically, of the 955 coded titles, more than half (57%) dealt with either family or other personal relationships (e.g., lovers). Of 704 titles that alluded to a description of individual attributes (for a total of 785 attributes; namely, some titles had more than one attribute description), the most frequent one dealt with sexual activity (19.5%). In other words, close to one in five individual attributes described in the titles dealt with sexuality. The themes that individuals are most interested in viewing are those that are most relevant to our innate Darwinian nature (i.e., sexuality, family conflicts, friendships, etc.). Being socialization-based theorists, the authors instead state that "a determination of which television world messages are actually presented on television talk shows is an important first step in assessing how viewers might construct social reality subsequent to viewing these shows" (p. 177). Thus, products of popular culture are construed as arbitrary socialization agents rather than reflections of our human nature. Numerous other scholars have uncovered roughly the same set of ubiquitous talk show topics and themes. For example, Woo and Dominick (2003) concluded:

In this genre, human relationships are seldom portrayed as positive. Instead the emphasis is on interpersonal conflict, betrayal, disloyalty, cheating, and lying. Almost all of the content features broken or abnormal relationships among members of primary groups: parents and children, siblings, spouses, romantically involved couples, friends. (p. 112)

Similarly, J. H. Wang (2000) stated, "By the 1995 syndicated season, a glut of daytime talk shows (up to twenty-three) were competing for the attention of younger daytime viewers with a menu of sexual conquests, family conflicts, and feuding friends" (p. 22). The most dramatic topics, which incidentally pull the highest ratings, are those that address issues of substantial Darwinian import.

Much research has sought to determine the effects of viewing talk shows, typically via the use of cultivation theory. In general, the findings suggest that cultivating effects are minimal (if any). For example, S. Davis and Mares (1998) did not find strong evidence that teens' viewing of talk shows had a deleterious effect on them. The authors state, "Although talk shows may offend some people, these data do not suggest that the youth of the U.S. is corrupted by watching them" (p. 84). More recently, Rössler and Brosius (2001) reached the same conclusion while studying German teenagers. They proclaimed, "The findings of this experimental study suggest that the content of German daily talk shows had limited cultivation effects on (adolescent) viewers" (p. 158). More generally, they proposed that "there is no evidence so far that talk show viewing leads to a general corruption or disorientation of adolescents" (p. 159). When cultivation effects are found, they are typically minimally useful. An example of a cultivation effect found by Rössler and Brosius was the overestimation of gays in the general population following the viewing of talk shows dealing with gays. This is a likely manifestation of the availability heuristic (see Kahneman et al., 1982, for a description of the heuristics and biases program); namely, a stimulus that is available and vivid in memory will have its frequency of occurrence overestimated. This is not an instantiation of a pernicious effect of television viewing. Woo and Dominick (2003) found that international students (mainly from Asia) who were not well acculturated to American culture and who watched a lot of daytime television talk shows were likely to yield a cultivation effect regarding the negativity of human relationships in the United States. That said, the same authors cite work that did not find any evidence of cultivation effects using two Korean samples within the United States. Hence, cultivation effects appear to be only sporadically found while being fleeting in nature. Nonetheless, the need to identify pernicious socialization agents maintains the interest of countless SSSM-based scholars in this less than promising research agenda.

To the extent that talk shows yield harmful effects on the viewing audience, it is much more likely due to the "experts" on such shows who offer baseless recommendations founded on an erroneous view of human nature. Robinson (1982) demonstrated that so-called experts on talk shows provide value-laden statements and scientifically unsubstantiated or unreferenced statements as truths. One could simply watch any current episode of *Dr. Phil* (or similar "gurus" such as Deepak Chopra) to arrive at the same conclusion. In discussing the values and beliefs held by talk show experts, Robinson mentions two that are particularly indicative of the social constructivist worldview. In referring to life forces that are external to one's locus of control, she states that experts held "a belief that people were controlled externally and that people are often not able to control their fates (e.g., 'biology is destiny')" (p. 375). This is a manifestation of the incorrect yet oft-repeated belief that one's biology is deterministic and hence is outside one's control. Second, Robinson highlights the overwhelming importance that experts placed on parents in shaping their children. She concludes, "The emphasis on the parent's almost unlimited ability to mold children is an assumption the experts on talk shows frequently made" (p. 377). The reader is referred to the recent book by J. R. Harris (1998) titled *The Nurture Assumption* for a critique of the latter premise. That said, Dr. Spock's views on parenting continue to dominate the layperson's understanding of parent–child dynamics, much of it diffused via the talk show medium.

To summarize, talk shows constitute a successful cultural product because they cater to our evolved need to gossip about topics of evolutionary import. Having spent considerable time discussing the evolutionary roots behind the themes and images covered on the small screen, I next turn to movies, the artistic medium that creates popular culture's version of royalty, namely the big-screen celebrity.

Movies

Film theory is dominated by the same intellectual courants as those found in literary criticism. Hence, one can analyze the key themes of a movie or the dialogue in a given scene using psychoanalytic theory, postmodernism, deconstructionism, or feminism (or a combination of these). An evolutionary-based analysis of the contents of film would suggest that many of the universally recurring themes are manifestations of our evolved nature. In other words, movies are able to elicit a roller coaster of emotions from the viewing audience because they address dramatic themes that speak to our evolved minds and that are congruent with our human nature. Grodal (2004) states:

> Evolutionary psychology provides an explanation for the fact that films are comprehended much more universally than radical culturalism alone

can explain. For example, viewers are often able to understand films set in unfamiliar cultural and historical contexts. While emotions are molded differently, they are shared universally, so that viewers can often understand films that portray different boundaries of modesty and explicitness than they are accustomed to. There is even a certain moral gratification in recognizing that *the production and reception of cultural products have their roots in a shared, universal human nature* [italics added], distinctly shaped by culture and individual experience, for it is this shared human nature that is the foundation of empathy and tolerance. (p. 43)

I am not suggesting that every imaginable movie scene or film has a direct link to our Darwinian heritage. Rather, I am referring to major cinematic plots or movie contents that universally occur in the same manner irrespective of a movie's country of origin. For example, certain sexual dynamics between men and women occur in perfectly predictable ways independently of whether the movies originate from the Egyptian, Hindi, French, or American film industries.

Prior to providing an evolutionary-based analysis of a few recent movies, I briefly discuss a representative study stemming from the dominant research stream within film theory. Hedley (2002) conducted a content analysis of popular movies covering the years 1986 through 2000. His goal was to explore the manner by which gender conflicts are depicted in films. The conceptual assumption was that the media teaches men and women which conflicts are relevant and how these should be resolved. Hedley states:

In terms of the meaning of conflict between women and men, then, popular films play a significant role in defining the applicable norms, values, and expectations. ... This meaning may have more to do with systemic stereotypes and hegemonic ideology than with empirical reality. (p. 203)

This mind control is supposedly shaped by the "rape culture," "which posits that popular culture serves as a motivational force for men's violence against women, and related work in men's studies, which analyzes the social construction of masculinity in relation to men's active participation in the domination of women" (Hedley, 2002, p. 201). In explaining the roots of popular culture, Hedley adds, "Through its application of technological advances, popular culture in modernity has been able to define what is real. A system-world of ideological control, therefore, has replaced the life-world of authentic experience as the primary source of meaning" (p. 202). Hedley concludes that "this devaluation of women by popular culture invites the distrust of women by men, and perhaps, the perceived need by some men to control their romantic/sexual partners" (p. 207). Hence, central to this research stream is the tenet that popular culture shapes otherwise empty minds via a conspiratorial political agenda.

I briefly highlight some of the key findings from Hedley's (2002) qualitative content analysis and subsequently provide an evolutionary explanation for each of his findings. Hedley's analysis yielded that male
characters were shown in positions of greater social power. Cheating husbands were forgiven by their wives in both *Fatal Attraction* and *The Firm,* as
was sexual deceit in *Cocktail.* As Hedley states, "It is also expected that,
once they have overcome temptation, men will be welcomed back by the
women they love with open arms" (p. 209). Hedley enumerates several
prevalent sex-specific archetypes such as the whore–madonna,
prince–scoundrel, and hero–villain dichotomies. Finally, regarding the dynamics between men and women, Hedley concludes, "Thus, absent information to the contrary, one may expect conflict between a man and a
woman to be based upon a foundation of sexual tension" (p. 212), and
"Typically, it is men who compete with each other for the attention of a
woman" (p. 212). The totality of his findings leads Hedley to conclude that
most movies are shown from the privileged male perspective. Furthermore, common to this research stream is the adversarial nature of the analysis (i.e., men pitted in a group-level conflict against women). Does the
reality depicted in movies correspond to specific elements of an innate human nature? Data spanning hundreds of cultures and all of recorded history suggest that men are much more concerned with social ascendancy as
compared to women. This does not imply that women are uninterested in
social status (e.g., in many professional degree programs, women now
outnumber men), however it is well accepted that, evolutionarily speaking, social status has been a predominant means by which men engage in
intrasexual competition. Thus, that men's social status is more clearly
highlighted in movies reflects the latter phylogenetic reality. That women
are more forgiving of an extramarital dalliance is in line with extensive
cross-cultural and longitudinal evidence demonstrating the differential
tolerance of the two sexes toward such dalliances. This behavioral dimorphism is rooted in the differential threat associated with such behaviors
(much greater for men given the threat of cuckoldry). The whore–madonna, prince–scoundrel, and hero–villain dichotomies are prevalent in
the movies because they cater to the sexes' evolved psychology. They do
not come to be via arbitrary and/or conspiratorial cultural learning. That
the female archetypes are based on sexuality whereas the male archetypes
are based on power accords with an evolutionary perspective regarding
mate preferences. That the dynamics between men and women are fraught
with sexual tension is expected given that *Homo sapiens* are a sexually reproducing species. Finally, that men compete for women's attention is in
line with the interspecies Darwinian reality that sexual selection typically
operates through female choice. The sexual dynamics as depicted in movies are a reflection of our innate nature as sexually reproducing organisms.

Movies capture an existing universal reality rather than create an arbitrary social order.

In the 1993 movie titled *Indecent Proposal,* a wealthy man (Robert Redford) offers a married couple (played by Demi Moore and Woody Harrelson) $1 million to spend the night with the wife. The offer is made as a result of a discussion wherein the husband suggests to the wealthy man that not all things or people could be bought. I contend that the story line did not occur in the opposite form (wealthy woman offering $1 million to sleep with a married man) because it would not present the same emotionally agonizing dilemma in light of the differential costs associated with an extramarital dalliance. *Shallow Hal* (2001) is a comedy wherein an otherwise shallow buffoon (played by Jack Black) is "reprogrammed" by Anthony Robbins (the motivational guru) to view the internal beauty of women as external beauty markers. Hence, an unattractive and morbidly obese woman who is otherwise kind-hearted is perceived as beautiful and thin by the reprogrammed Shallow Hal whereas a vain, self centered, and mean-spirited supermodel is seen as ugly. There are two telling points here. First, note that the story line stipulates that a man have his definition of physical beauty reprogrammed. This is in line with the universal reality that men place greater import on beauty because it is rooted in their evolved sexuality. Second, the reprogramming story line is congruent with the SSSM position regarding tabula rasa minds. In other words, the mundane realism of this story line holds true only if it is assumed that Hal's innate and universal definition of beauty could indeed be drastically altered. In *Forty Days and Forty Nights* (2002), a young man (played by Josh Hartnett) decides to abstain from engaging in any sexual activity (including masturbation) as part of Lent. Would this central movie premise have been equally effective, believable, and relevant if the protagonist were a woman? Men and women do not respond in the same manner to the challenges of restraining from sexual release for 40 days, hence the story line is unlikely to have occurred in its opposite form. This reality is not due to arbitrary social construction. Rather, it is rooted in the evolved physiology of the two sexes in response to selection pressures associated with the mating module. In the 2002 movie titled *Dummy,* one of the lead female characters (Illeana Douglas) is seeking to disassociate from a sinister exboyfriend. She instructs her brother (Adrien Brody) to lie to the exboyfriend by telling him that she is dating a lawyer. Her logic is that this would infuriate the exboyfriend because he is "merely" an accountant. In other words, the likelihood of triggering jealousy and causing pain is in this case related to evolved cues of intrasexual rivalry. Men compete for status. As such, what better way to derogate the exboyfriend than to humiliate him by highlighting his defeat to a higher ranked competitor? In *25th Hour* (2002), Edward Norton's character (Monty Brogan) states the following in reference to how special his girlfriend is: "She's the only girl I've ever kept fantasizing about after I slept with her" (Kilik, Benioff, & Lee, 2002). In other words, Brogan is articulating the fact that he did not succumb to the Coolidge effect (loss of sexual interest in a female that one has already mated with), a phenomenon that has been documented in males across a wide range of species. Incidentally, the central story line of *Someone Like You* (2001) starring Ashley Judd and Hugh Jackman is based on the male-specific Coolidge effect (which is referred to at several points in the movie albeit via another term). Returning to *25th Hour,* as Brogan prepares to report to prison to serve a 7-year sentence, a Russian mobster provides him with some unsolicited advice regarding survival in prison. Brogan is told that he must beat up a man badly during his first night in prison as a means of cementing his reputation. This is a form of Zahavian signaling. Such an act would likely extend Brogan's sentence as well as expose him to injuries. This is why it would serve as an honest signal of his toughness and would accordingly augment his status while in prison. Honest signals have to be costly. Hence, the newcomer that is willing to incur such costs is viewed as dangerous and accordingly is avoided.

The 1995 movie *Braveheart* (starring and directed by Mel Gibson) chronicled the life of a 13th-century Scottish heroic warrior named William Wallace. At the start of the movie, a representative of the English king (Edward the Longshanks), upon entering a Scottish village with the king's soldiers, advises the Scottish peasants that it is within his right to invoke *jus primae noctis.* Wettlaufer (2000) provides evolutionary explanations for two sex-related behaviors, the *jus primae noctis* and ritual defloration, which were found in numerous disparate cultures and accordingly were discussed in various literary forms and local folklores. The *jus primae noctis* or *droit du seigneur* in French (which translates to right of the lord) was a practice found in several European cultures whereby a lord or other high-status male had the right of first sexual access to any woman under his rule who was about to wed. On a related note, ritual defloration was a practice whereby someone other than the groom-to-be would deflower a virgin in preparation of her impending wedding. More often than not, males of high status such as chiefs and priests would perform the defloration. Wettlaufer discusses several possible ultimate explanations for the latter institutionalized cultural practices. He proposes that both practices are manifestations of the ubiquitous link between despotic rule and reproductive success. In other words, men of high status implement policies that ensure that they have maximal access to nubile women who are under their rule. That said, Wettlaufer argues that in many instances, the right was not instantiated; rather, it served as an intrasexual display of male dominance. Irrespective of which is the correct ultimate explanation, these sexual practices are a window to evolved male sexuality. Providing evolutionary explanations for *jus primae noctis* and ritual defloration should not be confused with its condoning. However, as has been repeatedly shown in countless cultures spanning numerous distinct eras, despotic rule has its reproductive advantages (cf. Betzig, 1986). Hence, a literary scholar who wishes to analyze the discussion of such issues in the context of European literature of the Middle Ages could do so more completely by recognizing the Darwinian etiology behind the behaviors in question. Cultural forms (in this case, specific contents within this epic film) contain themes that are manifestations of our human nature.

In the current section, I have tried to show that movie themes contain universal elements that are indicative of a shared human nature. This is one of the reasons that successful movies will oftentimes achieve global reach irrespective of their country of origin. This is not to imply that there are no cross-cultural differences in cinematic genres. Rather, emotional triggers inherent to movie plots and themes are consumed in similar manners around the world because of a universally shared nature. I next turn to an analysis of song lyrics and accordingly demonstrate that the great majority of songs contain universal sex-specific elements that are highly indicative of men's and women's evolved sexualities.

Songs

Perhaps the most unequivocal finding when conducting an analysis of song lyrics is the overwhelming focus on romantic love, lust, and mating. Recently, B. L. Cooper (1999) concluded that "romantic involvements undergird the thematic attention of most singers and songwriters" (p. 354). Horton (1957, see Table 1, p. 575) found that more than 85% of the songs analyzed dealt with love. Furthermore, this general pattern held true irrespective of the musical genres. Horton states:

> Though the country-song and Negro magazines belong in different musical subcultures and address different audiences from those of "standard" popular songs, all our major content categories are found in strikingly similar proportions in all four magazines (Table 2). There are minor differences in vocabulary and thematic emphasis but nothing to invalidate the supposition that these songs belong to a *common universe of discourse*. [italics added] (p. 570, footnote 4)

Not only are these themes common to the various musical genres within the United States, but they are also universally ubiquitous. Spanish, French, Arabic, or Hindi songs are no less focused on matters of the heart. Ostlund and Kinnier (1997) investigated the key themes addressed in the top 25 songs (as measured by *Billboard*) of each of four decades (1950s through the 1980s). Consistent with works that they cite, the authors found that romantic love was the overwhelmingly most frequent theme covered in each of the four decades. They conclude that the universal focus on romantic love is unaffected by societal trends. An evolutionary perspective explains why such a universal drive might exist and accordingly why it would be impervious to any societal and other environmental changes. Finally, and contrary to social constructivists who propose that song lyrics shape teenagers' behaviors and value systems, Ostlund and Kinnier state that the literature hardly warrants such an unequivocal conclusion (see Weisfeld, 1999, for an evolutionary account of adolescence). The evolutionary framework recognizes that it is the innate drives behind teenage sexuality that shape the contents of song lyrics rather than the opposite causal link. Dukes, Bisel, Borega, Lobato, and Owens (2003) conducted a content analysis of the 100 all-time most popular songs covering the period 1958–1998. They cite several studies highlighting that not only are love songs the most common types of songs written but also they can be found in all important demographic groups including distinct cultural and racial groups, gender lines, and age cohorts. In their content analysis, Dukes et al. found that the proportion of love songs within the covered time period did not change. Thus, despite both the universality of love songs and their ubiquity across temporal periods, the authors did not construe this as being indicative of an innate human nature (in this case linked to the mating module). Rather, song lyrics were analyzed from a socialization-based and environment-centric perspective. For example, the opening sentence of the article reads as follows: "Popular music lyrics follow cultural trends, and lyrics chronicle new societal developments" (p. 643). On the same page, the authors add, "Kalof (1993) argued that the sexual imagery of many songs is so powerful that it ultimately defines what is masculine and what is feminine." Hence, the SSSM served as the theoretical base for the subsequent analysis. Instead of positing that in part song lyrics serve as a forum wherein innate sex-based issues dealing with human mating are expressed, the opposite causal relationship is proposed. Specifically, it is argued that masculinity and femininity among many other behaviors and norms are learned via the songs that people listen to, a proposition congruent with the empty-slate premise. Evolutionists would certainly concede that song lyrics do reflect shifting societal trends. For example, the lyrics of Motown love songs of the 1960s are sexually less graphic as compared to those in gangsta rap songs. This is in part due to the societal shifts regarding the overt discussion of sexuality. Hence, when Dukes et al. state, "Additionally, the trends in music may be a response to teenage pregnancy, single parenthood, abuse and sexually transmitted diseases" (p. 649), they are correct that social movements are reflected in song lyrics. That said, despite the fact that song lyrics may contain contents that are both culture-specific and temporally bound, there exists a set of themes that are universally present. It is these ubiquitous themes that are within the purview of the evolutionist.

In the last chapter, I explored the depiction of women in advertising from an evolutionary perspective. A similar endeavor can be performed in the context of song lyrics. B. L. Cooper (1998) provided an exhaustive set of references that have explored the manner by which women are depicted in song lyrics. As is the case for the great majority of popular-culture scholars, the assumption is that lyrical images serve as key socialization agents. For example, Cooper states, "Hopefully, these print resources will add light to the ongoing discussion and debate concerning the role of popular music imagery in *socialization processes* [italics added]" (p. 81). Social constructivists reject the possibility that temporally and culturally invariant images and themes might be indicative of a universal human nature. More recently, B. L. Cooper (1999) proposed that in analyzing the depiction of women in song lyrics, one should move away from politicized ideologies (e.g., radical feminism). Rather, Cooper argues that women are portrayed in countless manners, all of which correspond to the multiplicity of roles that women occupy in any given society. That said, Cooper did not recognize that recurring themes and contents exist in their particular forms (e.g., extolling of women's beauty) because they are manifestations of a universal human nature. Scheurer (1990) provided a qualitative analysis of the depiction of women in popular songs of the 1930s. He argues that contrary to songs from an earlier era that seemed to have a clear dichotomy between the virgin and the vixen, the types of women depicted in the songs of the 1930s were more varied and included the femme fatale, the goddess, the golddigger, and the sophisticated lady. Scheurer proposes several environmental factors that apparently led to the changes in the depiction of women in popular music (e.g., the economic strife of the Depression). The importance of the environment in shaping culture, and its influence as a socialization agent, is implicit in Scheurer's analysis. An evolutionary perspective proposes that although societal and economic conditions might affect the contents of popular culture, many themes are temporally invariant and culturally universal. For example, the whore–madonna dichotomy can just as easily be found in today's rap lyrics as it was in the songs of the 1920s. This particular dichotomy speaks to men's differential sexual behaviors as a function of whether they are engaging in short- versus long-term mating (as per sexual strategies theory). The golddigger (and possibly femme fatale) is an archetype that describes an important element of female mating behavior, namely the predisposition to seek males with resources. This is not a strategy that is exclusively bound to the 1930s; rather, it is found across all eras and cultures (see Kanye West's 2005 Grammy-winning song titled "Gold Digger" wherein he refers to cuckoldry as an additional attack on men's interests). Scheurer concludes:

> There is, however, an element of consistency in all the images in that they contribute to an iconology of "woman" in general. ... In this way the culture is able to reconcile the immediate present with the ideal and the transcendent or what they feel to be universal. (p. 36)

The universal element that Scheurer speaks of is due to evolved sex-specific realities that are not bound by time or place.

E. D. Kuhn (1999) explored the alluring lyrics found in blues songs using speech act theory. This approach to understanding sexual dynamics via a methodical analysis of linguistic categories is reminiscent of deconstructionism with its central focus on language as a means by which reality is constructed. Kuhn's approach is surprising given that her introductory paragraph alludes to the fact that blues songs contain lyrics that carry much ecological validity (i.e., blues lyrics capture real-life speech). For example, she pronounces, "They are sung in a way that each woman in the audience could feel herself addressed directly. And the forms the requests in them take show that that assessment is quite realistic" (p. 533). To understand this form of communication with its sexually laden connotations, a greater focus on evolved human sexuality and lesser so on linguistic deconstructionism is needed. I provide herein a few examples to highlight the differences between the two approaches. Kuhn states (p. 529) that the lyrics contain numerous long-term promissory statements of loyalty and devotion as made by male singers. That men would display a proclivity to provide long-term investments to a prospective mate is central to evolved courtship rituals. She then adds that when seeking sex, male singers will highlight the fact that they are providing resources and hence women should reciprocate by agreeing to mate. An evolutionary perspective recognizes that the resources-for-sex exchange almost always occurs in the same sex-specific direction irrespective of the cultural setting. Kuhn concludes as follows:

> This preliminary study has focused on songs written and mostly performed by men because those were the most numerous. There are some songs by women singers in which they, the women, try to convince a man to make love to them. However, such songs are rarer. *That may be because this particular speech act has been used traditionally by men* [italics added]. Women, when they were assertive, approached the issue from the opposite end as in "Baby get lost," or they were singing to a lover who needed no convincing as in "Do what you did last night." (p. 533)

Hence, Kuhn proposes that the reason that men are more likely to be the ones to convince women to have sex is due to the fact that they are the ones more likely to engage in this particular speech act. The Darwinian framework recognizes the existence of a differential proclivity of each sex to seek mating opportunities. This sex-specific and universal difference is rooted in the evolved mating strategies of the two sexes and accordingly has little to do with the frequency with which each sex might or might not engage in a given speech act. For a more complete understanding of song lyrics (especially as relating to human mating), one should look to evolutionary psychology with its focus on the innate forces that shape human sexuality.

Manuel (1998) investigated gender dynamics in Caribbean songs via both analyses of relevant song lyrics and interviews with consumers of these musical genres. Although he did not utilize an evolutionary framework in guiding his research, the findings were compatible with Darwinian-based expectations. For example, an evolutionary account of human mating would suggest that men are much more likely to sing about multiple sexual conquests and about the dangers of cuckoldry. This is what Manuel found in his analysis when he states:

> While men boast of their sexual conquests and demand that women submit to them, they denounce promiscuous women and rail against perceivedly [sic] false accusations of paternity. Male irresponsibility is celebrated, and women are repeatedly portrayed as valuable only for sex. Jamaican dancehall deejays typically clarify that they offer women only sex, rather than commitment, while at the same time deriding as prostitutes women who demand some material compensation for their favors. (p. 12)

> Several Latino students referred to incidents sparked by song lyrics, such as alleged murders in Puerto Rico supposedly provoked by men being taunted as "*venado*" [italics in original] or cuckold, in the wake of Ramon Orlando's popular *merengue* [italics in original] by that name. (In local folklore, the horns of the *venado* [italics in original], or stag, grow when it is being cuckolded.) (p. 15)

The same expression exists in Arabic (Lebanese dialect). Specifically, a woman who cuckolds her husband is said to be "constructing him horns." As such, there appears to be a cross-cultural commonality in the use of this term. Given the substantial linguistic and cultural differences not to mention the geographic distance between Puerto Rico and Lebanon, the common term speaks to a universal male concern with paternity uncertainty. Hence, not only are humans equipped with a universal and innate module for language acquisition (as per the works of Noam Chomsky and Steven Pinker), but also certain linguistic expressions are shared across otherwise disparate languages because they describe a phenomenon of universal evolutionary import.

Manuel (1998) provides numerous examples of the ubiquitous themes that are addressed by leading male dance hall artists. He states, "In dancehall, as in much hardcore rap music, male boasting and the portrayal of women only as sex objects have in fact become stock themes" (p. 17). He makes reference to a song by Beenie Man wherein men who spread their genes extensively are viewed with much admiration. He provides an excerpt from Lord Shorty's song titled "Sixteen Commandments" regarding male infidelity and male insistence of female fidelity (p. 20). Thus, it would seem that these Jamaican male artists sing about short-term sexual dalliances with multiple women. They condone the sexual double standard, which stipulates that it is acceptable for them to sleep around but not for their women to do so. They appear to be concerned about paternity uncertainty. What can explain these lyrical contents? According to Manuel (p. 18), socioeconomic reasons are to be blamed for these sexist song lyrics. Specifically, the increased social and economic emancipation of Jamaican women has caused a backlash against them. Manuel proposes that male singers can participate in this backlash by writing sexist lyrics. No culture has yet to be uncovered where men are uninterested in sexual variety and/or in short-term mating opportunities. Similarly, the concerns regarding the threats of cuckoldry as well as the existence of the sexual double standard are not restricted to Jamaican society. Manuel's "backlash" explanation fails to explain why men's recorded sexual behaviors display robust similarities across innumerable cultures and epochs.

Politicized analyses, as discussed by Manuel, oftentimes yield contradictory positions. For example, the Jamaican female singer Patra is both hailed for being overtly sexual (hence challenging the sexual double standard) while being blamed for positioning herself as a sexual object. Similarly, it is difficult to reconcile the feminist notion that popular music has a devastating effect on women's sense of self with the fact that they constitute such an important market for such products. Manuel (1998) states:

> One woman related that derogatory, hedonistic songs "let us know what guys are all about and warn us to be on the lookout." Several others stated that regardless of their attitudes toward perceivedly [sic] sexist music videos, they and their female acquaintances watched the women in them in order to keep up with fashions and know what to buy. (p. 17)

The socialization effect appears to be serving a valuable role here, namely by being an informational source regarding men's sexuality and more innocuously as a purveyor of fashion advice. Products cater to consumers' needs and wants. Hence, the contents of raunchy dance hall lyrics exist in their particular forms because these cater to the evolved sexualities of women and men respectively.

E. G. Armstrong (2002) analyzed the contents of blues and rap lyrics with an explicit focus on the presence of sexual violence in both musical genres. As alluded to by Armstrong (e.g., Table 1, p. 183), rap is a male-centered cultural form. In seeking to understand the reasons behind the greater consumption of this cultural form by males, evolutionary and politicized analyses arrive at radically different conclusions. An evolutionary perspective proposes that to the extent that males dominate the consumption of rap, its contents will reflect the evolved male psyche (e.g., multiple matings with beautiful, nubile, and willing women, cues of extravagant wealth). In other words, a Darwinian analysis recognizes that successful cultural products are congruent with the innate predispositions of the members of the relevant target market. On the other hand, a politicized analysis yields conclusions such as "Gangsta rap is rape" (Armstrong, 2002, p. 184) and "The very act of singing is an exercise in the assertion of male control" (Armstrong, 2002, p. 188).

Black music, be it soul, hip-hop, R & B, or rap, provides an opportunity to explore our innate human nature because these cultural forms are irreverent to concerns of political correctness. In other words, there is a raw truth that is communicated in such lyrics that is candid and honest. I am not speaking here of objectionable language or of overtly misogynistic contents as examples of candor. Rather, I am referring to the fact that men and women openly sing about their respective desires for beautiful women and powerful men. I recently began a project to explore the lyrical contents of contemporary Black music as well as the images found in Black videos in order to explore various evolutionary-based predictions regarding universal mate preferences. For example, I predict that men are much more likely to sing about the physical attributes of women, to brag about their resources, and to display an interest in multiple mating partners. On the other hand, I posit that women are much more likely to seek resources and cues of power in prospective mates, and to be much less interested in engaging in indiscriminate sex. Anecdotally speaking, these findings manifest themselves in a clear manner in both song lyrics and music videos, of which I provide a few concrete instantiations next. I begin by identifying a few popular songs spanning a period of close to 30 years wherein female singers are highlighting the importance that they place on prospective mates having resources. In the classic soul song titled "Go Away Little Boy" sung by Marlena Shaw, she denigrates her soon-to-be ex-lover for lacking drive and ambition. Despite her proclamations to the contrary, she is equating manhood with a man's ability to amass resources. In the late 1970s and early 1980s, Sister Sledge had a string of successful disco songs including "We Are Family" and "He's the Greatest Dancer." In the latter song, the female singers hail the attractiveness of the dancer in question as determined in part by the social status that he is displaying via his attire. Several evolutionary-based studies have found that women judge the attractiveness of a man as a function of the status that is communicated via his wardrobe (cf. Townsend & Levy, 1990a). In the mid-1980s, Gwen

Guthrie's dance hit "Ain't Nothin' Goin' On but the Rent" made it clear that poor males need not approach her. The "romance without finance" chorus line subsequently made it into the popular-culture vernacular in part because it captures one of the central principles guiding women's mating behavior. More recently, two highly successful female groups namely TLC and Destiny's Child have each had a huge cross-over hit that specifically addresses the undesirability of a poor, lazy, and unambitious man as a prospective mate ("No Scrubs" and "Bills, Bills, Bills"). Finally, Missy Elliott, a contemporary female R & B artist, pushes the point further in her song titled "Hot Boyz" in arguing that the men who she finds most attractive are those who have the resources to drive luxury cars, and who can afford to shower her with expensive gifts.

An evolutionary-based analysis recognizes that if women seek generous men with resources, then male singers will boast about possessing these and corresponding willingness to invest them in a given mate. Countless hip-hop songs with their corresponding videos depict young males showing off their extravagant resources while surrounded by innumerable young and beautiful women. This phenomenon is so prevalent that one simply needs to watch any block of videos on BET to confirm this finding. That said, I wish to briefly describe a behavior that is consistently depicted in videos wherein male singers engage in a form of Zahavian signaling. In his recent hit song titled "I'm So Fly," Lloyd Banks, a currently popular hip-hop artist and rapper, is shown throwing away a large wad of money. This action is repeatedly found in rap and hip-hop videos (e.g., Chingy's "Balla Baby"). It is a manifestation of Zahavian signaling; namely, the artist (typically male) is conveying the fact that he is so fit (i.e., rich) that he is capable of engaging in extravagantly wasteful actions such as throwing his money away.

Song lyrics have served as the impetus for a well-known psychology study. Pennebaker et al. (1979) found that men's minimal acceptable levels of physical attractiveness when seeking prospective partners at a bar are relaxed the closer that it gets to closing time (i.e., when desperation sets in). The research was prompted by song lyrics in a country-and-western song by Mickey Gilley (1975) titled "Don't the Girls All Get Prettier at Closing Time". An evolutionary perspective based on the parental investment hypothesis (Trivers, 1972) would posit that only men's criteria might be relaxed, especially when seeking a mate for a short-term dalliance. That women are much less likely to have malleable minimal criteria is due to the greater costs they will accrue if a suboptimal suitor is chosen.

To summarize, the contents of song lyrics are fertile ground for studying human mating for they provide a direct window to the psyche of the two sexes. Rather than proposing that song lyrics are a source of "arbitrary" socialization, a more accurate causal link suggests that to the extent that songs have universally common elements, these are indicative of an evolved human nature. Troubadours, lyricists, and poets generate material that has broad reach because the themes that are typically addressed are culturally invariant and temporally unbound. In the ensuing section, I turn to a cultural form that has become indispensable to contemporary pop musicians, namely the music video, and similarly assert that its contents are indicative of our evolved sexuality.

Music Videos

Research on music videos has largely consisted of either content analyses (e.g., how each sex is portrayed), or studies that explore the effects of this cultural product on the viewing audience. Generally speaking, the premise that music videos yield harmful effects has not been supported by the research. Furthermore, the assumption that the postulated damaging effects will be sex-specific (e.g., women's self-concepts will be negatively affected) has also been invalidated. Andsager and Roe (2003) have concluded that "research findings indicate that gender is not the main determinant of an individual's liking or understanding of a video's message" (p. 84). In light of the paucity of evidence arising from the latter research stream, I restrict my discussion to content-analytic studies.

Baxter, De Riemer, Landini, Leslie, and Singletary (1985) identified 23 content areas that were most often depicted on MTV videos. Sex, friendship, and wealth were in the top eight categories, which is perhaps not surprising given their evolutionary import. Because of the utilized coding scheme, the other five categories cannot be easily mapped onto specific Darwinian domains (visual abstraction, dance, violence, celebration, or isolation). For example, the depiction of violence might be intra- or intersexual (i.e., all-male fight vs. male–female conflict); as such, the evolutionarily relevant domain is somewhat different depending on the contextual setting. That said, the key themes that continue to be shown in music videos are those that cater to our evolved Darwinian modules (i.e., sex, friendship, and status). In referring to the sexual stimuli shown in videos, Baxter et al. conclude, "Questions regarding the impact of this portrayal [sexual stimuli] on adolescent socialization, peer relationships, and modeling are raised" (p. 336). Hence, according to the latter scholars, sexuality does not seem to contain any innate elements; rather, in part it is learned via the viewing of music videos.

How are the two sexes depicted in music videos? Countless studies have found that women are much more likely to be represented as sexual objects. In a longitudinal study of music videos, Vincent (1989) found that although women were shown as equal to men, there was an increase in both female provocative attire and nudity. Vincent, Davis, and Boruszkowski (1987) also found that women were more likely to be sexually depicted, as did Andsager and Roe (1999) in their study of country-music videos. They concluded that there is a "symbolic annihilation" of women via the images that are used to depict them in music videos. Andsager and Roe (2003) recently reviewed two decades of research on the use of sexual imagery in music videos. They conclude that not only does such imagery contain certain recurring forms (e.g., women are more likely to be shown as sexual objects) but also it appears to be increasing. The literature was interpreted from an SSSM and "victimization" perspective. For example, they discuss (p. 87) the fact those female artists in country music who engaged in "ritualized subordination" (e.g., by being scantily clad) were more likely to be thinner and younger than those who did not. This would likely be a good example of "the ways that sexual imagery in particular is employed to convey messages through symbolism and stereotypical portrayals" (p. 80). Later in the article, they refer to videos where male artists are depicted as picking female audience members for casual liaisons. They conclude:

> The notion of displaying an artist's influence by implying that his status drives women's sexuality is powerful for both male and female audiences. Males learn that women are easily swayed sexually, that intimacy is not important. Females are shown, once again, that their bodies are what men desire, not their minds or ideas. Thus, music video can be readily criticized for its reinforcement of outdated, harmful sexual mores. (p. 94)

Thus, "outdated" socialization forces apparently teach women to be attracted to high-status males while informing men to be sexually interested in women's bodies. However, universal mating preferences suggest both that women are desirous of high-status males, and that men are sexually aroused by women's bodies. Hence, video images exist in their particular forms because they are an accurate representation of our evolved sexuality. No one questions the fact that both women and men are multidimensional beings who should not be solely judged on their beauty and status respectively. That said, to argue that videos are one of the mediums that teaches us these otherwise universal sex-specific preferences is misguided. Video directors are in the business of making commercially successful products. Hence, the images that they create within this medium correspond to those that appeal to their target market's innate preferences, wants, and needs. Music videos are shaped by our innate human nature. Social constructivists within this research stream postulate the opposite causal link.

In addition to exploring the prevalence in which men and women are sexually depicted, content analyses have also investigated the behavioral traits that seem to appear in consistently sex-specific manners. Among their key findings, Sommers-Flanagan, Sommers-Flanagan, and Davis (1993) found that men were depicted as both more dominant and more aggressive, whereas women were more likely to be the recipient of various forms of sexual advances. Seidman (1992) explored the manner by which men and women are depicted on MTV videos along 14 coded behaviors. He found that men were depicted as more adventuresome, more aggressive, more dominant, more victimized, and more violent. On the other hand, women were represented as more affectionate, more dependent, more fearful, more nurturing, more likely to both pursue and be pursued sexually, and more likely to wear sexually revealing clothes (strongest effect). Seidman provides socialization-based explanations with regard to the latter findings; namely, they are supposed manifestations of the sex-role stereotypes of American culture. An evolutionary perspective recognizes that these sex-specific findings are not restricted to American culture given that men are the more dominant, violent, and aggressive sex in all documented cultures. Seidman (1999) conducted a follow-up study using the same 14 behaviors, of which 6 yielded sex differences. Men were depicted as more adventuresome and more violent, whereas women were more affectionate, nurturing, more likely to be pursued sexually, and more likely to wear sexually revealing clothes. This last effect was by far the most significant one. Thus, the pattern of findings was the same as that of his earlier study, albeit fewer variables yielded significant effects. Congruent with the tabula rasa premise, he proclaimed, "Sex-role behavior and stereotyping of occupational roles are learned beginning at an early age, with the mass media, especially television, exerting a powerful influence" (p. 18). As such, despite the cross-cultural and temporal invariance of these sex-specific effects, Seidman relies on the social constructivist paradigm in interpreting his findings.

Thus far, I have concentrated on newer cultural forms including those found in television, movies, and contemporary music. I next turn to a much older cultural form, namely literature. This is followed by a discussion of one of the most successful forms of contemporary books, namely the self-help genre. I conclude the chapter by exploring two of the oldest instantiations of human culture, namely religion and art.

Literature

Literary criticism, as an academic discipline, has been recently dominated by a courant of intellectual relativism. Hence, a given novel can be studied from a Marxist, Foucaultian, Lacanian, Freudian, feminist, queer, Afro-centric, poststructuralist, and/or countless other perspectives. It can be deconstructed as per the guidelines established by Jacques Derrida. This deconstruction is supposedly necessary because reality is constructed by language. In other words, there is no such thing as reality outside of the inherent linguistic constraints. Language creates reality. Joseph Carroll, who has been at the forefront of applying Darwinian theory in understanding literature, provides caustic rebuttals to many of these tenets. Next, I provide two of his representative quotes that capture the folly of desconstructionist rhetoricians and related movements:

> If the human sciences and the humanities, as twentieth-century academic disciplines, had become intimately affiliated with the biological conception of human nature, it seems likely that they would have achieved a much higher degree of reasoned consensus within and among their own disciplines, and they would thus have presented a stronger defensive front to the overt irrationalism that now dominates the humanities and that has also begun to invade the social sciences. (Carroll, 1995, pp. 124–125)

> The belief that merely by changing the names of things we can change the things themselves—is naturally most prominent among people whose rhetoric normally has no immediate practical impact on anything except their own position within the academic bureaucracy; it is prominent above all, that is, among literary academics. People whose verbal formulations are susceptible to falsification through experience—say scientists, engineers, businessmen, or soldiers—would very likely be astonished by the declaration that "we make things what they are by naming them in one way or another." (Carroll, 1995, pp. 125–126)

Several other evolutionary-minded literary scholars have joined in the mordant criticism of these movements. For example, Boyd (1998) states:

> Literature departments around the world became mesmerized by the way of Roland Barthes, Jacques Derrida, Michel Foucault, and Jacques Lacan drew on the limited linguistics of Ferdinand de Saussure to concur that "Man does not exist prior to language, either as a species or as an individual." The new gospel of Theory, propelled with the messianic self-assurance of its prophets, spread through the humanities and the social sciences. What their converts failed to realize was that to follow parochial Paris intellectual fashion meant not only to exclude the world outside language but to ignore some of the major intellectual developments of our time in the understanding of human nature. (p. 1)

How do evolutionists propose that one should study literary creations? The answer is the same as for all other products of culture that I have addressed thus far. Specifically, literature moves us because it typically addresses universal themes that are evolutionarily relevant. Returning to Joseph Carroll's work, he states, "Consider that the vast bulk of fiction consists in personal interactions constituted primarily by combinations of motives involving mating strategies, family dynamics, and social strategies devoted to seeking status and forming coalitions" (Carroll, 1999, p. 373). He then adds:

All formal literary structures are prosthetic developments of evolved cognitive structures that serve adaptive functions. So long as theorists think of literature as purely emotional and expressive, they will be impeded in the effort to analyze the cognitive mechanisms and sociobiological functions of formal literary structures. (Carroll, 1999, p. 376)

In the remainder of this section, I describe studies that have investigated specific literary products from an evolutionary perspective.

Stiller, Nettle, and Dunbar (2003) conducted a sociometric study of the social networks within some of the most famous Shakespearean plays. Specifically, their goal was to demonstrate that the sociometric reality as depicted in fictional works conforms to that which has defined the phylogenetic history of our species. For example, the number of characters constituting a social network, the number of characters engaging in a given interaction, and the connectedness of the characters were in line with actual metrics derived from numerous real-world networks (e.g., hunter-gatherer societies). In accordance with Hamlet's edict that a successful drama should serve as an accurate reflection of the natural world (Act 3, Scene 2), Shakespearean plays are in part universally successful because they accurately capture social dynamics and networks that ring true across cultures and settings. Gottschall, Martin, Quish, and Rea (2004) performed a content analysis of two rich, albeit infrequently used, sources of data with the hope of establishing the universality of mate selection criteria. Specifically, they analyzed folktales and European literature to determine whether the mate preferences captured in these narratives, such as the differential importance placed on physical attractiveness and social status by men and women respectively, are indeed universal. The data set on folktales originated from an extraordinarily varied set of cultures, making it difficult for social constructivists to argue that a universal pattern is due to cultural transfer or social construction. The aggregate findings were highly supportive of the evolutionary literature on human mating, namely men (women) place greater value on physical attractiveness (wealth/social status), and both sexes value kindness, albeit this trait is valued more by women. Thiessen and Umezawa (1998) concentrated on a single Japanese novel (*The Tale of Genji*) written approximately a thousand years ago, which captured life in a society that was fully removed from Western ideals and norms. Hence, it would be difficult if not impossible for critics to argue that Western media and other socialization agents influenced the novel's contents. Thiessen and Umezawa found that the key themes were fully congruent with the universal tenets of evolutionary theory. Hence, a temporally distant and geographically isolated society manifested the same set of behavioral patterns as that of any contemporary culture.

Salmon and Symons (2003) provided an evolutionary account of slash fiction, which is a genre of romance novel that is predominantly targeted to and read by women. In doing so, they proposed that the contents of products of popular culture are demonstrative of various facets of human nature. For example, they state:

> One way in which erotica can be used to illuminate human sexual psychologies is to compare commercially successful products with less successful ones. ... Best-selling romance novels, for example, almost never feature gentle, sensitive heroes, because women readers prefer to fantasize about strong, confident men who ultimately are tamed only by their love for the heroine." (p. 58)

On pages 63–64, the authors describe a study conducted by April Gorry wherein she performed a content analysis of 45 romance novels (i.e., a cultural product that caters to women's evolved sexuality). Gorry obtained several findings, all congruent with evolutionary expectations. First, men were almost always older than their female counterparts, and in the 20 novels where both ages were provided, the average difference in age was 7 years. Second, heroes were always described as taller than was the heroine. In 44 of the novels, the hero was described as being tall. Third, the most frequent physical characteristics used to describe heroes (number of novels in which a description appears is shown in parentheses) were muscular (45), handsome (44), strong (42), large (35), tanned (35), masculine (33), and energetic (32). Fourth, the most frequently occurring adjectives used to describe a hero's physical and social competence included being sexually bold (40), calm (39), confident (39), intelligent (38), and impulsive (34). The authors conclude, "In not a single case was a hero described as short, skinny, fat, non-muscular, ugly, weak, small, pale, effeminate or lethargic" (p. 64). They continue, "No hero was described as sexually inhibited, nervous, timid, clumsy, or fearful in the face of a life-threatening challenge. ... No heroes were described as unintelligent" (p. 64). Finally, the most common feelings that the hero had toward the heroine included (as listed on p. 64) being sexually desirous (45), declaring his love (45), wanting the heroine more than he has ever wanted a woman (45), having never been so deeply in love (45), experiencing intrusive thoughts about the heroine (44), being gentle with the heroine (but not in general) (44), considering the heroine unique (43), wanting to protect the heroine (41), being possessive of the heroine (39), and being sexually jealous of the heroine (36). The study revealed that not a single hero was described as possessing the opposite of the latter traits and/or feelings. Most social constructivists would argue that romance novels are providing an arbitrary (or perhaps patriarchal) definition of masculinity, which then serves to socialize otherwise empty minds. On the other hand, evolutionists propose that culturally and temporally invariant depictions of masculinity exist in their particular form because they cater to women's evolved preferences regarding ideal prospective suitors (see Whissell, 1996, for another evolutionary-based analysis of mating issues as discussed in women's fiction).

E. O. Wilson's call for consilience across disparate human endeavors (Wilson, 1998) is particularly relevant when studying literature because literary theory has historically been isolated from the key developments in the natural and biological sciences. We now have the necessary tools and theories to develop an all-encompassing meta-theory of literary content. Carroll (1999) proclaimed:

> If we can formulate a theory and a methodology that link our deep evolu-
> tionary history, our evolved psychological structures, our cultural his-
> tory, and the formal structures of literary texts, we shall have made a
> major contribution to the advancement of scientific knowledge. This is a
> goal worth working towards, and it is within our reach. (p. 379)

A supratheory of literary content rooted in Darwinian principles not only would recognize that some story lines possess universal appeal but also would provide ultimate-based explanations for these (cf. Gottschall & Wilson, 2006).

Self-Help Books

Over the past 20 years, the self-help literature has constituted one of the most read genres of books. Countless books have been written about innu-merable self-help topics. That said, I propose that the most frequently ad-dressed issues map onto the key Darwinian modules. In other words, the domains along which people require and seek help are, evolutionarily speaking, those that are instrumental. I do not wish to imply that every sin-gle self-help book that has ever been written caters to a Darwinian drive, for this would certainly be indicative of just-so storytelling. The *For Dum-mies* series contains countless books that have little to do (directly, that is) with innate motives (e.g., *Sewing for Dummies, eBay Timesaving Techniques for Dummies, Senior Dogs for Dummies,* and *Fly Fishing for Dummies*). How-ever, a great majority of self-help books deal with a very restrained set of is-sues including dieting, exercise, relationships, sexuality, parenting, and the attainment of power and acquisition of resources. The infamous Atkins diet regime has amassed exceptional commercial success in an otherwise cluttered market, because its central tenets are in line with our evolved gustatory preferences. Imagine telling someone that they can engage in guilt-free all-you-can-eat fat. This is a diet that most individuals would not mind being permanently on. Dr. Spock, the notorious pediatrician and one-time U.S. presidential candidate, was instrumental in influencing a generation of parents in terms of their rearing techniques. Spock was able to latch onto the neuroses of a generation of parents that had experienced parental guilt stemming from the psychoanalytical movement (with its focus on blaming parents for every imaginable ill). Countless exercise programs offer promissory selling points that are instinctively attractive because they guarantee great results with minimal effort. The phylogenetic history of most species is such that energy and caloric conservation is a highly desirable objective, as evidenced by its central position in optimal foraging models. Hence, most individuals are more than happy to buy into the promise of an otherwise fictional account of reaping maximal exercise-related health and aesthetic benefits in minimal time spent. Status-related self-help books fall into one of two types, those that provide strategies for becoming wealthy and those that provide tools for social ascendancy. The former include numerous books on investment strategies (e.g., how to invest in real estate and/or the stock market), and personal financial responsibility (e.g., how to save more than spend). On the other hand, books that provide mechanisms for ascending the social hierarchy include the classic Dale Carnegie treatise on winning and influencing friends, the more recent *Seven Habits of Highly Effective People,* and Anthony Robbins' *Awaken the Giant Within.* Finally, many self-help books promise better relationships (less conflict, more understanding, greater prospects for mutual growth), hotter monogamous sex, guaranteed female orgasms, the ability to tell when one's partner is cheating, and the ability to eradicate a partner's (typically a man's) desire to cheat.

Coleman and Ganong (1987) conducted a content analysis of 11 self-help books meant to address problems that arise in stepfamilies. There were several noteworthy findings, all of which are congruent with an evolutionary perspective of stepfamilies (cf. Daly & Wilson, 1988, for such an account). Of the 11 books, 10 addressed loyalty conflicts, 9 tackled the "wicked" stepparent issue (see Daly & Wilson, 1999, for an evolutionary account of the so-called Cinderella effect), and 8 discussed step-sibling conflicts. Other popular topics included jealousy, territory, and changes in birth order, all issues seemingly related to parental investment. One of the analyzed books apparently mentioned that stepfathers are concerned about the waste of resources (e.g., gas, food, etc.). Once again, this makes evolutionary sense in that stepfathers are unlikely to be particularly pleased at the idea of having to invest in their nonbiological children. This suboptimal use of one's paternal investment is handled in exceptionally brutal manners in certain species such as when an incoming dominant male lion seeks out and kills cubs that could not have been sired by him. Hence, when the authors concluded that the self-help books were much more likely to address negative aspects of being in a stepfamily as compared to the positives, this is expected from an evolutionary perspective. Stepfamilies are fertile ground for familial conflicts, the genesis of which is rooted in the Darwinian module of kin selection. Coleman and Ganong concluded that not a single book provided any empirical or clinical references in support of their contentions. On a related note, Johnson and Johnson (1998) cite research suggesting that self-help books are not founded on any empirically validated treatments, approaches, and/or findings. The therapeutic advice found in self-help books does not adhere to norms of scientific rigor (e.g., as is required by the Food and Drug Administration when testing the efficacy of drugs) because none of the self-help areas are guided by integrative meta-theories. To the extent that the majority of self-help topics deal with issues of evolutionary import, Darwinian principles might serve as the organizing rubric from which to test the validity of specific therapeutic advice.

Johnson and Johnson (1998, Table 3, p. 463) provide summary statistics of the frequency of self-help book recommendations made by therapists to their clients, as captured by 14 categories of self-help topics. These were addiction, anxiety, depression, child development and parenting, family, grief/loss, interpersonal skills, personal adjustment/improvement, spirituality, marriage, gender issues, sexuality, relationships, and top classics (consists of books included in the previous categories). If one were to loosely group the first three under the "health" heading, the next three under "family-related issues," the next three under "personal development," and finally the last four under "sexuality and relationships," one sees that there is a rather restricted set of topics that are addressed. This is a rough categorization given that some topics such as sexual addiction under the "health" category could have been reassigned to the "sexuality and relationships" category, or grief/loss could be categorized in either "family-related" issues or "sexuality and relationships" depending on who is being grieved. Notwithstanding the approximate nature of the latter categorization, I calculated that more than 50% of the recommended self-help books could be categorized within the "family" and "sexuality and relationships" categories. Regarding the original breakdown of 14 categories, I calculated that self-help books on depression were the most frequently recommended followed by those on marriage, sexuality, and child development and parenting. Given that depression is oftentimes symptomatic of failures in evolutionarily relevant pursuits (cf. Nesse, 2001), it would seem that most self-help books address a rather limited set of issues, all of which have evolutionary links.

Using a social constructionist and poststructuralist approach, Lyons and Griffin (2003) sought to explore the manner by which menopause is depicted in the self-help literature. They begin by describing four approaches in understanding menopause, namely the biomedical, sociocultural, feminist, and postmodernist approaches. They claim that whereas the biomedical approach consists of negative depictions of menopause, the other three modes of analysis provide positive views of meno-pause. In describing the feminist approach, Lyons and Griffin state:

> In a related approach, researchers working within the feminist paradigm view menopause as yet another biological experience which has been used to suppress women's positions and led to the social control of women via medicalisation. Menopause is seen as a natural female process which often has social and class implications. (p. 1630)

Regarding the postmodernist approach, the authors propose, "Physio-logical, social, historical and cultural dimensions of knowledge about menopause are attended to in this paradigm, and no one form of knowl-edge (i.e. empirical) is privileged above another" (p. 1630). In other words, the medical experts are merely espousing one viewpoint that is no better or superior to that which might be espoused by laypeople. All viewpoints are valid. In reviewing one of the four self-help books written by a journalist and supposedly informed by a feminist outlook, the authors claim, "Women's voices appear throughout the text and are given as much status as those of medical 'experts'" (p. 1633). Lyons and Griffin warn the readers that their analysis is constrained by the fact that they are White Western women approaching middle age, implying that the realities of menopause change as a function of who is conducting the analysis. Menopausal reali-ties including hot flashes, decreased libidinal drive, osteoporosis, mood swings, sleep disturbances (e.g., insomnia), drier skin, increased growth of body and facial hair, irregular heartbeat, vaginal dryness, incontinence, and weight gain are apparently socially constructed by the sexist medical community. The authors pit the "menopause as a disease" medical ap-proach against the "menopause as natural" feminist stance implying that the two positions are mutually exclusive. Menopausal symptoms are an inherent element of senescence and hence are natural. That said, seeking to alleviate menopausal symptoms that affect a woman's health and her quality of life is fully congruous with the realization that the symptoms are natural. Finally, the authors deconstructed the meaning of the word *com-plaint* (as used by one of the medical-oriented books) as when a meno-pausal patient has a complaint regarding her symptoms. They provide a dictionary definition to argue that the word *complaint* refers to being dis-satisfied. The implication here is that the medicalization of menopause causes women to be dissatisfied with their bodies. They add, "Within the care of a doctor, women are constructed as passive patients, being 'monitored' and 'looked after'" (p. 1638).

Rimke (2000) provided an equally conspiratorial analysis of the self-help literature, albeit in this case the government is the culprit. Using an amalgamation of Durkheimian and Marxist tenets, Rimke (p. 62) argues that the self-help literature misleads people into believing that they are in-dependent individuals capable of affecting changes in their lives, whereas in reality the self-help literature is apparently a means by which govern-ments control us. I provide two relevant quotes:

> Rather than viewing individuals and individualism as the historical product of intersecting social processes and cultural discourses, propo-nents of the principle of individuality, which is crucial in self-help rheto-ric, assume the social world to be the sum aggregation of atomized, autonomous and self-governing individual persons. Popular psychol-ogy's unilateral focus on individuals contributes to a world-view which erroneously postulates that people can exercise control and mastery of themselves and their lives. (p. 62)

> Practices of self-help are thus connected to the management and govern-ment of populations. Governing psychologized subjectivities through liberal political choice, freedom and autonomy ensures that norms of ob-ligation, accountability and responsibility continually turn the subject back on itself. This form of political rule shifts the necessity for social re-sponsibilities to the domain of hyper-individual responsibility. Through these norms, self-helpers are induced to assume the ultimate politics of personal self-rule. (p. 72)

It is unclear how much scientific value can be reaped from the construal of the self-help literature as a means by which the medical community and/or the government controls the populace.

Starker (1988) administered a survey to mental health professionals and found that a substantial majority read, found useful, and accordingly pre-scribed some of the leading self-help book titles to their patients. This was construed as particularly problematic given that "self-help titles, by and large, are repositories of unproven, sometimes unprovable, advice on mat-ters of considerable importance and complexity" (Starker, 1988, p. 453). In terms of the topics most often addressed by the leading self-help titles, per-sonal growth and family-related issues seemed to dominate. Starker states, "In an earlier study, parenting was the area most often selected for the pre-scription of self-help books; the next most often selected were personal growth and relationships" (p. 453). Though it is unclear why in this particu-lar study sexuality and relationships were minimally covered, the general consensus is rather unequivocal; namely, family and mating related issues are two of the most common topics discussed in the self-help literature.

Because sexuality and romantic relationships are some of the most fre-quently addressed topics in the self-help literature, it is perhaps not surpris-ing that of the few content analyses that have explored this literature, most have explored books that deal with these issues. True to the SSSM, the analy-ses are approached from a social constructivist (i.e., sexuality is constructed) and more often than not from a feminist perspective. I describe herein three recent studies that are representative of this approach. Zimmerman, Holm, and Haddock (2001) conducted a content analysis of the top 10 best-selling self-help books (as listed on the *New York Times* bestseller list) for the period 1988 to 1998. The goal of the analysis was to determine the extent to which a self-help book was viewed as either empowering or disempowering in promoting resistance to so-called gender socialization. The classification was based on whether the advice supported the ascribed gender roles or whether it taught men and women to break free of these supposedly "arbitrary" shackles. Hence, whenever a woman's looks or a man's professional prestige were mentioned as important mating preferences, this was indicative of disempowerment. Barbara DeAngelis was taken as an example of a self-help author who is particularly empowering. Given the authors' starting premise that gender roles are socially constructed, it is not surprising that DeAngelis would be perceived as the epitome of the "liberating" author because she views everything as due to socialization. For example, Zimmerman, Holm, and Haddock provide a quote by DeAngelis (p. 129) wherein she chastises women for caring about a man's earning potential when there are so many loving and loyal low-status males ready to commit. DeAngelis proposes that women have been programmed (supposedly by societal norms) to care about a man's status. Women's mating preferences are rooted in the dual forces of natural and sexual selection, and as such are not due to arbitrary socialization. To the extent that socialization teaches women to be attracted to high-status males, evolutionists would expect that such learning would be consistent with evolved mating preferences. Books that were coded as disempowering by Zimmerman, Holm, and Haddock were those that proposed that there does exist innate differences between the two sexes. Zimmerman, Holm, and Haddock state, "No books explicitly stated that the author supported oppression or sexism. Nonetheless, *several books supported the status quo of oppression and sexism by maintaining that gender differences are innate* [italics added] and the way they are supposed to be" (p. 127). Later, the authors add:

> The more disempowering books were based on a thesis that gender differences are innate and the "way things are supposed to be;" the more empowering books emphasized the influence of socialization on perceived gender differences and the importance of resisting this socialization. (p. 129)

The authors also explored who the targeted readership was and which books achieved the greatest popularity. They conclude that of the 10 top-selling relationship maintenance books for 1988–1998, none were targeted solely to men. The authors were dismayed at the fact that the 4 most popular self-help books (of the 10 analyzed) were those that were apparently most disempowering (i.e., supporting stereotypical gender roles).

This is particularly problematic to feminists because women consume the great majority of these books. One proposed explanation regarding the latter finding was that although people may wish to change the ascribed gender roles, they are afraid of societal change, and hence passively accept the status quo. Accordingly, that women seem to read the most "sexist" books is a mere reflection of their fear of change.

In a related project, Zimmerman, Holm, and Starrels (2001) explored the number of the relevant top self-help books that were supportive of a feminist perspective when conducting relationship therapy or dispensing relationship advice. The coding mechanism was defined as follows:

> A score of 1 refers to gender being conceptualized as an inherent and immutable fact. Books that reflect this notion implicitly encourage readers to accept traditional (i.e., nature vs. nurture) gender roles. ... Books that address gender as socially constructed through processes such as socialization were assigned a score of 3. These books have the potential to empower readers, because they suggest that change is possible. (p. 168)

The authors add, "This view of gender [i.e., innately determined] does not empower readers to change or to make different choices for themselves due to the belief that these are unchangeable aspects of biology" (p. 168). There are several noteworthy theoretical errors in the latter two quotes, all part and parcel of the SSSM. This includes the belief in the moot nature–nurture dichotomy, as well as antiquated concerns regarding biological determinism, which are used to argue against innate sex differences and in favor of socialization. The belief that all sex differences are due to socialization implies that these can be unlearned. As the Darwinian literary critic Joseph Carroll (1995) remarked, "Biological thinking threatens to constrain the range of wishful thinking" (p. 126). Returning to Zimmerman, Holm, and Starrels (2001), Barbara DeAngelis is once more hailed as the bastion of a "healthy" feminist perspective as evidenced by the quotes that are attributed to her (see, e.g., on p. 171) regarding the fact that women should not care about a man's social status and men should cease to focus on a woman's beauty. In other words, DeAngelis purports that the latter preferences have nothing to do with innate forces shaping human mating despite the fact that every culture across every era has displayed these exact preferences. DeAngelis proposes that one simply needs to "unlearn" these supposed shallow preferences, and accordingly women could become irresistibly drawn to unemployed men and men might begin to solely focus on women's inner glow while forgoing any interest in their outer appearances. Zimmerman, Holm, and Starrels found that the five most popular (i.e., best-selling) books yielded the lowest "egalitarian" scores. In other words, the latter five books were the least likely to have a feminist outlook. The authors claim that the popularity of such books reflects a bias (on the part of both men and women) toward the status quo.

The latter explanation could not explain the second key finding, namely that a temporal analysis revealed that this nonfeminist outlook was becoming more pronounced. Thus, despite the efforts made by second-wave feminists to "reeducate" the masses regarding gender roles, the most popular self-help books are those that are least congruent with feminism, with this pattern becoming longitudinally more pronounced.

A third study conducted by Zimmerman, Holm, Daniels, and Haddock (2002) sought to identify the manner by which the relevant self-help books provide advice that either facilitates or hinders the attainment of intimacy and mutuality in relationships (e.g., mutual sexual pleasure). They set forth their theoretical premise by stating, "When considering which aspects of sexuality to analyze, the authors felt it was important to consult feminist literature because so much of sexuality is constructed through gender socialization (Gilbert & Scher, 1999)" (p. 291). Accordingly, the paper is replete with passages wherein numerous sexual behaviors and preferences are all attributed to socialization forces. For example, that men assiduously pursue women for sex, that they are more likely to initiate sex, that they focus on a woman's appearance, and that they seek unencumbered sexual liaisons, are elements of male sexuality that are supposedly merely learned. Thus, to the extent that the latter serve as hinderances to intimate and mutually satisfying relationships, individuals must extinguish their prior learning and accordingly must relearn "healthier" sex-based norms, behaviors, and preferences. Viewpoints that suggest that sex differences might be innate and not socially constructed are coded as an example of a barrier to intimacy and mutuality. For example, in coding one of the self-help books, the authors state, "In *Mars and Venus Starting Over,* Gray (1998) constructed a barrier to intimacy when he described men and women as innately different with regard to sexuality and intimacy" (p. 299). It is again erroneously assumed that to argue that something has a biological basis (e.g., sex-based differences in sexuality) is tantamount to arguing for biological determinism. The ascription of socialization forces to sexuality takes on a fevered pitch when the authors propose:

> Finally, men may respond to social messages that male sexual pleasure is more important than women's by disregarding their partners' sexual pleasure. On the other hand, given social expectations that men are knowledgeable about and skilled at sex, men may feel undue pressure to "perform" for female partners, prioritizing their partners' satisfaction over their own. (p. 294)

The latter quote covers all possible outcomes while attributing each to socialization. In this particular case, regardless of whether a man displays behaviors corresponding to his being a selfish or selfless lover, this is demonstrative of the pervasive influence of socialization in shaping human sexuality.

Providing accurate descriptions of sexual dynamics should be based on sound science instead of charlatanism (e.g., at least two of the most famous professed self-help gurus hold doctoral degrees from fictitious schools). The problem is further exacerbated when social scientists investigating the contents of self-help books (e.g., Zimmerman and her colleagues) perpetuate the inaccuracies via distorted ideological lenses. For example, one of the analyzed self-help books by Zimmerman et al. (2002) was coded as a barrier to mutuality because it suggested that men display sexual confidence and a take-charge attitude in the bedroom. Yet countless romance novels, soap operas, and erotica (which cater to women's sexuality) show that women prefer such men rather than tentative, sexually insecure, and weak men. Hence, an evolved preference that most women would agree is desirable for a man to sexually possess is viewed as a hindrance to mutuality when analyzed from a feminist perspective. The conclusions of Zimmerman et al. (2002) amount to a mix of feminist accusations and deconstructionist pronouncements. First, they conclude that "the gender-based messages in self-help books appear to be consistent with those in other forms of mass media" (p. 304). From their perspective, the patriarchy is likely to blame because it apparently controls all of the various mass media in question. In order to overcome this onslaught of sexism, they propose the following deconstructionist strategy:

> Therefore, when people use these books for relationships advice, they are not provided with the necessary information and tools for analyzing their relationships with a critical "gender lens," which is helpful in efforts to improve sexual relationships. More specifically, in order to achieve intimacy and mutuality in sexual relationships, couples must "deconstruct" or unlearn constraining messages that they have integrated about what it means to be a sexual man or woman. … An awareness of the larger social context with regard to gender socialization is essential in understanding the origin of these gender-based expectations in deconstructing the thoughts, emotions, and behaviors related to sexuality. (pp. 306–307)

Where do men learn the "harmful" relationship patterns that must subsequently be deconstructed and unlearned? According to Zimmerman et al. (2002), the pornography industry is in part to blame. They conclude:

> Unfortunately, few materials in the mass media provide examples of sexuality based on intimacy and mutuality. Instead, an abundance of materials are available that promote sexuality based on power differentials and stereotypic gender behaviors, which is epitomized by materials generated by the pornography industry. (p. 307)

An accurate worldview based on rigorous science rather than ideology is particularly important in the context of self-help books given that the consumers of such sources oftentimes constitute an emotionally fragile readership.

Though it might be argued that self-help books are useful in that they market hope and faith in one's self, perhaps no cultural practice has been more successful in providing humans with hope and solace as has religion. I turn to an analysis of this universal cultural form in the ensuing section.

Religion

The phylogenetic history of *Homo sapiens* is replete with several thousand religions, cults, and belief systems. Despite wide cross-cultural differences in belief systems (e.g., paganism vs. monotheistic religions or verbal vs. written religious traditions), religiosity is a human universal (cf. Grinde, 1996). The consumption of religion constitutes one of the most important cultural practices that *Homo sapiens* have engaged in over the past 10,000 years. It has shaped every imaginable human endeavor including literature, science, medicine, philosophy, morality, art, politics, warfare, as well as the consumption arena. Close to 500 years ago, one of the central complaints ushered by Martin Luther against the Catholic Church was directly linked to a "consumption" ritual that he felt was spiritually corrupt, namely the purchase of indulgences as a means of seeking salvation. In the contemporary setting, there are innumerable manifestations of religion that are relevant to the consumer scholar. Retail sales are dominated by the Christmas season. Television evangelism is a hugely profitable industry. The all-time best-selling book is the Bible. The sale of alcohol is prohibited in Islamic countries. Kosher dietary laws dictate food consumption for practicing Jews. That said, consumer scholars have been largely uninterested in studying the consumption-relevant aspects of religiosity. A recent search that I conducted on December 7, 2004, on ABI/INFORM revealed only four papers in the *Journal of Consumer Research* that included the words *religion* and *consumer* within the citation and abstract index. Consumer researchers who have investigated religion have typically sought to determine its relevance as a segmentation variable. That said, the actual consumption of religion (i.e., religion construed as an experiential product to be consumed) has largely been ignored (but see Goff & Gibbs, 1993, for an exploration of religious affiliation as a form of brand choice).

It is easy when studying religion to focus on the apparent cross-cultural differences in belief systems. Accordingly, religion is one area of study that is particularly emblematic of the apparent importance of culture in shaping human rituals. However, beneath the veneer of wide cross-cultural differences in religious traditions, there exist key universals (e.g., that all cultures possess a religious/spiritual narrative; see Shermer, 2003). Whenever human universals are uncovered, it typically falls on the evolutionists to provide parsimonious explanations for the existence of such cross-cultural commonalities. Dawkins (1976, 2003) has been at the forefront of applying memetics in explaining the persistence of religion as an integral element of human cultures. Dawkins argues that in the same manner that biological and computer viruses infect their respective hosts, the religion memeplex (a complex of interrelated memes) is particularly well suited to infect human minds (see also Blackmore, 1999). For example, religion utilizes our innate tendency to segment the world using the "us versus them" mentality (in-group vs. out-group logic) to create a sense of appartenance. In other words, the religion meme usurps our innate proclivity to engage in coalitional thinking (see also Kirkpatrick, 1999). From a memetic perspective, religion need not confer any adaptive advantage to have evolved as a viable element of human cultures. Rather, the mere fact that the religion memeplex contains certain properties that makes it accurately replicable and easily transmissible ensures that it will continue to spread within human populations. Other evolutionists have proposed radically different perspectives regarding the founding and maintenance of religious beliefs. One group has sought to identify the adaptive value of religiosity. The argument is that if religion is a universal phenomenon, it must confer adaptive advantage to those that hold onto such a belief system (cf. Steadman & Palmer, 1995, pp. 159–160). This is the position taken by Grinde (1998) regarding religion, when he states,"Anything which is universal to human culture is likely to have contributed to human survival, and anything that contribute [sic] to human survival will be selected for. Genes favoring such behavior will permeate the genetic pool of the species" (p. 20). Other evolutionists have made similar arguments regarding the adaptive advantages conferred by religion, albeit they have done so from a group selectionist perspective (D. S. Wilson, 2002; see MacDonald, 1994, for a discussion of Judaism as a group selection strategy). On a related note, Sosis and Bressler (2003) obtained mixed support for the hypothesis that the imposition of costly rituals to members of a group (e.g., religious group) improves group cohesion and hence predicts commune longevity. A third group of evolutionists has proposed that religion is a mere exaptation or by-product of an adaptive process. For example, Kirkpatrick (1999) proposes that religious narratives and rituals are replete with elements originating in key Darwinian modules. For example, Kirkpatrick argues that religions typically espouse a reciprocal relationship between the divine and humans, which is at times explicitly referred to as a covenant. The kin selection module is triggered whenever religious figures are addressed using kin terms such as *father, brother,* and *sister*. Other evolutionarily relevant mechanisms triggered by religion according to Kirkpatrick include attachment, coalitional thinking, and status concerns. Boyer (2001, 2003) also argues that religion is a by-product of evolution, although in his case he uses a computational approach in identifying the evolved cognitive processes and neural circuitry that are "borrowed" in the service of religious and spiritual thinking. Finally, another evolutionary-based approach for studying religion was applied by Richerson and Boyd (1989). They discuss the manner by which a specific religious belief can spread via gene–culture coevolution. Hence, from their perspective, neither memetic/cultural transmission nor gene-based formalisms can alone adequately explain certain forms of cultural learning. Rather, they have been staunch proponents of the dual-inheritance approach when modeling the evolution of cultural practices.

Not only can an evolutionary-based approach be used to study why religious narratives exist as human universals but also recurring themes contained within these narratives are amenable to a Darwinian-based analysis. Irrespective of whether one believes that religious texts and codes are divine revelation or are produced by mere mortals, one should expect that their contents be congruent with our evolved human nature. Hence, I would predict that religious narratives contain certain universally recurring contents precisely because they are reflective of our common Darwinian heritage. I provide herein one contemporary example, although many others could be discussed. The horrors of September 11th have made *Jihad* a household term understood by the majority of Americans. Most Westerners are now all too familiar with the terror that is inflicted by suicide bombers. One might question how such a behavior that has dire Darwinian consequences to the suicidal terrorist could be promulgated so easily to the masses of disenfranchised young Muslim men. If one wishes to "market" such an idea, how should they go about it? The best approach is to create a narrative with promissory rewards of great evolutionary import. Hence, prospective suicide bombers are told that they will be immortalized both in terms of their memory on earth and in their ascending to Heaven. Their families will typically receive money and increased status within the community. Finally, the suicide bomber in addition to being reunited with his Maker can engage in countless earthly pursuits such as having 72 virgins as mates (some have argued that the correct number is 70). Hence, within one religious narrative, the suicide bombers have been assured spiritual immortality, increased social status to both them and their families, and exceptional (and eternal) mating opportunities with young nubile virgins. On the other hand, young female suicide bombers are not promised 72 young virgin males once they reach Heaven. Undoubtedly, the marketers of this "religious" act are well aware that this is not a particularly persuasive selling point when targeting female suicide bombers.

Though suicide bombers are much more likely to be men, it is interesting to note that overall religiosity is much stronger in women. Stark

(2002) reviewed various explanations that have been proposed regarding the universal finding that women display greater religiosity as compared to men. In a first analysis, he listed data from 49 countries and showed that in 48 of these women claimed to be more religious. The listed countries originated from Oceania, South America, North America, Europe, Asia, and Africa. In a second analysis, he turned his focus to non-Christian countries (e.g., Islamic and Pacific Rim nations) and found that of 36 differences that were explored, 35 yielded that women were more religious. Furthermore, he reviewed historical data demonstrating that not only is the sex difference in question culturally invariant but also it appears to be longitudinally stable. He states that most of the existing explanations rely either directly or indirectly on socialization-based arguments, these being incomplete, inaccurate, and/or tautological (see also A. S. Miller & Stark, 2002). Instead, he is strongly supportive of the argument proposed by A. S. Miller and Hoffman (1995) wherein they argued that the lesser religiosity of men is a manifestation of the consistent finding that men are more risk seeking across a wide range of domains. How is religiosity related to risk taking? Miller and Hoffman utilize Blaise Pascal's 17th-century wager to link risk and religiosity. In perhaps one of the earliest examples of game theoretic logic, Pascal argued that there are four possible states of the world; namely, one can either believe or not believe in the existence of God, and God either does or does not exist. Pascal's payoff matrix was structured in such a manner that he concluded that it was always better to believe in God. Of course, as Stark points out, believing in God and being religious involves adhering to religious edicts and moral constraints that many individuals are unwilling to assume. Hence, that men are more willing to forgo a pious existence and accordingly are less likely to be religious is construed as a manifestation of men's greater proclivity toward risk. Stark agrees with Miller and Hoffman's assertion that there exists a physiological basis for the sex differences in risk-taking proclivity and he refers to the biological-based arguments regarding sex differences in criminality as supportive of his position. An evolutionary perspective posits that men's greater proclivity both to commit violent crimes and to partake in countless other forms of risk-taking activities is rooted in their evolved physiology.

In the next and final section of this chapter, I analyze evolutionary-based explanations of art, perhaps the oldest of all human cultural forms (dating to at least 10,000 years ago).

Art

Most discussions of art over the past 50 years have been in line with the central tenets of the SSSM. Specifically, given that the SSSM assumes that

humans are born with empty minds, and in light of the supposed importance of culture-specific learning, it is assumed that art is hence by definition culturally constrained (cf. Dutton, 2002, 2003, for a discussion of
aesthetic relativism vs. aesthetic universals). Hence, according to such a
view it is impossible to speak of art appreciation and/or art production as
innate human universals. On the surface, this idea seems quite intuitive
and plausible given the ease with which people can point to cross-cultural
differences in artistic traditions. Tribal masks from Central Africa bear little resemblance to Renaissance paintings, and these appear quite distinct
from cave paintings produced 10,000 years ago. However, the logic is
flawed in that this would be similar to using the apparent morphological
differences between various dog breeds to conclude that they are not part
of the same species. On a related note, this would be equivalent to arguing
that because languages seem to be so radically different around the world,
there could not be an innate mental faculty that could be responsible for
the production of such varied linguistic traditions. However, famed lin-
guists such as Noam Chomsky and Steven Pinker have demonstrated that
beneath the surface differences in languages lies a universal language faculty. In the same spirit, scholars have sought to provide evolutionary-based explanations of art. As is true in studying other cultural forms,
art can be studied from an evolutionary perspective along several independent lines. Some have sought to develop theories that explain the
adaptive value of art. In other words, given that art is a human universal
(see Mithen, 1996, for an evolutionary-based archaelogical account of art),
it is argued that it must have conferred an adaptive advantage within our
phylogenetic history. Perhaps the most famous proponent of this view is
Ellen Dissanayake. Briefly put, she argues that humans have an innate proclivity to endow objects and rituals with special meaning, which she calls
"making special." This process of making special is typically experienced
within a group setting, thus yielding group cohesion and cementing social
bonds (cf. Dissanayake, 1992). It would thus appear that her explanation
operates at the group selection level, which most evolutionists now discount as a viable level of selection. Geoffrey Miller is another evolutionist
who has argued for the adaptive significance of art (cf. G. F. Miller, 2000,
chap. 8). However, in his case, he proposes that sexual selection is the evolutionary mechanism through which the adaptive advantage is conferred
to the producer of art. Thus, in the same manner that a male peacock's tail
is wasteful and costly, and hence serves as an honest signal of his quality,
the creation of cultural products (including art) is the equivalent wasteful
signal that serves to tickle the fancy of women's minds in the mating arena.

The specific contents of art (e.g., representation of beauty in a paint-
ing) can also be explored from an evolutionary perspective. The idea in
this case is that there exist universal icons and themes that recur in count-

less artistic traditions because these are representations of evolutionarily relevant cues. Facial symmetry is as important in the art produced by the Wodaabe in Africa as it is in Renaissance paintings because facial symmetry is an indicator of beauty irrespective of time or place. Hersey (1996) demonstrated how visual cues that are relevant in sexual selection (i.e., within the mating arena) have shaped products of art (e.g., represented body shapes). Along the same lines, Singh (2002b, pp. 90–92; see also Singh, Frohlich, & Haywood, 1999) has shown that statues emanating from widely diverse cultures and epochs tend to display female body shapes that are within the evolutionarily prescribed standards of beauty (in terms of waist-to-hip [WTH] ratios). Although there might be small differences in the depicted female WTH ratios across cultures (undoubtedly linked to culture-specific ecological conditions), there is no culture where men's bodies were not depicted as possessing larger WTH ratios as compared to that of women. In other words, representational art contains universal depictions that appear to be impervious to temporal or cultural settings because these are evolutionarily defined. Note that instantiations of nonrepresentational art (e.g., abstract tradition) do not lend themselves to the latter type of content analyses. That said, Martindale (1990) has proposed an all-encompassing theory to explain the evolution of artistic movements and fads. He argues that art (or any other artistic product) can be viewed as an "organism" prone to the forces of Darwinian selection. Hence, the evolution of art is conceptually similar to the evolution of any other organism. The idea is to identify the evolutionary mechanisms that are relevant within the context of this particular cultural organism. Martindale proposed that selection pressures driven by a need for novelty (i.e., an avoidance of habituation or tedium) shape the "speciation" of new art movements. Viewed from this perspective, nonrepresentational art was selected precisely because it contained sufficient variation from its predecessors as to forstall tedium and tickle the novelty-seeking mind of *Homo sapiens*.

A third evolutionary-inspired courant in the study of art argues that our universal appreciation of visually pleasing stimuli is in fact an evolutionary by-product. For example, Grinde (1996) proposed that visual art is universally pleasurable because it typically contains features that our evolved visual system codes as rewarding (from an adaptive sense). Grinde associates the artistic use of vivid colors to our evolved preference for ripe fruits (which are typically bright in color). Additionally, he proposes that symmetry is a universal cue of aesthetics because it signals genetic quality in a prospective mate. This is congruent with the point made in chapter 3 regarding the importance that the Wodaabe place on symmetry in their judging of cattle, art, or prospective mates. Grinde's position is plausible; namely, he is espousing that it is not art itself that is adaptive, but that rather, our evolved neural circuitry attends to elements in art that contain adaptively rewarding information and hence are experienced as pleasurable. In a sense, he is proposing that one's visual appreciation of art is a by-product of our evolved visual system, a position reminiscent of Boyer's (2001, 2003) account regarding the existence of religion. That said, some of Grinde's explanations appear to be manifestations of just-so storytelling. For example, though bright colors can plausibly be linked to ripe and juicy fruits, they have also evolved as aposematic signals to warn potential predators that an animal is highly venomous. Grinde might retort that both interpretations demonstrate that bright colors carry adaptive value; however, one account promotes approach behavior whereas the second results in avoidance. Perhaps a clearer example of just-so theorizing is his postulated link between a preference for balanced images and our innate fear of falling from trees as rooted in our arboreal phylogenetic past. The reader interested in a thorough discussion of the "art as an evolutionary by-product" approach is referred to Aiken (1998).

Given the experiential, cultural, and economic importance of art (see Frey, 2000, for the links between economics and art), it is surprising to see the paucity of research that has explored arts consumption within the consumer behavior tradition. The majority of studies that have addressed the topic have done so from a managerial perspective such as identifying the demographic profiles of arts patrons or identifying variables that could serve as predictors of a cultural product's likely success (e.g., movie receipts). In the instances where the experiential value of consuming art was explored, it was done with a postmodernist bent (cf. Joy & Sherry, 2003). As Dutton (2002, 2003) explains, numerous intellectual giants including Aristotle, Hume, and Kant (his *Sensus Communis*) have highlighted the universality of aesthetic and artistic appreciation. As I have shown in the current section, this universality is steeped in evolutionary mechanisms, be it in explaining the origins and existence of art, the contents of art, or the evolution of artistic forms. Accordingly, consumer scholars interested in studying the consumption of art and aesthetics might expand their research agendas by incorporating the evolutionary-based approaches discussed herein. This is especially true when one recognizes not only the universality of the arts consumption experience but also the ever-increasing importance of globalization. The consumption of art is truly a human universal.

CHAPTER SUMMARY

E. O. Wilson, the world-renowned evolutionist and Harvard entomologist, has cogently remarked that culture is held on a leash by biology. The current chapter has sought to demonstrate the veridicality of his assertion. Specifically, I have explored various cultural forms, including television shows, movie themes, song lyrics, music videos, self-help books, literary works, artistic creations, and religious narratives, and I argued that these exist in their particular forms because they are a reflection of a universal human nature. Beneath the veneer of cross-cultural differences in cultural forms exists a layer of universals that unites the manner by which individuals create, experience, and consume instantiations of cultural expression. A complete theory of culture should take into account both the myriad of unique and idiosyncratic cultural expressions along with the underlying cultural commonalities that binds all people under a universal and invariant human nature.

In the next chapter, I tackle consumption acts that yield deleterious effects to those engaging in them. What are the reasons that cause people to succumb to eating disorders, addictive pornography, pathological gambling, and compulsive shopping? Why do individuals sunbathe religiously when they are well aware of the cancer risks associated to sun exposure? Are there specific demographic groups that are more likely to succumb to any of the latter self-harming behaviors? I argue that the answer to each of the latter questions inherently recognizes that these forms of "dark-side" consumption are rooted in a Darwinian etiology. Hence, though proximate explanations might be relevant in understanding such acts, a complete theory of addictive, compulsive, and pathological consumption should recognize the evolutionary forces that predispose individuals to succumb to the allure of such actions.

6

The Darwinian Roots
of "Dark-Side" Consumption

Darwinian psychiatry conceptualizes mental health and disease on the basis of two basic ideas. First, the capacity to achieve biological goals is the best single attribute that characterizes mental health. Second, the assessment of the disease status of a behavioral or psychological condition cannot be properly made without consideration of both the environment in which the individual currently lives and the environment where Homo sapiens evolved as a species.

—Troisi (2003, p. 55)

Individuals succumb to countless consumption behaviors that potentially yield destructive outcomes (e.g., consuming a high-fat diet). As such, consumer researchers have much to offer in terms of the development of efficacious public service announcements meant to curtail such behaviors. That said, a complete and accurate understanding of these destructive behavioral patterns would be difficult to achieve without an explicit recognition of the innate mechanisms and motives driving such behaviors. Because most "dark-side" consumption patterns can be linked to one or more of the seven deadly sins, I begin this chapter by demonstrating the Darwinian etiology of these sins. This is followed by a brief introduction of Darwinian medicine and evolutionary-based health promotion. Subsequently, I explore five specific dark-side consumption behaviors and demonstrate how in each case, a full understanding of the phenomenon in question will require that both proximate and ultimate causes be addressed.

THE DARWINIAN ETIOLOGY
OF THE SEVEN DEADLY SINS

Dante's "Inferno," one of the three poems comprising the *Divine Comedy* written close to 700 years ago, is timeless because it powerfully captures the frailties of the human condition. Specifically, it discusses the seven deadly (cardinal) sins of sloth (apathy), envy, gluttony, lust, pride (vanity), revenge (wrath), and greed (avarice). These ubiquitous human weaknesses, which transcend cultures and historical epochs, have been addressed by several traditions of scholarship including those originating from Jewish, Christian, and Classical (e.g., ancient Greece) roots (cf. Schimmel, 1997). Whereas many ancient scholars might have attributed the roots of our human weaknesses to supernatural forces or religious struggles (e.g., the conflict between good and evil, Satanic temptation), I propose that the deadly sins are alluring and difficult to eradicate because their genesis lies deep in our Darwinian heritage. In other words, individuals' insatiable desire to engage in actions that violate the cardinal rules of moral conduct is because these are inextricably linked to pursuits that are relevant to one's inclusive fitness. This does not imply that we are helpless executors of our genes' instructions, for evolution has also equipped us with the capacity for moral reasoning and ethical fortitude. Nonetheless, as elucidated by Burnham and Phelan (2000), some of our biological imperatives (which they refer to as *mean genes*) require taming and temperance especially when it comes to pursuits that relate to evolutionarily relevant domains such as sex, food, money, and status. On a related note, J. Medina (2000) provides an interesting albeit predominantly proximate account of the links between our evolved physiology and the seven deadly sins.

How is the latter discussion relevant to consumer behavior? Most of the consumption choices that we partake in cater to innate drives that can become manifestations of "sinful" behavior when taken to the extremes. The consumption of pornography, the soliciting of prostitutes, and the pursuit of extramarital dalliances (with all of the requisite purchases involved in such a ritual) relate to our lustful tendencies. The obesity epidemic, super sizing and add-on food sales, all-you-can eat buffets, and all-inclusive vacation packages cater to our gluttonous nature. The need to keep up with the Joneses and the associated positional conspicuous consumption is meant to attenuate our covetousness of others' material possessions. The fashion, cosmetics, and plastic surgery industries cater to one's vanity. The positional arms race that has taken place in certain industries with regard to the number of hours worked per week (e.g., junior investment bankers or young lawyers in large law firms) is driven by greed. Needless to say, countless ethical breaches that occur at both the macro and micro economic levels with the subsequent deleterious effects on the everyday consumer are clearly rooted in greed (e.g., the Savings and Loans Crisis, the Enron and WorldCom scandals, Martha Stewart's recent conviction, and fraudulent insurance claims). Perhaps at no time was it as socially condoned to display one's wanton greed as in the booming 1980s. The pursuit of greed for its sheer sake was immortalized in the highly successful movie *Wall Street* (Pressman & Stone, 1987). The main antagonist, a ruthless and morally bankrupt takeover capitalist named Gordon Gekko (played by Michael Douglas), states the following as he addresses the stakeholders of a company that he is about to break up and liquidate:

> The new law of evolution in corporate America seems to be "survival of the unfittest." Well in my book, you either do it right or you get eliminated. … The point is, ladies and gentlemen, greed is good. Greed works, greed is right. Greed clarifies, cuts through, and captures the essence of the evolutionary spirit. Greed in all its forms, greed for life, money, love, knowledge, has marked the upward surge of mankind—and greed, mark my words—will save not only Teldar Paper but that other malfunctioning corporation called the USA. … Thank you. (quote accessed at http://www.dailyscript.com/scripts/wall_street.html on June 6, 2004)

To the sheer delight of advertisers, sloth promotes the sedentary lifestyle that has been adopted by a substantial number of contemporary consumers, wherein the passive and mind-numbing viewing of endless hours of television on the proverbial couch has become the preferred activity. Despite any institutional and social barriers that might hinder an individual's progress in society, it is difficult to justify why families can require welfare assistance for five or six contiguous generations. As such, apathy and sloth are likely two of several causative agents in explaining the ever-widening social safety net that is needed to support all members of countries with a socialist ethos. Finally, wrath manifests itself in a myriad of ways in contemporary settings. The ever-increasing incidences of road rage, the burgeoning spa and relaxation industries (meant in part to alleviate anger and stress), and the highly litigious culture that has become part and parcel of the American ethos are in part rooted in wrath.

To the extent that many behavioral afflictions are rooted in our Darwinian heritage, it would seem reasonable that health practitioners and public health policymakers should in part utilize evolutionary-based frameworks to address these. Accordingly, I turn to a brief explanation of Darwinian medicine and evolutionary health promotion in the ensuing two sections. My hope here is to propose novel approaches for tackling the myriad of important societal problems that is typically within the purview of social marketing.

DARWINIAN MEDICINE
AND THE PROMOTION OF HEALTH

Both the practice of medicine and the development of health-related public policy have typically occurred with minimal if any evolutionary-based theorizing. The focus has commonly been on identifying the proximate mechanisms of a particular disease or unhealthy practice. That said, a full and accurate understanding of health would recognize that the human body is a product of natural and sexual selection. Darwinian medicine specifically recognizes this fact and accordingly seeks to comprehend human diseases in light of our phylogenetic history (cf. Nesse & Williams, 1996; Stearns & Ebert, 2001). As mentioned in chapter 1, the suppression of symptoms associated with a cold (fever, running nose, and cough), and those linked with pregnancy sickness yield suboptimal results because the symptoms in question are adaptive responses (reducing the viral load, and expelling ingested teratogens), and hence should not be suppressed. An evolutionary perspective recognizes that the astonishing rise in many lethal albeit preventable diseases (e.g., heart disease, stroke, and type 2 diabetes) is predominantly due to a mismatch between the environment of evolutionary adaptedness and current environments (Eaton, Cordain, & Lindeberg, 2002; Eaton, Strassman et al., 2002). Thus, not only are there theoretical implications in understanding medicine from an ultimate perspective but also an evolutionary-based approach to health provides concrete and actionable programs that at times are contrary to the accepted wisdom.

The journal *Addiction* recently dedicated one of its 2002 issues to the application of evolutionary approaches in understanding various facets of addictions. Panksepp, Knutson, and Burgdorf (2002) propose, "In comparison to cultural, environmental, biological and pathological accounts, evolutionary explanations for addiction have received scant elaboration (Nesse & Berridge 1997)" (p. 459). This quote should highlight the fact that studying a phenomenon from a biological perspective is not synonymous with ultimate-based theorizing. In other words, though many addiction researchers have explored the biological underpinnings of addictions, few have sought to develop their research programs using Darwinian frameworks. In the latter special issue, one of the articles demonstrates how evolutionary theory can be used to integrate findings across multiple levels of analyses. Specifically, Lende and Smith (2002) provided an adaptationist account of addiction at three levels of analyses, namely the biological, psychological, and social levels. I provide herewith a brief summary of some of their ideas. First, they explored evolutionary-based explanations of the dopamine system and its relevance in the consumption of rewarding experiences (e.g., drugs). Second, they analyzed the adaptive importance of parent–child attachments and argued that in many instances drug addicts have poor attachments with their parents. Third, they proposed an analogy between the manner by which depressives foster dependency by assuming the submissive role in their relationships, and that fostered by drug addicts as they navigate their social environments and addictions. Social dependency, be it as manifested by depressives or drug addicts, is one of several adaptive strategies that are available to *Homo sapiens,* a highly social albeit hierarchical animal. Notwithstanding the speculative nature of some of their ideas, the importance of their work lies in demonstrating how evolutionary-based theorizing can serve as the integrative rubric for a given phenomenon (addiction) across multiple levels of analyses (biological, psychological, and social).

An offshoot of Darwinian medicine particularly relevant to the study of dark-side consumption is Darwinian psychiatry (see McGuire & Troisi, 1998). Specifically, evolutionary-minded psychiatrists and clinical psychologists seek to understand the Darwinian etiology that gives rise to a particular psychiatric disorder (cf. Nesse, 1998, for an evolutionary treatise of emotional afflictions). As is discussed later in this chapter, numerous disorders that have a clear universal pattern of sex-specific morbidity or symptomatology are candidates for an evolutionary-based explanation. For example, using an evolutionary perspective, Brüne (2001) analyzed 246 cases originating from 28 countries of De Clérambault's syndrome, a rare psychiatric disorder whereby patients have delusional thoughts of being loved by a particular individual. Specifically, Brüne explored sex differences in terms of the incidence of the disease, the characteristics of both the patients and the love interests, and specific behaviors targeted at the love interests. There were several important sex differences (see Brüne, 2001, p. 412, Table 1, for a summary of these), which Brüne proposes as being consistent with sexual strategies theory (Buss & Schmitt, 1993). Some of the findings include that women were much more likely to be afflicted with the disorder and that the love interests of women patients were older and of higher status whereas those of male patients were younger and more sexually attractive. Male patients engaged in behaviors typically associated with strategies to ensure paternity certainty including harassment (e.g., stalking) and jealousy, and were more likely to show off resources as a means of appearing attractive to the love interest. On the other hand, female patients were more likely to improve their physical appearance as a mate attraction strategy. Incidentally, Brüne states that "the core features of the disorder have been found strikingly similar irrespective of the cultural background or ethnicity (as also confirmed by the uniformity of the syndrome over different historical epochs)" (p. 413). Thus, whenever a phenomenon appears to transcend cultures and eras, this is suggestive of it having a Darwinian etiology.

PUBLIC SERVICE ANNOUNCEMENTS
AND EVOLUTIONARY THEORY

One of the central assumptions in the development of public service announcements is that consumers need to be educated about healthy behaviors. Specifically, the premise is that if consumers engage in "irrational" behavior (i.e., that which yields negative consequences on them), it must be the case that they are ignorant about the relevant issues that would permit for more informed and "rational" behaviors. A related view of rationality has been applied by some in arguing that advertisers create irrational wants. For example, Cohan (2001) states, "A successful advertising campaign can persuade people to do all sorts of things—to consume products harmful to themselves such as tobacco, junk food, colas, or alcoholic drinks—or products that are relatively useless—such as cosmetics" (p. 324). These definitions of rationality are misguided because they fail to explore the Darwinian motives that drive these particular behaviors.

Individuals engage in a bewildering number of behaviors that have severe consequences on their health and related life expectancies. People frequently engage in unprotected sex despite several negative consequences that can arise from such behaviors (e.g., sexually transmitted diseases and unwanted pregnancy). There has apparently been a recent increase in the number of HIV infections in young gay males as a result of an increase with which they engage in unprotected anal sex. Millions of Americans not only are morbidly obese but also lead sedentary lifestyles. Skin cancer is one of the most common yet most easily preventable types of cancers yet millions of people insist on obtaining the healthy glow associated with a suntan. It is unlikely that each of the latter behaviors is due either to irrationality and/or to misinformation. Are young gay males unaware of the risks of HIV? Are Americans simply misinformed about the dangers of being a hundred pounds overweight? Are most sunbathers simply oblivious to the link between skin cancer and sun exposure? Based on the contents of public service announcements, one would quickly surmise that the working assumption is that negative behaviors can be altered solely via a reeducation of the consumer. This assumption yields suboptimal outcomes, as evidenced by the fact that the majority of the targeted behaviors have been tenaciously resistant to change, despite dogged efforts on the parts of public health officials. Next, I provide a discussion of sun-tanning behavior as an example of the incongruity between the contents of the antitanning public service messages and the ultimate motives for engaging in such an unhealthy and dangerous practice.

Saad and Peng (2006) identified key findings from the behavioral sun-tanning literature and subsequently proposed that these are congruent with an evolutionary perspective. First, women are much more likely to tan as compared to men and this holds true across all sources of exposure including natural sun tanning, artificial tanning booths, and sun-tanning creams. This sex effect has been consistently found across countless cultures. Second, young and single individuals are more likely to sunbathe as compared to their older married counterparts. Finally, individuals seem to discount future costs (e.g., developing melanoma) for immediate benefits (looking good). The evolutionary explanation for each of the latter findings is straightforward. Suntans have become associated with health and beauty in most Western societies. Hence, the demographic variables most likely to predict the extent of sun-tanning behavior are those associated with the mating module. From a self-presentational perspective, women care more about appearance-related matters and hence it would seem reasonable to expect that they are the overwhelmingly greater participants in the sunbathing ritual. Being single and young implies that one is currently in the mating market, thus the need to look good is accentuated. Finally, the immediate benefits of looking good at tonight's party outweigh the costs of potentially developing melanoma in 30 years. Discounting future costs for immediate benefits is the mechanism by which senescence is thought to have evolved (see Nesse & Williams, 1996). Specifically, a trait that is beneficial early in one's reproductive life might have negative repercussions later in life. Natural selection could "accept" such a trade-off if the net effect is one that maximizes fitness. Hence, looking good at tonight's party (replete with attractive mates) looms much larger than a probabilistically remote chance of developing melanoma in the distant future. As Saad and Peng point out, in comparison to men, women are more knowledgeable about the deleterious effects of sun exposure yet they are more likely to engage in the behavior. Thus, it does not seem to be the case here that unhealthy behaviors are due to lack of relevant information.

In a highly related approach to that employed by Saad and Peng, E. M. Hill and Chow (2002) proposed that young, single, childless males originating from unstable environments would be those most likely to engage in risky drinking patterns because of evolutionary reasons rooted in life-history theory, a model that has been frequently used by behavioral ecologists. The key idea is that a given behavior carries differential fitness costs and benefits depending on which life stage an individual is currently in. Hence, exceptionally risky behaviors are consistently most likely to be carried out by young males because of the differential payoffs associated with such behaviors given the reproductive pressures that they face. Risky behaviors manifest themselves in the same sex-specific manner across several domains. For example, Nell (2002) provides an evolutionary explanation of why young men drive unsafely; namely, this risky behavior is an evolved Zahavian honest signal, which amounts to advertising that "I have the ability to survive despite the fact that I am engaging in activities frought with grave danger." Nell argues that this is in part the reason why fear appeals have not been effective when targeting young men regarding the dangers of unsafe driving.

One criminal manifestation of reckless and dangerous driving is car stealing (or carjacking) followed by joyriding. This crime is commissioned in numerous cultural settings by the same culprit profile; namely, young and disenfranchised males are overwhelmingly the most likely to commit such crimes. A few years ago, the city of Newark (New Jersey) faced a particularly dangerous form of carjacking and joyriding. The culprits would seek and subsequently taunt the police in the hope of baiting them into a dangerous high-speed chase. More recently, Dawes (2002) conducted interviews with Aboriginal and Torres Strait Islander youths to explore the reasons that they stole cars and engaged in excessively dangerous joyriding. As is true in every other society where criminality has been investigated, Australian data demonstrates that males are exceptionally more likely to commit violent crimes (including car stealing followed by joyriding). Dawes provides several explanations and postulates regarding the exceptionally robust male effect. First, he wonders why women do not engage in this activity to a greater extent given that it would permit them to gain greater "freedom" (e.g., by increasing their mobility). Second, he proposes that the disenfranchised males are likely engaging in such destructive criminal behaviors in order to subvert colonialization. The veridical causative force driving these youths to engage in joyriding has a Darwinian etiology. Young and otherwise powerless males have little other than their street reputations to protect. Hence, they will go to extraordinary lengths to obtain and protect their status within their relevant social networks. Dawes recognizes that being an accomplished carjacker yields high status. Furthermore, he states that not only do the joyriders ignore the consequences of driving fast but also incarcerating them has had no effect. As such, the commission of high risk–taking crimes such as joyriding has little to do with a backlash against the "colonial oppressors" and much to do with the differential mechanisms that young males will seek to gain social status. Thus, returning to the point made by Nell (2002), public policy programs that are rooted in inaccurate causal theories will likely fail. Young disenfrenchised males do not curb their risky driving behaviors despite being exposed to images of mortality (via a given public service announcement). It is precisely the highly salient risk of dying that motivates these young males to engage in this behavior.

How well have marketing scholars fared in their investigation of those public policy issues deemed most relevant to the consumer? Sprott and Miyazaki (2002) analyzed the publications of the *Journal of Public Policy & Marketing* (*JPP&M*), the premier journal in the field, for its first

20-year period (1982–2001). The most frequently addressed topic dealt with consumer information (22.9% of articles published in *JPP&M* dealt with information provision). Additionally, a great majority of the most cited *JPP&M* articles explored various issues dealing with the provision of information. A typical topic might be to explore the links between how information is presented and its subsequent processing. This focus on information processing is expected given that the operative assumption within this research stream is that the "education" of consumers is the means by which aversive behaviors can be eliminated. Although the provision of relevant information in appropriate formats might curb destructive behaviors, this is insufficient in of itself. Most harmful behaviors have a Darwinian etiology, and as such require ultimate-based theorizing to be fully understood. Incidentally, Sprott and Miyazaki conducted a citation analysis as part of their review of the literature and concluded that *JPP&M* articles seem minimally influential outside of the marketing discipline. Given the important societal problems that it addresses, *JPP&M* should be a leading contender for generating interdisciplinary interest. Though evolutionary psychology might not be the panacea here, it might provide a parsimonious meta-framework for studying problems of great societal import.

In the following section, I turn to an analysis of four dark-side consumption forms while providing a possible Darwinian etiology for each.

ANALYSIS OF SPECIFIC
DARK-SIDE CONSUMPTION BEHAVIORS

The four dark-side consumption acts explored herewith are the addictive consumption of pornography, eating disorders, pathological gambling, and compulsive buying. In each case, I demonstrate that the pattern of morbidity is such that one's biological sex is the strongest predictor of succumbing to the particular affliction. I propose that the sex-specificity in each case is a "behavioral misfiring" rooted in the mating module. That behavioral-based afflictions are highly sex-specific is expected given that "sex is the most common human polymorphism that affects health and illness through the life cycle" (Grumbach, 2004, p. 12). That said, many forms of dark-side consumption are not linked to the mating module, and as such do not yield a sex-specific effect. For example, both men and women succumb to the allure of high-fat foods because the evolved gustatory preferences driving this consumption act are rooted in an adaptive problem equally relevant to both sexes (i.e., caloric scarcity and caloric uncertainty in the environment of evolutionary adaptedness). Notwithstanding the latter example, my focus is restricted to dark-side consumption acts linked to the mating module.

Pornography

Sales figures associated with the consumption of pornography are astounding. W. A. Fisher and Barak (2001, p. 314) cite findings by *Blue Money* wherein it was reported that 69% of online purchases were sexually related. This is consistent with data reported in Li (2000), wherein online revenues attributed to adult sites for the years 1998 through 2001 were 69.09%, 68.27%, 66.12%, and 66.10% (projected) respectively of the total online revenues. Weitzer (2000b) reports that Americans spent $9 billion in 1996 on various pornographic products (phone sex, videos, etc.). The profit potential of pornography is so pronounced that it has driven technological advances meant to find increasingly effective distribution and delivery systems of pornographic products. S. E. Stern and Handel (2001) provide a historical synopsis of research that has explored the incidence of sexual material in various mediums (e.g., print, radio, television, telephone, VCRs, and the Internet) and in products of popular culture (e.g., movies, music videos, songs, advertising, video games). One apparent point stemming from their analysis is that technological advances have translated into new means by which sexual materials are diffused to the ravenous masses (mainly comprised of men). As soon as a new medium is developed, clever marketers are able to put it to use as a distribution channel for the selling of pornographic and sexually explicit materials. Hence, irrespective of the cultural setting, epoch, or medium, there are extraordinary financial opportunities in the peddling of sexuality. Despite consumers' persistent interest in pornographic materials, most social scientists have largely ignored (or are unaware of) the fact that Darwinian forces drive the human fascination with sexually explicit stimuli.

Much of the research on pornography has sought to identify links between its consumption and various social ills. Antipornography advocates seem to "link" it to numerous individual, familial, and/or social problems including rape, infidelity, domestic violence, the objectification of women, institutionalized sexism, pedophilia, sexual addiction, marital problems, and the disintegration of moral and family values to name but a few examples. Accordingly, much of the academic research within the social sciences has typically approached the study of pornography with a moral agenda, namely that pornography should be condemned given the pernicious harm that it causes throughout all levels of society. It is beyond the current scope to provide a thorough review of this vast literature. Instead, I provide a few telling examples of this research stream. In the same vein that some strands of feminism promulgated the mantra that rape has nothing to do with sex and everything to do with violence, a similar viewpoint has been diffused with regard to pornography. According to this worldview, "pornography is not really about sex, it is about gender" (Elliott et al., 1995, p. 188). Hence, not only rape but also pornography has apparently little to do with sex and everything to do with violence against women. The antipornography movement as exemplified by Andrea Dworkin and Catharine A. MacKinnon has been influential in providing "explanations" regarding the astonishing sex effect when it comes to the consumption of pornography (and other sexual products or services) as well as in providing motives for such consumption. MacKinnon (1989) has stated:

> In pornography, the violence is the sex. The inequality is sex. The humiliation is sex. The debasement is sex. The intrusion is sex. Pornography does not work sexually without gender hierarchy. If there is no inequality, no violation, no dominance, no force, there is no sexual arousal. (as quoted in Norton, 1999, p. 122)

The latter position as espoused by many radical feminists is not shared by all relevant parties within the SSSM tradition. Though many feminists are against prostitution and pornography, others are fully supportive of a woman's freedom of choice. Simmons (1999) provides a contrast of two opposing camps of feminists (Feminists Against Systems of Prostitution and Prostitutes' Rights) regarding these matters.

The work by Cowan and Campbell (1994) is a representative example of research that explores facets of pornography from a victimization perspective. Specifically, they sought to demonstrate the supposed sexist and racist agenda of pornographers via a content analysis of interracial pornographic movies. Because the findings must be supportive of the "correct" moral and ideological position, the coding scheme was developed such that a majority of the depicted acts would likely be coded as either sexist and/or racist. For example, most acts that would be considered reasonably common and desired by both men and women within the confines of standard heterosexual sex (e.g., spanking, and dirty talking) were viewed as aggressive and physically violent to women. The authors state that perhaps White and Black men can "bond" in the context of pornography for they are joining in their attack on women. As argued by Buss (1994), evolutionarily speaking, intrasexual rivalry is much more common than group-level intersexual conflicts. Hence the contention that Black and White men put aside the racist feelings that they might otherwise feel for one another, in order to band in their common desire to oppress women, is both empirically and theoretically baseless. In defining what might constitute "appropriate" pornography, Cowan and Campbell refer to Gloria Steinem's distinction between "erotica" and hardcore porn. It is indeed true that erotica is a more appealing form of pornography when targeting women consumers; however, it is hardly equally interesting to men.

Cross-cultural and longitudinal sales figures from around the world attest to this fact. However, in the same manner that queer theory seeks to challenge the "heterosexist" view that heterosexuality is the more common form of human sexuality, radical feminists wish to create a worldview wherein they "redefine" what is considered sexually arousing to men (e.g., alter men's preferences from hardcore pornography to erotica).

The accumulated scientific evidence does not support the premise that pornography causes a wide range of devastating ills. Potter (1999) conducted a study to explore the link between pornography and attitudes toward women. He found "no support for the contention that consumption of sexually explicit materials leads to a more generalized and insidious hatred of women" (p. 80). More important, Potter provided a summary of the findings from the extant literature and concluded, "Evidence in support of a causal link between 'pornographic' materials and aggression or attitudes toward women is at best scant" (pp. 65–66). Refutations of the standard antipornographic mantra have been obtained using a wide range of data collection procedures including surveys and content analyses. For example, W. A. Fisher and Barak (2001, p. 316, Figure 1) showed that despite an exponential growth in the availability of sexually explicit materials available on the Internet from 1995 to 1999, the rate of forcible rape (as obtained from FBI data) during that period has steadily declined. Palys (1986) found that depictions of sexual aggression were more prevalent in X-rated as compared to triple-X-rated movies. My goal in demonstrating the lack of evidence in support of the antipornography position should not be taken as my providing implicit support of this industry. Rather, I wish to merely highlight the fact that the mixing of science with political, ideological, and moral positions inevitably leads to shoddy work.

The recent paper by Bernstein (2001) is an illustrative examplar of sex-related research (in this case the consumption of sex) stemming from an ideological-based and social constructivist perspective. For example, in describing the literature that has sought to identify the reasons that men seek prostitutes, Bernstein states:

> The primary motivations identified by these authors include clients' desire for sexual variation, sexual access to partners with preferred ages, racialized features and physiques, the appeal of an "emotion-free" and clandestine sexual encounter, loneliness, marital problems, the quest for power and control, the desire to be dominated or to engage in "exotic" sex acts, and the thrill of violating taboos. *While provocative and insightful, this literature has often failed to explain client motives with historical specificity, or to link these motives to social and economic institutions that might themselves structure the relations of gender domination implied by many of the explanatory categories above. In general, typologies are presented as if based on distinct attributes of a transhistorical and unwavering masculinity* .[italics added] (p. 396)

That men are interested in seeking unencumbered sex with multiple new partners is not a reality that is restricted to a particular era or culture. However, this is what Bernstein is arguing; namely that men's sexuality is not temporally and culturally invariant but rather is influenced by historical contingencies. Furthermore, she is proposing that male sexuality must be understood in light of the economic and social institutions that are set up to promote the patriarchal goal of dominating women. According to Bernstein and many of her colleagues (e.g., gender theorists), that men are practically the exclusive consumers of sexual services is in part a reflection of capitalism (which commodifies sex), as well as the economic and social defeat that men have faced at the hands of the second-wave feminists. Hence, men retaliate by exploiting female prostitutes via a form of recreational sex that has been promulgated by the patriarchal capitalist system. Bernstein cites the work of Carole Pateman (on p. 404) in support of the view that men seek prostitutes as a means of exploiting and demeaning women. Apparently, Pateman has proposed that because men oftentimes seek manual stimulation as the desired sexual service, an act that could ostensibly be self-performed, this demonstrates that the real purpose of the sexual interaction is male dominance. Because most men are incapable of performing "self-fellatio," one would have to conclude according to Pateman's logic that the purchase of this act should be deemed as nonexploitative. Bernstein proposes several additional causative demographic factors that have supposedly led to "a new set of erotic dispositions" (p. 399) as displayed by men, including increased divorce rates and increases in single-person households.

Bernstein reports several findings and conclusions, all of which are congruent with an evolutionary perspective. For example, she quotes one of her interviewees, who states: "My wife has never understood my desire to do this. I have no problem with my wife. We have a good sexual relationship. There's a Vietnamese restaurant on 6th and Market that I love, but I don't want to eat there every day" (p. 397). She concludes that the second-wave feminist assumption that johns seek prostitutes for services that would not be performed by their regular partners does not hold true. Additionally, she describes research (p. 412, note 3) showing that men seeking heterosexual female prostitutes constituted two thirds of the sex market, whereas the other third was comprised of men seeking male prostitutes. She claims that there is very little evidence that either heterosexual women or lesbians ever sought prostitutes. She concludes, "The lack of such a market reveals a great deal about the persistently gendered nature of commercial sexual consumption" (p. 412). Each of the latter findings and conclusions are in line with evolutionary principles linked to the mating module. Men have a predisposition toward greater sexual variety (i.e., the Coolidge effect) and this desire can coexist with the fact that they are fully satisfied (sexually and emotionally) within the context of their long-term union. This duality is expected from an evolutionary perspective. That men are the sole consumers of sexual services has nothing to do with gender roles, demographic variables, forms of societies (preindustrial vs. capitalist), or historical contingencies. Men in every known culture and epoch have been the main purchasers of sex. The adage "the world's oldest profession" predates both capitalist societies and rising divorce rates.

What have other authors proposed regarding men's motives for seeking the services of a prostitute? Men seek prostitutes in order to have emotionally unencumbered sex with many different partners (see discussion in Monto, 2000). They do not seek prostitutes for any "deviant" or unusual sex; rather, they wish to have a variety of body types (Lever & Dolnick, 2000), a finding consistent with the Coolidge effect. Johns are not "damaged" by prior sexual abuse as only 14% of johns had had prior childhood abuse (Monto, 2000). Furthermore, most johns were in relationships that were sexually satisfying; nonetheless, they sought prostitutes despite the havoc that it oftentimes caused in their lives (Weitzer, 2000a). Each of the latter findings is consistent with an evolutionary-informed perspective. The consumption of both hardcore heterosexual pornography and sexual services appeals to specific facets of male evolved sexuality. The depiction of men engaging in unencumbered and easily available sex with countless young and beautiful women is central to men's fantasies (cf. Ellis & Symons, 1990) and is rooted in the differential costs and benefits of engaging in indiscriminate mating for the two sexes.

As discussed in the previous chapter, the specific contents of cultural products are oftentimes indicative of our Darwinian heritage (e.g., song lyrics or literary themes). No cultural product is as amenable to such a content-analytic approach as is pornography given its direct links to men's evolved sexuality. Because pornographers are in the profit-making business, they will seek to create products that appeal to the preferences of their target market. Given men's evolved preference to mate with young and beautiful women, it would seem logical that pornographic films would contain images of such women. This is not a manifestation of oppressive sexism and ageism; rather, it is a foundational marketing tenet, namely providing one's target market with the desired product. The reader is referred to Symons (1979), Shepher and Reisman (1985), and Malamuth (1996) for discussions of evolutionary-based approaches to pornography.

Pound (2002) applied an evolutionary perspective to explain the greater prevalence of polyandrous (i.e., one female with multiple males) as compared to polygynous (i.e., one male with multiple females) matings in pornographic movies targeted at heterosexual males. Furthermore, he conducted both an online survey and a process-tracing online study to respectively investigate the stated preferences and click-on behaviors associated with this issue. One might expect that heterosexual males would prefer depictions of polygynous matings more so than polyandrous ones. Polygyny is an inherent part of male sexuality (spreading one's genes) whereas polyandry is typically abhored given that it triggers the greatest threat to a man's genetic interests, namely paternity uncertainty. Anthropologists have established the fact that polygyny is an exceptionally more frequent form of mating arrangement. That said, Pound found that irrespective of whether conducting a content analysis of pornographic material, eliciting preferences via online surveys, or tracking online Web behavior, men seem to have a pronounced preference for viewing polyandrous situations. What can explain the discrepancy between the standard evolutionary prediction regarding male sexuality (disdain for polyandry) and the greater depiction and preference of such mating situations in pornographic settings? Pound argues that polyandrous scenarios trigger cues of sperm competition, which have been found to be arousing to males across a wide range of species. In other words, though it is true that men are not amenable to sharing their mates, they have evolved an adaptive response (becoming sexually aroused) to cues that signal the increased presence of sperm competition. A nonevolutionary approach (e.g., as might be conducted by an academic feminist) to tackling this issue would likely conclude that given that pornography exists to degrade and exploit women, polyandrous depictions are expected. In other words, if a pornographer's goal is to depict violent and demeaning images of women, what better way is there to do so than to have multiple males mating with one woman? Contrary to the "victimization" tenet, Pound states, "It should be noted that explicit signs of physical control, aggression, and violence were extremely rare in the material included in content analyses reported here" (p. 461).

Evolutionary forces not only should affect the differential consumption of pornography but also should manifest themselves when exploring sex differences in the motives and characteristics of the service providers (i.e., pornographic actors and actresses). Abbott (2000) explored various facets along which male and female adult actors differ, albeit void of any evolutionary-based theorizing. Abbott found that male actors join this industry with the prime motivation of obtaining sexual opportunities, and they are more likely to depend on how much they are enjoying the sex in deciding whether to stay in this profession. Women's motives are predominantly financial based, as evidenced by the fact that female porn stars make more than their male counterparts. In terms of personal characteristics, Abbott states that female actors are expected to look good via any means (e.g., cosmetic surgeries) and are typically younger than their male counterparts. Anecdotally, the most famous current male pornographic actor is Ron

Jeremy, a man who happens to be grossly overweight and well into his 50s. Abbott proposes that new actresses produce the greatest number of videos in the first year of their career. That male consumers would lose interest in familiar faces and would accordingly view these as monotonous is a manifestation of the Coolidge effect. Each of the latter findings is congruent with an evolutionary perspective regarding human sexuality.

Though some might argue that any consumption of sexual products or services constitutes dark-side consumption, this categorization is typically established via clinical rather than moral guidelines. In terms of sexual compulsivity and addiction, the sex effect is unequivocal and is the same irrespective of time or place. Men are overwhelmingly more likely to be addicted consumers of sexual products and/or services. This finding has recently been replicated within the context of online behavior. Specifically, Griffiths (2001) explored various demographic traits of Internet sex addicts. Of the few studies that have been conducted in this area and that were accordingly cited by Griffiths, one incontestable conclusion is that men are much more likely to be Internet sex addicts. In those instances when women outnumbered men in terms of being compulsive cybersex users, the focus of the compulsion was quite different across the two sexes. Male addicts were much more likely to be classified as suffering from a sexual-based addiction. Griffiths (2001) states:

> Females preferred chat rooms to other mediums whereas males preferred the Web. No female cybersex compulsives reported using newsgroups for sexual pursuits. Since newsgroups are primarily for the exchange of erotic pictures, this supported the finding that women tend to desire cybersex in the context of a "relationship" rather than simply viewing images or text. (p. 339)

A. Cooper, Scherer, Boies, and Gordon (1999), who explored various facets of the consumption of sexuality on the Internet, obtained results well in line with those found by Griffiths. Men were more than six times more likely to view sexually graphic material, and were more than twice more likely to view softer erotica, whereas women were more than twice as likely to use chat rooms to foster relationships. Hence, dark-side consumption in the context of the sex industry is overwhelmingly sex-specific because of Darwinian reasons that transcend cultures and epochs.

Despite the universality and robustness of the sex effect regarding the consumption of sexual products and services, the majority of social scientists do not recognize that this behavior might have a Darwinian etiology. The ignoring of biological principles in explaining the consumption of sexuality is not restricted to the antipornography camp. Most social scientists, including those who do not pronounce an ideological position regarding pornography, are immersed in proximate-based theorizing. For example,

W. A. Fisher and Barak (2001) use the Sexual Behavior Sequence, a proximate-based social psychological approach, in tackling the issue of Internet sexuality and pornography. They claim that several other proximate theories might prove relevant in understanding Internet sexuality including the theory of reasoned action, excitation transfer theory, social-cognitive theory, and the confluence model (p. 317). Thus, in discussing issues revolving around sexuality, the innate Darwinian forces behind such behaviors were missing from within the authors' theoretical purview. It seems unreasonable to expect that the theory of reasoned action is more relevant in explaining sexuality than are evolved biological mechanisms.

What can explain the erroneous causal attributions within the SSSM-based and "victimization" research streams? I propose that the view of the human mind as a blank slate, with the utopic hope for infinite human malleability, generates these worldviews. If one believes that male sexuality is merely learned (via capitalism, television, *Penthouse,* or the patriarchy), this implies that it is malleable and hence can be "relearned." Bernstein (2001) provides a telling quote in support of this position when she states, "Some have attributed recent attempts to reform male sexuality to the gains of second-wave feminism" (p. 393). Bernstein proceeds to describe some of these attempts including "john schools" and "client reeducation projects." As remarked by Pinker (2002), the most brutal regimes of the 20th century have all subscribed to the blank-slate proposition and have accordingly sought to reeducate the masses at a cost of several hundred million lives lost. Though I am certainly not implying that john schools are equivalent to Khmer Rouge reeducation camps, the central theoretical premise behind each movement is identical and rests on the firm belief that the human mind is infinitely "reeducatable." John Stoltenberg, who is both the partner of Andrea Dworkin and a staunch feminist author in his own right, has supposedly pronounced that "pornography tells lies about women. But pornography tells the truth about men." He is correct albeit for the wrong reasons. Pornography lies about the ease with which women are willing to engage in unencumbered sex while speaking the truth about men's evolved sexuality. Men's sexuality is not rooted in a desire to oppress and subjugate women. Rather, men have an evolved desire for multiple short-term mating opportunities with attractive, young, and perennially receptive women. These are the images and themes that are available in pornographic material that is targeted to men.

To conclude, evolutionary psychology provides ultimate explanations regarding the universal finding that men are much more likely to succumb to pornographic addictions. In the next section, I turn to another form of dark-side consumption wherein in this case the sex-specificity of the morbidity rates is universally dominated by women.

Eating Disorders

Eating disorders such as bulimia and anorexia nervosa afflict millions of individuals in North America, most of whom are women. The American Psychiatric Association (1994) has estimated that women outnumber men by a factor of 10 in terms of eating disorders. One of the tragic realities of eating disorders is that they predominantly afflict young and otherwise vibrant women who end up withering away while battling the ravages of this cruel illness. Perhaps no example is more vivid than that of Karen Carpenter, the lead singer of the Carpenters, who eventually succumbed to this dreadful disease. Accordingly, policymakers, physicians, mental health professionals, and behavioral scientists are well justified in their search for the etiology of this common cluster of disorders. Most scholars working to elucidate the causative agent of eating disorders are in agreement as to the likely culprit. The media, with its focus on thin, young, and beautiful women, is apparently to be blamed for the eating disorders epidemic. Incidentally, the same media is also blamed for the obesity epidemic. For example, Jeffrey, McLellarn, and Fox (1982, as cited by Harrison & Cantor, 1997) have estimated that a child is exposed to 11,000 junk-food ads, implicitly arguing that television induces unhealthy eating practices (consumption of high-fat foods) resulting in obesity. Hence, according to this research stream, the same causative agent is responsible for both anorexia nervosa and morbid obesity. I begin by summarizing representative studies from the social constructivist stream (e.g., the media causes eating disorders) followed by a discussion of evolutionary-based studies.

Social Constructivist Perspective. How much evidence exists in support of the contention that media images cause eating disorders? Even those who have spent much effort trying to establish the existence of this link are candid regarding the paucity of evidence. For example, despite citing numerous examples meant to show the pernicious effects of the media in creating eating disorders, Harrison and Cantor (1997) state, "Very little empirical evidence has been produced to show that exposure to media images of thinness leads directly to disordered eating" (p. 43). Apparently, only one such study existed up to that point. As such, Harrison and Cantor conducted their study to hopefully establish the existence of such a link. In discussing their findings, the authors state:

> Why does body dissatisfaction appear to be more strongly related to television viewing than magazine reading, whereas drive for thinness is more strongly related to magazine reading than television viewing? Similarly, why is body dissatisfaction related to viewing heavy shows and not thin shows? (p. 61)

On the next page, they add, "When men's overall endorsement of thinness for women was tested as a criterion variable, regression analyses yielded no significant effects for the media use variables" (p. 62). In sum, Harrison and Cantor did not find support for the postulated causal links between eating disorders and the media. Additional examples of the "media causes eating disorder" research stream are provided next.

Harrison (1997) sought to determine whether viewers' liking of thin media personalities might be responsible for the development of eating disorders. Data was collected on seven measures associated with eating disorders, seven variables capturing the extent of one's exposure to seven media, and three attitudinal measures capturing one's affinity toward thin, average, and heavy media personalities. The seven media variables coupled with the seven measures associated with eating disorders yielded only four significant relationships (based on a multiple hierarchical regression analysis; see Table 4, p. 492, of the article). In other words, only 4 out of 49 possible effects were significant, not all of which were in the expected directions. This seems to invalidate the premise that exposure to the media is related to or better yet causes eating disorders.

Harrison (2000) conducted another study to explore the relationship between the symptomatology of eating disorders and exposure to various media outlets. When it comes to female viewers, Harrison seems to have found that exposure to any body type other than a perfectly average one "causes" eating disorders. For example, Harrison found that exposure to "fat-character" television correlated with bulimia whereas exposure to "thin-ideal" magazines correlated with anorexia (for females, that is). Exposure to sports magazines yielded an increase in body dissatisfaction solely for females in the 12th grade (a rather specific effect). That said, exposure to fat-character television programming was associated with increased body dissatisfaction in males but only if they were in the sixth grade. Finally, contrary to the intuition within this research stream, which assumes that these media effects are particularly potent in shaping younger minds, Harrison found that older females were more susceptible. The latter findings appear haphazard and as such do not seem to support the premise that media causes eating disorders.

Posavac, Posavac, and Posavac (1998) used an experimental design to investigate whether a woman's dissatisfaction with her body moderated how she might react to being exposed to media depictions of attractive women. The authors state:

> Despite the popular belief that the thin standard of female attractiveness currently presented in the media is a primary contributor to the high level of concern with body weight among women, experimental studies have not shown that exposure to media images increases women's weight concern. (p. 187)

In other words, contrary to the accepted premise linking media images of attractive women with a wide range of social ills, there currently exists very little *causal* evidence in support of it. This erroneous yet staunchly held belief is driven by two factors, namely ideological dogma (e.g., the patriarchy creates oppressive images to exploit women) and the intellectual doctrine of the SSSM with its overemphasis on socialization forces. Returning to the study by Posavac et al. (1998), they found that only those women who were a priori dissatisfied with their bodies were adversely affected by the latter images, via an increased concern with their body weight.

Botta (2003) sought to establish a relationship between teenagers' exposure to magazines and their body image and eating disorder scores. These consisted of five variables, namely body satisfaction, drive toward thinness, anorexic and bulimic behaviors, and drive toward muscularity. The collected data included demographic information as well as the extent to which the teenagers read each of three types of magazines (fashion, health/fitness, and sports). Of 30 correlations between the measures of eating disorders and the extent of reading magazines (five measures of eating disorders × three types of magazines × two sexes), only 7 reached marginal significance or better (see Tables II and III, pp. 394–395). Furthermore, several of the significant correlations were counterintuitive. For example, health/fitness magazines were the most significant media "culprits" for girls as opposed to perhaps the expected fashion magazines. In sum, few significant correlations were obtained between measures of eating disorders and the extent to which one is exposed to the so-called culprit media sources.

Bissell and Zhou (2004) discussed several theories relevant to the manner by which women internalize expectations and standards regarding ideal body types (e.g., being thin) including social comparison theory, objectification theory, and social cognitive theory. The working hypothesis was that women are taught to care about their body image via exposure to specific television shows (Must-See TV and ESPN sports programs). After much data mining, it was found that exposure to thin-ideal programming (e.g., Must-See TV) predicted scores on four dimensions of disordered eating in women whereas exposure to sports shows did not. The authors conclude, "The goal for future research is to continue to find ways to combat the negative messages often found in entertainment media" (p. 20). Most studies within this paradigm including that by Bissell and Zhou succumb to the same methodological biases, namely identifying illusory correlations and confounding correlation with causality. For example, one might be able to show that men who watch NFL games on television can bench press heavier weights as compared to those men that never watch football games. It would be erroneous to conclude that the two variables are correlated in a meaningful manner or that one variable caused the other.

Ferron (1997) explored and contrasted the body image concerns of French and American adolescents. The findings were consistent with evolutionary principles. For example, given the universal preference for clear skin (cue of health), it is not surprising that the surveyed adolescents worried about skin issues. Numerous commercials targeting adolescents deal with the perceived social costs of having facial pimples and acne. This concern is not an arbitrary aesthetic cue imposed by Machiavellian advertisers; rather, it is an evolved preference that carries evolutionarily relevant information (cf. Kellett & Gilbert, 2001). Similarly, both the French and American adolescent girls wished to possess facial traits that are predicted from an evolutionary perspective including neotenous traits (e.g., large eyes) and full lips. On a related note, Ferron cites research showing that adolescent boys aspire to have mesomorphic body types. This sex-specific preference makes evolutionary sense in that the latter body type is the clearest indicator of physical dominance. Ferron states, "Cross-cultural studies have shown that body image depends more on gender differences than on cultural differences among adolescents who have different ethnic origins but live in the same country" (p. 737). This is expected from an evolutionary perspective, given that the mating module, which is driven by sex-specific differences that are culturally invariant, guides preferred body types. Accordingly, the roots of body dissatisfaction and subsequent eating disorders are unlikely to be driven by media images given that the findings occur in the same sex-specific manner in countless cultures.

Turner, Hamilton, Jacobs, Angood, and Dwyer (1997) exposed two groups of women to either four fashion magazines or four news magazines and subsequently gauged various measures dealing with body image, dieting, and concerns with thinness. The authors stated, "Although previous researchers (i.e., Spillman & Everington, 1989) have implied that the media have changed our perceptions of the female body, few studies have actually tested this hypothesis empirically" (p. 605). In the first part of the post-experimental questionnaire, using nine drawn female silhouettes varying in level of thinness, the female participants had to identify the silhouettes that most closely corresponded to their body, their ideal body, as well as the societal ideal of a body type. The two groups did not differ on any of the three measures. The second part of the experimental questionnaire contained 31 items, of which 21 yielded null effects between the two groups. Despite the preponderance of null effects, Turner et al. proclaimed that the latter findings supported the tenet that media images cause body image dissatisfaction and other eating-related attitudes and behaviors. It would seem that the mantra is impervious to falsification even by those who are fully aware that scant evidence exists in support of the tenet.

Waller et al. (1994) provided a succinct review of the postulated links between the media and eating-related psychopathology. When discussing the postulated effects of using slim models, they state, "However, there has been little evidence to date that the media's use of such models has any effect upon women's eating psychopathology" (p. 287). In reviewing their research, they conclude that women who already had eating disorders were affected by media images whereas those who did not suffer from any such disorder were unaffected. They then added that the latter effect was not replicated for television images but was restricted to still images of women's bodies. This is a rather curious effect, especially if media images are the supposed culprits in causing eating disorders. Finally, Waller et al. proposed, "It cannot be concluded that fashion magazines act as initial antecedents to eating disorders. However, they may be potent maintaining factors in part of the psychopathology" (p. 287). Given that an anorexic patient looks at her emaciated body and views it as too fat, it is not surprising that media images might be equally powerful in shaping her self-concept. This does not imply that media images are the causative agent.

Groesz, Levine, and Murnen (2002) conducted a meta-analysis of experiment-based studies that sought to gauge the effects of exposing women to thin-ideal images. They conclude that such a deleterious effect exists and state that "body satisfaction for women is significantly lower after viewing thin media images than after viewing media images of average size models, of cars or houses, or of overweight models" (p. 11). That women would react more adversely upon viewing images of thin women (who are also typically beautiful because the images oftentimes stem from fashion magazines) as opposed to inanimate objects does not demonstrate that the media are responsible for such an attribution. One can safely expect that images of same-sex rivals would engender greater concern as compared to those of inanimate items in all documented cultures. A central expectation within this research stream proposes that because specific media images are harmful to women's self-concept, increased exposure to such images should be positively correlated to the harm caused. Groesz et al. obtained findings that contradicted the latter expectation. Not only did they find that younger women (i.e., less than 19) were more susceptible to the effect but also the strongest effect sizes occurred when the number of exposures (to the thin ideal) was small. In order to "explain" the otherwise problematic findings, they conclude that "the experimental effect is seen most clearly in the activation—not the cultivation—of a thinness schema" (p. 12). Hence in this new interpretation, it is not the fact that women are cumulatively assailed with media images of thin models that causes them distress (which is the common postulate); rather, a mere one or two exposures is what is most detrimental to their self-concept. Irrespective of the obtained findings, the interpretation is consistent with the starting premise, namely that media images are harmful to women's self-concepts.

M. N. Miller and Pumariega (2001) reviewed the cross-cultural incidence of eating disorders. They suggest that such disorders transcend time
and place. For example, they state:

> Although contemporary emphasis on the Western ideal of beauty has
> been blamed for increases in the prevalence of eating disorders across the
> last several decades, a more thorough review of history reveals that these
> disorders have been present in other eras. (p. 94)

They add, "Disordered eating behaviors documented throughout most
of history raise much question about whether eating disorders are in fact a
product of current social pressures (Bemporad, 1996)" (p. 96). They recognized the fact that eating disorders (including anorexia nervosa) have existed since antiquity, albeit their prevalence rates have changed over time.
The Greek physician Hippocrates had documented the incidence of such
disorders several millennia ago. What might explain the changing prevalence rates in the disease cross-culturally and longitudinally? Miller and
Pumariega conclude, "Throughout history, self-starvation has been more
common during periods of affluence but only if combined with greater
freedom for women" (p. 104). Polivy and Herman (2002) have also confirmed that eating disorders tend to occur mainly in cultures where food is
abundant. To the extent that Western cultures comprise the majority of
such environments of plenty, it is perhaps not surprising that the eating
disorders tend to occur more frequently in First World economies. In all instances where Miller and Pumariega (2001) identified the sex of the pa-
tients/participants in their cross-cultural review, the instantiation of the
disease occurred in the same sex-specific manner, albeit they did not recognize the possible evolutionary roots of the disorder. Though Thai, Egyptian, and American women might have a different probability of
succumbing to the disorder, what is unequivocally clear is that irrespective
of culture or epoch, women are the overwhelming sufferers. Thus, although it is certainly relevant to discuss the importance of culture and
acculturation in shaping this disorder, it is perhaps more important to seek
an explanation for the universal sex effect.

Whereas social constructivists have typically sought to link the incidence of eating disorders to advertising and related media images, other
theories have been proposed with equal aplomb. For example, M. N.
Miller and Pumariega (2001) discuss feminist theories that have espoused that the root of eating disorders might lie in the contradictory societal roles that women are now expected to adhere to (e.g., that women
must be pretty and nurturing while being assertive and professional).
Hence, according to feminist theorizing, not only does showing a thin,
beautiful, and perfect-looking model cause eating disorders but also
showing the same woman in the role of a neurosurgeon will be equally

detrimental to women's self-concepts. The celebrated feminist Camille Paglia has proclaimed her abhorence for such feminist theorizing because it depicts women as fragile creatures in need of constant protection. Not only are such worldviews offensive in their depiction of women but also they are extremely easy to falsify. Out of 100 women who view unrealistic images of female perfection and who are also exposed to "contradictory" gender roles, 1 to 3 of these might develop an eating disorder. What explains the fact that the remaining 97% to 99% of women are unaffected by these "causal" factors? Additionally, why are men not succumbing to eating disorders given the contradictory expectations inherent in contemporary definitions of masculinity, comprised of both unbridled virility and emotional sensitivity?

Polivy and Herman (2002) conducted a thorough review of the various research streams that have sought to identify the causes of eating disorders. Their outlook regarding the state of the literature was rather bleak. For example, they explicitly recognized the incessant error committed throughout the literature in thinking of correlational relationships as implying causality. They sum up their evaluation of the field as follows:

> Finally, much of the literature consists of atheoretical attempts to measure and correlate particular researchers' favorite variables, rather than attempting to test etiological hypotheses about EDs [eating disorders]. This is not to say that there are not theoreticians doing systematic studies testing conceptual views of the disorder, but such research is often overshadowed by the myriad studies in this area that do not rely on theoretical underpinnings. The noise-to-signal ratio in the literature is thus higher than one would like. (p. 205)

Though no mention of the evolutionary forces behind the disorder was made, the authors expeditiously dismissed the "media causes eating disorder" mantra. They state, "Exposure to the media is so widespread that if such exposure were *the* cause of EDs, then it would be difficult to explain why anyone would *not* be eating-disordered" [italics in original] (p. 192). They then add, "Media and peer pressure no doubt impinge more powerfully on females than on males, but we should not be too complacent about explaining the huge disproportion of females among ED patients solely in terms of these influences" (p. 193).

Even those scholars who have explored a wide range of likely causes of eating disorders other than the supposed influence of the media have typically done so from a proximate perspective. Polivy and Herman (2002) review various individual-level variables that might predict why some women develop an eating disorder. For example, they propose that what differentiates women who develop eating disorders from those who do not is that the former view weight-related control as a means to gain identity and achieve control in their lives. This is a tautological explanation for it merely conflates the outcome of the disease as a viable antecedent. Countless other personality traits and biological markers have been investigated as likely causes of eating disorders. For example, Polivy and Herman discuss the relevance of perfectionism in the context of eating disorders. Because both men and women can suffer from clinical instantiations of perfectionism, this research stream does not explain why it is predominantly women who might succumb to perfectionism in the context of eating disorders. As far as biological-based studies are concerned, these typically cannot establish whether a given physiological marker (e.g., serotonin imbalance) is the cause or the effect of the disease. By solely focusing on proximate issues, the most robust finding is lost namely that eating disorders manifest themselves in the same sex-specific manner across cultures and eras.

Evolutionary Perspective.   Evolutionists have provided ultimate explanations not only of the Darwinian etiology of eating disorders but also of the ecological factors that are likely to trigger the onset of the disease. Several evolutionary-based frameworks have been proposed to explain the sex-specific nature of eating disorders. For example, that women are overwhelmingly more likely to succumb to the aesthetic-based versions of the disease, as opposed to religiously-inspired self-starvation, irrespective of cultural setting and historical context suggests that its etiology is linked to sex-specific components within the reproductive module (cf. McGuire & Troisi, 1998, pp. 201–206). Surbey (1987) applied the reproduction suppression model (Wasser & Barash, 1983) in explaining anorexia nervosa. The basic tenet of the model is that females across a wide range of mammalian species can shut off their reproductive potential if the ecological conditions are nonconducive to a pregnancy. The suppression in women can take on many forms including delayed menarche (primary amenorrhea) or the shutting off of the menses for women who have already gone through menarche (secondary amenorrhea). Viewed from this perspective, anorexia nervosa is an instantiation of reproductive suppression, which can at times be taken to maladaptive extremes. Given that environmental stressors have been found to influence the onset of menarche (see Ellis, 2004, for a thorough review of theories of female pubertal maturation), it would seem reasonable to contrast the demographic profiles and environmental conditions of girls that mature early to those of anorexics (Surbey, 1987). Using the reproductive suppression hypothesis as the explicative framework, Juda, Campbell, and Crawford (2004) demonstrated that dieting symptomatology is negatively correlated with perceptions of family and partner support. They also found that dieting symptomatology was negatively correlated with readiness to become a parent but positively correlated with stress. In other words, an increase in an important environmental stressor (lack of familial and mate support) can trigger the suppression of one's reproductive potential, which in this case is instantiated via an increase in dieting symptomatology. In their review of the causes of eating disorders, Polivy and Herman (2002) suggest that family stress and other stressors seem to be correlated with the incidence of eating disorders. This seems to confirm the evolutionary-based prediction as derived from the reproductive suppression hypothesis; namely, poor environments will serve as catalysts to the suppression of one's reproductive potential.

Voland and Voland (1989) discuss specific ecological variables that are likely to trigger reproductive suppression. For example, they propose that the fact that anorexia nervosa occurs more frequently in Westernized countries is congruent with the reproductive suppression hypothesis in that this disorder should be more likely to occur in countries with lower adult mortality (i.e., where life is better). Suppressing one's reproductive potential makes sense only if one will live long enough to experience superior mating opportunities in the future. Hence, whereas the macroenvironments conducive to anorexia should be ones of plenty, the specific microenvironments of potential anorexics are predicted to contain important stressors. Voland and Voland propose that some of these stressors include the incidence of sexual attacks and poor family life. Additionally, they argue that reproductive suppression can operate via kin selection as a form of "helper at the nest" mechanism (not unlike insect eusociality). They propose the possibility that an anorexic can at times be manipulated to suppress reproduction by her parents, as a form of biased parental investment. This parental manipulation is thought to favor the parents to the detriment of the anorexic. Evolutionists have discovered that depending on various ecological conditions, parents are expected to engage in sex-specific biased parenting (i.e., favoring either sons or daughters). For example, in polygynous societies, high-status families oftentimes have son-biased investments. On the other hand, societies with increased risks of paternity uncertainty are more likely to have daughter-biased parenting (see Holden, Sear, & Mace, 2003, pp. 103–105, for a model to predict the direction of parental bias). Hence, given that anorexia nervosa has typically been linked to higher social classes, this might be a manifestation of son-biased parenting (although there appears to be a democratization of the disease in terms of its incidence across social classes). Viewed from this perspective, anorexia is a form of daughter-based negatively biased parental investment, which if taken to its most morbid extreme becomes a form of female infanticide. The findings within the literature on eating disorders seem to be congruent with many of the ideas espoused by Voland and Voland. For example, in their cross-cultural review of eating disorders, M. N. Miller and Pumariega (2001) cite research suggesting that parental overprotection is correlated with eating disorder scores. This is consistent with the parental manipulation mechanism that promotes anorexia in female patients as proposed by Voland and Voland (1989).

Although the reproductive suppression model is perhaps the most frequently applied evolutionary mechanism in explaining eating disorders, other Darwinian-inspired frameworks have been proposed. Abed (1998) provided an alternate evolutionary account of eating disorders, which he coined the sexual competition hypothesis. Specifically, he proposed that the maladaptive concern for thinness is triggered via a runaway form of intrasexual competition between women (see also Campbell, 2004). Abed argues that the current environments in Western countries contain a set of demographic realities that accentuate female intrasexual rivalry. For example, he proposes that the delayed age at which women now bear children has effectively increased the time span in which they maintain nubile figures. Additionally, he argues that a greater number of postmenopausal women now seem to maintain "pseudo-nubile" figures (e.g., to "recompete" in the mating market in light of rising divorce rates). This effectively creates an environment that is ripe for female-based intrasexual rivalry, which for some women results in eating disorders. Note that Abed's hypothesis accords with the reproductive suppression model in that he is proposing a specific environmental stressor (i.e., greater perceived intrasexual competition) as the trigger for reproductive suppression. Additionally, as Abed concedes, media images might indeed expose women to a greater number of intrasexual rivals who possess nubile figures. Hence, viewed from this perspective, media images can exacerbate intrasexual competition but for reasons rooted within the evolved sexuality of women and not because of patriarchal forces. For additional evolutionary-based discussions of eating disorders, the reader is referred to Condit (1990), Anderson and Crawford (1992), Mealy (2000), Guisinger (2003), and Faer, Hendriks, Abed, and Figueredo (2005).

Gambling

The aggregate consumption figures of gambling are staggering. In 1991, U.S. $304 billion were wagered in the United States (Volberg, 1994). In 1996, revenues from gambling exceeded those of five combined leisure industries, namely the film box office, recorded music, cruise ships, spectator sports, and live-entertainment industries (Christiansen, 1998, as cited by Shaffer & Korn, 2002, p. 175). The latter finding is congruent with a more recent one reported by Potenza, Kosten, and Rounsaville (2001) wherein they noted that in 1998, legalized gambling grossed more than three major entertainment industries combined (movies, theme parks, and music) and amounted to U.S. $50 billion. In 1999, 0.74% of personal income was spent on gambling in the United States (Shaffer & Korn, 2002). Though gambling can serve as an important economic catalyst (e.g., economic impact of casinos on federal reserves), few consumption activities yield as many deleterious effects as does pathological gambling. Legarda, Babio, and Abreu (1992) estimated that the prevalence of pathological gambling was six times greater than that for opiate addiction in Spain. Potenza et al. (2001) cite the Gambling Impact and Behavior Study that found that the costs (perhaps underestimated) of pathological gambling are U.S. $5 billion, a figure also reported by Shaffer and Korn (2002, p. 180). Lamberton and Oei (1997) cite research from the 1980s that had explored the socioeconomic and occupational costs of pathological gambling. Reported findings include that problem gamblers have twice the unemployment rate, that they owe from U.S. $50,000 to U.S. $90,000 in average accumulated gambling debts, and that they operate at 50% of their productivity when at work (see the relevant references in Lamberton & Oei, 1997, p. 86).

In light of the economic and social repercussions of gambling, it is not surprising that scholars from several disciplines have sought to explore numerous facets of gambling behavior. That said, Blanco, Ibáñez, Sáiz-Ruiz, Blanco-Jerez, and Nunes (2000) state, "After more than 10 000 years of the existence of the disorder, the field of pathological gambling research and treatment is still in its infancy" (p. 406). Additionally, there does not appear to be any integrative framework to organize the otherwise disjointed findings. This holds true even for those topics that have been most often studied such as the prevalence rate of gambling in various populations. In their review of the literature on the prevalence rates of gambling, Shaffer and Korn (2002) state, "With few exceptions, the prevalence estimates reviewed here seem to have been promulgated, at best, by the question of 'let's find out,' and, at worst, in a conceptual vacuum" (p. 199). Later in this section, I argue that evolutionary psychology can help provide the needed conceptual and theoretical guidance to the gambling literature.

Despite the lack of theoretical frameworks within this research stream, scholars have obtained robust findings that appear to be cross-culturally invariant. For example, Shaffer, Hall, and Bilt (1999) conducted a meta-analysis of studies that have addressed the prevalence rates of gambling. The meta-analysis included 134 prevalence estimates (originating from 119 studies) and a very large sample size ($N = 122,286$). No differences were found in the prevalence estimates across population segments when comparing the United States with Canada. The prevalence of problem/pathological gambling is around 1% of the general population. Shaffer and Korn (2002) conclude, "Perhaps most notable about this evidence is the relative consistency of the prevalence rates observed in different venues, using different measures and methods" (p. 184). That said, not only are the prevalence rates of pathological gambling roughly the same across cultures but also the demographic profile of the typical pathological gambler seems universally invariant (cf. Shaffer & Korn, 2002, p. 203). Thus, that the gambling literature has amassed a set of universally valid findings is indicative of a possible Darwinian etiology for this particular behavioral phenomenon.

Demographic Risk Factors Associated With Pathological Gambling.
Shaffer and Korn (2002) provide a review of the gambling literature with an eye to its public health implications. Despite the fact that the majority of gambling-related problems occur in men, little mention of this fact is made. Rather, there appeared to be a need to "democratize" the disease. One would find it irrational to democratize diseases of the ovaries, of the breasts, or of the prostate. However, when it comes to behavioral-related problems, it seems politically incorrect to focus on one sex even if the epidemiological data is unequivocal in highlighting that the sufferers are overwhelmingly members of one of the two sexes. For example, Welte, Barnes, Wieczorck, Tidwell, and Parker (2002) state, "It appears that the increased availability of gambling opportunities in our society has led to the 'democratization' of gambling" (p. 336). This is misleading because those behaviors that constitute gambling have been redefined in a way that makes it appear as though a more heterogeneous group of people now gamble (e.g., church bingo). Regarding the truly impactful statistics (e.g., pathological gambling), little if any democratization has occurred. The great majority of studies, covering several decades and a wide range of cultures, have yielded the same pattern of findings. Men are much more likely to be pathological gamblers. Other risk factors include being young, poor, uneducated, and unmarried. In the ensuing paragraphs, I provide brief descriptions of a small subset of such studies. The countries covered include Canada, the United States, Spain, Switzerland, Sweden, Norway, and Hong Kong.

Volberg (1994) conducted a study to gauge the prevalence of pathological gambling across five American states (New Jersey, Maryland, Massachusetts, Iowa, and California). The demographics of the gamblers were roughly the same across the five states. Most strikingly, the percentage of males comprising the gambling population (in terms of gamblers in treatment programs) in each of the five states were 93, 91, 93, 86, and 93 respectively. In the latter cases, the data correspond to the demographics of pathological gamblers who had sought professional treatment. The authors make the point that women gamblers are less likely to seek treatment and hence might be underrepresented in such statistics. The opposite and contradictory position is taken by researchers who investigate compulsive buying (see later in this chapter) wherein it is argued that the reason that women appear to be the majority of compulsive buyers is that they are more likely to seek treatment. Incidentally, Petry (2003) compared Gamblers Anonymous (GA) attendees and non-attendees on a wide slew of variables including both gambling-related ones as well as demographics to see whether the profiles of those who attend are different from those who do not. The two groups did not differ along education levels or gender, hence casting doubt on the notion that women gamblers are less likely to seek treatment. In addition to collecting data from pathological gamblers who had sought treatment, Volberg administered a survey, which yielded that 76% of those that scored as probable pathological gamblers were male. Additionally, individuals who were categorized as probable pathological gamblers were more likely to be unmarried and less educated as compared to members of the general population. More recently, Welte et al. (2002) conducted a national survey ($N = 2,630$) whereby both self-reported measures of participation in various forms of gambling were elicited as was a psychometric scale to measure pathological gambling. The findings provide unequivocal support for the ubiquitous male effect. Specifically, men who gambled did so more often, they placed larger bets, had greater variance in terms of the absolute amounts won and lost (i.e., larger absolute gains and losses), and were more involved in gambling. Additionally, men engaged in greater gambling in all forms of games where they felt that they have control over the possible outcomes (e.g., cards, pool, and sports betting). Finally, problem gamblers were more likely to be males. The authors also explored the relationship between gambling and socioeconomic status (SES). They obtained a negative correlation between SES and problem/pathological gambling. Specifically, the highest SES quartile had a problem/pathological gambling rate of 1.6% whereas the lowest quartile's rate was 5.3% (an extremely significant difference). Additionally, SES and gambling involvement were negatively correlated, with the lowest and highest quartiles spending $400 and $176 per year respectively. Canadian data yield roughly the same profile of the pathological gambler as that uncovered in the United States. For example, Doiron and Nicki (2001) sought to determine whether the characteristics defining problematic gamblers in Prince Edward Island (a Canadian province in the Maritimes) were similar to those throughout the rest of Canada. Not surprisingly, the authors conclude, "The profile of problem gamblers is also relatively uniform. In general, Canadians experiencing problems with gambling are more likely to be male, single, and younger than the general population" (p. 413).

Data from Europe replicate the standard demographic profile of the pathological gambler irrespective of whether it originates in Northern Europe (Switzerland), Southern Europe (Spain), or Scandinavia (Sweden and Norway). Using telephone surveys, Bondolfi, Osiek, and Ferrero (2000) explored pathological gambling in Switzerland ($N = 2,526$). In line with several papers that they cited, Bondolfi et al. found that being male, young (in this case under 29 years old), and single were key demographic predictors of problem or pathological gamblers. Contrary to the bulk of the existing literature, the latter problematic gamblers were underrepresented in terms of low household incomes, and they were more likely to be employed full-time (wage earners). Götestam and Johansson (2003) conducted a nationwide telephone survey ($N = 2{,}014$) in Norway wherein specific questions related to gambling habits were asked (e.g., how often one gambled, amount bet, etc.). Young males (less than 30 years old) were most likely to be categorized as problematic gamblers (pathological and at-risk gambling). Additionally, the relationship between degree of gambling and various demographics was explored. Both education and employment status were correlated with degree of gambling in the expected directions (i.e., being less educated and unemployed were predictors of problematic gambling). Surprisingly, civil status was not correlated with degree of gambling (typically being unmarried is a risk factor). For the most part, the latter results accord with those of Volberg and Abbott (1994), who listed the following key risk factors: young (under 30), unmarried, unemployed, low education, low income, non-White males. Volberg, Abbott, Rönnberg, and Munck (2001) administered a national telephone and mail survey ($N = 7{,}139$) in Sweden to explore the rate of pathological gambling along with the associated risk factors. The specific demographic variables were chosen (as prospective risk factors) because as Volberg et al. state, "These variables, including gender, age, country of birth and education, were selected on the basis of research showing that these factors are the major predictive variables for gambling problems in many jurisdictions internationally" (p. 253). Ceteris paribus, men were found to have a 271% higher risk of succumbing in their lifetime to problem or pathological gambling. The next most important variable was an individual's age, with those less than 25 years old having a 151% greater risk of exhibiting pathological or problem gambling in their lifetimes. Additionally, those receiving social welfare payments (a proxy measure of low SES) were at greater risk of developing problematic gambling behaviors. The authors state, "For both youth and marginalized minority groups, little is known about why problem gambling rates are higher than among majority adults in the same population" (p. 250). They then conclude that "a striking finding of the present study is the similarity in the sociodemographic profile of problem gamblers in Sweden and those in other countries in the world" (p. 255). The universal links between specific demographic variables and problematic gambling are due to evolutionary-based reasons, explained shortly. Finally, although no statistical results were provided, Legarda et al. (1992) concluded that Spanish men were much more likely to be pathological or problem gamblers. Other demographic variables yielded mixed findings (e.g., the effect of age on gambling etc.). The ubiquitous sex effect is not restricted to North America and Europe for it has also been documented in Asia. Wong and So (2003) administered a telephone survey on pathological gambling in Hong Kong. They found that being male, of low education, and middle-income were important risk factors. The odds ratio of sex (male) was 2.26. There does not appear to be one documented culture wherein the latter sex effect is reversed (but see Welte, Barnes, Wieczorek, Tidwell, & Parker, 2004, for a rare null effect for gender).

Most studies wherein authors have cited research with regard to the sex of the typical pathological gambler have yielded the same conclusions. Young males of low social status comprise the majority of pathological gamblers. Potenza et al. (2001) cite research showing that men have two to three times the likelihood of being pathological gamblers. They also cite research that has found that pathological gamblers are more likely to be adolescents, African Americans, and individuals originating from the lower socioeconomic strata. Shaffer et al. (1999) concluded that two risk factors for developing pathological gambling habits were being male and adolescence. Welte et al. (2002) cited the first national gambling survey (Kallick, Suits, Dielman, & Hybels, 1979), which showed that males were more likely than females to be heavy bettors. Surprisingly (from an evolutionary psychology perspective), those classified as heavy bettors, were more likely to be in a higher income bracket. Shaffer and Korn (2002) concluded that lower-income households spend a greater proportion of their resources on gambling. They also cited work showing that young people are more prone to suffer from gambling-related problems as are people of lower socioeconomic standing (see p. 187). On the same page, they refer to research that has shown that men are much more likely to suffer from gambling-related addictions and that adolescent boys are four times more likely to be pathological gamblers as compared to their female counterparts. The explanations that they provided to explain these robust sex differences are lacking. For example, they state, "Gender differences reflect complex attitudes and opportunities about recreational activities and the social milieus within which these occur" (p. 187). An evolutionary perspective proposes that men will assiduously seek to acquire resources because this is one of the most important intersexual cues along which women will judge them. Accordingly, for the same reasons that bank robbers are predominantly men, pathological gamblers are equally dominated by the male sex. Pathological gambling is one approach by which men can amass resources. Hence, it is particularly important to understand the innate motives that drive this particular behavior.

Domain-General Perspective of Addiction. Many scholars who explore compulsive or addictive behaviors do so from a comorbidity perspective. Namely, it is argued that the specific affliction (e.g., pathological gambling) is a manifestation of a more general "addictive" personality, a position congruent with a domain-general viewpoint of addiction. Shaffer and Korn (2002, p. 194) claim that because kleptomania, pyromania, and trichotillomania are impulse disorders (as posited to be the case for pathological gambling), this implies that all of these diseases should have similar origins. Illusory "diseases" as originating from the self-help literature such as the codependency syndrome are also typically construed from a domain-general perspective. In discussing the latter "syndrome," Rimke (2000) states, "The emergence of the concept of codependency arose from the self-help recovery experts' conviction that the essence of all addictions is an unhealthy dependence upon *any* [italics in original] pathological relationship, whether with persons, activities, or substances" (p. 66). The domain-general viewpoint is a reasonable assumption only if one assumes that the etiology of addictions transcends domains. That a cluster of disorders might for example be linked to impulse control does not imply that they have the same etiology. The comorbidity findings do not seem to accord with the domain-general perspective. For example, Shaffer and Korn cite research that has shown that there is no comorbidity between pathological gambling and eating and/or sexual addictions. Similarly, Petry (2003) found that very few of the pathological gamblers had active drug addictions. In many instances, there is no reason to expect that such a correlation should exist. This can be expected only when one assumes that the mechanism driving these addictions is domain-general (e.g., reward deficiency syndrome). However, I propose that many addictions have a domain-specific etiology linked to a specific adaptive problem (even if in this case the behavior is maladaptive). Accordingly, that individuals succumb to a given "behavioral misfiring," which results in a very specific addiction, does not imply that they will succumb to other addictions. For example, pornographic addiction, anorexia nervosa, and pathological gambling have domain-specific etiologies, all linked in sex-specific manners to the Darwinian module of reproduction. That said, there is no reason to think that a woman who suffers from an eating disorder is more likely to be addicted to pornography because of a domain-general addictive personality trait. As such, I contend that pathological gambling is a primary and not secondary disorder. Hence, its etiology is unique and does not fall within a cluster of conditions. Accordingly, a domain-specific perspective is incongruous with Shaffer and Korn's contention that problematic gambling should be construed as a syndrome of some other illness. It is a singular manifestation of one of many possible strategies for acquiring resources.

Notwithstanding the questionable theoretical assumptions implicit in much of the comorbidity research, there does exist a substantial amount of evidence that has linked pathological gambling with other disorders. That said, in many instances the comorbidity findings are difficult to interpret given the difficulty in establishing the veridical causal link between the comorbid disorders. This is the conclusion reached by Shaffer and Korn (2002, p. 177) when they proclaimed that the cause–effect confound is endemic within the gambling literature. Does crime cause gambling or vice versa? Does depression result in gambling or does gambling result in depression (Blanco et al., 2000)? Thus, to establish a pattern of comorbidity between pathological gambling and one or more other disorders does not necessarily elucidate much about the ultimate causes behind the behavior.

Proximate Theories of Gambling.   There exist several thorough reviews of the pathological-gambling literature, all of which address theories at the proximate level and that inherently espouse domain-general theorizing (cf. El-Guebaly & Hodgins, 2000; Raylu & Oei, 2002). For example, Lamberton and Oei (1997) describe four proximate theories, namely affective theory, behaviour theory, arousal theory, and cognitive theory, that have been applied in studying pathological gambling. Some of these are useful from a proximate perspective whereas others are questionable (e.g., childhood pain causes affective problems that are attenuated via gambling). Potenza et al. (2001) discuss key neurobiological theories of pathological gambling, namely those associated with problems with impulse control and those related with addictive predispositions (e.g., comorbidity with substance addiction). Dickerson and Baron (2000, Table 2, pp. 1153–1154) list a wide range of proximate issues that have been investigated within the gambling literature. Blanco et al. (2000) reviewed four theoretical approaches that have been applied in addressing the etiology of disordered gambling, a summary of which I provide here. Perhaps the least valuable of all such theories are psychodynamic approaches stemming from the Freudian movement. As explained by Blanco et al., some Freudian-inclined scholars have sought to link pathological gambling with either the Oedipal complex and/or with pre-Oedipal conflicts associated with denial and omnipotence. Hence, given that gamblers engage in behaviors that have low probabilities of yielding positive outcomes, it is argued that they must be suffering from narcissism with its associated denial and sense of omnipotence. A second class of theories explores various learning mechanisms that drive gambling behavior. Accordingly, such theories are heavily influenced by the domain-general approaches of behaviorism. For example, some scholars within this tradition have explored how behavioral reinforcement (e.g., in the Skinnerian sense) can occur either in terms of the sporadic and intermittent positive outcomes (i.e., monetary wins) and/or in terms of the actual heightened excitement arising from the risk-taking activity. A third class of theories are those that explore the cognitive processes and corresponding cognitive biases that gamblers succumb to when engaging in gambling-related behaviors. For example, several scholars have documented the recall bias wherein gamblers are much more likely to remember wins while forgetting losses. This cognitive bias likely serves as a faciliatory mechanism for engaging in additional gambling. Another common cognitive bias that gamblers succumb to is the illusion of control over random events. Casino operators take advantage of this particular bias by providing roulette players with tally cards that permit players to count the number of times that a particular number or color (black or red) has occurred. The erroneous logic here is that random events have an auto-corrective mechanism such that if a particular number or color has occurred less frequently, its likelihood of "hitting" is greater. An unbiased roulette machine is a random generator such that each spin of the wheel is an independent event. However, many gamblers moniter a night's hit patterns with the goal of having greater "informational" value and hence supposed control over the upcoming wheel spins. This is in line with another "irrational" behavior whereby avid lottery players refuse to trade in their "carefully chosen" tickets for a greater number of tickets consisting of randomly chosen numbers (cf. Bar-Hillel & Neter, 1996, for some reasons that make individuals reluctant to trade their lottery tickets). The probabilistic calculus would suggest that any rational consumer should prefer to trade in their lottery tickets for some larger number of tickets (i.e., increased probability of winning). Nonetheless, many consumers refuse the offer. A fourth class of theories reviewed by Blanco et al. seeks to identify neurobiological substrates and physiological markers that discriminate between pathological gamblers and members of the general population. Included here are the effects of seretonin, dopamine, and other neurotransmitters on mechanisms that relate to gambling such as arousal, impulse control, and the processing and integration of reward-related information. Along these lines, several groups of neuroscientists have begun to explore the neuronal activation patterns that occur when individuals are making risk-related decisions (cf. Breiter, Aharon, Kahneman, Dale, & Shizgal, 2001; Gonzalez, Dana, Koshino, & Just, 2005; K. Smith, Dickhaut, McCabe, & Pardo, 2002) albeit not necessarily in the context of pathological gambling. For example, neuroeconomics is a newly founded field that specifically seeks to explore the neuronal substrates behind economic decision making (see the work by Colin Camerer and Paul Zak).

To recapitulate, numerous theoretical approaches have been applied in seeking to understand pathological gambling. That said, these have operated at the proximate level while espousing domain-general mechanisms. In light of the fact that specific demographic risk factors associated with pathological gambling seem remarkably similar across cultures and temporal periods, the phenomenon appears to be within the purview of evolutionary theory. In their discussion of the gambling literature, Blaszczynski and Nower (2002) conclude, "At the moment, there is no single conceptual theoretical model of gambling that adequately accounts for the multiple biological, psychological and ecological variables contributing to the development of pathological gambling" (p. 487). Accordingly, they proposed an integrative model (see Fig. 2, p. 493) similar in spirit to those espoused during the utopian grand theories phase of consumer research (see Ekström, 2003). However, successful integrative frameworks are not those that posit innumerable links between potentially relevant variables. Rather, one must identify a meta-theory that permeates through all levels of analyses and that accordingly organizes the literature in a coherent and consilient manner. Evolutionary theory can help achieve this unity of knowledge within the gambling literature, a topic that is explored next.

Evolutionary Explanation of Pathological Gambling. Few scholars have applied evolutionary-based theorizing in understanding pathological gambling. Spinella (2003) has argued that humans have an evolved neural circuitry for calculating risks and rewards, which is usurped by gambling stimuli. He states:

> The genetic underpinnings of the reward system would have adapted to maximize survival and reproductive success throughout human evolutionary history. Thus, its neuroanatomical, neurophysiological, and neurochemical configurations would be best suited to manage risks and rewards under conditions most typical of a hunter-gatherer existence. However, modern gambling represents an abrupt departure from risktaking in this context. In modern gambling, the contingencies for reward and punishment are intentionally calculated and adjusted to maximize gambling: the element of chance inherent in naturalistic situations has been refined into games of chance. Environmental conditions are carefully manipulated to intensify the impact of experience. Alcohol is supplied to alter judgment and risk-taking tendencies, and to minimize impulse control.
>
> In the evolutionary context, the losses and gains provided by risk taking were often more immediate and tangible, affecting one's food availability, mating opportunities, and physical safety. In contrast, the losses in modern gambling are abstract and delayed, represented by symbolic chips and numerical digits. Their relation to material items is only through associative conditioning. (pp. 509–510)

Though both men and women possess the evolved neuronal circuitry to calculate risks and rewards, some of the relevant ecological triggers are likely sex-specific in manners that are congruent with sex-specific adaptive problems. Hence, given that in countless status-related domains, men are much more likely to engage in risky behaviors (e.g., the young male syndrome as described by M. Wilson & Daly, 1985), it is not surprising that gambling is an ecological trigger that is more likely to usurp men's evolved neuronal circuitry that is dedicated to the processing of risks and rewards. P. B. Gray (2004) applied this form of evolutionary theorizing by looking at three separate cross-cultural data sets in order to explore the idea that young males are most likely to be gamblers. Cross-cultural data from the Human Relations Area File, a literature review of gambling studies conducted in numerous countries, and an observational study of gambling behaviors in American casinos served as the relevant data sets. Gray confirmed the cross-cultural robustness of the male effect although the predicted hypothesis regarding age, namely that young adults were more likely to gamble, was not.

It is important to note that by providing an evolutionary explanation of pathological gambling does not imply that the behavior is adaptive. Zuckerman and Kuhlman (2000) state:

> Foraging for food or mates was risky but necessary for survival. Those who enjoyed it had an advantage over those who only did it out of necessity. Modern forms of human sensation seeking such as drug abuse, reckless driving, mountain climbing and parachuting are not adaptive. They are merely a testimony to the persistence of traits produced by the selective pressures of the distant evolutionary history of our species. (pp. 1024–1025)

Hence, though pathological gambling typically yields maladaptive outcomes, its Darwinian roots lie in the adaptive solution to a survival problem that was relevant in the phylogenetic history of our species.

Compulsive Buying

The literature on compulsive buying shares at least four common points with that of pathological gambling. First, each behavior is overwhelmingly dominated by one sex. Whereas men constitute the majority of pathological gamblers, most compulsive buyers are women. In his recent review of the compulsive-buying literature, Black (2001) states:

> Compulsive buying appears to overlap with other impulse control disorders, particularly pathological gambling. Pathological gambling is primarily a disorder of men, but the two disorders are similar in terms of cognitive and behavioural symptoms; each could represent gender-specific manifestations of an underlying impulsive tendency. (pp. 18–19)

This is an incomplete account in that no attempt is made to explain why the impulse control disorder should manifest itself in these particular sex-specific manners. A second commonality between the two research streams is that they are both void of integrative theoretical frameworks capable of organizing the findings. In their review of two books on compulsive buying, Villarino and Otero-López (2001) conclude:

> This growing interest was not, however, accompanied by the development of a theoretical and methodological "corpus." While the last few decades have witnessed the appearance of descriptive studies which have brought forth a remarkable abundance, dispersion, and diversity of findings, both theoreticians and researchers agree that it is necessary to go beyond these partial and fragmentary approaches and to provide the field with a greater coherence. (pp. 443–444)

A third common point between the compulsive-buying and pathological-gambling literature is that scholars in both areas make the assumption that the particular affliction is part of a domain-general etiology. Fourth, the cause-and-effect problem is endemic in both disciplines. Does depression cause pathological gambling and/or compulsive buying or vice versa? Is low self-esteem the precursor or the consequence of compulsive buying (O'Guinn & Faber, 1989)?

Women and Compulsive Buying. J. A. Roberts (1998) conducted a survey-based study to explore various predictors of compulsive buying. Gender was correlated with compulsive buying; namely, women were more likely to engage in this behavior. Additionally, a hierarchical regression analysis found that gender was the second most important predictor after credit card use. Approximately 6% of the surveyed sample were classified as compulsive buyers. The gender effect was explained using standard socialization-based arguments, such as that young men are supposedly taught to be more careful with their money. As mentioned in chapter 3, there is convincing evidence to suggest that women are more risk aversive when it comes to financial decisions. Hence, the socialization-based explanation is in stark contradiction with the accumulated evidence, as well as being silent as to the genesis of this particular form of sex-based learning. O'Guinn and Faber (1989) found that 92% of the compulsive buyers were females. The authors provide several methodological reasons to explain this strong sex effect. They claim that women seek help more readily and hence might be overrepresented within the sampled group. This contradicts the working assumption in the gambling literature wherein it is typically claimed that women are less likely to seek help for their gambling habits (hence explaining why men constitute the majority of pathological gamblers). In the sample studied by Faber and Christenson (1996), 22 of the 24 participants who volunteered were women. Black, Repertinger, Gaffney, and Gabel (1998) found that 94% of compulsive buyers were women and suggested that compulsive buying might run in families matrilineally. In his extensive review of the compulsive-buying literature, Black (2001) cites six sources all showing a pronounced sex-specific effect (namely women more so than men) ranging from 80% to 95% of all compulsive buyers. That said, no reasons were provided as to why the disorder predominantly afflicts women. In the study conducted by De Sarbo and Edwards (1996), 82% of the sample was comprised of women. Finally, in those instances when the researchers determine a priori to restrict the studied sample to only one sex, it is always comprised of women.

Despite the latter unequivocal sex effect, the leading compulsive-buying scales have been developed without any compelling explanation as to why such an effect should exist and how this might impact the development of an accurate and reliable scale. Valence, d'Astous, and Fortier (1988) proposed a conceptual model of compulsive buying prior to the development of their scale. The ubiquitous sex effect was not mentioned despite the amassed evidence suggesting that roughly 90% of compulsive buyers are women. More recently, Faber and O'Guinn (1992) developed the definitive scale in the field using a compulsive-buying sample that was predominantly comprised of women (92%). They cited several studies that have each found a preponderance of women in their samples of compulsive buyers. Regarding the skewed gender distribution, they state:

> This is not surprising since compulsive buying is most likely an impulse control disorder (Christenson et al. 1992; McElroy et al., 1991), and all of the impulse control disorders are skewed on the basis of gender (American Psychiatric Association 1987; Popkin 1989). For example, pathological gambling tends to afflict mostly men, while kleptomania predominantly affects women (American Psychiatric Association 1987). (p. 461)

Missing from the latter statement is why specific disorders manifest themselves in sex-specific manners. Faber and O'Guinn conclude, "Finally, the relationship between compulsive buying and gender needs to be explored more fully, particularly in terms of its social construction" (p. 467). Hence, to the extent that consumer scholars have identified this robust sex effect, their explanation is that this is due to socialization.

Domain-General Perspective of Compulsive Buying.   Within this research stream, it is typically assumed that compulsive buyers are likely to be afflicted with a cluster of compulsive disorders. For example, O'Guinn and Faber's (1989) investigation of compulsive buying assumed that all such behaviors fit within a domain-general model of addiction. They conclude that exploring the commonalities across compulsive behaviors (e.g., excessive working or excessive participation in sports) is a superior approach to exploring the differences between such behaviors. The authors can arrive at this conclusion only if they assume that addictions can be subsumed within a domain-general etiology.

In establishing the nomological validity of their scale, Valence et al. (1988) used other "compulsive" behaviors including alcoholism, toxicomania, and bulimia. This speaks to the domain-general approach that is inherently assumed when studying addictions and compulsions. Along those lines, some scholars have sought to identify personality profiles that are more predisposed to succumbing to one or more addictions (including compulsive buying). However as mentioned earlier, some behavioral pathologies are likely linked to or triggered by domain-specific pursuits and hence cannot be fully investigated without a specific focus on the relevant domain in question.

Numerous scholars have sought to empirically demonstrate the comorbidity of compulsive buying with other psychiatric afflictions. Black et al. (1998) found that compulsive buyers had a higher lifetime chance of having a clinical depression and of suffering from more than one psychiatric condition as compared to a sample of noncompulsive buyers. Furthermore, they demonstrated that first-degree family members (i.e., close kin) of the compulsive buyers were more likely to suffer from psychiatric conditions (e.g., depression), alcoholism, and heavy drug use. This genre of comorbidity research contains the same cause–effect problem that is endemic to the pathological-gambling literature. In other words, it need not be the case that these disorders are comorbid because of a common domain-general etiology. Rather, it might simply be that the deleterious consequences of compulsive buying lead to depression, alcoholism, and drug abuse (or vice versa). Faber and O'Guinn (1992) discuss research suggesting a link between compulsive buying and other forms of negative behaviors. Paradoxically, they cite research showing that compulsive buying is linked to obesity, as well as to binge eating and bulimia. On the other hand, both Black et al. (1998) and Mitchell et al. (2001) found that compulsive buyers were not more likely to suffer from eating disorders. Despite the equivocal findings arising from comorbidity research, Black (2001) concluded that there is much evidence in support of the comorbidity of various psychiatric disorders when it comes to compulsive buyers. He discusses the Minnesota Impulsive Disorder Interview, which is utilized to determine the incidence of the following conditions: compulsive buying, kleptomania, trichotillomania, intermittent explosive disorder, pathological gambling, compulsive sexual behavior, and compulsive exercise. That one inventory or procedure is used to gauge the incidence of each of the latter compulsions speaks to the domain-general focus inherent to such an approach.

A domain-general perspective regarding addictive and compulsive behaviors can result in the wrong research questions being asked. For example, O'Guinn and Faber (1989) conclude:

Further research is needed on the commonalities and differences between compulsive buying and other forms of compulsive consumption. Both of our research and others' suggest there are a number of commonalities underlying these behaviors. Studies comparing people with different forms of compulsive behaviors may further illuminate this issue and help explain why some people manifest a compulsive disorder through buying rather than in some other way. (p. 156)

Note the domain-general assumptions implicit within the latter quote. It is assumed that individuals possess a general compulsive proclivity, which is instantiated into a specific compulsion (e.g., compulsive buying vs. sexual compulsion) by some hitherto unknown factors. A domain-specific perspective recognizes that there are few meaningful commonalities between male sexual addicts and bulimic women other than that they are both suffering from a psychiatric disorder. To reiterate, epidemiological data suggest that many addictions and compulsions have an unequivocal sex-specific morbidity, which is best understood from a domain-specific outlook, namely that the disorders are maladaptive manifestations of evolved sex-specific modules.

Proximate Issues Addressed by Marketing Scholars.   Marketing scholars have investigated numerous proximate issues dealing with compulsive buying, albeit void of a meta-framework to guide the research stream. Kwak, Zinkhan, and Crask (2003, Table 1, p. 164) cite several studies that have explored the relationship between compulsive buying and specific variables including credit card use, binge eating, buying impulsiveness, mood shift, disrupted family, shopping attitudes, impulsive buying, and money attitudes. This sample of variables is indicative of the haphazard strategy employed by marketing scholars when studying compulsive buying, wherein the key focus is to uncover statistically significant correlations without any integrative theorizing. That said, as often occurs with a disjointed research stream, the panacea is to suggest a grand and all-encompassing model, which it is hoped will provide order and coherence to the amassed findings. For example, O'Guinn and Faber (1989) proposed the use of a multifactor approach in understanding compulsive buying including physiological, genetic, psychological, social, and cultural factors. Without the necessary meta-framework to organize this multitude of variables, it is unclear how much value can be reaped from such a proposal. Hassay and Smith (1996) found that compulsive buyers not only were more likely to return products but also were more likely to care about return policies. Additionally, compulsive buyers did not engage in greater amounts of nonstore purchases as compared to their noncompulsive counterparts. These findings are used to suggest that one must come up with a typology of motives when discussing compulsive consumption behaviors.

Numerous scholars have argued that the key motive for engaging in compulsive buying is to regulate one's affective state. For example, O'Guinn and Faber state that because compulsive buyers have little interest in the products once purchased, it would seem that these are not purchased for a specific utilitarian or hedonic purpose; rather, the act of purchasing attenuates the feelings of anxiety of the compulsive buyer. On a related note, Miltenberger et al. (2003) sought to establish that compulsive buying is used as a mood-regulating mechanism. Although the results were equivocal, there seemed to be support that engaging in this behavior ameliorates one's mood. Lacking here is an explanation as to why it should be women who utilize this behavior in regulating their affective states. Furthermore, to argue that the motive behind a given behavior is to regulate one's mood carries little explanatory power. Miltenberger et al. add that similar mood regulation occurs with binge eating and chronic hair pulling, highlighting their implicit domain-general assumption with regard to addictions and compulsions. Faber and Christenson (1996) have also proposed that compulsive buyers engage in this behavior as a means of regulating their affective states. Although they provided several supposed causes of compulsive buying, no mention is made of an individual's sex as the key predictor of compulsive buying although gender roles are mentioned as one of several possible sociological causes (i.e., a social constructivist view of one's sex is assumed).

Marketing scholars have attempted to identify key characteristics of compulsive buyers and/or characteristics that differentiate between various groups of compulsive buyers. For example, Mowen and Spears (1999) explored the relationship between the Big Five personality traits and compulsive buying. Overall, they obtained support for their posited directional hypotheses between each of the traits and compulsive buying. The two fitted structural equation models explained 19% and 28% of the variance respectively. Although these are encouraging results, what is perhaps surprising about this research is that no mention of the sex-specific effect was made. It is difficult to fathom how a literature review of compulsive buying can omit the variable that yields the highest predictive ability when it comes to identifying risk factors associated with becoming a compulsive buyer. DeSarbo and Edwards (1996) sought to create two clusters of compulsive shoppers using 15 variables thought linked to compulsive buying. In choosing their final list of discriminating variables, they conducted an extensive literature review of the compulsive-buying literature. No mention was made of the sex effect other than the finding that sex did not discriminate between the two groups of compulsive buyers. This is expected given that the majority of compulsive buyers are women.

To summarize, marketing scholars have explored a myriad of proximate issues, none of which has adequately addressed the one universal and robust finding within this literature, namely that women are over-whelmingly more likely to be compulsive buyers. Breast cancer afflicts both men and women albeit it is highly sex-specific in its manifestation. Medical researchers studying breast cancer recognize that it predominantly afflicts women. However, when a behavioral disorder is overwhelmingly sex-specific in its manifestation, social scientists typically find ways to ignore, reject, or explain away such a finding, a position congruent with the empty-slate premise.

Evolutionary Explanation of Compulsive Buying.   Several clues seem to suggest that there might be a Darwinian etiology to this disorder. First, the incidence of compulsive buying seems to occur globally. For example, Kwak et al. (2003) proposed that because materialism is a human universal ("pervasive human trait" in their terminology), compulsive buying should be construed as occurring globally. They cite research that has investigated the phenomenon in Germany, Canada, Mexico, and Korea (in addition to the United States, of course). Black (2001) proposes:

> Compulsive buying disorder is found worldwide. Reports on the disorder have come from Brazil, England, France, Germany and the US. However, the disorder appears confined to the developed countries; compulsive consumption in an undeveloped country seems unlikely except among the wealthy elite. (p. 21)

Hence, as long as the necessary economic conditions are present (i.e., economic development), compulsive buying will likely occur irrespective of cultural environment. Second, the epidemiology of the disorder is such that the majority of sufferers are women. Third, given the equivocal evidence with regard to the comorbity of compulsive buying with other behavioral disorders, it would appear that a domain-specific account might prove superior to a domain-general model of compulsive behavior. Hence, though none of the latter clues would in of themselves serve as evidence of the Darwinian etiology of the disorder, taken together the argument becomes much more compelling. I provide herewith one possible, albeit speculative, avenue for future research.

Though compulsive buying might not qualify as a manifestation of hoarding behavior (an instantiation of obsessive-compulsive disorder or OCD), both disorders involve the accumulation of objects that are otherwise not strictly needed (see Frost et al., 1998, for links between OCD [hoarding] and compulsive buying). Along those lines, Abed and de Pauw (1998) have provided an evolutionary-based account of OCD. First, they cite research demonstrating that the incidence of OCD is cross-culturally invariant. Second, they argue that the spectrum of obsessions and compulsions is linked to either physical or social risks whose attenuation is adaptive if the triggered response is within a certain acceptable range. The problem with OCD is that the trigger lies at the extreme end of an otherwise adaptive set of mechanisms meant to handle current and future risks and dangers. In other words, for most individuals the evolved "flag" that signals to our brain that something needs to be attended to, is turned off once the potential danger is addressed (e.g., checking to see that the oven is off). However, for OCD sufferers, the flag is reactivated in a never-ending compulsive or obsessive loop. Rapoport and Fiske (1998) have also drawn links between evolutionary psychology and OCD. Specifically, they argued that not only is OCD universally found but also the symptomatology is very similar across a wide range of otherwise dissimilar cultures. The reason for this universality is thought to arise because the OCD symptoms map onto meaningful rituals (both religious and secular) that transcend cultures. In other words, OCD is an overactivation of neural circuitry that is otherwise applied in roughly similar manners across countless cultural rites and actions. Rapoport and Fiske state:

> Around the world, weddings, curing rites, and religious observances are characteristically composed of similar elements. This universal repertoire corresponds closely to the symptoms of OCD.
>
> This suggests that despite their manifest diversity, culturally meaningful rituals are composed in part from a universal repertoire of elements corresponding closely to the symptoms of OCD. These behaviors and ideas do not fundamentally depend on any particular cultural meaning system: direct innate neural control appears to be a most parsimonious explanation for the invariance of these actions, affects, and ideas. (pp. 166–167)

I propose that from an evolutionary perspective it might be reasonable to expect that the specific compulsions and obsessions that men and women are more likely to succumb to are linked to sex-specific evolutionarily relevant domains (see Saad, 2006b, for additional details). For example, men are much more likely to suffer from sexual compulsions whereas women are more likely to experience intrusive thoughts relating to the harming of their newborn infants. These two sex-specific instantiations of OCD symptomatology are in line with evolutionary-based predictions regarding the differential attention assigned to mating versus parenting by each of the two sexes (on a related note, see Frost, Meagher, & Riskind, 2001, for links between OCD and pathological gambling). Of the little research that has explored sex differences in OCD symptomatology, none has provided a compelling theoretical explanation regarding the sex-specific distribution of symptoms. Though some OCD scholars have argued that the sex-specific symptoms might be related to societally imposed gender roles, sex differences in the symptomatology of

OCD are typically explored void of an integrative framework (cf. Bogetto, Venturello, Albert, Maina, & Ravizza, 1999; Lochner et al., 2004; Lochner & Stein, 2001; Matsunaga et al., 2000). To the extent that a link exists between OCD and compulsive buying, that women are more likely to be compulsive buyers makes sense in light of the evolutionary-based hypothesis presented earlier. Specifically, because most purchases made by women in a compulsive-buying episode seem to be linked to appearance-enhancing products, this suggests that in this case the compulsive "loop" is related to the social risks associated with looking unattractive. O'Guinn and Faber (1989) found that the types of products most purchased during a compulsive-buying episode were clothing, cosmetics, and gifts for significant others. Black (2001) obtained very similar results; namely, women compulsively bought clothes, jewelry, and makeup, whereas male compulsive buyers bought some of the same items as women but also purchased electronics, car-related products, and hardware items. Note that the products purchased by women compulsive buyers are predominantly publicly consumed whereas those bought by their male counterparts are much more likely to be privately consumed.

Though appearance enhancement might be one motive driving a woman's compulsive-buying habits, another ubiquitous motive that has been uncovered by several scholars is the need to signal prestige. Using a middle-class sample in Mexico, J. A. Roberts and Sepulveda (1999) explored predictors of compulsive buying. The five predictors consisted of factors arising from a scale measuring one's attitude toward money. The authors obtained two significant betas, the strongest of which was "power-prestige." They concluded, "The present study's results suggest compulsive buying is partially an attempt to display one's wealth to others as a means of trying to prove one's superiority" (p. 67). On a related note, social status, as linked to the purchase, ownership, and possession of products, was discussed as a relevant factor with regard to the phenomenon of compulsive buying (J. A. Roberts, 1998). Black (2001) describes a psychodynamic case wherein a female patient who was a compulsive buyer fantasized that she was the wife of a wealthy and powerful man who possessed the resources to offer her anything that she desired at will. Thus, although the need to display status is a human universal typically associated with male mating strategies (e.g., sexual signaling via conspicuous consumption), women can be desirous of engaging in status signaling, albeit for likely different motives than those of men.

CHAPTER SUMMARY

Throughout recorded history, moral philosophers and theologians alike have repeatedly warned against the allure of succumbing to certain ubiquitous human drives. The seven deadly sins, which have been documented in various forms for several millennia, fully recognize the universal human weakness in tempering such drives. I have argued in the current chapter that these drives are rooted in a Darwinian etiology, albeit these are expressed within a maladaptive range. Not surprisingly, the seven deadly sins manifest themselves in countless acts of dark-side consumption. These include pornographic addictions, eating disorders, pathological gambling, and compulsive buying. I proposed that each of these four case examples has a sex-specific Darwinian etiology, thus each yields the universal pattern of highly sex-specific epidemiological rates. Additionally, I have demonstrated that the majority of research that has explored such acts is rooted within the SSSM. Specifically, there is an exclusive focus on proximate causes, environmental forces, and domain-general mechanisms. However, evolutionary-based approaches as espoused by recently founded fields such as Darwinian medicine recognize that numerous physiological and behavioral-based illnesses are rooted in a Darwinian etiology. As such, a more complete theory of addiction, compulsion, and other obsessive patterns of behaviors will likely require that scholars recognize the evolutionary forces that can predispose individuals to succumb to such devastating consumption acts.

    In the next and final chapter, I provide a summary of some of the key benefits that might be reaped if consumer researchers were to incorporate evolutionary frameworks within their theoretical toolboxes.

Benefits of Darwinizing Consumer Research

Nisbett introduced the series [on evolution and social cognition at the University of Michigan] by saying that he once thought every psychology department would need to hire an evolutionary psychologist, but he had changed his mind. Instead, Nisbett predicted that evolutionary theory will come to play the same role in psychology as it currently assumes in biology: "Not every psychologist will be an evolutionary psychologist, but every psychologist will be aware of the perspective and will have to address its explanations and constraints in his or her own work" (Nisbett, 1995, personal communication).

—Kenrick and Simpson (1997, pp. 16–17)

A key objective in this final chapter is to demonstrate that Richard Nisbett's position is equally à propos in the context of the consumer behavior discipline. Specifically, I wish to show the multitude of ways by which evolutionary theory might complement and enrich existing consumer behavior research streams.

CONSILIENCE, FULLER EXPLANATIONS, AND NOVEL HYPOTHESES

In his laudable call for consilience, Henriques (2003) states the following:

What is needed is a meta-theoretical framework that crisply defines the subject matter of psychology, demonstrates how psychology exists in relationship to the other sciences, and allows one to systematically integrate the key insights from the major perspectives in a manner that results in cumulative knowledge. Metaphorically, each "key insight" can be viewed as a piece of the larger puzzle. And, as with completing a puzzle, the more pieces that are filled in, the clearer the overall picture. Furthermore, as the puzzle is completed, it will become increasingly clear as to which theoretical pieces do not fit into the overarching scheme.

In fitting the pieces together, what have traditionally been "either–or" epistemological splits become "both-and-neither" answers. The argument here is that the schisms between cognitive and behavioral science perspectives, distal/nature and proximate/nurture perspectives, psychodynamic and behavioral therapeutic perspectives, and constructivist and empiricist epistemological perspectives are the consequences of incomplete, partially correct knowledge systems being defined against one another in a manner that is more political than scientific. These fragmented, politically antagonistic mini-epistemologies create a buzzing, confusing mass of information that prevents cumulative understanding. (p. 152)

This state of affairs applies just as easily to the consumer behavior discipline. We have certainly achieved methodological plurality in our discipline. Surveys, in-depth interviews, mathematical models, focus groups, laboratory experiments, content analyses, and observational studies are but a few of the data collection methods available to consumer researchers. All of these approaches should continue to be championed, as should efforts that have sought to create a stronger rapprochement between the behavioral and quantitative camps. That said, the latter artificial schisms are not the key challenges facing our discipline. Without a meta-theory to help organize our discipline, we will continue to generate disjointed findings that are difficult to amass into a coherent tree of knowledge. Thus, the first and most important benefit of infusing evolutionary theory into the consumer behavior discipline is that we will have an organizing meta-framework that will yield a consilient, coherent, and cumulative body of knowledge. The drive toward a more consilient discipline will likely begin once consumer scholars forgo their unquestioned allegiance to the foundational tenets of the SSSM, with its exclusive focus on domain-general modules and proximate-level explanations, and its ascription of all phenomena to socialization and learning. I return to these two key issues in the ensuing paragraphs.

A second beneficial outcome of having Darwinian theory guide our discipline is that it will permit consumer researchers to address scientific issues at both the proximate and ultimate levels. By definition, ultimate causes are those that are linked to an adaptive understanding of the phenomenon in question. This level of analysis cannot be tackled if we restrict our focus to proximate mechanisms. Both levels are needed to make substantial and consilient progress when studying any living organism. The two levels feed off each other in an epistemological feedback loop resulting in a more accurate and complete understanding of the organism in question. If one were to use an electronic microscope to study the cosmos, this would yield the same phenomenological blindness as would the use of the Hubble telescope to investigate cellular structures. It is not that one tool is superior to the other; rather, both are needed to study the panoply of natural phenomena. In a similar vein, consumer researchers are partially blinded by solely exploring the world of proximate phenomena. Let me reiterate that proximate and ultimate theories are not engaged in a zero-sum game of epistemological influence. A large number of important consumption phenomena should indeed be studied at the proximate level. That said, both levels of explanations are needed in order to achieve an accurate and complete understanding of such phenomena.

A third beneficial outcome of Darwinizing our discipline is that consumer researchers will recognize the importance of both domain-general and domain-specific mental modules as integral components of the human mind. As it currently stands, there are no articles in the consumer behavior and marketing disciplines that have explicitly explored a domain-specific mental process (in the evolutionary sense of the term). As mentioned in chapter 2, the term *domain-specific* as used to categorize phenomena in the consumer behavior discipline explicitly assumes that the human mind consists of general-purpose domain-independent mental processes. For example, in their recent comparison of content areas covered in the *Journal of Consumer Research (JCR)* and the *Journal of Consumer Psychology (JCP)* between 1992 and 1998, Alon, Morrin, and Bechwati (2002, see Table 1, p. 18) used domain-specific in such a manner. The following headings were listed as examples of domain-specific research: information processing (sensation and perception; attention; categorization; inference making; information search; memory); attitudes (formation and persuasion; conditioning; attitudes and behavior); affect (as independent or dependent variables); and choice (heuristics and biases; variety seeking and decision timing; satisfaction). On a related note, Bettencourt and Houston (2001) conducted both citation and reference diversity analyses of articles that appeared in *JCR*, the *Journal of Marketing Research (JMR)*, and the *Journal of Marketing (JM)* between 1991 and 1995. The 13 content areas that they used for *JCR* included affect/emotion, attitudes, cognition/information processing, and choice (see p. 329 of the article in question for a listing of all 13 categories used). Although there is nothing inherently incorrect about creating the latter nomenclatures, that it is organized in this manner is fully indicative of the exclusive focus on domain-general processes.

If consumer scholars were to recognize the importance of both domain-specific and domain-general modules, and of proximate and ultimate explanations, many new research streams will likely be identified. Some scholars might decide to revisit previously published findings in order to provide ultimate-based Darwinian explanations for these (see Saad & Gill, 2000). For example, robust sex differences regarding the efficacy of sexual ads would be attributed to evolutionary factors in addition to the current range of proximate explanations. Consumption motives that have historically been linked to unsubstantiated theories (e.g., Maslow's hierarchy of needs) might now be categorized onto a restricted set of universally valid Darwinian modules. Countless previous findings that have been explained in terms of socialization, learning, and culture could be revisited in the hope of explaining the ultimate genesis of such socialization processes. For example, product categories and consumption habits that are dominated by one sex (e.g., cosmetics, gambling, prostitution, eating disorders, pornography, sports cars, and extreme sports) will no longer be explained solely in terms of socialization and learning. Cross-cultural research will be revisited in order to identify human universals in the consumption arena. This will allow marketers to have a better understanding of when one should focus on cross-cultural differences versus cross-cultural similarities. Furthermore, when cross-cultural differences are identified, it will permit consumer scholars to apply the approach of behavioral ecologists, namely understanding the adaptive reasons (if any) that led to these emic manifestations (i.e., adapting to a local niche). This revisiting of previous findings will be an important step in the pursuit of greater consilience.

Perhaps most important, evolutionary psychology will permit consumer scholars to posit novel hypotheses that would have been difficult to identify without an evolutionary psychology lens. It is unlikely that a nonevolutionist could have discovered the link between ovulatory cycle and provocative attire (see chap. 3), or uncovered differential grandparental solicitude (Euler & Weitzel, 1996). That mothers are much more likely to state that a newborn resembles the father as a means of attenuating the threats of paternity uncertainty is an effect that could have solely been visible to the evolutionist (Daly & Wilson, 1982). On a related note, that men's parental investments are correlated to the perceived resemblance of the child to the father is yet another finding that would have been impossible to uncover from anyone other than an evolutionist (Apicella & Marlowe, 2004). It would be difficult to imagine how anyone who was not biologically informed and evolutionary-inspired could have documented the phenomenon of menstrual synchrony (cf. McClintock, 1998; Weller & Weller, 1995). Not only are countless human phenomena solely within the purview of the evolutionist but also in most instances evolutionary-based findings adhere to the criteria of "interestingness" as espoused by a large number of philosophers of science (e.g., M. S. Davis, 1971). For example, Cole (1994) proclaimed, "Thus, in all sciences the theories that develop counterintuitive or unexpected results are more likely to be judged to be additions to knowledge" (p. 143). Recently, Small (2004) conducted a content analysis of the responses given by authors of highly cited papers in 22 disciplines regarding why they think that their papers get cited. Small found that the four key dimensions were a paper's interest, novelty, utility, and significance (in decreasing order of frequency). Comparing the evolutionary psychology literature to that in consumer behavior on any of the latter metrics yields unequivocal conclusions. The evolutionary psychology literature is defined by the novelty, impact, and "interestingness" of its amassed findings, whereas, as has been concluded by numerous consumer and marketing scholars, the consumer behavior discipline performs less well on many of these epistemological metrics (cf. J. S. Armstrong, 1991, 2003; November, 2004).

EVOLUTIONARY PSYCHOLOGY AS AN EPISTEMOLOGICAL HEURISTIC

Kanazawa (2004b) proposes the savanna principle as a meta-heuristic, which can be used by social scientists in predicting the likelihood that a theory will yield consistent empirical support for its central tenets. Specifically, he argues that if the central premises of a proposed theory are in disaccord with the environment of evolutionary adaptedness (i.e., the collection of ancestral environments within which *Homo sapiens* evolved), the theory will ultimately be falsified. Subsequently, he applied the savanna principle in the context of specific microeconomic theories. Kanazawa explored four theories, two of which have received consistent empirical support whereas two others have had their central tenets repeatedly falsified. Kanazawa chose network exchange theory and competitive price theory (as tested in double-auction markets) as examples of successful theories. On the other hand, he focused on noncooperative game theory and public choice theory as examplars of theories that have yielded consistent falsifications of their central predictions (e.g., cooperating in the prisoner's dilemma and not engaging in free riding in the context of a public good). Why do people cooperate in the prisoner's dilemma and why do they contribute to a public good? Kanazawa argues that this is because the conditions under which these theories are typically tested (e.g., anonymity of players and anonymity of actions) are counterintuitive to the social dynamics that have defined our phylogenetic history. Specifically, humans have evolved in small bands defined by face-to-face exchanges and public accountability of one's actions. Hence, our mental calculus for social exchanges is incongruent with the phylogenetically invalid environments tested by many microeconomic theories. In a related manner, many of the most influential theories that have been used in consumer behavior and that have ultimately proven to be less than useful, could have been identified as such upon espousing them, had evolutionary psychology been used as the epistemological heuristic.

Saad and Gill (2001) applied principles from evolutionary psychology in studying the effects that the sex makeup of a dyad has on offers made in the Ultimatum Game (cf. Güth, Schmittberger, & Schwartze, 1982). In this economic game, an offerer (Player A) is given a fixed amount of money and is asked to split it with a receiver (Player B). Player A's offer can be either accepted or rejected by Player B. If Player B accepts the split, both parties keep their respective amounts. However, if Player B refuses it (e.g., he or she views the offer as unfair), both players receive nothing. Both players are aware of the amount to be split and they cannot negotiate with one another other than communicating the offer and the subsequent decision to either accept or reject it. This game has repeatedly been used in the literature on behavioral economic games to demonstrate violations of axioms of rational choice (cf. Camerer & Thaler, 1995; Thaler, 1988). The tenet of income maximization posits that Player A should offer the smallest possible denomination to the recipient given that from the latter's perspective the utility of receiving something is higher than the utility of receiving nothing. Using evolutionary psychology as the theoretical framework, Saad and Gill predicted and found that the highest and lowest offers occurred in the male–female and male–male cells respectively. In other words, men are strategic in their generosity depending on whom they are playing against. When facing women, they seek to display cues of generosity whereas when placed against other males, this triggers intrasexual resource-based rivalry. Women make equally fair offers irrespective of the sex of Player B.

Congruent with Kanazawa's savanna principle, Saad and Gill (2001) implemented their ultimatum experiment via face-to-face interactions. In other words, they recognized that the evolutionary based effect that they were positing was less likely to occur in contexts where the relevant ecologically valid environment was not operative. Thus, experimental settings such as when players are making anonymous choices while facing anonymous players do not trigger the conditions relevant for the postulated evolutionary mechanism. This is the reason that numerous previous studies that had explored sex effects in laboratory games did not yield results congruent with those obtained by Saad and Gill.

Kanazawa's savanna principle is applicable in any field that explores human behavior including the consumer discipline. For example, the selectivity hypothesis, which posits that women are more comprehensive information processors irrespective of the domain in question, is incongruent with the savanna principle. As such, it is not surprising that it has received mixed empirical support. As mentioned in chapter 3, there is no compelling evolutionarily viable reason to expect such a sex main effect across all purposive domains. Hence, evolutionary psychology can serve as an epistemological sieve by which implausible theories can be identified and rejected without the need for extensive empirical testing.

DOES EVOLUTIONARY THEORY YIELD INACTIONABLE AND/OR IMPRACTICAL INFORMATION?

Given that numerous scholars, including marketing and consumer researchers, erroneously associate evolutionary theory with biological determinism, it is easy to see how they might not see the practical implications of Darwinian-based theories. The fallacious logic proposes that because a behavior is "inscribed" in the genotype it must lie outside of the marketer's sphere of influence. What is the point of studying the links between menstrual cycles and consumption given the fact that marketers cannot manipulate a woman's menstrual cycle? Who cares that men are much more likely to prefer younger women as prospective mates? In what way does understanding our evolved gustatory preferences help a food marketer develop a better product? How could such information be actionable if it is already "hardwired" as an integral element of our Darwinian heritage? At its most basic level, this line of argumentation is flawed given that evolutionary theory does not in any way imply biological determinism. As explained by countless evolutionists, Darwinian modules interact with idiosyncratic environments in generating unique behaviors. Hence, though at the population level men might prefer to mate with younger women, this does not imply that there does not exist a context where a particular male might choose to mate with an older woman. Though most men desire to obtain social status (this is the Darwinian goal), they will likely do so in idiosyncratic ways as a function of their unique talents and environments. Biological determinism is a relevant issue solely to those that miscomprehend evolutionary theory and/or those that reject it on ideological grounds.

On a related note, numerous scholars argue that evolutionary theory provides theories that have little or no practical implications. From an epistemological perspective, it is unclear why the value of academic research should be determined according to ephemeral guidelines of practicality. No one could have imagined that Fermat's work in number theory, which he conducted several centuries ago, would have yielded current practical applications in cryptography. It is unlikely that Gregory Mendel was aware that his work with garden peas would spawn the field of genetics and the clear practical implications of genetic engineering (e.g., in developing genetically modified foods and genetic approaches to combating human diseases). I fully agree here with Holbrook (1987) when he stated, "The need to ground consumer research in a central preoccupation with consumption, independent of any relevance that subject might carry for marketing managers or, indeed, for any other external interests" (p. 130). From a practical perspective, both consumer researchers and practitioners alike are in the business of understanding the consumer. One cannot fully understand the complexities of human behavior as manifested in the consumption arena *without* any discussion of the biological and evolutionary forces that shape most consumption acts. The foods that we eat, the advertisements that appeal to us, the clothes that we wear, the conspicuous purchases that we show off, the gifts that we offer, and the mating choices that we make are all due to our biological heritage. Our consumption habits are manifestations of our innate human nature. As consumers, we do not navigate in a parallel universe where biology and evolution cease to matter. However, the socialization worldview is particularly appealing to marketers for there is nothing more alluring from a practical perspective than to imagine that the human mind is infinitely malleable.

One of the attacks frequently levied against evolutionary psychology is that it can be used to explain every imaginable phenomenon. Evolutionary psychology cannot and does not claim to provide an adaptive explanation for every conceivable consumption act. Darwinian theory cannot explain why some people prefer bowling to scuba diving but it certainly can predict that the majority of participants in violent sports are males. It cannot explain why a given consumer prefers chicken more than beef but it can explain why evolved gustatory preferences are universal in that fatty foods are typically preferred to raw cabbage. Evolutionary theory cannot explain why two specific people fell in love but it can explain evolved and universal sex-specific patterns of mate preferences. Kin selection does not claim to explain why a particular father might love his daughter more than his son but it does predict that the presence of stepparents in a home increases the likelihood of child abuse. In other words, evolutionary psychology cannot necessarily elucidate the idiosyncratic preferences of each individual consumer. However, it can help in identifying universal patterns of consumption that are manifestations of an innate human nature. These universal patterns can be mapped onto a restrained set of Darwinian modules, each of which has been empirically confirmed across innumerable studies spanning countless eras, cultures, and species.

THE "DARWINIZING" OF THE COGNATE DISCIPLINES CLOSEST TO CONSUMER BEHAVIOR

At the end of chapter 2, I provided a brief overview of the multitude of disciplines that have adopted Darwinian principles within their theoretical purview. What of the disciplines closest to consumer behavior? A growing number of scholars, in each of the cognate disciplines that consumer scholars have historically relied on for their theoretical frameworks, have begun infusing Darwinian theory into their respective disciplines. The closest disciplinary ally of consumer behavior, namely psychology, is witnessing a rapid infusion of Darwinian-based theorizing across both its research and pedagogic fronts. Anthropologists have been at the forefront of both pro-Darwinian movements (e.g., physical, biological, Darwinian, and evolutionary anthropology) and anti-Darwinian intellectual courants (e.g., cultural relativism). That said, the pro-Darwinian anthropologists are growing in stature as evidenced by the founding of several journals that are exclusively dedicated to evolutionary-based approaches to anthropological work (e.g., *Human Nature* and *Evolutionary Anthropology*). Even sociology, the bastion of anti-Darwinism within the social sciences, has evolutionary-minded scholars calling for epistemological change (cf. 1996 summer special issue of *The American Sociologist* (Vol. 27, issue 2); Dietz, Burns, & Buttel, 1990; Freese, Li, & Wade, 2003; Lopreato & Crippen, 1999; Nielsen, 1994; Sanderson, 2001; van den Berghe, 1990). Whereas economists have been inspired by evolutionary theory for close to two centuries (see Zak & Denzau, 2001), scholars are now seeking to explicitly incorporate evolutionary psychology within the foundational tenets of economic theory (cf. Cohen & Dickens, 2002; Cosmides & Tooby, 1994; Hoffman, McCabe, & Smith, 1998). Gowdy and Carbonell (1999) propose, "In the neoclassical theory of the consumer, only human preferences count. It does not matter where these preferences come from or what the consequences for the rest of the world are" (p. 342). Evolutionary theory recognizes that many human preferences are a manifestation of our evolved biological heritage. For example, Ben-Ner and Putterman (2000) state, "A scientific theory of preferences, grounded in evolutionary psychological and biological theory, can avoid resort to ad hoc assumptions" (p. 91). As might be expected, ecological economics is one subdiscipline that appears to be at the forefront of applying Darwinian principles within its theoretical purview (cf. Jackson, 2002). In their invited paper commemorating the 10th-year anniversary of *Ecological Economics*, Gowdy and Carbonell, (1999) proclaim:

> Ecological economics has played a valuable role in putting economics on a firm footing with respect to biological reality. We argue above that this is because ecological economics has taken interdisciplinarity seriously. Following the traditional division of economics into consumption and production, ecological economics has helped ground the consumer in social and ecological context, and to ground the firm in biophysical reality.
>
> Science has entered the age of the breakdown of disciplinary boundaries. For some sciences this transition is going smoothly, for others it is not. For the natural sciences, perhaps, the change is relatively easy because it does not involve a rethinking of basic assumptions. The integration of economics with the physical and biological sciences has proved far more difficult. (p. 345)

The latter proclamation regarding the need for developing consilient and interdisciplinary research programs is antithetical to the manner by which most of the social sciences have defined themselves. In addressing the isolationist stance typical of the social sciences, Carroll (1995) states:

> All such declarations of disciplinary autonomy stultify the discipline they are meant to protect. By sealing off the phenomena it studies from causal relations to phenomena within other disciplines, a science places severe restrictions on its capacity for causal explanation and thus for development as a science. (p. 126)

Carroll's caveat is particularly à propos when it comes to the existing schism between the consumer behavior discipline and the Darwinian revolution that has been so influential across a wide range of scientific fields. Given the richness of phenomena addressed by consumer scholars, our discipline is ideally placed within the social sciences to serve as the epitome of an interdisciplinary yet highly consilient field.

Zaltman (2000) implored consumer researchers to explore disciplines outside their traditional paradigmatic lenses in order to achieve the next wave of important and lasting contributions. As an example, he proposes that advances in the neurosciences provide fertile opportunities for consumer researchers. Though he did not explicitly mention evolutionary psychology, he referred to evolutionarily based principles such as human universals and biofeedback. Additionally, he alluded to the importance of our evolutionary history in shaping our perceptions, actions, preferences, and emotions. Several of the scholars that he cites as having the potential of opening new avenues in consumer research are biologically inspired evolutionists (e.g., Gerald Edelman and Antonio Damasio). Zaltman (2000) concludes:

> To make substantial leaps of progress in understanding consumer behavior will require dedicated hiking into other fields and overcoming the substantial barriers to seeing the relevance of their insights as we define consumer research questions and create strategies for answering them. (p. 428)

Breaking down discipline boundaries is never an easy task. In an autobiographical article, the eminent psychologist Paul Meehl (1989) proposed:

> (1) Bright, scientifically trained persons may become grossly irrational when issues of territory, dominance, and bonding are involved; (2) when you become alpha baboon, the communication tends to deteriorate. One knows these facts intellectually, but sitting in that chair gives a real appreciation of their power. Ethology rules the academy more than logic. (p. 356)

In other words, academics are Darwinian beings who succumb to coalitional and affiliational thinking, territorial defense, and adherence to dominance hierarchies. In the current context, to the extent that evolutionary theory might be construed as intellectually threatening, consumer scholars are likely to entrench themselves within their familiar paradigms. However, reiterating that evolutionary theory can complement and enrich the existing consumer behavior paradigms can hopefully avert this instinctual defensive reaction.

On the occasion of the *Journal of Marketing*'s 60th anniversary, Kerin (1996) wrote a commemorative essay wherein he highlighted the key intellectual movements that have spanned the history of this illustrious journal. He identified six key periods along with the driving theme within each period. According to Kerin (see Table 1, p. 4), marketing has been contiguously construed as applied economics, managerial activity, quantitative science, behavioral science, decision science, and most recently, integrative science. Hence, within the current era of supposed marketing integration, the most grand of integrative frameworks (i.e., evolutionary theory) is missing from within the purview of all marketing theories. In his discussion of consilience, Henriques (2003) states:

> This unification [modern synthesis of Darwinian theory] had a tremendous impact on the capacity of the field to organize itself. A shared mission, a shared language, and a shared conceptual foundation have allowed for much greater consistency, novelty of discovery, and accumulation of knowledge. (p. 151)

Hence, although the biological sciences have made exponential strides this past century as a result of having adopted the consilience-inducing and highly integrative Darwinian framework, marketing and consumer scholars have in large part ignored or rejected biology and evolutionary theory as relevant to their intellectual pursuits.

CHAPTER SUMMARY

In the same manner that the natural sciences operate under consilient meta-frameworks, consumer scholars might ameliorate the level of consilience of their discipline by recognizing that consumption phenomena are rooted in our evolved biological heritage. Many additional epistemological benefits would likely be forthcoming if consumer researchers were to Darwinize the discipline including providing more complete explanations (e.g., at both the proximate and ultimate levels), identifying new hypotheses that would have been otherwise impossible to posit, and creating a taxonomy of consumption universals that transcend cultural settings and temporal periods. The incorporation of evolutionary psychology into the consumer behavior discipline should not be construed as a means by which existing theories are supplanted. Rather, evolutionary theory should be viewed as a means of enriching our discipline with the latest knowledge arising from the biological sciences. The Darwinian revolution has extended beyond the natural sciences and is accordingly diffusing into the cognate disciplines that consumer scholars typically borrow their theories from. As argued throughout the current book, we stand a good chance of missing many of the exciting opportunities afforded to us by the biological revolution if we fail to recognize the role of evolution in shaping consumption phenomena.

CONCLUDING REMARKS

Individuals consume countless products, services, and activities in their daily lives. These pursuits are shaped by various factors including a universal Darwinian heritage that defines one's human nature as well as idiosyncratic life experiences, environmental forces, and a phenotypic expression that defines one's uniqueness as an individual. Each of the important domains defining our human existence is a manifestation of the evolutionary forces that have shaped our common humanity. To the extent that consumption is the nexus where many of these evolutionarily relevant domains meet, it would seem impossible to investigate accurately and fully consumption phenomena void of any Darwinian-based and biologically inspired theorizing. *Homo consumericus* has evolved via the same Darwinian forces that have shaped all other living organisms. As has been cogently argued by Kanazawa (2004c), the social sciences should be subsumed within the grander field of biology. In other words, our behaviors including our consumption habits are best understood as manifestations of the interaction between our biological heritage and our unique circumstances. E. O. Wilson's aphorism regarding human culture being held on a leash by our biology is equally valid if we were to replace *culture* with *consumption*. Theodor Dobzhansky, the renowned evolutionist, famously stated, "Nothing in biology makes sense except in the light of evolution." While addressing the disunity of psychology, Henriques (2003) proposed, "Nothing in psychology makes sense" (p. 151). The latter two quotes would be equally relevant if one were to replace *biology* and *psychology* with *consumer behavior* in the quotes of Dobzhansky and Henriques respectively.

I hope to have achieved two goals in writing this book, namely demonstrating the relevance of evolutionary theory in understanding consumption phenomena while identifying new areas in which evolutionists might apply Darwinian-based ideas and frameworks. In other words, I hope that both SSSM-based scholars (including consumer researchers) as well as evolutionists have found value in reading this book. I thank the reader for having undertaken this intellectual journey with me.

References

Aaker, J., & Maheswaran, D. (1997). The effect of cultural orientation on persuasion. *Journal of Consumer Research, 24,* 315 328.

Abbey, A. (1982). Sex differences in attributions for friendly behavior: Do males misperceive females' friendliness? *Journal of Personality and Social Psychology, 32,* 830–838.

Abbott, S. A. (2000). Motivations for pursuing an acting career. In R. Weitzer (Ed.), *Sex for sale: Prostitution, pornography, and the sex industry* (pp. 17–34). New York: Routledge.

Abed, R. T. (1998). The sexual competition hypothesis for eating disorders. *British Journal of Medical Psychology, 71,* 525–547.

Abed, R. T., & de Pauw, K. W. (1998). An evolutionary hypothesis for obsessive compulsive disorder: A psychological immune system? *Behavioural Neurology, 11,* 245–250.

Agrawal, M. (1995). Review of a 40-year debate in international advertising. *International Marketing Review, 12,* 26–48.

Aharon, I., Etcoff, N., Ariely, D., Chabris, C. F., O'Connor, E., & Breiter, H. C. (2001). Beautiful faces have variable reward value: fMRI and behavioral evidence. *Neuron, 32,* 537–551.

Aiken, N. E. (1998). *The biological origins of art.* Westport, CT: Praeger.

Ajzen, I., & Fishbein, M. (1980). *Understanding attitudes and predicting social behavior.* Englewood Cliffs, NJ: Prentice-Hall.

Alcock, J. (2001). *The triumph of sociobiology.* New York: Oxford University Press.

Alden, D. L., Hoyer, W. D., & Lee, C. (1993). Identifying global and culture-specific dimensions of humor in advertising: A multinational analysis. *Journal of Marketing, 57,* 64–75.

Alexander, G. M. (2003). An evolutionary perspective of sex-typed toy preferences: Pink, blue, and the brain. *Archives of Sexual Behavior, 32,* 7–14.

Alexander, G. M., & Hines, M. (2002). Sex differences in response to children's toys in nonhuman primates (*Cercopithecus aethiops sabaeus*). *Evolution and Human Behavior, 23,* 467–479.

278

Alon, A., Morrin, M., & Bechwati, N. N. (2002). Comparing *Journal of Consumer Psychology* and *Journal of Consumer Research*. *Journal of Consumer Psychology, 12*, 15–20.

American Psychiatric Association. (1994). *Diagnostic and statistical manual of mental disorders* (4th ed.). Washington, DC: Author.

Anderson, J. L., & Crawford, C. B. (1992). Modeling costs and benefits of adolescent weight control as a mechanism for reproductive suppression. *Human Nature, 3*, 299–334.

Andrews, P. W., Gangestad, S. W., & Matthews, D. (2002). Adaptationism—How to carry an exaptationist program. *Behavioral and Brain Sciences, 25*, 489–504.

Andsager, J., & Roe, K. (2003). "What's your definition of dirty, baby?": Sex in music video. *Sexuality & Culture, 7*, 79–97.

Andsager, J. L., & Roe, K. (1999). Country music video in country's Year of the Woman. *Journal of Communication, 49*, 69–82.

Antonides, G. (1989). An attempt at integration of economic and psychological theories of consumption. *Journal of Economic Psychology, 10*, 77–99.

Apicella, C. L., & Marlowe, F. W. (2004). Perceived mate fidelity and paternal resemblance predict men's investment in children. *Evolution and Human Behavior, 25*, 371–378.

Aranyosi, E. F. (1999). Wasteful advertising and variance reduction: Darwinian models for the significance of nonutilitarian architecture. *Journal of Anthropological Archaeology, 18*, 356–375.

Ariely, D., & Loewenstein, G. (2006). The heat of the moment: The effect of sexual arousal on sexual decision making. *Journal of Behavioral Decision Making, 19*, 87–98.

Armstrong, E. G. (2002). Devil music and gangsta rap: A comparison of sexual violence in blues and rap lyrics. *Arkansas Review: A Journal of Delta Studies, 33*, 182–193.

Armstrong, J. S. (1991). Prediction of consumer behavior by experts and novices. *Journal of Consumer Research, 18*, 251–256.

Armstrong, J. S. (2003). Discovery and communication of important marketing findings: Evidence and proposals. *Journal of Business Research, 56*, 69–84.

Ashton, M. C., Paunonen, S. V., Helmes, E., & Jackson, D. N. (1998). Kin altruism, reciprocal altruism, and the Big Five personality factors. *Evolution and Human Behavior, 19*, 243–255.

Aunger, R. (Ed.). (2000). *Darwinizing culture: The status of memetics as a science*. Oxford, England: Oxford University Press.

Aunger, R. (2002). *The electric meme: A new theory of how we think*. New York: The Free Press.

Axelrod, R. (1984). *The evolution of cooperation*. New York: Basic Books.

Axelrod, R., & Hamilton, W. D. (1981). The evolution of cooperation. *Science, 211*, 1390–1396.

Bagwell, L. S., & Bernheim, B. D. (1996). Veblen effects in a theory of conspicuous consumption. *The American Economic Review, 86*, 349–373.

Baker, M. J., & Churchill, G. A., Jr. (1977). The impact of physically attractive models on advertising evaluations. *Journal of Marketing Research, XIV*, 538–555.

Baker, R. (1996). *Sperm wars: The science of sex*. Toronto, Ontario, Canada: HarperCollins.

Baker, R., & Bellis, M. A. (1995). *Human sperm competition*. London: Chapman & Hall.

Bar-Cohen, Y. (2005). Biomimetics: Mimicking and inspired-by biology. In *Proceedings of the SPIE Smart Structures Conference* (SPIE Vol. 5759-02, pp. 1–8). Bellingham, WA: SPIE Press.

Bar-Hillel, M., & Neter, E. (1996). Why are people reluctant to exchange lottery tickets? *Journal of Personality and Social Psychology, 70,* 17–27.

Barkow, J. H., Cosmides, L., & Tooby, J. (Eds.). (1992). *The adapted mind: Evolutionary psychology and the generation of culture.* New York: Oxford University Press.

Barton, C. M., & Clark, G. A. (Eds.). (1997). *Rediscovering Darwin: Evolutionary theory and archeological explanation.* Arlington, VA: American Anthropological Association.

Bartsch, R. A., Burnett, T., Diller, T. R., & Rankin-Williams, E. (2000). Gender representation in television commercials: Updating an update. *Sex Roles, 43,* 735–743.

Batten, M. (1992). *Sexual strategies: How females choose their mates.* New York: Tarcher/Putnam.

Baumeister, R. F., & Leary, M. R. (1995). The need to belong: Desire for interpersonal attachments as a fundamental human motivation. *Psychological Bulletin, 117,* 497–529.

Baumgartner, H. (2002). Toward a personology of the consumer. *Journal of Consumer Research, 29,* 286–292.

Baxter, R. L., De Riemer, C., Landini, A., Leslie, L., & Singletary, M. W. (1985). A content analysis of music videos. *Journal of Broadcasting & Electronic Media, 29,* 333–340.

Beatty, S. E., & Smith, S. M. (1987). External search effort: An investigation across several product categories. *Journal of Consumer Research, 14,* 83–95.

Belk, R. W. (1988). Possessions and the extended self. *Journal of Consumer Research, 15,* 139–168.

Bell, D. (1991). Reciprocity as a generating process in social relations. *Journal of Quantitative Anthropology, 3,* 251–260.

Ben-Ner, A., & Putterman, L. (2000). On some implications of evolutionary psychology for the study of preferences and institutions. *Journal of Economic Behavior and Organization, 43,* 91–99.

Berenbaum, S. A., & Hines, M. (1992). Early androgens are related to childhood sex-typed toy preferences. *Psychological Science, 3,* 203–206.

Bergstrom, T. C. (1995). On the evolution of altruistic ethical rules for siblings. *The American Economic Review, 85,* 58–81.

Berl, R. L., Williamson, N. C., & Powell, T. E. (1984). Industrial salesforce motivation: A critique and test of Maslow's hierarchy of need. *The Journal of Personal Selling & Sales Management, 4,* 32–39.

Berlim, M. T., & Abeche, A. M. (2001). Evolutionary approach to medicine. *Southern Medical Journal, 94,* 26–32.

Bernard, A., Adelman, M. B., & Schroeder, J. E. (1991). Two views of consumption in mating and dating. In R. H. Holman & M. R. Solomon (Eds.), *Advances in consumer research* (Vol. 18, pp. 532–537). Provo, UT: Association for Consumer Research.

Bernhardt, P. C., Dabbs, J. M., Jr., Fielden, J. A., & Lutter, C. D. (1998). Testosterone changes during vicarious experiences of winning and losing among fans at sporting events. *Physiology & Behavior, 65,* 59–62.

Bernstein, E. (2001). The meaning of the purchase: Desire demand and the commerce of sex. *Ethnography, 2,* 389–420.

Berry, J. W. (1989). Imposed etics-emics-derived etics: The operationalization of a compelling idea. *International Journal of Psychology, 24,* 721–735.

Bettencourt, L. A., & Houston, M. B. (2001). The impact of article method type and subject area on article citations and reference diversity in *JM, JMR,* and *JCR. Marketing Letters, 12,* 327–340.

Betz, M., O'Connell, L., & Shepard, J. M. (1989). Gender differences in proclivity for unethical behavior. *Journal of Business Ethics, 8,* 321–324.

Betzig, L. (Ed). (1997). *Human nature.* New York: Oxford University Press.

Betzig, L. L. (1986). *Despotism and differential reproduction: A Darwinian view of history.* Hawthorne, NY: Aldine.

Bierly, C., McSweeney, F. K., & Vannieuwkerk, R. (1985). Classical conditioning of preferences for stimuli. *Journal of Consumer Research, 12,* 316–323.

Bissell, K. L., & Zhou, P. (2004). Must-see TV or ESPN: Entertainment and sports media exposure and body-image distortion in college women. *Journal of Communication, 54,* 5–21.

Bjorklund, D. F., & Pellegrini, A. D. (2002). *The origins of human nature: Evolutionary developmental psychology.* Washington, DC: American Psychological Association.

Bjorklund, D. F., & Shackelford, T. K. (1999). Differences in parental investment contribute to important differences between men and women. *Current Directions in Psychological Science, 8,* 86–89.

Black, D. W. (2001). Compulsive buying disorder: Definition, assessment, epidemiology and clinical management. *CNS Drugs, 15,* 17–27.

Black, D. W., Repertinger, S., Gaffney, G. R., & Gabel, J. (1998). Family history and psychiatric comorbidity in persons with compulsive buying: Preliminary findings. *American Journal of Psychiatry, 155,* 960–963.

Blackmore, S. (1999). *The meme machine.* Oxford, England: Oxford University Press.

Blanco, C., Ibáñez, A., Sáiz-Ruiz, J., Blanco-Jerez, C., & Nunes, E. V. (2000). Epidemiology, pathophysiology and treatment of pathological gambling. *CNS Drugs, 13,* 397–407.

Blaszczynski, A., & Nower, L. (2002). A pathways model of problem and pathological gambling. *Addiction, 97,* 487–499.

Bloch, F., Rao, V., & Desai, S. (2004). Wedding celebrations as conspicuous consumption: Signaling social status in rural India. *The Journal of Human Resources, 39,* 675–695.

Bloom, D. F. (2004). Is acne really a disease?: A theory of acne as an evolutionarily significant, high-order psychoneuroimmune interaction timed to cortical development with a crucial role in mate choice. *Medical Hypotheses, 62,* 462–469.

Blum, D. (1998). *Sex on the brain: The biological differences between men and women.* New York: Penguin.

Boddewyn, J. J. (1981). Comparative marketing: The first twenty-five years. *Journal of International Business Studies, 12,* 61–79.

Boddewyn, J. J. (1991). Controlling sex and decency in advertising around the world. *Journal of Advertising, 20,* 25–35.

Boen, F., Vanbeselaere, N., & Feys, J. (2002). Behavioral consequences of fluctuating group success: An Internet study of soccer-team fans. *The Journal of Social Psychology, 142,* 769–781.

Bogetto, F., Venturello, S., Albert, U., Maina, G., & Ravizza, L. (1999). Gender-related clinical differences in obsessive-compulsive disorder. *European Psychiatry, 14,* 434–441.

Bondolfi, G., Osiek, C., & Ferrero, F. (2000). Prevalence estimates of pathological gambling in Switzerland. *Acta Psychiatrica Scandinavica, 101,* 473–475.

Boote, A. S. (1983). Psychographic segmentation in Europe. *Journal of Advertising Research, 22,* 19–25.

Botta, R. A. (2003). For your health? The relationship between magazine reading and adolescents' body image and eating disturbances. *Sex Roles, 48,* 389–399.

Bouchard, T. J., Jr., & Loehlin, J. C. (2001). Genes, evolution, and personality. *Behavior Genetics, 31,* 243–273.

Bovin, M. (2001). *Nomads who cultivate beauty: Wodaabe dances and visual arts in Niger.* Uppsala, Sweden: Nordiska Afrikainstitutet.

Bower, A. B. (2001). Highly attractive models in advertising and the women who loathe them: The implications of negative affect for spokesperson effectiveness. *Journal of Advertising, 30,* 51–63.

Boyd, B. (1998). Jane, meet Charles: Literature, evolution, and human nature. *Philosophy and Literature, 22,* 1–30.

Boyd, R., & Richerson, P. (1985). *Culture and the evolutionary process.* Chicago: University of Chicago Press.

Boyer, P. (2001). *Religion explained: The evolutionary origins of religious thought.* New York: Basic Books.

Boyer, P. (2003). Religious thought and behaviour as by-products of brain function. *Trends in Cognitive Sciences, 7,* 119–124.

Breiter, H. C., Aharon, I., Kahneman, D., Dale, A., & Shizgal, P. (2001). Functional imaging of neural responses to expectancy and experience of monetary gains and losses. *Neuron, 30,* 619–639.

Brinson, S. L., & Winn, J. E. (1997). Talk shows' representations of interpersonal conflicts. *Journal of Broadcasting & Electronic Media, 41,* 25–39.

Brodie, R. (1996). *Virus of the mind: The new science of the meme.* Seattle, WA: Integral Press.

Brown, D. E. (1991). *Human universals.* New York: McGraw-Hill.

Brown, W. M., Cronk, L., Grochow, K., Jacobson, A., Liu, C. K., Popovic, Z., et al., (2005). Dance reveals symmetry especially in young men. *Nature, 438,* 1148–1150.

Brown, W. M., & Moore, C. (2000). Is prospective altruist-detection an evolved solution to the adaptive problem of subtle cheating in cooperative ventures? Supportive evidence using the Wason selection task. *Evolution and Human Behavior, 21,* 25–37.

Brüne, M. (2001). De Clérambault's syndrome (erotomania) in an evolutionary perspective. *Evolution and Human Behavior, 22,* 409–415.

Burnham, T., & Phelan, J. (2000). *Mean genes—from sex to money to food: Taming our primal instincts.* Cambridge, MA: Perseus.

Burnham, T. C., Chapman, J. F., Gray, P. B., McIntyre, M. H., Lipson, S. F., & Ellison, P. T. (2003). Men in committed, romantic relationships have lower testosterone. *Hormones and Behavior, 44,* 119–122.

Burnstein, E., Crandall, C., & Kitayama, S. (1994). Some neo-darwinian rules for altruism: Weighing cues for inclusive fitness as a function of the biological importance of the decision. *Journal of Personality and Social Psychology, 67,* 773–789.

Buss, D. M. (1989). Sex differences in human mate preferences: Evolutionary hypotheses tested in 37 cultures. *Behavioral and Brain Sciences, 12,* 1–49.

Buss, D. M. (1990). Toward a biologically informed psychology of personality. *Journal of Personality, 58,* 1–16.

Buss, D. M. (1991). Evolutionary personality psychology. *Annual Review of Psychology, 42,* 459–491.

Buss, D. M. (1994). *The evolution of desire: Strategies of human mating.* New York: Basic Books.

Buss, D. M. (1995). Evolutionary psychology: A new paradigm for psychological science. *Psychological Inquiry, 6,* 1–30.

Buss, D. M. (1998). Sexual strategies theory: Historical origins and current status. *The Journal of Sex Research, 35,* 19–31.

Buss, D. M. (1999). *Evolutionary psychology: The new science of the mind.* Needham Heights, MA: Allyn & Bacon.

Buss, D. M. (2000). *The dangerous passion: Why jealousy is as necessary as love and sex.* New York: The Free Press.

Buss, D. M. (Ed.). (2005). *The handbook of evolutionary psychology.* New York: Wiley.

Buss, D. M., Larsen, R. J., Westen, D., & Semmelroth, J. (1992). Sex differences in jealousy: Evolution, physiology, and psychology. *Psychological Science, 3,* 251–255.

Buss, D. M., & Schmitt, D. P. (1993). Sexual strategies theory: An evolutionary perspective on human mating. *Psychological Review, 100,* 204–232.

Byrne, R. W., & Whiten, A. (Eds.). (1988). *Machiavellian intelligence: Social expertise and the evolution of intellect in monkeys, apes and humans.* Oxford, England: Clarendon.

Byrnes, J., & Miller, D. (1999). Gender differences in risk taking: A meta analysis. *Psychological Bulletin, 125,* 367–383.

Camerer, C., & Thaler, R. H. (1995). Anomalies: Ultimatums, dictators and manners. *Journal of Economic Perspectives, 9,* 209–219.

Campbell, A. (2002). *A mind of her own: The evolutionary psychology of women.* New York: Oxford University Press.

Campbell, A. (2004). Female competition: Causes, constraints, content, and contexts. *The Journal of Sex Research, 41,* 16–26.

Campos, L. de S., Otta, E., & Siqueira, J. de O. (2002). Sex differences in mate selection strategies: Content analyses and responses to personal advertisements in Brazil. *Evolution and Human Behavior, 23,* 395–406.

Cárdenas, R. A., & Harris, L. J. (2006). Symmetrical decorations enhance the attractiveness of faces and abstract designs. *Evolution and Human Behavior, 27,* 1–18.

Carroll, J. (1995). Evolution and literary theory. *Human Nature, 6,* 119–134.

Carroll, J. (1999). Wilson's *Consilience* and literary study. *Philosophy and Literature, 23,* 361–381.

Carroll, J. (2004). *Literary Darwinism: Evolution, human nature, and literature.* New York: Routledge.

Cartwright, J. (2000). *Evolution and human behavior: Darwinian perspectives on human nature.* Cambridge, MA: MIT Press.

Cary, M. S. (2000). Ad strategy and the stone age brain. *Journal of Advertising Research, 40,* 103–106.

Case, A., Lin, I.-F., & McLanahan, S. (2001). Educational attainment of siblings in stepfamilies. *Evolution and Human Behavior, 22,* 269–289.

Celsi, R. L., Rose, R. L., & Leigh, T. W. (1993). An exploration of high-risk leisure consumption through skydiving. *Journal of Consumer Research, 20,* 1–23.

Cervone, D. (2000). Evolutionary psychology and explanation in personality psychology. *The American Behavioral Scientist, 43,* 1001–1014.

Chao, A., & Schor, J. (1998). Empirical tests of status consumption: Evidence from women's cosmetics. *Journal of Economic Psychology, 19,* 107–131.

Chavanne, T. J., & Gallup, G. G., Jr. (1998). Variation in risk taking behavior among female college students as a function of the menstrual cycle. *Evolution and Human Behavior, 19,* 27–32.

Cheng, H. (1997). "Holding up half the sky?" A sociocultural comparison of gender-role portrayals in Chinese and U.S. advertising. *International Journal of Advertising, 16,* 295–319.

Chiappe, D., & MacDonald, K. (2005). The evolution of domain-general mechanisms in intelligence and learning. *The Journal of General Psychology, 132,* 5–40.

Choi, J., & Silverman, I. (2002). The relationship between testosterone and route-learning strategies in human. *Brain and Cognition, 50,* 116–120.

Cialdini, R. B., Borden, R. J., Thorne, A., Walker, M. R., Freeman, S., & Sloan, L. R. (1976). Basking in reflected glory: Three (football) studies. *Journal of Personality and Social Psychology, 34,* 366–375.

Clark, R., Guilmain, J., Saucier, P. K., & Tavarez, J. (2003). Two steps forward, one step back: The presence of female characters and gender stereotyping in award-winning picture books between the 1930s and the 1960s. *Sex Roles, 49,* 439–449.

Claxton, R. P. (1995). Birth order as a market segmentation variable. *Journal of Consumer Marketing, 12,* 22–39.

Claxton, R. P. (1999). Birth order and two marketing related measures of aggression. *Psychological Reports, 84,* 236–238.

Clements, K. W., & Chen, D. (1996). Fundamental similarities in consumer behaviour. *Applied Economics, 28,* 747–757.

Cohan, J. A. (2001). Towards a new paradigm in the ethics of women's advertising. *Journal of Business Ethics, 33,* 323–337.

Cohen, J. (1996). The search for universal symbols: The case of right and left. *Journal of International Consumer Marketing, 8,* 187–210.

Cohen, J. L., & Dickens, W. T. (2002). A foundation for behavioral economics. *The American Economic Review, 92,* 335–338.

Colarelli, S. M. (1998). Psychological interventions in organizations: An evolutionary perspective. *American Psychologist, 53,* 1044–1056.

Colarelli, S. M. (2003). *No best way: An evolutionary perspective on human resource management.* Westport, CT: Praeger.

Colarelli, S. M., & Dettman, J. R. (2003). Intuitive evolutionary perspectives in marketing practices. *Psychology & Marketing, 20,* 837–865.

Cole, S. (1994). Why sociology doesn't make progress like the natural sciences. *Sociological Forum, 9,* 133–154.

Coleman, M., & Ganong, L. (1987). An evaluation of the stepfamily self-help literature for children and adolescents. *Family Relations, 36,* 61–65.

Collins, D. (2000). The quest to improve the human condition: The first 1 500 articles published in *Journal of Business Ethics. Journal of Business Ethics, 26,* 1–73.

Commuri, S., & Gentry, J. W. (2000). Opportunities for family research in marketing. *Academy of Marketing Science Review, 8.* Retrieved March 22, 2004, from http://www.amsreview.org/articles/commuri08–2000.pdf

Condit, V. K. (1990). Anorexia nervosa: Levels of causation. *Human Nature, 1,* 391–413.

Congleton, R. D. (1989). Efficient status seeking: Externalities, and the evolution of status games. *Journal of Economic Behavior and Organization, 11,* 175–190.

Conway, L. G., III, & Schaller, M. (2002). On the verifiability of evolutionary psychological theories: An analysis of the psychology of scientific persuasion. *Personality and Social Psychology Review, 6,* 152–166.

Cooper, A., Scherer, C. R., Boies, S. C., & Gordon, B. L. (1999). Sexuality on the Internet: From sexual exploitation to pathological expression. *Professional Psychology–Research and Practice, 30,* 154–164.

Cooper, B. L. (1998). Images of women in popular song lyrics: A bibliography. *Popular Music & Society, 22,* 79–89.

Cooper, B. L. (1999). "From Lady Day to Lady Di: Images of women in contemporary recordings, 1938–1998." *International Journal of Instructional Media, 26,* 353–358.

Cooper, W. S. (1987). Decision theory as a branch of evolutionary theory: A biological derivation of Savage axioms. *Psychological Review, 94,* 395–411.

Cosmides, L. (1989). The logic of social exchange: Has natural selection shaped how humans reason? Studies with the Wason selection task. *Cognition, 31,* 187–276.

Cosmides, L., & Tooby, J. (1992). Cognitive adaptations for social exchange. In J. H. Barkow, L. Cosmides, & J. Tooby (Eds.), *The adapted mind: Evolutionary psychology and the generation of culture* (pp. 163–228). New York: Oxford University Press.

Cosmides, L., & Tooby, J. (1994). Better than rational: Evolutionary psychology and the invisible hand. *American Economic Review, 84,* 327–332.

Cowan, G., & Campbell, R. R. (1994). Racism and sexism in interracial pornography. *Psychology of Women Quarterly, 18,* 323–338.

Cronin, H. (1991). *The ant and the peacock: Altruism and sexual selection from Darwin to today.* Cambridge, England: Cambridge University Press.

Cronk, L. (1991). Human behavioral ecology. *Annual Review of Anthropology, 20,* 25–53.

Cronk, L., & Dunham, B. (2003, June). *Engagement rings as signals in American courtship.* Paper presented at the annual meeting of the Human Behavior and Evolution Society, Lincoln, NE.

Cziko, G. (1995). *Without miracles: Universal selection theory and the second Darwinian revolution.* Cambridge, MA: MIT Press.

Cziko, G. (2000). *The things we do: Using the lessons of Bernard and Darwin to understand the what, how, and why of our behavior.* Cambridge, MA: MIT Press.

Daly, M., & Wilson, M. (1988). *Homicide.* New York: Aldine de Gruyter.

Daly, M., & Wilson, M. (1999). *The truth about Cinderella: A Darwinian view of parental love.* New Haven, CT: Yale University Press.

Daly, M., Wilson, M., & Weghorst, S. J. (1982). Male sexual jealousy. *Ethology and Sociobiology, 3,* 11–27.

Daly, M., & Wilson, M. I. (1982). Whom are newborn babies said to resemble? *Ethology and Sociobiology, 3,* 69–78.

Darley, W. K., & Smith, R. E. (1995). Gender differences in information processing strategies: An empirical test of the selectivity model in advertising response. *Journal of Advertising, 24,* 41–56.

Darwin, C. (1985). *The origin of species.* New York: Penguin. (Original work published 1859)

Darwin, C. (1871). *The descent of man, and selection in relation to sex* (2 vols.). London: Murray.

Davis, H., & McLeod, S. L. (2003). Why humans value sensational news: An evolutionary perspective. *Evolution and Human Behavior, 24,* 208–216.

Davis, M. S. (1971). That's interesting! Towards a phenomenology of sociology and a sociology of phenomenology. *Philosophy of Social Science, 1,* 309–344.

Davis, S., & Mares, M.-L. (1998). Effects of talk show viewing on adolescents. *Journal of Communication, 48,* 69–86.

Dawar, N., & Parker, P. (1994). Marketing universals: Consumers' use of brand name, price, physical appearance, and retailer reputation as signals of product quality. *Journal of Marketing, 58,* 81–95.

Dawes, G. (2002). Figure eights, spin outs and power slides: Aboriginal and Torres Strait islander youth and the culture of joyriding. *Journal of Youth Studies, 5,* 195–208.

Dawkins, R. (1976). *The selfish gene.* New York: Oxford University Press.

Dawkins, R. (1982). *The extended phenotype: The long reach of the gene.* Oxford, England: Oxford University Press.

Dawkins, R. (1991). *The blind watchmaker.* London: Penguin.

Dawkins, R. (2003). *A devil's chaplain: Reflections on hope, lies, science, and love.* New York: Houghton Mifflin.

Denison, R. F., Kiers, E. T., & West, S. A. (2003). Darwinian agriculture: When can humans find solutions beyond the reach of natural selection? *The Quarterly Review of Biology, 78,* 145–168.

Dennett, D. C. (1991). *Consciousness explained.* New York: Little, Brown.

Dennett, D. C. (1995). *Darwin's dangerous idea: Evolution and the meanings of life.* London: Penguin.

DeSarbo, W. S., & Edwards, E. A. (1996). Typologies of compulsive buying behavior: A constrained clusterwise regression approach. *Journal of Consumer Psychology, 5,* 231–262.

DeSteno, D., Bartlett, M. Y., Braverman, J., & Salovey, P. (2002). Sex differences in jealousy: evolutionary mechanism or artifact of measurement? *Journal of Personality and Social Psychology, 83,* 1103–1116.

Dickemann, M. (1979). Female infanticide, reproductive strategies, and social stratification: A preliminary model. In N. A. Chagnon & W. Irons (Eds.), *Evolutionary biology and human social behaviour* (pp. 321–367). North Scituate, MA: Duxbury Press.

Dickerson, M., & Baron, E. (2000). Contemporary issues and future directions for research into pathological gambling. *Addiction, 95,* 1145–1159.

Dietz, T., Burns, T. R., & Buttel, F. H. (1990). Evolutionary theory in sociology: An examination of current thinking. *Sociological Forum, 5,* 155–171.

Dimberg, U., & Öhman, A. (1996). Behold the wrath: Psychological responses to facial stimuli. *Motivation and Emotion, 20,* 149–182.

Dissanayake, E. (1992). *Homo aestheticus: Where art comes from and why.* New York: The Free Press.

Doiron, J. P., & Nicki, R. M. (2001). Epidemiology of problem gambling in Prince Edward Island: A Canadian microcosm? *Canadian Journal of Psychiatry, 46,* 413–417.

Dombrovsky, Y., & Perrin, N. (1994). On adaptive search and optimal stopping in sequential mate choice. *American Naturalist, 144,* 355–361.

Douglas, S. P., & Wind, Y. (1987). The myth of globalization. *Columbia Journal of World Business, 22,* 19–29.

Dukes, R. L., Bisel, T. M., Borega, K. N., Lobato, E. A., & Owens, M. D. (2003). Expressions of love, sex, and hurt in popular songs: A content analysis of all-time greatest hits. *The Social Science Journal, 40,* 643–650.

Dunbar, R. I. M. (1996). *Grooming, gossip, and the evolution of language.* Cambridge, MA: Harvard University Press.

Dunbar, R. I. M. (2003). The social brain: Mind, language, and society in evolutionary perspective. *Annual Review of Anthropology, 32,* 163–181.

Durvasula, S., Andrews, J. C., Lysonski, S., & Netemeyer, R. G. (1993). Assessing the cross-national applicability of consumer behavior models: A model of attitude toward advertising in general. *Journal of Consumer Research, 19,* 626–636.

Dutton, D. (2002). Aesthetic universals. In B. Gaut & D. M. Lopes (Eds.), *The Routledge companion to aesthetics* (pp. 203–214). New York: Routledge.

Dutton, D. (2003). Aesthetics and evolutionary psychology. In J. Levinson (Ed.), *The Oxford handbook for aesthetics* (pp. 693–705). New York: Oxford University Press.

Eagly, A. (1987). *Sex differences in social behavior: A social role theory interpretation.* Hillsdale, NJ: Lawrence Erlbaum Associates.

Eagly, A. H., Ashmore, R. D., Makhijani, M. G., & Longo, L. C. (1991). What is beautiful is good, but … : A meta-analytic review of research on the physical attractiveness stereotype. *Psychological Bulletin, 110,* 109–128.

Eaton, S. B., Cordain, L., & Lindeberg, S. (2002). Evolutionary health promotion: A consideration of common counterarguments. *Preventive Medicine, 34,* 119–123.

Eaton, S. B., Strassman, B. I., Nesse, R. M., Neel, J. V., Ewald, P. W., Williams, G. C., et al. (2002). Evolutionary health promotion. *Preventive Medicine, 34,* 109–118.

Edelman, G. M. (1987). *Neural Darwinism: The theory of neuronal group selection.* New York: Basic Books.

Eens, M., & Pinxten, R. (2000). Sex-role reversal in vertebrates: Behavioural and endocrinological accounts. *Behavioural Processes, 51,* 135–147.

Eibl-Eibesfeldt, I. (1989). *Human ethology.* New York: Aldine de Gruyter.

Ekström, K. M. (2003). Revisiting the family tree: Historical and future consumer behavior research. *Academy of Marketing Science Review, 1*. Retrieved January 12, 2004, from http://www.amsreview.org/articles/ekstrom01–2003.pdf

El-Guebaly, N., & Hodgins, D. C. (2000). *Pathological gambling: The biopsychological variables and their management.* Retrieved from http://www.abgaminginstitute.ualberta.ca/literature_reviews.cfm

Elliott, R., Jones, A., Benfield, A., & Barlow, M. (1995). Overt sexuality in advertising: A discourse analysis of gender responses. *Journal of Consumer Policy, 18,* 187–217.

Ellis, B. J. (1992). The evolution of sexual attraction: Evaluative mechanisms in women. In J. H. Barkow, L. Cosmides, & J. Tooby (Eds.), *The adapted mind: Evolutionary psychology and the generation of culture* (pp. 267–288). New York: Oxford University Press.

Ellis, B. J. (2004). Timing of pubertal maturation in girls: An integrated life history approach. *Psychological Bulletin, 130,* 920–958.

Ellis, B. J., & Symons, D. (1990). Sex differences in sexual fantasy: An evolutionary psychological approach. *The Journal of Sex Research, 27,* 527–555.

Elster, J. (1998). Emotions and economic theory. *Journal of Economic Literature, 36,* 47–74.

Emlen, S. T. (1995). An evolutionary theory of the family. *Proceedings of the National Academy of Sciences, 92,* 8092–8099.

Emlen, S. T. (1997). The evolutionary study of human family systems. *Social Science Information, 36,* 563–589.

Englis, B. G., Solomon, M. R., & Ashmore, R. D. (1994). Beauty before the eyes of the beholders: The cultural encoding of beauty types in magazine advertising and music television. *Journal of Advertising, 23,* 49–61.

Ernst, C., & Angst, J. (1983). *Birth order: Its influence on personality.* Berlin: Springer-Verlag.

Etcoff, N. (1999). *Survival of the prettiest: The science of beauty.* New York: Doubleday.

Euler, H. A., & Weitzel, B. (1996). Discriminative grandparental solicitude as reproductive strategy. *Human Nature, 7,* 39–59.

Evans, L., & Davies, K. (2000). No sissy boys here: A content analysis of the representation of masculinity in elementary school reading textbooks. *Sex Roles, 42,* 255–270.

Evans, M. G., & Chang, Y. C. (1998). Cheater detection and altruistic behavior: An experimental and methodological exploration. *Managerial and Decision Economics, 19,* 467–480.

Faber, R. J., & Christenson, G. A. (1996). In the mood to buy: Differences in the mood states experienced by compulsive buyers and other consumers. *Psychology & Marketing, 13,* 803–819.

Faber, R. J., & O'Guinn, T. C. (1992). A clinical screener for compulsive buying. *Journal of Consumer Research, 19,* 459–469.

Faer, L. M., Hendriks, A., Abed, R. T., & Figueredo, A. J. (2005). The evolutionary psychology of eating disorders: Female competition for mates or for status? *Psychology and Psychotherapy: Theory, Research and Practice, 78,* 397–417.

Farber, P. L. (1998). *The temptations of evolutionary ethics.* Berkeley: University of California Press.

Fay, M., & Price, C. (1994). Female body-shape in print advertisements and the increase in Anorexia Nervosa. *European Journal of Marketing, 28,* 5–18.

Feinberg, R. A. (1986). Credit cards as spending facilitating stimuli: A conditioning interpretation. *Journal of Consumer Research, 13,* 348–356.

Feingold, A. (1992). Gender differences in mate selection preferences: A test of the parental investment model. *Psychological Bulletin, 112,* 125–139.

Ferguson, J. H., Kreshel, P. J., & Tinkham, S. F. (1990). In the pages of *Ms.*: Sex role portrayals of women in advertising. *Journal of Advertising, 19,* 40–51.

Ferron, C. (1997). Body image in adolescence: Cross-cultural research—results of the preliminary phase of a quantitative survey. *Adolescence, 32,* 735–745.

Fessler, D. M. T. (2003). No time to eat: An adaptationist account of periovulatory behavioral changes. *The Quarterly Review of Biology, 78,* 3–21.

Fiddick, L., Cosmides, L., & Tooby, J. (2000). No interpretation without representation: The role of domain-specific representations and inferences in the Wason selection task. *Cognition, 77,* 1–79.

Fink, B., &, Penton-Voak, I. (2002). Evolutionary psychology of facial attractiveness. *Current Directions in Psychological Science, 11,* 154–158.

Fisher, R. A. (1930). *The genetical theory of natural selection.* Oxford, England: Clarendon.

Fisher, W. A., & Barak, A. (2001). Internet pornography: A social psychological perspective on Internet sexuality. *Journal of Sex Research, 38,* 312–323.

First, A. (1998). Nothing new under the sun? A comparison of images of women in Israeli advertisements in 1979 and 1994. *Sex Roles, 38,* 1065–1077.

Fitch, W. T. (2006). The biology and evolution of music: A comparative perspective. *Cognition, 100,* 173–215.

Floyd, K., & Haynes, M. T. (2005). Applications of the theory of natural selection to the study of family communication. *Journal of Family Communication, 5,* 79–101.

Ford, J. B., LaTour, M. S., & Clarke, I. (2004). A prescriptive essay concerning sex role portrayals in international advertising contexts. *American Business Review, 22,* 42–55.

Ford, J. B., LaTour, M. S., Honeycutt, E. D., Jr., & Joseph, M. (1994). Female sex role portrayals in international advertising: Should advertisers standardize in the Pacific Rim? *American Business Review, 12,* 1–10.

Ford, J. B., LaTour, M. S., & Lundstrom, W. J. (1991). Contemporary women's evaluation of female role portrayals in advertising. *The Journal of Consumer Marketing, 8,* 15–28.

Ford, J. B., Voli, P. K., Honeycutt, E. D., Jr., & Casey, S. L. (1998). Gender role portrayals in Japanese advertising: A magazine content analysis. *Journal of Advertising, 27,* 113–124.

Fouts, G., & Burggraf, K. (1999). Television situation comedies: Female body images and verbal reinforcements. *Sex Roles, 40,* 473–481.

Fouts, G., & Vaughan, K. (2002). Television situation comedies: Male weight, negative references, and audience reactions. *Sex Roles, 46,* 439–442.

Foxall, G. R. (1987). Radical behaviorism and consumer research. Theoretical promise and empirical problems. *International Journal of Research in Marketing, 4,* 111–129.

Foxall, G. R. (1994). Behavior analysis and consumer psychology. *Journal of Economic Psychology, 15,* 5–91.

Frank, R. H. (1985). *Choosing the right pond: Human behavior and the quest for status.* New York: Oxford University Press.

Frank, R. H. (1988). *Passions within reason: The strategic role of the emotions.* New York: Norton.

Frank, R. H., & Cook, P. J. (1995). *The winner-take-all society: Why the few at the top get so much more than the rest of us.* New York: Penguin.

Franzoi, S. L. (2001). Is female body esteem shaped by benevolent sexism? *Sex Roles, 44,* 177–188.

Freeman, D. (1999). *The fateful hoaxing of Margaret Mead: A historical analysis of her Samoan research.* Boulder, CO: Westview Press.

Freese, J., Li, J. C. A., & Wade, L. D. (2003). The potential relevances of biology to social inquiry. *Annual Review of Sociology, 29,* 233–256.

Freese, J., & Meland, S. (2002). Seven tenths incorrect: Heterogeneity and change in the waist-to-hip ratio of *Playboy* centerfolds and Miss America pageant winners. *The Journal of Sex Research, 39,* 133–138.

Frey, B. S. (2000). *Arts and economics: Analysis and cultural policy.* Berlin: Springer.

Frost, R. O., Kim, H.-J., Morris, C., Bloss, C., Murray-Close, M., & Steketee, G. (1998). Hoarding, compulsive buying and reasons for saving. *Behaviour Research and Therapy, 36,* 657–664.

Frost, R. O., Meagher, B. M., & Riskind, J. H. (2001). Obsessive-compulsive features in pathological lottery and scratch-ticket gamblers. *Journal of Gambling Studies, 17,* 5–19.

Fullerton, J. A., & Kendrick, A. (2000). Portrayal of men and women in U.S. Spanish-language television commercials. *Journalism & Mass Communication Quarterly, 77,* 128–142.

Furnham, A. (1999). The saving and spending habits of young people. *Journal of Economic Psychology, 20,* 677–697.

Furnham, A., & Mak, T. (1999). Sex-role stereotyping in television commercials: A review and comparison of fourteen studies done on five continents over 25 years. *Sex Roles, 41,* 413–437.

Furnham, A., Tan, T., & McManus, C. (1997). Waist-to-hip ratio and preferences for body shape: A replication and extension. *Personality and Individual Differences, 22,* 539–549.

Gallistel, C. R. (1998). The modular structure of learning. In M. Gazzaniga & J. S. Altman (Eds.), *Brain and mind: Evolutionary perspectives* (Vol. 5, pp. 56–68). Strasbourg, France: Human Frontiers Science Program.

Gallistel, C. R. (2000). The replacement of general-purpose learning with adaptively specialized learning modules. In M. S. Gazzaniga (Ed.), *The new cognitive neurosciences* (pp. 1179–1191). Cambridge, MA: MIT Press.

Ganahl, D. J., Prinsen, T. J., & Netzley, S. B. (2003). A content analysis of prime time commercials: A contextual framework of gender representation. *Sex Roles, 49,* 545–551.

Gandolfi, A. E., Gandolfi, A. S., & Barash, D. P. (2002). *Economics as an evolutionary science: From utility to fitness.* Piscataway, NJ: Transaction.

Gangestad, S. W., & Buss, D. M. (1993). Pathogen prevalence and human mate preferences. *Ethology and Sociobiology, 14,* 89–96.

Gangestad, S. W., & Simpson, J. A. (2000). The evolution of human mating: Trade-offs and strategic pluralism. *Behavioral and Brain Sciences, 23,* 573–587.

Gangestad, S. W., & Thornhill, R. (1998). Menstrual cycle variation in women's preferences for the scent of symmetrical men. *Proceedings of the Royal Society of London: Series B, Biological Sciences, 265,* 927–933.

Gangestad, S. W., Thornhill, R., & Yeo, R. A. (1994). Facial attractiveness, developmental stability, and fluctuating asymmetry. *Ethology and Sociobiology, 15,* 73–85.

Garfein, R. T. (1989). Cross-cultural perspectives on the dynamics of prestige. *The Journal of Services Marketing, 3,* 17–24.

Garst, J., & Bodenhausen, G. V. (1997). Advertising's effects on men's gender role attitudes. *Sex Roles, 36,* 551–572.

Geary, D. C. (1998). *Male, female: The evolution of human sex differences.* Washington, DC: American Psychological Association.

Geary, D. C., & Flinn, M. V. (2001). Evolution of human parental behavior and the human family. *Parenting: Science and Practice, 1,* 5–61.

Gibson, J. J. (1979). *The ecological approach to visual perception.* Boston: Houghton Mifflin.

Gigerenzer, G. (2000). *Adaptive rationality: Rationality in the real world.* New York: Oxford University Press.

Gigerenzer, G., & Goldstein, D. G. (1996). Reasoning the fast and frugal way: Models of bounded rationality. *Psychological Review, 103,* 650–669.

Gigerenzer, G., & Todd, P. M. (1999). Fast and frugal heuristics: The adaptive toolbox. In G. Gigerenzer, P. M. Todd, & the ABC Research Group (Eds.), *Simple heuristics that make us smart* (pp. 3–34). New York: Oxford University Press.

Gigerenzer, G., Todd, P. M., & the ABC Research Group (1999). *Simple heuristics that make us smart.* New York: Oxford University Press.

Gilovich, T., Griffin, D., & Kahneman, D. (Eds.). (2002). *Heuristics and biases: The psychology of intuitive judgment.* Cambridge, England: Cambridge University Press.

Gintis, H., Smith, E. A., & Bowles, S. (2001). Costly signaling and cooperation. *Journal of Theoretical Biology, 213,* 103–119.

Goff, B. G., & Gibbs, M. C. (1993). Denominational affiliation change: Application of the consumer decision model. *Journal of Consumer Affairs, 27,* 227–257.

Goffman, E. (1979). *Gender advertisements.* Cambridge, MA: Harvard University Press.

Goldstein, D. G., & Gigerenzer, G. (1999). The recognition heuristic: How ignorance makes us smart. In G. Gigerenzer, P. M. Todd, & the ABC Research Group (Eds.), *Simple heuristics that make us smart* (pp. 37–58). New York: Oxford University Press.

Gonzalez, C., Dana, J., Koshino, H., & Just, M. (2005). The framing effect and risky decisions: Examining cognitive functions with fMRI. *Journal of Economic Psychology, 26,* 1–20.

Gorn, G. J. (1982). The effects of music in advertising on choice behavior: A classical conditioning approach. *Journal of Marketing, 46,* 94–101.

Götestam, K. G., & Johansson, A. (2003). Characteristics of gambling and problematic gambling in the Norwegian context: A DSM-IV-based telephone interview study. *Addictive Behaviors, 28,* 189–197.

Gottschall, J., Martin, J., Quish, H., & Rea, J. (2004). Sex differences in mate choice criteria are reflected in folktales from around the world and in historical European literature. *Evolution and Human Behavior, 25,* 102–112.

Gottschall, J., & Wilson, D. S. (Eds.). (2006). *The literary animal: Evolution and the nature of narrative.* Evanston, IL: Northwestern University Press.

Gowdy, J. M., & Carbonell, A. F. (1999). Toward consilience between biology and economics: The contribution of ecological economics. *Ecological Economics, 29,* 337–348.

Graham, J. F., Stendardi, E. J., Jr., Myers, J. K., & Graham, M. J. (2002). Gender differences in investment strategies: An information processing perspective. *International Journal of Bank Marketing, 20,* 17–26.

Grammer, K. (1996, June). *The human mating game: The battle of the sexes and the war of signals.* Paper presented at the annual meeting of the Human Behavior and Evolution Society, Evanston, IL.

Grammer, K. (1998). Sex and gender in advertisements: Indoctrination and exploitation. In I. Eibl-Eibesfeldt & F. K. Salter (Eds.), *Indoctrinability, ideology and warfare: Evolutionary perspectives* (pp. 219–240). New York: Berghahn Books.

Grammer, K., Dittami, J., & Fischmann, B. (1993, September). *Changes in female sexual advertisement according to menstrual cycle.* Paper presented at the *23rd International Ethological Conference.* Torremolinos, Spain.

Grammer, K., & Thornhill, R. (1994). Human (*homo sapiens*) facial attractiveness and sexual selection: The role of symmetry and averageness. *Journal of Comparative Psychology, 108,* 233–242.

Gray, P. B. (2004). Evolutionary and cross-cultural perspectives on gambling. *Journal of Gambling Studies, 20,* 347–371.

Greenberg, B. S., Sherry, J. L., Busselle, R. W., Hnilo, L. R., & Smith, S. W. (1997). Daytime television talk shows: Guests, content and interactions. *Journal of Broadcasting & Electronic Media, 41,* 412–426.

Greenberg, B. S., & Woods, M. G. (1999). The soaps: Their sex, gratifications, and outcomes. *The Journal of Sex Research, 36,* 250–257.

Greenlees, I. A., & McGrew, W. C. (1994). Sex and age differences in preferences and tactics of mate attraction: Analysis of published advertisements. *Ethology and Sociobiology, 15,* 59–72.

Gresham, L. G., & Shimp, T. A. (1985). Attitude toward the advertisement and brand attitudes: A classical conditioning perspective. *Journal of Advertising, 14,* 10–18.

Grether, D. M., & Plott, C. R. (1979). Economic theory of choice and the preference reversal phenomenon. *American Economic Review, 69,* 623–638.

Griffiths, M. (2001). Sex on the Internet: Observations and implications for Internet sex addiction. *Journal of Sex Research, 38,* 333–342.

Grinde, B. (1996). The biology of visual aesthetics. *Journal of Social and Evolutionary Systems, 19,* 31–40.

Grinde, B. (1998). The biology of religion: A Darwinian gospel. *Journal of Social and Evolutionary Systems, 21,* 19–28.

Grodal, T. (2004). Love and desire in the cinema. *Cinema Journal, 43,* 26–46.

Groesz, L. M., Levine, M. P., & Murnen, S. K. (2002). The effect of experimental presentation of thin media images on body satisfaction: A meta-analytic review. *International Journal of Eating Disorders, 31,* 1–16.

Grossman, R. P., & Till, B. D. (1998). The persistence of classically conditioned brand attitudes. *Journal of Advertising, 27*, 23–32.

Grossman, R. P., & Wisenblit, J. Z. (1999). What we know about consumers' color choices. *Journal of Marketing Practice: Applied Marketing Science, 5*, 78–88.

Grosvenor, P. C. (2002). Evolutionary psychology and the Intellectual Left. *Perspectives in Biology and Medicine, 45*, 433–448.

Grumbach, M. M. (2004). To an understanding of the biology of sex and gender differences: "an idea whose time has come." *Journal of Men's Health & Gender, 1*, 12–19.

Guisinger, S. (2003). Adapted to flee famine: Adding an evolutionary perspective on anorexia nervosa. *Psychological Review, 110*, 745–761.

Gulas, C. S., & McKeage, K. (2000). Extending social comparison: An examination of the unintended consequences of idealized advertising imagery. *Journal of Advertising, 29*, 17–28.

Güth, W., Schmittberger, R., & Schwartze, B. (1982). An experimental analysis of ultimatum bargaining. *Journal of Economic Behavior and Organization, 3*, 367–388.

Habimana, E., & Massé, L. (2000). Envy manifestations and personality disorders. *European Psychiatry, 15*, 15–21.

Hagen, E. H. (2005). Controversial issues in evolutionary psychology. In D. M. Buss (Ed.), *The handbook of evolutionary psychology* (pp. 145–173). New York: Wiley.

Hagen, E. H., & Bryant, G. A. (2003). Music and dance as a coalition signaling system. *Human Nature, 14*, 21–51.

Hagerty, M. R., & Aaker, D. A. (1984). A normative model of consumer information processing. *Marketing Science, 3*, 227–246.

Hamilton, W. D. (1964). The genetical evolution of social behavior. *Journal of Theoretical Biology, 7*, 1–52.

Hanna, M. T., & Freeman, J. (1977). The population ecology of organizations. *The American Journal of Sociology, 82*, 929–964.

Hanna, M. T., & Freeman, J. (1989). *Organizational ecology.* Cambridge, MA: Harvard University Press.

Hargreaves, D. A., & Tiggemann, M. (2003). Female "thin ideal" media images and boys' attitudes toward girls. *Sex Roles, 49*, 539–544.

Harrington, C. L., & Bielby, D. D. (1991). The mythology of modern love: Representations of romance in the 1980s. *Journal of Popular Culture, 24*, 129–144.

Harris, C. R. (2003). Factors associated with jealousy over real and imagined infidelity: An examination of the social-cognitive and evolutionary psychology perspectives. *Psychology of Women Quarterly, 27*, 319–329.

Harris, G., & Attour, S. (2003). The international advertising practices of multinational companies: A content analysis study. *European Journal of Marketing, 37*, 154–168.

Harris, J. R. (1998). *The nurture assumption: Why children turn out the way they do.* New York: The Free Press.

Harrison, K. (1997). Does interpersonal attraction to thin media personalities promote eating disorders? *Journal of Broadcasting & Electronic Media, 41*, 478–500.

Harrison, K. (2000). The body electric: Thin-ideal media and eating disorders in adolescents. *Journal of Communication, 50,*119–143.

Harrison, K. (2003). Television viewers' ideal body proportions: The case of the curvaceously thin woman. *Sex Roles, 48,* 255–264.

Harrison, K., & Cantor, J. (1997). The relationship between media consumption and eating disorders. *Journal of Communication, 47,* 40–67.

Haselton, M. G. (2003). The sexual overperception bias: Evidence of a systematic bias in men from a survey of naturally occurring events. *Journal of Research in Personality, 37,* 43–47.

Haselton, M. G., & Buss, D. M. (2000). Error management theory: A new perspective on biases in cross-sex mind reading. *Journal of Personality and Social Psychology, 78,* 81–91.

Hassan, S. S., Craft, S. H., & Kortam, W. (2003). Understanding the new bases for global market segmentation. *The Journal of Consumer Marketing, 20,* 446–462.

Hassay, D. N., & Smith, M. C. (1996). Compulsive buying: An examination of the consumption motive. *Psychology & Marketing, 13,* 741–752.

Hayward, L. S., & Rohwer, S. (2004). Sex differences in attitudes toward paternity testing. *Evolution and Human Behavior, 25,* 242–248.

Heath, C., Bell, C., & Sternberg, E. (2001). Emotional selection in memes: The case of urban legends. *Journal of Personality and Social Psychology, 81,* 1028–1041.

Hedley, M. (2002). The geometry of gendered conflict in popular film: 1986–2000. *Sex Roles, 47,* 201–217.

Henrich, J., & Gil-White, F. J. (2001). The evolution of prestige: Freely conferred deference as a mechanism for enhancing the benefits of cultural transmission. *Evolution and Human Behavior, 22,* 165–196.

Henriques, G. (2003). The tree of knowledge system and the theoretical unification of psychology. *Review of General Psychology, 7,* 150–182.

Hersey, G. L. (1996). *The evolution of allure: Sexual selection from Medici Venus to the Incredible Hulk.* Cambridge, MA: MIT Press.

Heyes, C., & Hull, D. L. (Eds.). (2001). *Selection theory and social construction: The evolutionary naturalistic epistemology of Donald T. Campbell.* Albany: State University of New York Press.

Hill, E., & Wenzl, P. A. (1981, June). *Variation in ornamentation and behavior in a disco theque for females observed at different menstrual phases.* Paper presented at the meeting of the Animal Behavior Society, Knoxville, TN.

Hill, E. M., & Chow, K. (2002). Life-history theory and risky drinking. *Addiction, 97,* 401–413.

Hill, E. M., Grabel, D., & McCurren, R. (2003). Impairment in family caregiving: A biological perspective. *Medical Hypotheses, 61,* 248–258.

Hill, R. A., & Dunbar, R. I. M. (2003). Social network size in humans. *Human Nature, 14,* 53–72.

Hinsz, V. B., Matz, D. C., & Patience, R. A. (2001). Does women's hair signal reproductive potential? *Journal of Experimental Social Psychology, 37,* 166–172.

Hirsch, F. (1976). *Social limits to growth.* Cambridge, MA: Harvard University Press.

Hirschberger, G., Florian, V., Mikulinger, M., Goldenberg, J. L., & Pyszczynski, T. (2002). Gender differences in the willingness to engage in risky behavior: A terror management perspective. *Death Studies, 26,* 117–141.

Hirschfeld, L. A., & Gelman, S. A. (Eds.). (1994). *Mapping the mind: Domain specificity in cognition and culture.* New York: Cambridge University Press.

Hirschman, E. C. (1987). People as products: Analysis of a complex marketing exchange. *Journal of Marketing, 51,* 98–108.

Hoffman, E., McCabe, K. A., & Smith, V. L. (1998). Behavioral foundations of reciprocity: Experimental economics and evolutionary psychology. *Economic Inquiry, 36,* 335–352.

Hofstede, G. (1997). *Cultures and organizations: Software of the mind.* New York: McGraw-Hill.

Holbrook, M. B. (1987). What is consumer research? *Journal of Consumer Research, 14,* 128–132.

Holden, C. J., Sear, R., & Mace, R. (2003). Matriliny as daughter-biased investment. *Evolution and Human Behavior, 24,* 99–112.

Horton, D. (1957). The dialogue of courtship in popular songs. *American Journal of Sociology, 62,* 569–578.

Huber, J., Payne, J. W., & Puto, C. (1982). Adding asymmetrically dominated alternatives: Violations of regularity and the similarity hypothesis. *Journal of Consumer Research, 9,* 90–98.

Hui, C. H., & Triandis, H. C. (1985). Measurements in cross-cultural psychology: A review and comparison of strategies. *Journal of Cross-Cultural Psychology, 16,* 131–152.

Hull, D. L. (2001). *Science and selection: Essays on biological evolution and the philosophy of science.* Cambridge, England: Cambridge University Press.

Hupfer, M. (2002). Communicating with the agentic woman and the communal man: Are stereotypic advertising appeals still relevant? *Academy of Marketing Science Review.* Retrieved March, 15, 2004, from http://www.amsreview.org/articles/hupfer03-2002.pdf

Iyer, G. R. (1997). Comparative marketing: An interdisciplinary framework for institutional analysis. *Journal of International Business Studies, 28,* 531–561.

Jackson, T. (2002). Evolutionary psychology in ecological economics: Consilience, consumption and contentment. *Ecological Economics, 41,* 289–303.

Jacoby, J., Johar, G. V., & Morrin, M. (1998). Consumer behavior: A quadrennium. *Annual Review of Psychology, 49,* 319–344.

Jankowiak, W., & Diderich, M. (2000). Sibling solidarity in a polygamous community in the USA: Unpacking inclusive fitness. *Evolution and Human Behavior, 21,* 125–139.

Jianakoplos, N. A., & Bernasek, A. (1998). Are women more risk averse? *Economic Inquiry, 36,* 620–630.

Johnson, W. B., & Johnson, W. L. (1998). Self-help books used by religious practitioners. *Journal of Counseling & Development, 76,* 459–466.

Johnston, V. S., Hagel, R., Franklin, M., Fink, B., & Grammer, K. (2001). Male facial attractiveness: Evidence for hormone-mediated adaptive design. *Evolution and Human Behavior, 22,* 251–267.

Jones, D. (2000). Group nepotism and human kinship. *Current Anthropology, 41,* 779–809.

Jones, D. (2003a). The generative psychology of kinship: Part 1. Cognitive universals and evolutionary psychology. *Evolution and Human Behavior, 24,* 303–319.

Jones, D. (2003b). The generative psychology of kinship: Part 2. Generating variation from universal building blocks with optimality theory. *Evolution and Human Behavior, 24,* 320–350.

Jones, M. Y., Stanaland, A. J. S., & Gelb, B. D. (1998). Beefcake and cheesecake: Insights for advertisers. *Journal of Advertising, 27,* 33–51.

Jones, O. D., & Goldsmith, T. H. (2005). Law and behavioral biology. *Columbia Law Review, 105,* 405–502.

Joy, A., & Sherry, J. F., Jr. (2003). Speaking of art as embodied imagination: A multisensory approach to understanding aesthetic experience. *Journal of Consumer Research, 30,* 259–282.

Juda, M. N., Campbell, L., & Crawford, C. B. (2004). Dieting symptomatology in women and perceptions of social support: An evolutionary approach. *Evolution and Human Behavior, 25,* 200–208.

Kahneman, D., Slovic, P., & Tversky, A. (Eds.). (1982). *Judgment under uncertainty: Heuristics and biases.* Cambridge, England: Cambridge University Press.

Kahneman, D., & Tversky, A. (1979). Prospect theory: An analysis of decision under risk. *Econometrica, 47,* 263–291.

Kahneman, D., & Tversky, A. (2000). *Choices, values, and frames.* Cambridge, England: Cambridge University Press.

Kanazawa, S. (2004a). General intelligence as a domain-specific adaptation. *Psychological Review, 111,* 512–523.

Kanazawa, S. (2004b). The savanna principle. *Managerial and Decision Economics, 25,* 41–54.

Kanazawa, S. (2004c). Social sciences are branches of biology. *Socio-Economic Review, 2,* 371–390.

Kang, M.-E. (1997). The portrayal of women's images in magazine advertisements: Goffman's gender analysis. *Sex Roles, 37,* 979–996.

Katz, L. D. (Ed.). (2000). *Evolutionary origins of morality: Cross-disciplinary perspectives.* Thorverton, England: Imprint Academic.

Katz, S. H. (1990). An evolutionary theory of cuisine. *Human Nature, 1,* 233–259.

Keller, H. (2000). Human parent–child relationships from an evolutionary perspective. *The American Behavioral Scientist, 43,* 957–969.

Keller, L. (Ed.). (1999). *Levels of selection in evolution.* Princeton, NJ: Princeton University Press.

Kellett, S., & Gilbert, P. (2001). Acne: A biopsychosocial and evolutionary perspective with a focus on shame. *British Journal of Health Psychology, 6,* 1–24.

Kellett, S. C., & Gawkrodger, D. J. (1999). The psychological and emotional impact of acne and the effect of treatment with isotretinoin. *British Journal of Dermatology, 140,* 273–282.

Kenrick, D. T., Groth, G. E., Trost, M. R., & Sadalla, E. K. (1993). Integrating evolutionary and social exchange perspectives on relationships: Effects of gender, self-appraisal and involvement level on mate selection criteria. *Journal of Personality and Social Psychology, 64,* 951–969.

Kenrick, D. T., & Keefe, R. C. (1992). Age preferences in mates reflect sex differences in human reproductive strategies. *Behavioral and Brain Sciences, 15,* 75–133.

Kenrick, D. T., Maner, J. K., Butner, J., Li, N. P., Becker, D. V., & Schaller, M. (2002). Dynamical evolutionary psychology: Mapping the domains of the new interactionist paradigm. *Personality and Social Psychology Review, 6,* 347–356.

Kenrick, D. T., Sadalla, E. K., Groth, G., & Trost, M. R. (1990). Evolution, traits, and the stages of human courtship: Qualifying the parental investment model. *Journal of Psychology, 58,* 97–116.

Kenrick, D. T., & Simpson, J. A. (1997). Why social psychology and evolutionary psychology need one another. In J. A. Simpson & D. T. Kenrick (Eds.), *Evolutionary social psychology* (pp. 1–20). Mahwah, NJ: Lawrence Erlbaum Associates.

Kerin, R. A. (1996). In pursuit of an ideal: The editorial and literary history of the *Journal of Marketing. Journal of Marketing, 60,* 1–13.

Kerin, R. A., Lundstrom, W. J., & Sciglimpaglia, D. (1979). Women in advertisements: Retrospect and prospect. *Journal of Advertising, 8,* 37–42.

Ketelaar, T., & Ellis, B. J. (2000). Are evolutionary explanations unfalsifiable? Evolutionary psychology and the Lakatosian philosophy of science. *Psychological Inquiry, 11,* 1–21.

Kilik, J. (Producer), Benioff, D. (Writer), & Lee, S. (Director). (2002). *25th hour* [Motion picture]. United States: Touchstone Pictures.

Kim, J., Allen, C. T., & Kardes, F. R. (1996). An investigation of the mediational mechanisms underlying attitudinal conditioning. *Journal of Marketing Research, 33,* 318–328.

Kim, J., Lim, J.-S., & Bhargava, M. (1998). The role of affect in attitude formation: A classical conditioning approach. *Journal of the Academy of Marketing Science, 26,* 143–152.

King, L. W. (1915a). *Hammurabi's code.* Retrieved October 20, 2003, from http://eawc.evansville.edu/anthology/hammurabi.htm

King, L. W. (1915b). *Hammurabi's code.* Retrieved October 20, 2003, from http://www.fordham.edu/halsall/ancient/hamcode.html

Kirkpatrick, L. A. (1999). Toward and evolutionary psychology of religion and personality. *Journal of Personality, 67,* 921–952.

Kleine, S. S., & Baker, S. M. (2004). An integrative review of material possession attachment. *Academy of Marketing Science Review, 1.* Retrieved from http://www.amsreview.org/articles/kleine01–2004.pdf

Knight, J. L., & Giuliano, T. A. (2001). He's a Laker; she's a "Looker": The consequences of gender-stereotypical portrayals of male and female athletes by the print media. *Sex Roles, 45,* 217–229.

Koehler, N., Rhodes, G., & Simmons, L. W. (2002). Are human female preferences for symmetrical male faces enhanced when conception is likely? *Animal Behaviour, 64,* 233–238.

Kors, A. C., & Silverglate, H. A. (1998). *The shadow university: The betrayal of liberty on America's campuses.* New York: The Free Press.

Kotler, P. (1986). Global standardization—courting danger. *The Journal of Consumer Marketing, 3,* 13–15.

Kowner, R., & Wiseman, R. (2003). Culture and status-related behavior: Japanese and American perceptions of interaction in asymmetric dyads. *Cross-Cultural Research, 37,* 178–210.

Koza, J. R. (1992). *Genetic programming: On the programming of computers by means of natural selection.* Cambridge, MA: MIT Press.

Krassas, N. R., Blauwkamp, J. M., & Wesselink, P. (2001). Boxing Helena and corseting Eunice: Sexual rhetoric in *Cosmopolitan* and *Playboy* magazines. *Sex Roles, 44,* 751–771.

Krauss, R. M., Curran, N. M., & Ferleger, N. (1983). Expressive conventions and the cross-cultural perception of emotion. *Basic and Applied Social Psychology, 4,* 295–305.

Krebs, J. R., & Davies, N. B. (1987). *An introduction to behavioural ecology.* Oxford, England: Blackwell Scientific.

Krug, R., Plihal, W., Fehm, H. L., & Born, J. (2000). Selective influence of the menstrual cycle on perception of stimuli with reproductive significance: An event-related potential study. *Psychophysiology, 37,* 111–122.

Kuhn, E. D. (1999). "I just want to make love to you"—Seductive strategies in blues lyrics. *Journal of Pragmatics, 31,* 525–534.

Kuhn, T. S. (1970). *The structure of scientific revolutions.* Chicago: University of Chicago Press.

Kwak, H., Zinkhan, G. M., & Crask, M. R. (2003). Diagnostic screener for compulsive buying: Applications to the USA and South Korea. *The Journal of Consumer Affairs, 37,* 161–169.

Laland, K. N., & Brown, G. R. (2002). *Sense and nonsense: Evolutionary perspectives on human behaviour.* Oxford, England: Oxford University Press.

Lamberton, A., & Oei, T. P. S. (1997). Problem gambling in adults: An overview. *Clinical Psychology and Psychotherapy, 4,* 84–104.

Langlois, J. H., Kalakanis, L., Rubenstein, A. J., Larson, A., Hallam, M., & Smoot, M. (2000). Maxims or myths of beauty? A meta-analytic and theoretical review. *Psychological Bulletin, 126,* 390–423.

Langlois, J. H., Roggman, L. A., & Reiser-Danner, L. A. (1990). Infants' differential social responses to attractive and unattractive faces. *Developmental Psychology, 26,* 153–159.

Laroche, M., Saad, G., Browne, E., Cleveland, M., & Kim, C. (2000). Determinants of in-store information search strategies pertaining to a Christmas gift purchase. *Canadian Journal of Administrative Sciences, 17,* 1–19.

LaTour, M. S., & Henthorne, T. L. (1993). Female nudity: Attitudes toward the ad and the brand, and implications for advertising strategy. *Journal of Consumer Marketing, 10,* 25–32.

Lauzen, M. M., & Dozier, D. M. (2002). You look mahvelous: an examination of gender and appearance comments in the 1999–2000 prime-time season. *Sex Roles, 46,* 429–437.

LeBlanc, R. P., & Herndon, N. C., Jr. (2001). Cross-cultural consumer decisions: Consideration sets—A marketing universal? *Marketing Intelligence & Planning, 19,* 500–506.

Lee, C., & Green, R. T. (1991). Cross-cultural examination of the Fishbein behavioral intentions model. *Journal of International Business Studies, 22,* 289–305.

Legarda, J. J., Babio, R., & Abreu, J. M. (1992). Prevalence estimates of pathological gambling in Seville (Spain). *British Journal of Addiction, 87,* 767–770.

Leger, D. W., Kamil, A. C., & French, J. A. (2001). Fear and loathing of evolutionary psychology in the social sciences. In J. A. French, A. C. Kamil, & D. W. Leger (Eds.), *Evolutionary psychology and motivation* (pp. xi–xxiii). Lincoln: University of Nebraska Press.

Leifer, C. (Writer), Mehlman, P. (Writer), & Ackerman, A. (Director). (1995). The beard [Television series episode]. In A. Ackerman et al. (Producers), *Seinfeld.* Los Angeles: Castle Rock Entertainment.

Leit, R. A., Pope, H. G., Jr., & Gray, J. J. (2000). Cultural expectations of muscularity in men: The evolution of *Playgirl* centerfolds. *International Journal of Eating Disorders, 29,* 90–93.

Lende, D. H., & Smith, E. O. (2002). Evolution meets biopsychosociality: an analysis of addictive behavior. *Addiction, 97,* 447–458.

Lever, J., & Dolnick, D. (2000). Clients and call girls: Seeking sex and intimacy. In R. Weitzer (Ed.), *Sex for sale: Prostitution, pornography, and the sex industry* (pp. 85–100). New York: Routledge.

Levitt, T. (1983). The globalization of markets. *Harvard Business Review, 61,* 92–102.

Li, K. (2000). Porn goes public. *Industry Standard, 3*(45), 94.

Liefeld, J. P., Wall, M., & Heslop, L. A. (1999). Cross cultural comparison of consumer information processing styles. *Journal of EuroMarketing, 8,* 29–43.

Lin, C. A. (1998). Uses of sex appeals in prime-time television commercials. *Sex Roles, 38,* 461–475.

Lochner, C., Hemmings, S. M. J., Kinnear, C. J., Moolman-Smook, J. C., Corfield, V. A., Knowles, J. A., et al. (2004). Gender in obsessive-compulsive disorder: Clinical and genetic findings. *European Neuropsychopharmacology, 14,* 105–113.

Lochner, C., & Stein, D. J. (2001). Gender in obsessive-compulsive disorder and obsessive-compulsive spectrum disorders. *Archives of Women's Mental Health, 4,* 19–26.

Loewenstein, G. (1996). Out of control: Visceral influences on behavior. *Organizational Behavior and Human Decision Processes, 65,* 272–292.

Loewenstein, G. (2001). The creative destruction of decision research. *Journal of Consumer Research, 28,* 499–505.

Lopreato, J., & Crippen, T. (1999). *Crisis in sociology: The need for Darwin.* New Brunswick, NJ: Transaction.

Lotem, A., Fishman, M. A., & Stone, L. (2002). From reciprocity to unconditional altruism through signalling benefits. *Proceedings of the Royal Society of London: Series B, 270,* 199–205.

Lueptow, L. B., Garovich, L., & Lueptow, M. B. (1995). The persistence of gender stereotypes in the face of changing sex roles: Evidence contrary to the sociocultural model. *Ethology and Sociobiology, 16,* 509–530.

Lueptow, L. B., Garovich-Szabo, L., & Lueptow, M. B. (2001). Social change and the persistence of sex typing: 1974–1997. *Social Forces, 80,* 1–35.

Luna, D., & Gupta, S. F. (2001). An integrative framework for cross-cultural consumer behavior. *International Marketing Review, 18,* 45–69.

Lycett, J. E., & Dunbar, R. I. M. (2000). Mobile phones as lekking devices among human males. *Human Nature, 11,* 93–104.

Lynch, A. (1996). *Thought contagion: How belief spreads through society.* New York: Basic Books.

Lynn, M., Kampschroeder, K., & Perriera, T. (1998, October). *Evolutionary perspectives on consumer behavior: An introduction.* Paper presented at the Twenty-Sixth Annual Conference of the Association for Consumer Research, Montreal, Canada.

Lyons, A. C., & Griffin, C. (2003). Managing menopause: A qualitative analysis of self-help literature for women at midlife. *Social Science & Medicine, 56,* 1629–1642.

MacDonald, K. (1995). Evolution, the five-factor model, and levels of personality. *Journal of Personality, 63,* 525–567.

MacDonald, K. (1998). Evolution, culture, and the five-factor model. *Journal of Cross-Cultural Psychology, 29,* 119–149.

MacDonald, K. B. (1991). A perspective on Darwinian psychology: The importance of domain-general mechanisms, plasticity, and individual differences. *Ethology and Sociobiology, 12,* 449–480.

MacDonald, K. B. (1994). *A people that shall dwell alone: Judaism as a group evolutionary strategy.* Westport, CT: Praeger.

MacKay, N. J., & Covell, K. (1997). The impact of women in advertisements on attitudes toward women. *Sex Roles, 36,* 573–583.

Maheswaran, D., & Shavitt, S. (2000). Issues and new directions in global consumer psychology. *Journal of Consumer Psychology, 9,* 59–66.

Malamuth, N. M. (1996). Sexually explicit media, gender differences, and evolutionary theory. *Journal of Communication, 46,* 8–31.

Maner, J. K., Kenrick, D. T., Becker, D. V., Delton, A. W., Hofer, B., Wilbur, C. J., et al. (2003). Sexually selective cognition: Beauty captures the mind of the beholder. *Journal of Personality and Social Psychology, 85,* 1107–1120.

Manuel, P. (1998). Gender politics in Caribbean popular music: Consumer perspectives and academic interpretation. *Popular Music & Society, 22,* 11–29.

Marsden, P. (2002). Brand positioning: Meme's the word. *Marketing Intelligence & Planning, 20,* 307–312.

Marsden, P. S. (1998). Memetics: A new paradigm for understanding customer behaviour and influence. *Marketing Intelligence & Planning, 16,* 363–368.

Martin, M. C., & Gentry, J. W. (1997). Stuck in the model trap: The effects of beautiful models in ads on female pre-adolescents and adolescents. *Journal of Advertising, 26,* 19–33.

Martindale, C. (1990). *The clockwork muse: The predictability of artistic change.* New York: Basic Books.

Mason, R. (2000). Conspicuous consumption and the positional economy: Policy and prescription since 1970. *Managerial and Decision Economics, 21,* 123–132.

Mason, R. S. (1981). *Conspicuous consumption: A study of exceptional consumer behaviour.* Hampshire, England: Gower.

Massey, G. R. (1999). Product evolution: A Darwinian or Lamarckian phenomenon? *The Journal of Product and Brand Management, 8,* 301–318.

Masters, R. D. (1989). *The nature of politics.* New Haven, CT: Yale University Press.

Matelski, M. J. (1988). *The soap opera evolution: America's enduring romance with daytime drama*. Jefferson, NC: McFarland.

Matsunaga, H., Kiriike, N., Matsui, T., Miyata, A., Iwasaki, Y., Fujimoto, K., et al. (2000). Gender differences in social and interpersonal features and personality disorders among Japanese patients with obsessive-compulsive disorder. *Comprehensive Psychiatry, 41,* 266–272.

Maynard, M. L., & Taylor, C. R. (1999). Girlish images across cultures: Analyzing Japanese versus U.S. *Seventeen* magazine ads. *Journal of Advertising, 28,* 39–48.

Maynard Smith, J. (1982). *Evolution and the theory of games*. Cambridge, England: Cambridge University Press.

Mayne, I. (2000). The inescapable images: Gender and advertising. *Equal Opportunities International, 19,* 56–61.

Mazalov, V., Perrin, N., & Dombrovsky, Y. (1996). Adaptive search and information updating in sequential mate choice. *American Naturalist, 148,* 123–137.

Mazurski, E. J., Bond, N. W., Siddle, D. A. T., & Lovibond, P. F. (1996). Conditioning with facial expressions of emotion: Effects of CS sex and age. *Psychophysiology, 33,* 416–425.

McAndrew, F. T., & Milenkovic, M. A. (2002). Of tabloids and family secrets: The evolutionary psychology of gossip. *Journal of Applied Social Psychology, 32,* 1–20.

McClintock, M. K. (1998). Whither menstrual synchrony? *Annual Review of Sex Research, 9,* 77–95.

McCort, D. J., & Malhotra, N. K. (1993). Culture and consumer behavior: Toward an understanding of cross-cultural consumer behavior in international marketing. *Journal of International Consumer Marketing, 6,* 91–126.

McGuire, M., & Troisi, A. (1998). *Darwinian psychiatry*. New York: Oxford University Press.

Mealy, L. (2000). Anorexia: A losing strategy? *Human Nature, 11,* 105–116.

Mealy, L., Daood, C., & Krage, M. (1996). Enhanced memory for faces of cheaters. *Ethology and Sociobiology, 17,* 119–128.

Medina, J. (2000). *The genetic inferno: Inside the seven deadly sins*. Cambridge, England: Cambridge University Press.

Medina, J. F., & Duffy, M. F. (1998). Standardization vs globalization: A new perspective of brand strategies. *The Journal of Product and Brand Management, 7,* 223–243.

Meehl, P. (1989). Autobiography of Paul Meehl. In G. Lindzey (Ed.), *A history of psychology in autobiography* (Vol. 8, pp. 337–389). Stanford, CA: Stanford University Press.

Mesko, N., & Bereczkei, T. (2004). Hairstyle as an adaptive means of displaying phenotypic quality. *Human Nature, 15,* 251–270.

Meyers-Levy, J. (1989). Gender differences in information processing: A selectivity interpretation. In P. Cafferata & A. Tybout (Eds.), *Cognitive and affective responses to advertising* (pp. 219–260), Lexington, MA: Lexington.

Meyers-Levy, J., & Maheswaran, D. (1991). Exploring differences in males' and females' processing strategies. *Journal of Consumer Research, 18,* 63–70.

Meyers-Levy, J., & Sternthal, B. (1991). Gender differences in the use of message cues and judgments. *Journal of Marketing Research, 28,* 84–96.

Mick, D. G., & Politi, L. G. (1989). Consumers' interpretations of advertising imagery: A visit to the hell of connotation. In E. C. Hirschman (Ed.), *Interpretive consumer research* (pp. 85–96). Provo, UT: Association for Consumer Research.

Miller, A. S., & Hoffman, J. P. (1995). Risk and religion: An explanation of gender differences in religiosity. *Journal of the Scientific Study of Religion, 34,* 63–75.

Miller, A. S., & Stark, R. (2002). Gender and religiousness: Can socialization explanations be saved? *American Journal of Sociology, 107,* 1399–1423.

Miller, G. F. (1998). How mate choice shaped human nature: A review of sexual selection and human evolution. In C. Crawford & D. Krebs (Eds.), *Handbook of evolutionary psychology: Ideas, issues, and applications* (pp. 87–129). Mahwah, NJ: Lawrence Erlbaum Associates.

Miller, G. F. (1999a). Sexual selection for cultural displays. In R. Dunbar, C. Knight, & C. Power (Eds.), *The evolution of culture* (pp. 71–91). New Brunswick, NJ: Rutgers University Press.

Miller, G. F. (1999b, February). Waste is good. *Prospect,* pp. 18–23.

Miller, G. F. (2000). *The mating mind: How sexual choice shaped the evolution of human nature.* New York: Doubleday.

Miller, G. F., & Todd, P. M. (1998). Mate choice turns cognitive. *Trends in Cognitive Sciences, 2,* 190–198.

Miller, M. N., & Pumariega, A. J. (2001). Culture and eating disorders: A historical and cross-cultural review. *Psychiatry, 64,* 93–110.

Milner, L. M., & Collins, J. M. (2000). Sex-role portrayals and the gender of nations. *Journal of Advertising, 29,* 67–79.

Miltenberger, R. G., Redlin, J., Crosby, R., Stickney, M., Mitchell, J., Wonderlich, S., et al. (2003). Direct and retrospective assessment of factors contributing to compulsive buying. *Journal of Behavior Therapy and Experimental Psychiatry, 34,* 1–9.

Mitchell, J. E., Redlin, J., Wonderlich, S., Crosby, R., Faber, R., Miltenberger, R., et al. (2001). The relationship between compulsive buying and eating disorders. *International Journal of Eating Disorders, 32,* 107–111.

Mithen, S. (1996). *The prehistory of the mind: The cognitive origins of art, religion, and science.* New York: Thames & Hudson.

Mittal, B., & Lassar, W. M. (2000). Sexual liberalism as a determinant of consumer response to sex in advertising. *Journal of Business and Psychology, 15,* 111–127.

Monto, M. A. (2000). Why men seek out prostitutes. In R. Weitzer (Ed.), *Sex for sale: Prostitution, pornography, and the sex industry* (pp. 67–83). New York: Routledge.

Mowen, J. C., & Spears, N. (1999). Understanding compulsive buying among college students: A hierarchical approach. *Journal of Consumer Psychology, 8,* 407–430.

Mueller, B. (1991). Multinational advertising: Factors influencing the standardised vs. specialised approach. *International Marketing Review, 8,* 7–18.

Murnen, S. K., Smolak, L., Mills, J. A., & Good, L. (2003). Thin, sexy women and strong, muscular men: Grade-school children's responses to objectified images of women and men. *Sex Roles, 49,* 427–437.

Neave, N., & Wolfson, S. (2003). Testosterone, territoriality, and the "home advantage." *Physiology & Behavior, 78,* 269–275.

Neiman, F. (1998). Conspicuous consumption as wasteful advertising: A Darwinian perspective on spatial patterns in classic Maya terminal monument dates. In C.

M. Barton & G. A. Clark (Eds.), *Rediscovering Darwin: Evolutionary theory in archeological explanation* (pp. 267–290). Arlington, TX: American Anthropological Association.

Nell, V. (2002). Why young men drive dangerously: Implications for injury prevention. *Current Directions in Psychological Science, 11*, 75–79.

Nesse, R. (1998). Emotional disorders in evolutionary perspective. *British Journal of Medical Psychology, 71*, 397–415.

Nesse, R. M. (1990). Evolutionary explanations of emotions. *Human Nature, 1*, 261–289.

Nesse, R. M. (2001). Motivation and melancholy: A Darwinian perspective. *Nebraska Symposium on Motivation, 47*, 179–203.

Nesse, R. M., & Williams, G. C. (1996). *Why we get sick: The new science of Darwinian medicine*. New York: Vintage Books.

Neto, F., & Pinto, I. (1998). Gender stereotypes in Portuguese television advertisements. *Sex Roles, 39*, 153–164.

Nicholson, N. (1997). Evolutionary psychology: Toward a new view of human nature and organizational society. *Human Relations, 50*, 1053–1078.

Nicholson, N. (1998). How hardwired is human behavior? *Harvard Business Review, 76*, 135–147.

Nielsen, F. (1994). Sociobiology and sociology. *Annual Review of Sociology, 20*, 267–303.

Nisbett, R. E., & Kanouse, D. E. (1969). Obesity, food deprivation, and supermarket shopping behavior. *Journal of Personality and Social Psychology, 12*, 389–394.

Nord, W. R., & Peter, J. P. (1980). A behavior modification perspective on marketing. *Journal of Marketing, 44*, 36–47.

Norton, J. (1999). Invisible man: A queer critique of feminist anti-pornography theory. In B. M. Dank & R. Refinetti (Eds.), *Sex work & sex workers* (Sexuality & Culture, Vol. 2, pp. 113–124). New Brunswick, NJ: Transaction.

November, P. (2004). Seven reasons why marketing practitioners should ignore marketing academic research. *Australasian Marketing Journal, 12*, 39–50.

Nuwer, H. (1999). *Wrongs of passage: Fraternities, sororities, hazing, and binge drinking*. Bloomington: Indiana University Press.

O'Cass, A., & Frost, H. (2002). Status brands: Examining the effects of non-product-related brand associations on status and conspicuous consumption. *Journal of Product and Brand Management, 11*, 67–86.

Odekerken-Schröder, G., De Wulf, K., & Hofstee, N. (2002). Is gender stereotyping in advertising more prevalent in masculine countries? A cross-national analysis. *International Marketing Review, 19*, 408–419.

O'Guinn, T. C., & Faber, R. J. (1989). Compulsive buying: A phenomenological exploration. *Journal of Consumer Research, 16*, 147–157.

Olsen, R. A., & Cox, C. M. (2001). The influence of gender on the perception and response to investment risk: The case of professional investors. *Journal of Psychology and Financial Markets, 2*, 29–36.

Olson, B. (1994). Sex and the soaps: A comparative content analysis of health issues. *Journalism and Mass Communication Quarterly, 71*, 840–850.

Orians, G. H., & Heerwagen, J. H. (1992). Evolved responses to landscapes. In J. H. Barkow, L. Cosmides, & J. Tooby (Eds.), *The adapted mind: Evolutionary psychology and the generation of culture* (pp. 555–580). New York: Oxford University Press.

Orth, U. R., & Holancova, D. (2004). Men's and women's responses to sex role portrayals in advertisements. *International Journal of Research in Marketing, 21, 77–88.*

Ostlund, D. R., & Kinnier, R. T. (1997). Values of youth: Messages from the most popular songs of four decades. *Journal of Humanistic Education & Development, 36, 83–91.*

Palmer, A. (2000). Co-operation and competition: A Darwinian synthesis of relationship marketing. *European Journal of Marketing, 34, 687–704.*

Palys, T. S. (1986). Testing the common wisdom: The social content of video pornography. *Canadian Psychology, 27, 22–35.*

Panksepp, J., Knutson, B., & Burgdorf, J. (2002). The role of brain emotional systems in addictions: a neuro-evolutionary perspective and new "self-report" animal model. *Addiction, 97, 459–469.*

Papavassiliou, N., & Stathakopoulos, V. (1997). Standardization versus adaptation of international advertising strategies: Towards a framework. *European Journal of Marketing, 31, 504–527.*

Parker, P. M., & Tavassoli, N. T. (2000). Homeostasis and consumer behavior across cultures. *International Journal of Research in Marketing, 17, 33–53.*

Payne, J. W., Bettman, J. R., & Johnson, E. J. (1993). *The adaptive decision maker.* Cambridge, England: Cambridge University Press.

Pech, R. J. (2003). Memetics and innovation: Profit through balanced meme management. *European Journal of Innovation Management, 6, 111–117.*

Penn, D. J. (2003). The evolutionary roots of our environmental problems: Toward a Darwinian ecology. *The Quarterly Review of Biology, 78, 275–301.*

Pennebaker, J. W., Dyer, M. A., Caulkins, R. S., Litowitz, D. L., Ackreman, P. L., Anderson, D. B., et al. (1979). Don't the girls get prettier at closing time: A country and western application to psychology. *Personality and Social Psychology Bulletin, 5, 122–125.*

Penton-Voak, I. S., & Perrett, D. I. (2000). Female preference for male faces changes cyclically: Further evidence. *Evolution and Human Behavior, 21, 39–48.*

Peter, J. P., & Nord, W. R. (1982). A clarification and extension of operant conditioning principles in marketing. *Journal of Marketing, 46, 102–107.*

Peterson, S. A., & Somit, A. (Eds.). (2001). *Evolutionary approaches in the behavioral sciences: Toward a better understanding of human nature—research in biopolitics* (Vol. 8). Greenwich, CT: JAI.

Petry, N. M. (2003). Patterns and correlates of Gamblers Anonymous attendance in pathological gamblers seeking professional treatment. *Addictive Behaviors, 28, 1049–1062.*

Petty, R. E., & Cacioppo, J. T. (1986). The elaboration likelihood model of persuasion. In L. Berkowitz (Ed.), *Advances in experimental social psychology* (Vol. 19, 123–205). New York: Academic Press.

Petty, R. E., Rucker, D. D., Bizer, G. Y., & Cacioppo, J. T. (2004). The elaboration likelihood model of persuasion. In J. S. Seiter & R. H. Gass (Eds.), *Perspectives on persuasion, social influence, and compliance gaining* (pp. 65–89). Boston: Allyn & Bacon.

Petty, R. E., & Wegener, D. T. (1999). The elaboration likelihood model: Current status and controversies. In S. Chaiken & Y. Trope (Eds.), *Dual process theories in social psychology* (pp. 41–72). New York: Guilford.

Pierce, B. D., & White, R. (1999). The evolution of social structures: Why biology matters. *Academy of Management Review, 24,* 843–853.

Pillsworth, E. G., Haselton, M. G., & Buss, D. M. (2004). Ovulatory shifts in female sexual desire. *The Journal of Sex Research, 41,* 55–65.

Pinker, S. (1994). *The language instinct.* New York: Morrow.

Pinker, S. (1997). *How the mind works.* New York: Norton.

Pinker, S. (2002). *The blank slate: The modern denial of human nature.* New York: Viking.

Polivy, J., & Herman, C. P. (2002). Causes of eating disorders. *Annual Review of Psychology, 53,* 187–213.

Pope, H. G., Jr., Olivardia, R., Gruber, A., & Borowiecki, J. (1999). Evolving ideals of male body image as seen through action toys. *International Journal of Eating Disorders, 26,* 65–72.

Pornpitakpan, C., & Francis, J. N. P. (2001). The effect of cultural differences, source expertise, and argument strength on persuasion: An experiment with Canadians and Thais. *Journal of International Consumer Marketing, 13,* 77–101.

Posavac, H. D., Posavac, S. S., & Posavac, E. J. (1998). Exposure to media images of female attractiveness and concern with body weight among young women. *Sex Roles, 38,* 187–201.

Potenza, M. N., Kosten, T. R., & Rounsaville, B. J. (2001). Pathological gambling. *Journal of the American Medical Association, 286,* 141–144.

Potter, R. H. (1999). Long-term consumption of "X-Rated" materials and attitudes toward women among Australian consumers of X-rated videos. In B. M. Dank & R. Refinetti (Eds.), *Sex work & sex workers* (Sexuality & Culture, Vol. 2, pp. 61–85). New Brunswick, NJ: Transaction.

Pound, N. (2002). Male interest in visual cues of sperm competition risk. *Evolution and Human Behavior, 23,* 443–466.

Powell, M., & Ansic, D. (1997). Gender differences in risk behavior in financial decision-making: An experimental analysis. *Journal of Economic Psychology, 18,* 605–628.

Pressman, E. R. (Producer), & Stone, O. (Writer/Director). (1987). *Wall street* [Motion picture]. United States: 20th Century Fox.

Profet, M. (1992). Pregnancy sickness as adaptation: A deterrent to maternal ingestion of teratogens. In J. H. Barkow, L. Cosmides, & J. Tooby (Eds.), *The adapted mind: Evolutionary psychology and the generation of culture* (pp. 327–365). New York: Oxford University Press.

Putrevu, S. (2001). Exploring the origins and information processing differences between men and women: Implications for advertisers. *Academy of Marketing Science Review, 10.* Retrieved March 15, 2004, from http://www.amsreview.org/articles/putrevu10-2001.pdf

Rajala, A. K., & Hantula, D. A. (2000). Towards a behavioral ecology of consumption: Delay-reduction effects on foraging in a simulated online mall. *Managerial and Decision Economics, 21,* 145–158.

Rapoport, J. L., & Fiske, A. (1998). The new biology of obsessive-compulsive disorder: Implications for evolutionary psychology. *Perspectives in Biology and Medicine, 41*, 159–174.

Raylu, N., & Oei, T. P. S. (2002). Pathological gambling: A comprehensive review. *Clinical Psychology Review, 22*, 1009–1061.

Reichert, T. (2002). Sex in advertising research: A review of content, effects, and functions of sexual information in consumer advertising. *Archives of Sex Research, 13*, 241–273.

Reichert, T., & Lambiase, J. (Eds.). (2006). *Sex in consumer culture: The erotic content of media and marketing*. Mahwah, NJ: Lawrence Erlbaum Associates.

Reichert, T., Lambiase, J., Morgan, S., Carstarphen, M., & Zavoina, S. (1999). Cheesecake and beefcake: No matter how you slice it, sexual explicitness in advertising continues to increase. *Journalism & Mass Communication Quarterly, 76*, 7–20.

Reidenbach, R. E., & McCleary, K. W. (1983). Advertising and male nudity: An experimental investigation. *Journal of the Academy of Marketing Science, 11*, 444–454.

Revelle, W. (1995). Personality processes. *Annual Review of Psychology, 46*, 295–328.

Rhodes, G., Roberts, J., & Simmons, L. W. (1999). Reflections on symmetry and attractiveness. *Psychology, Evolution & Gender, 1*, 279–295.

Rhodes, G., Yoshikawa, S., Clark, A., Lee, K., McKay, R., & Akamatsu, S. (2001). Attractiveness of facial averageness and symmetry in non-Western cultures: In search of biologically based standards of beauty. *Perception, 30*, 611–625.

Richerson, P. J., & Boyd, R. (1989). The role of evolved predispositions in cultural evolution: Or, human sociobiology meets Pascal's Wager. *Ethology and Sociobiology, 10*, 195–219.

Richerson, P. J., & Boyd, R. (2005). *Not by genes alone: How culture transformed human evolution*. Chicago: University of Chicago Press.

Ridley, M. (1993). *The Red Queen: Sex and the evolution of human nature*. London: Penguin.

Riegel, H. (1996). Soap operas and gossip. *Journal of Popular Culture, 29*, 201–209.

Rimke, H. M. (2000). Governing citizens through self-help literature. *Cultural Studies, 14*, 61–78.

Roberts, G. (1998). Competitive altruism: From reciprocity to the handicap principle. *Proceedings of the Royal Society of London: Series B, 265*, 427–431.

Roberts, J. A. (1998). Compulsive buying among college students: An investigation of its antecedents, consequences, and implications for public policy. *The Journal of Consumer Affairs, 32*, 295–319.

Roberts, J. A., & Sepulveda M., C. J. (1999). Money attitudes and compulsive buying: An exploratory investigation of the emerging consumer culture in Mexico. *Journal of International Consumer Marketing, 11*, 53–74.

Robinson, B. E. (1982) Family experts on television talk shows: Facts, values, and half-truths. *Family Relations, 31*, 369–378.

Rohlinger, D. A. (2002). Eroticizing men: cultural influences on advertising and male objectification. *Sex Roles, 46*, 61–74.

Rosenblitt, J. C., Soler, H., Johnson, S. E., & Quadagno, D. M. (2001). Sensation seeking and hormones in men and women: Exploring the link. *Hormones and Behavior, 40*, 396–402.

Rössler, P., & Brosius, H.-B. (2001). Do talk shows cultivate adolescents' views of the world? A prolonged-exposure experiment. *Journal of Communication, 51,* 143–163.

Rubin, P. H. (2002). *Darwinian politics: The evolutionary origin of freedom.* New Brunswick, NJ: Rutgers University Press.

Ruse, M. (1999). Evolutionary ethics: What can we learn from the past. *Zygon, 34,* 435–451.

Ryans, J. K., Jr., Griffith, D. A., & White, S. D. (2003). Standardization/adaptation of international marketing strategy: Necessary conditions for the advancement of knowledge. *International Marketing Review, 20,* 588–603.

Saad, G. (1998). The experimenter module of the DSMAC (dynamic sequential multiattribute choice) interface. *Behavior Research Methods, Instruments, & Computers, 30,* 250–254.

Saad, G. (2003). Evolution and political marketing. In S. A. Peterson & A. Somit (Eds.), *Human nature and public policy: An evolutionary approach* (pp. 121–138). New York: Palgrave Macmillan.

Saad, G. (2004). Applying evolutionary psychology in understanding the representation of women in advertisements. *Psychology & Marketing, 21,* 593–612.

Saad, G. (2006a). Applying evolutionary psychology in understanding the Darwinian roots of consumption phenomena. *Managerial and Decision Economics, 27,* 189–201.

Saad, G. (2006b). Sex differences in OCD symptomatology: An evolutionary perspective. *Medical Hypotheses, 67,* 1455–1459.

Saad, G., & Eba, A. (2005). *Sequential mate choice within pairs of prospective suitors.* Manuscript submitted for publication.

Saad, G., & Gill, T. (1999). [Departmental affiliations of authors in *Ethology and Sociobiology/Evolution and Human Behavior* (1979–1998)] Unpublished raw data.

Saad, G., & Gill, T. (2000). Applications of evolutionary psychology in marketing. *Psychology and Marketing, 17,* 1005–1034.

Saad, G., & Gill, T. (2001). Sex differences in the ultimatum game: An evolutionary psychology perspective. *Journal of Bioeconomics, 3,* 171–193.

Saad, G., & Gill, T. (2003). An evolutionary psychology perspective on gift-giving among young adults. *Psychology & Marketing, 20,* 765–784.

Saad, G., Gill, T., & Nataraajan, R. (2005). Are laterborns more innovative and non-conforming consumers than firstborns? A Darwinian perspective. *Journal of Business Research, 58,* 902–909.

Saad, G., & Peng, A. (2006). Applying Darwinian principles in designing effective intervention strategies: The case of sun tanning. *Psychology & Marketing, 23,* 617–638.

Salamon, S. D., & Deutsch, Y. (2006). OCB as a handicap: an evolutionary psychological perspective. *Journal of Organizational Behavior, 27,* 185–199.

Salmon, C., & Symons, D. (2003). *Warrior lovers: Erotic fiction, evolution and female sexuality.* New Haven, CT: Yale University Press.

Salter, F., Grammer, K., & Rikowski, A. (2005). Sex differences in negotiating with powerful males. *Human Nature, 16,* 306–321.

Samuels, R. (1998). Evolutionary psychology and the massive modularity hypothesis. *British Journal for the Philosophy of Science, 49,* 575–602.

Samuels, R. (2000). Massively modular minds: Evolutionary psychology and cognitive architecture. In P. Carruthers & A. Chamberlain (Eds.), *Evolution and the human mind: Modularity, language and meta-cogntion* (pp. 13–46). Cambridge, England: Cambridge University Press.

Sanderson, S. K. (2001). *The evolution of human sociality: A Darwinian conflict perspective.* Lanham, MD: Rowman & Littlefield.

Sanfey, A. G., Rilling, J. K., Aronson, J. A., Nystrom, L. E., & Cohen, J. D. (2003). The neural basis of economic decision-making in the ultimatum game. *Science, 300,* 1755–1758.

Scalise Sugiyama, M. (1996). On the origins of narrative: Storyteller bias as a fitness-enhancing strategy. *Human Nature, 7,* 403–425.

Scheib, J. E. (2001). Context-specific mate choice criteria: Women's trade-offs in the contexts of long-term and extra-pair mateships. *Personal Relationships, 8,* 371–389.

Scheurer, T. E. (1990). Goddesses and golddiggers: Images of women in popular music of the 1930s. *Journal of Popular Culture, 24,* 23–38.

Schlenker, J. A., Caron, S. L. & Halteman, W. A. (1998). A feminist analysis of *Seventeen* magazine: Content analysis from 1945 to 1995. *Sex Roles, 38,* 135–149.

Schimmel, S. (1997). *The seven deadly sins: Jewish, Christian, and Classical reflections on human psychology.* New York: Oxford University Press.

Schmitt, D. P., & Buss, D. M. (1996). Strategic self-promotion and competitor derogation: Sex and context effects on the perceived effectiveness of mate attraction tactics. *Journal of Personality and Social Psychology, 70,* 1185–1204.

Schmitt, D. P., & Buss, D. M. (2000). Sexual dimensions of person description: Beyond or subsumed by the Big Five? *Journal of Research in Personality, 34,* 141–177.

Schmitt, D. P., & 118 Members of the International Sexuality Description Project. (2003). Universal sex differences in the desire for sexual variety: Tests from 52 nations, 6 continents, and 13 Islands. *Journal of Personality and Social Psychology, 85,* 85–104.

Schooler, C. (1972). Birth order effects: Not here, not now! *Psychological Bulletin, 78,* 161–175.

Schrader, M. P., & Wann, D. L. (1999). High-risk recreation: The relationship between participant characteristics and degree of involvement. *Journal of Sport Behavior, 22,* 426–441.

Schubert, G. (1989). *Evolutionary politics.* Carbondale: Southern Illinois University Press.

Schubert, J., & Curran, M. A. (2001, June). *Appearance effects in political careers: Do politicians with good genes get more votes.* Paper presented at the Human Behavior and Evolution Society meetings, London.

Schwartz, S. H. (1994). Are there universal aspects in the structure and contents of human values? *Journal of Social Issues, 50,* 19–45.

Scott, L. M. (2005). *Fresh lipstick: Redressing fashion and feminism.* New York: Palgrave Macmillan.

Segal, N. L., & Ream, S. L. (1998). Decrease in grief intensity for deceased twin and non-twin relatives: An evolutionary perspective. *Personality and Individual Differences, 25,* 317–325.

Segerstråle, U. (2001). *Defenders of the truth: The sociobiology debate.* New York: Oxford University Press.

Seidman, S. A. (1992). An investigation of sex-role stereotyping in music videos. *Journal of Broadcasting & Electronic Media, 36,* 209–216.

Seidman, S. A. (1999). Revisiting sex-role stereotyping in MTV videos. *International Journal of Instructional Media, 26,* 11–22.

Sesardic, N. (2003). Evolution of human jealousy: A just-so story or just-so criticism? *Philosophy of the Social Sciences, 33,* 427–443.

Shaffer, H. J., Hall, M. N., & Bilt, J. V. (1999). Estimating the prevalence of disordered gambling behavior in the United States and Canada: A research synthesis. *American Journal of Public Health, 89,* 1369–1376.

Shaffer, H. J., & Korn, D. A. (2002). Gambling related mental disorders: A public health analysis. *Annual Review of Public Health, 23,* 171–212.

Shepher, J. (1971). Mate selection among second generation kibbutz adolescents and adults: Incest avoidance and negative imprinting. *Archives of Sexual Behavior, 1,* 293–307.

Shepher, J., & Reisman, J. (1985). Pornography: A sociobiological attempt at understanding. *Ethology and Sociobiology, 6,* 103–114.

Sherman, P. W., & Billing, J. (1999). Darwinian gastronomy: Why we use spices. *BioScience, 49,* 453–463.

Sherman, P. W., & Hash, G. A. (2001). Why vegetable recipes are not very spicy. *Evolution and Human Behavior, 22,* 147–163.

Shermer, M. (2003). *How we believe: Science, skepticism, and the search for God.* New York: Holt.

Shimp, T. A., & Moody, M. P. (2000). In search of a theoretical explanation for the credit card effect. *Journal of Business Research, 48,* 17–23.

Shimp, T. A., Stuart, E. W., & Engle, R. W. (1991). A program of classical conditioning experiments testing variations in the conditioned stimulus and context. *Journal of Consumer Research, 18,* 1–12.

Shoemaker, P. J. (1996). Hardwired for news: Using biological and cultural evolution to explain the surveillance function. *Journal of Communication, 46,* 32–47.

Shoham, A. (1995). Global marketing standardization. *Journal of Global Marketing, 9,* 91–119.

Shoham, A. (1996). Effectiveness of standardized and adapted television advertising: An international field study approach. *Journal of International Consumer Marketing, 9,* 5–23.

Shoham, A., Rose, G. M., & Kahle, L. R. (1998). Marketing of risky sports: From intention to action. *Journal of the Academy of Marketing Science, 26,* 307–321.

Shoham, A., Rose, G. M., & Kahle, L. R. (2000). Practitioners of risky sports: A quantitative examination. *Journal of Business Research, 47,* 237–251.

Signorielli, N., McLeod, D., & Healy, E. (1994). Gender stereotypes in MTV commercials: The beat goes on. *Journal of Broadcasting & Electronic Media, 38,* 91–101.

Sijuwade, P. O. (1995). Counterfeit intimacy: A dramaturgical analysis of an erotic performance. *Social Behavior and Personality, 23,* 369–376.

Silverman, I., & Eals, M. (1992). Sex differences in spatial abilities: Evolutionary theory and data. In J. H. Barkow, L. Cosmides, & J. Tooby (Eds.), *The adapted mind: Evolutionary psychology and the generation of culture* (pp. 533–554). New York: Oxford University Press.

Silverman, I., & Phillips, K. (1993). Effects of estrogen changes during the menstrual cycle on spatial performance. *Ethology and Sociobiology, 14,* 257–269.

Silverman, I. W. (2003). Gender differences in delay gratification: A meta-analysis. *Sex Roles, 49,* 451–463.

Simmons, M. (1999). Theorizing prostitution: the question of agency. In B. M. Dank & R. Refinetti (Eds.), *Sex work & sex workers* (Sexuality & Culture, Vol. 2, pp. 125–148). New Brunswick, NJ: Transaction.

Simon, H. A. (1982). *Models of bounded rationality.* Cambridge, MA: MIT Press.

Simonson, I., Carmon, Z., Dhar, R., Drolet, A., & Nowlis, S. M. (2001). Consumer research: In search of identity. *Annual Review of Psychology, 52,* 249–275.

Simonton, D. K. (1999). *Origins of genius: Darwinian perspectives on creativity.* New York: Oxford University Press.

Simpson, J. A., & Kenrick, D. T. (Eds.). (1997). *Evolutionary social psychology.* Mahwah, NJ: Lawrence Erlbaum Associates.

Simpson, P. M., Horton, S., & Brown, G. (1996). Male nudity in advertisements: A modified replication and extension of gender and product effects. *Journal of the Academy of Marketing Science, 24,* 257–262.

Singh, D. (1993). Adaptive significance of female physical attractiveness: Role of waist-to-hip ratio. *Journal of Personality and Social Psychology, 65,* 293–307.

Singh, D. (2002a). Female mate value at a glance: Relationship of waist-to-hip ratio to health, fecundity and attractiveness. *Neuroendocrinology Letters, 23,* 81–91.

Singh, D. (2002b). Waist-to-hip ratio: An indicator of female mate value. In K. Aoki & T. Akazawa (Eds.), *Proceedings of Human Mate Choice and Prehistoric Marital Networks International Symposium* (Vol. 16, pp.79–99). Kyoto, Japan: International Research Center for Japanese Studies.

Singh, D., Frohlich, T., & Haywood, M. (1999, June). *Waist-to-hip ratio representation in ardent sculptures from four cultures.* Paper presented at the meeting of the Human Behavior and Evolution Society, Salt Lake City, UT.

Singh, D., & Luis, S. (1995). Ethnic and gender consensus for the effect of waist-to-hip ratio on judgment of women's attractiveness. *Human Nature, 6,* 51–65.

Slovic, P. (1975). Choice between equally-valued alternatives. *Journal of Experimental Psychology: Human Perception and Performance, 1,* 280–287.

Small, H. (2004). Why authors think their papers are highly cited. *Scientometrics, 60,* 305–316.

Smith, E. A., & Bliege Bird, R. L. (2000). Turtle hunting and tombstone opening: Public generosity as costly signaling. *Evolution and Human Behavior, 21,* 245–261.

Smith, E. A., & Bliege Bird, R. L. (2005). Costly signaling and cooperative behavior. In H. Gintis, S. Bowles, R. T. Boyd, & E. Fehr (Eds.), *Moral sentiments and material interests: On the foundations of cooperation in economic life* (pp. 115–148). Cambridge, MA: MIT Press.

Smith, E. O. (1999). High heels and evolution: Natural selection, sexual selection and high heels. *Psychology, Evolution & Gender, 1,* 245–277.

Smith, K., Dickhaut, J., McCabe, K., & Pardo, J. V. (2002). Neuronal substrates for choice under ambiguity, risk, gains, and losses. *Management Science, 48,* 711–718.

Smith, M. S., Kish, B. J., & Crawford, C. B. (1987). Inheritance of wealth as human kin investments. *Ethology and Sociobiology, 8,* 171–182.

Smith, S. W., Mitchell, M. M., Yun, J. A., Johnson, A. J., Orrego, V. O., & Greenberg, B. S. (1999). The nature of close relationships as presented in television talk show titles. *Communication Studies, 50,* 175–187.

Sober, E., & Wilson, D. S. (1998). *Unto others: The evolution and psychology of unselfish behavior.* Cambridge, MA: Harvard University Press.

Sommers-Flanagan, R., Sommers-Flanagan, J. & Davis, B. (1993). What's happening on music television? A gender role content analysis. *Sex Roles, 28,* 745–753.

Soper, B., Milford, G. E., & Rosenthal, G. T. (1995). Belief when evidence does not support theory. *Psychology & Marketing, 12,* 415–422.

Sosis, R., & Bressler, E. R. (2003). Cooperation and commune longevity: A test of the costly signaling theory of religion. *Cross-Cultural Research, 37,* 211–239.

South, S. J. (1991). Sociodemographic differentials in mate selection preferences. *Journal of Marriage and the Family, 53,* 928–940.

Speed, R., & Thompson, P. (2000). Determinants of sports sponsorship response. *Journal of the Academy of Marketing Science, 28,* 226–238.

Spero, A. (1988). "Conspicuous consumption" at Jewish functions. *Judaism, 37,* 103–110.

Spinella, M. (2003). Evolutionary mismatch, neural reward circuits, and pathological gambling. *International Journal of Neuroscience, 113,* 503–512.

Springer, K., & Berry, D. S. (1997). Rethinking the role of evolution in an ecological model of social perception. In J. A. Simpson & D. T. Kenrick (Eds.), *Evolutionary social psychology* (pp. 49–71). Mahwah, NJ: Lawrence Erlbaum Associates.

Sprott, D. E., & Miyazaki, A. D. (2002). Two decades of contributions to marketing and public policy: An analysis of research published in *Journal of Public Policy & Marketing. Journal of Public Policy & Marketing, 21,* 105–125.

Stanislaw, H., & Rice, F. J. (1988). Correlation between sexual desire and menstrual cycle characteristics. *Archives of Sexual Behavior, 17,* 499–508.

Stark, R. (2002). Physiology and faith: Addressing the "universal" gender difference in religious commitment. *Journal for the Scientific Study of Religion, 41,* 495–507.

Starker, S. (1988). Psychologists and self-help books: Attitudes and prescriptive practices of clinicians. *American Journal of Psychotherapy, 42,* 448–455.

Steadman, L. B., & Palmer, C. T. (1995). Religion as an identifiable traditional behavior subject to natural selection. *Journal of Social and Evolutionary Systems, 18,* 149–164.

Stearns, S. C., & Ebert, D. (2001). Evolution in health and disease: Work in progress. *Quarterly Review of Biology, 76,* 417–432.

Steenkamp, J.-B. E. M., & Burgess, S. M. (2002). Optimum stimulation level and exploratory consumer behavior in an emerging consumer market. *International Journal of Research in Marketing, 19,* 131–150.

Stephens, D. L., Hill, R. P., & Hanson, C. (1994). The beauty myth and female consumers: The controversial role of advertising. *The Journal of Consumer Affairs, 28,* 137–153.

Stern, B. (1993). Feminist literary criticism and the deconstruction of ads: A postmodern view of advertising and consumer responses. *Journal of Consumer Research, 19,* 556–566.

Stern, S. E., & Handel, A. D. (2001). Sexuality and mass media: The historical context of psychology's reaction to sexuality on the Internet. *Journal of Sex Research, 38,* 283–291.

Stewart, A. E., & Stewart, E. A. (1995). Trends in birth order research: 1976–1993. *Journal of Individual Psychology, 51,* 21–36.

Stigler, G. J. (1961). The economics of information. *Journal of Political Economy, 69,* 213–225.

Stiller, J., Nettle, D., & Dunbar, R. I. (2003). The small world of Shakespeare's plays. *Human Nature, 14,* 397–408.

Strassmann, B. I. (1992). The function of menstrual taboos among the Dogon: Defense against cuckoldry? *Human Nature, 2,* 89–131.

Strassmann, B. I. (1996). Menstrual hut visits by Dogon women: A hormonal test distinguishes deceit from honest signaling. *Behavioural Ecology, 7,* 304–315.

Streeter, S. A., & McBurney, D. H. (2003). Waist–hip ratio and attractiveness: New evidence and a critique of "a critical test." *Evolution and Human Behavior, 24,* 88–98.

Stuart, E. W., Shimp, T. A., & Engle, R. W. (1987). Classical conditioning of consumer attitudes: Four experiments in an advertising context. *Journal of Consumer Research, 14,* 334–349.

Studd, M. V., & Gattiker, U. E. (1991). The evolutionary psychology of sexual harassment in organizations. *Ethology and Sociobiology, 12,* 249–290.

Sugiyama, L. S. (2004). Is beauty in the context-sensitive adaptations of the beholder? Shiwiar use of waist-to-hip ratio in assessments of female mate value. *Evolution and Human Behavior, 25,* 51–62.

Sulloway, F. J. (1995). Birth order and evolutionary psychology: A meta-analytic overview. *Psychological Inquiry, 6,* 75–80.

Sulloway, F. J. (1996). *Born to rebel: Birth order, family dynamics and creative lives.* New York: Pantheon.

Sulloway, F. J. (2001). Birth order, sibling competition, and human behavior. In R. H. Holcomb, III (Ed.), *Conceptual challenges in evolutionary psychology: Innovative research strategies* (pp. 39–83). Dordrecht, Netherlands: Kluwer Academic.

Surbey, M. K. (1987). Anorexia nervosa, amenorrhea, and adaptation. *Ethology and Sociobiology, 8,* 47S–61S.

Sverdrup, S. G., & Stø, E. (1992). Regulation of sex discrimination in advertising: An empirical inquiry into the Norwegian case. *Journal of Consumer Policy, 14,* 371–391.

Symons, D. (1979). *The evolution of human sexuality.* New York: Oxford University Press.

Szymanski, D. M., Bharadwaj, S. G., & Varadarajan, P. R. (1993). Standardization versus adaptation of international marketing strategy: An empirical investigation. *Journal of Marketing, 57,* 1–17.

Tassinary, L. G., & Hansen, K. (1998). A critical test of the waist-to-hip-ratio hypothesis of female physical attractiveness. *Psychological Science, 9,* 150–155.

Thaler, R. H. (1988). Anomalies: The ultimatum game. *Journal of Economic Perspectives, 2,* 195–206.

Thiessen, D., & Umezawa, Y. (1998). The sociobiology of everyday life: A new look at a very old novel. *Human Nature, 9,* 293–320.

Thornhill, R., & Gangestad, S. W. (1993). Human facial beauty: Averageness, symmetry, and parasite resistance. *Human Nature, 4,* 237–269.

Till, B. D., & Priluck, R. L. (2000). Stimulus generalization in classical conditioning: An initial investigation and extension. *Psychology & Marketing, 17,* 55–72.

Tinbergen, N. (1963). On aims and methods of ethology. *Zeitschrift für Tierpsychologie, 20,* 410–433.

Todd, P. M., & Miller, G. F. (1999). From pride and prejudice to persuasion: Satisficing in mate search. In G. Gigerenzer, P. M. Todd, & the ABC Research Group (Eds.), *Simple heuristics that make us smart* (pp. 287–308). New York: Oxford University Press.

Tombs, S., & Silverman, I. (2004). Pupillometry: A sexual selection approach. *Evolution and Human Behavior, 25,* 221–228.

Tooby, J., & Cosmides, L. (1989). Evolutionary psychology and the generation of culture, part I: Theoretical considerations. *Ethology and Sociobiology, 10,* 29–49.

Tooby, J., & Cosmides, L. (1990). The past explains the present: Emotional adaptations and the structure of ancestral environments. *Ethology and Sociobiology, 11,* 375–424.

Tooby, J., & Cosmides, L. (1992). Psychological foundations of culture. In J. H. Barkow, L. Cosmides, & J. Tooby (Eds.), *The adapted mind: Evolutionary psychology and the generation of culture* (pp. 19–136). New York: Oxford University Press.

Townsend, J. M. (1987). Sex differences in sexuality among medical students: Effects of increasing socioeconomic status. *Archives of Sexual Behavior, 16,* 425–444.

Townsend, J. M., & Levy, G. D. (1990a). Effects of potential partners' costume and physical attractiveness on sexuality and partner selection. *The Journal of Psychology, 124,* 371–389.

Townsend, J. M., & Levy, G. D. (1990b). Effects of potential partners' physical attractiveness and socioeconomic status on sexuality and partner selection. *Archives of Sexual Behavior, 19,* 149–164.

Trigg, A. B. (2001). Veblen, Bourdieu, and conspicuous consumption. *Journal of Economic Issues, 35,* 99–115.

Trivers, R. L. (1971). The evolution of reciprocal altruism. *Quarterly Review of Biology, 46,* 35–57.

Trivers, R. L. (1972). Parental investment and sexual selection. In B. Campbell (Ed.), *Sexual selection and descent of man: 1871–1971* (pp. 136–179). Chicago: Aldine.

Trivers, R. L. (1985). *Social evolution.* Menlo Park, CA: Benjamin/Cummings.

Troisi, A. (2003). Sexual disorders in the context of Darwinian psychiatry. *Journal of Endocrinological Investigation, 26,* 54–57.

Tsui, E. (1999). *Evolutionary architecture: Nature as a basis for design.* New York: Wiley.

Turner, S. L., Hamilton, H., Jacobs, M., Angood, L. M., & Dwyer, D. H. (1997). The influence of fashion magazines on the body image satisfaction of college women: An exploratory analysis. *Adolescence, 32,* 603–614.

Tversky, A. (1969). Intransitivity of preferences. *Psychological Review, 76,* 31–48.

Tversky, A., & Kahneman, D. (1986). Rational choice and the framing of decisions. *Journal of Business, 59,* S251–S278.

Tybout, A. M., & Artz, N. (1994). Consumer psychology. *Annual Review of Psychology, 45,* 131–169.

Udry, J. R. (2000). Biological limits of gender construction. *American Sociological Review, 65,* 443–457.

Urbaniak, G. C., & Kilmann, P. R. (2003). Physical attractiveness and the "nice guy paradox": Do nice guys really finish last? *Sex Roles, 49,* 413–426.

Valence, G., d'Astous, A., & Fortier, L. (1988). Compulsive buying: Concept and measurement. *Journal of Consumer Policy, 11,* 419–433.

van den Berghe, P. L. (1990). Why most sociologists don't (and won't) think evolutionarily. *Sociological Forum, 5,* 173–185.

Vanhanen, T. (1999). Domestic ethnic conflict and ethnic nepotism: A comparative analysis. *Journal of Peace Research, 36,* 55–73.

van Honk, J., Tuiten, A., Verbaten, R., van den Hout, M., Koppeschaar, H., Thijssen, J., et al. (1999). Correlations among salivary testosterone, mood, and selective attention to threat in humans. *Hormones and Behavior, 36,* 17–24.

van Kempen, L. (2003). Fooling the eye of the beholder: Deceptive status signalling among the poor in developing countries. *Journal of International Development, 15,* 157–177.

van Mesdag, M. (2000). Culture-sensitive adaptation or global standardization—the duration-of-usage hypothesis. *International Marketing Review, 17,* 74–84.

van Raaij, W. F. (1997). Globalisation of marketing communication? *Journal of Economic Psychology, 18,* 259–270.

Veblen, T. (1899). *The theory of the leisure class.* New York: Macmillan.

Vigneron, F., & Johnson, L. W. (1999). A review and a conceptual framework of prestige-seeking consumer behavior. *Academy of Marketing Science Review, 1.* Retrieved March 15, 2004, from http://www.amsreview.org/articles/vigneron01-1999.pdf

Vigorito, A. J., & Curry, T. J. (1998). Marketing masculinity: gender identity and popular magazines. *Sex Roles, 39,* 135–152.

Viki, G. T., Abrams, D., & Hutchison, P. (2003). The "true" romantic: Benevolent sexism and paternalistic chivalry. *Sex Roles, 49,* 533–537.

Villarino, R. R., & Otero-López, J. M. (2001). [Review of the book *I shop therefore I am: Compulsive buying and the search for self*]. *Journal of Consumer Policy, 24,* 443–449.

Vincent, R. C. (1989). Clio's consciousness raised? The portrayal of women in rock videos reexamined. *Journalism Quarterly, 66,* 155–160.

Vincent, R. C., Davis, D. K., & Boruszkowski, L. A. (1987). Sexism on MTV: The portrayal of women in rock videos. *Journalism Quarterly, 64,* 750–755.

Voland, E., & Voland, R. (1989). Evolutionary biology and psychiatry: The case of anorexia nervosa. *Ethology and Sociobiology, 10,* 223–240.

Volberg, R. A. (1994). The prevalence and demographics of pathological gamblers: Implications for public health. *American Journal of Public Health, 84,* 237–241.

Volberg, R. A., & Abbott, M. W. (1994). Lifetime prevalence estimates of pathological gambling in New Zealand. *International Journal of Epidemiology, 23,* 976–983.

Volberg, R. A., Abbott, M. W., Rönnberg, S., & Munck, I. M. E. (2001). Prevalence and risks of pathological gambling in Sweden. *Acta Psychiatrica Scandinavica, 104,* 250–256.

Vyncke, P., Poels, K., & De Backer, C. (2003, June). *Maslow revisited: Towards a new motivation inventory based on evolutionary psychology.* Paper presented at the meeting of the Human Behavior and Evolution Society, Lincoln, NE.

Waller, G., Shaw, J., Hamilton, K., Baldwin, G., Harding, T., & Summer, A. (1994). Beauty is in the eye of the beholder: Media influences on the psychopathology of eating problems. *Appetite, 23,* 287.

Wallin, N. L., Merker, B., & Brown, S. (Eds.). (2000). *The origins of music.* Cambridge, MA: MIT Press.

Wang, J. H. (2000). "Everything's coming up Rosie": Empower America, Rosie O'Donnell, and the construction of daytime reality. *The Velvet Light Trap, 45,* 20–35.

Wang, X. T. (1996). Domain-specific rationality in human choices: Violations of utility axioms and social contexts. *Cognition, 60,* 31–63.

Ward, L. M. (2003). Understanding the role of entertainment media in the sexual socialization of American youth: A review of empirical research. *Developmental Review, 23,* 347–388.

Wasser, S. K., & Barash, D. P. (1983). Reproductive suppression among female mammals: Implications for biomedicine and sexual selection theory. *The Quarterly Review of Biology, 58,* 513–538.

Weaver, J. B., III, & Laird, E. A. (1995). Menstrual cycle through selective exposure to television. *Communication Quarterly, 72,* 139–146.

Weber, E. U., Blais, A.-R., & Betz, N. E. (2002). A domain-specific risk-attitude scale: Measuring risk perceptions and risk behaviors. *Journal of Behavioral Decision Making, 15,* 263–290.

Webster, G. D. (2003). Prosocial behavior in families: Moderators of resource sharing. *Journal of Experimental Social Psychology, 39,* 644–652.

Wee, C.-H., Choong, M.-L., & Tambyah, S.-K. (1995). Sex role portrayal in television advertising. *International Marketing Review, 12,* 49–64.

Weisfeld, G. (1999). *Evolutionary principles of human adolescence.* New York: BasicBooks.

Weitzer, R. (2000a). The politics of prostitution in America. In R. Weitzer (Ed.), *Sex for sale: Prostitution, pornography, and the sex industry* (pp. 159–180). New York: Routledge.

Weitzer, R. (2000b). Why we need more research on sex work. In R. Weitzer (Ed.), *Sex for sale: Prostitution, pornography, and the sex industry* (pp. 1–13). New York: Routledge.

Weller, L., & Weller, A. (1995). Menstrual synchrony: Agenda for future research. *Psychoneuroendocrinology, 20,* 377–383.

Welte, J. W., Barnes, G. M., Wieczorek, W. F., Tidwell, M.-C., & Parker, J. (2002). Gambling participation in the U.S.—results from a national survey. *Journal of Gambling Studies, 18,* 313–337.

Welte, J. W., Barnes, G. M., Wieczorek, W. F., Tidwell, M.-C. O., & Parker, J. C. (2004). Risk factors for pathological gambling. *Addictive Behaviors, 29,* 323–335.

Westen, D. (1997). Towards a clinically and empirically sound theory of motivation. *International Journal of Psycho-Analysis, 78,* 521–548.

Westermarck, E. (1891). *The history of human marriage.* New York: Macmillan.

Westman, A., & Marlowe, F. (1999). How universal are preferences for female waist-to-hip ratios? Evidence from the Hadza of Tanzania. *Evolution and Human Behavior, 20,* 219–228.

Wettlaufer, J. (2000). The *jus primae noctis* as a male power display: A review of historic sources with evolutionary interpretation. *Evolution and Human Behavior, 21,* 111–123.

Whipple, T. W., & Courtney, A. E. (1985). Female portrayals in advertising and communication effects: A review. *Journal of Advertising, 14,* 4–8, 17.

Whissell, C. (1996). Mate selection in popular women's fiction. *Human Nature, 7,* 427–447.

Whiten, A., & Byrne, R. W. (Eds.). (1997). *Machiavellian intelligence II: Extensions and evaluations.* Cambridge, England: Cambridge University Press.

Wiegmann, D. D., Mukhopadhyay, K., & Real, L. A. (1999). Sequential search and the influence of male quality on female mating decisions. *Journal of Mathematical Biology, 39,* 193–216.

Wilkie, W. L., & Moore, E. S. (2003). Scholarly research in marketing: Exploring the "4 eras" of thought development. *Journal of Public Policy & Marketing, 22,* 116–146.

Williams, C. T. (1994). Soap opera men in the '90s. *Journal of Popular Film & Television, 22,* 126–132.

Williams, G. C. (1966). *Adaptation and natural selection: A critique of some current evolutionary thought.* Princeton, NJ: Princeton University Press.

Williams, R. (2000). The business of memes: Memetic possibilities for marketing and management. *Management Decision, 38,* 272–279.

Williams, R. (2002). Memetics: A new paradigm for understanding customer behaviour? *Marketing Intelligence & Planning, 20,* 162–167.

Wilson, D. S. (2002). *Darwin's cathedral: Evolution, religion, and the nature of society.* Chicago: University of Chicago Press.

Wilson, D. S., Near, D., & Miller, R. R. (1996). Machiavellianism: A synthesis of the evolutionary and psychological literatures. *Psychological Bulletin, 199,* 285–299.

Wilson, E. O. (1975). *Sociobiology: A new synthesis.* Cambridge, MA: Belknap Press of Harvard University Press.

Wilson, E. O. (1998). *Consilience: The unity of knowledge.* London: Abacus.

Wilson, M., & Daly, M. (1985). Competitiveness, risk taking, and violence: The Young Male Syndrome. *Ethology and Sociobiology, 6,* 59–73.

Winterhalder, B., & Smith, E. A. (2000). Analyzing adaptive strategies: Human behavioral ecology at twenty-five. *Evolutionary Anthropology, 9,* 51–72.

Wolf, A. P. (1993). Westermarck redivivus. *Annual Review of Anthropology, 22,* 157–175.

Wolf, A. P. (1995). *Sexual attraction and childhood association: A Chinese brief for Edward Westermarck.* Stanford, CA: Stanford University Press.

Wolf, N. (1991). *The beauty myth: How images of beauty are used against women.* New York: Morrow.

Wong, I. L. K., & So, E. M. T. (2003). Prevalence estimates of problem and pathological gambling in Hong Kong. *American Journal of Psychiatry, 160,* 1353–1354.

Woo, H.-J., & Dominick, J. R. (2003). Acculturation, cultivation, and daytime TV talk shows. *Journalism and Mass Communication Quarterly, 80,* 109–127.

Wrangham, R., & Conklin-Brittain, N. L. (2003). "Cooking as a biological trait." *Comparative Biochemistry and Physiology Part A, 136,* 35–46.

Wyckham, R. G. (1993). Self-regulation of sex-role stereotyping: Educating the advertising industry. *Journal of Consumer Policy, 16,* 235–253.

Yamagishi, T., Tanida, S., Mashima, R., Shimoma, E., & Kanazawa, S. (2003). You can judge a book by its cover: Evidence that cheaters may look different from cooperators. *Evolution and Human Behavior, 24,* 290–301.

Zahavi, A. (1975). Mate selection: A selection for a handicap. *Journal of Theoretical Biology, 53,* 205–214.

Zahavi, A., & Zahavi, A. (1997). *The handicap principle: A missing piece of Darwin's puzzle.* New York: Oxford University Press.

Zajonc, R. B., & Mullally, P. R. (1997). Birth order: Reconciling conflicting effects. *American Psychologist, 52,* 685–699.

Zak, P. J., & Denzau, A. T. (2001). Economics is an evolutionary science. In S. A. Peterson & A. Somit (Eds.), *Evolutionary approaches in the behavioral sciences: Toward a better understanding of human nature—research in biopolitics* (Vol. 8, pp. 31–65). Greenwich, CT: JAI.

Zaltman, G. (2000). Consumer researchers: Take a hike! *Journal of Consumer Research, 26,* 423–428.

Zemanek, J. E., Claxton, R. P., & Zemanek, W. H. G. (2000). Relationship of birth order and the marketing related variable of materialism. *Psychological Reports, 86,* 429–434.

Zimmerman, T. S., Holm, K. E., Daniels, K. C., & Haddock, S. A. (2002). Barriers and bridges to intimacy and mutuality: A critical review of sexual advice found in self-help bestsellers. *Contemporary Family Therapy, 24,* 289–311.

Zimmerman, T. S., Holm, K. E., & Haddock, S. A. (2001). A decade of advice for women and men in the best-selling self-help literature. *Family Relations, 50,* 122–133.

Zimmerman, T. S., Holm, K. E., & Starrels, M. E. (2001). A feminist analysis of self-help bestsellers for improving relationships: A decade review. *Journal of Marital and Family Therapy, 27,* 165–175.

Zuckerman, M., & Kuhlman, D. M. (2000). Personality and risk-taking: Common biosocial factors. *Journal of Personality, 68,* 999–1029.

Zvoch, K. (1999). Family type and investment in education: A comparison of genetic and stepparent families. *Evolution and Human Behavior, 20,* 453–464.

Author Index

A

Aaker, D. A., 31
Aaker, J., 26
Abbey, A., 68
Abbott, M. W., 249
Abbott, S. A., 233, 234
ABC Research Group, 36, 37
Abeche, A. M., 9
Abed, R. T., 245, 261
Abrams, D., 137, 138
Abreu, J. M., 246, 249
Ackerman, A., 173
Ackreman, P. L., 195
Adelman, M. B., 59
Agrawal, M., 29, 152, 153
Aharon, I., 159, 253
Aiken, N. E., 217
Ajzen, I., 43
Akamatsu, S., 159
Albert, U., 263
Alcock, J., 3, 5
Alden, D. L., 154
Alexander, G. M., 70, 71
Allen, C. T., 21
Alon, A., 267
American Psychiatric Association, 236
Anderson, D. B., 195
Anderson, J. L., 245
Andrews, J. C., 28
Andrews, P. W., 7
Andsager, J., 196, 197
Andsager, J. L., 197
Angood, L. M., 239
Angst, J., 108
Ansic, D., 78
Antonides, G., 31
Apicella, C. L., 268

Aranyosi, E. F., 87
Ariely, D., 46, 159
Armstrong, E. G., 193, 194
Armstrong, J. S., 269
Aronson, J. A., 57
Artz, N., 19
Ashmore, R. D., 157, 158
Ashton, M. C., 51
Attour, S., 152
Aunger, R., 58, 167
Axelrod, R., 53

B

Babio, R., 246, 249
Bagwell, L. S., 87
Baker, M. J., 157
Baker, R., 62, 172
Baker, S. M., 88
Baldwin, G., 239, 240
Barak, A., 228, 230, 235
Barash, D. P., 31, 243
Bar-Cohen, Y., 57
Bar-Hillel, M., 253
Barkow, J. H., 7
Barlow, M., 146, 229
Barnes, G. M., 247, 248, 250
Baron, E., 252
Bartlett, M. Y., 48
Barton, C. M., 57
Bartsch, R. A., 149
Batten, M., 63
Baumeister, R. F., 114
Baumgartner, H., 49
Baxter, R. L., 196
Beatty, S. E., 33
Bechwati, N. N., 267
Becker, D. V., 38, 43, 59, 167

Subject Index

R

Radical scientific theories, xviii, 1, 110
Rationality
    bounded, 34, 37
    classical, 37
    ecological, 36–37
    Homo economicus, 31–32, 36, 46
    and maladaptive behaviors, 6
    normative, 36
    violations of, 32, 36
Reciprocity, 111–121
    amicable numbers and bonds of, 116
    friendship as a form of, 119–120
    indirect reciprocity, 111
    and marriage rituals, 112
    nonreciprocators, 117, see also Cheater
        detection
    reciprocal altruism, 4, 111, 117–118
    relationship marketing as a form of, 119,
        121
Recognition heuristic, 37
Religion
    as an adaptation, 212
    the Bible, 211
    and coalitional thinking, 212
    and consumption, 211
    as a costly signal, 212
    Darwinian modules in, 212–213
    eating disorders and, 243
    as an exaptation, 212–213
    gene–culture coevolution and, 213
    as a human universal, 211
    indulgences, purchase of, 211
    Jihad, 213
    Judaism, 13, 89–90, 211, 212
    as a memeplex, 212
    Mormons, 106
    Pascal's wager, 214
    religiosity as a form of risk aversiveness,
        214
    as a segmentation variable, 211
    Shariah law, 13
Reproductive fitness, 10, 12
    and despotic rule, 187–188
    and high-status males, 187
    in songs, 193
Risk taking
    in athletic and/or physical activities, 78,
        80–84
    in financial investments, 78–79
Rites of passage
    and fraternities and sororities, 81
    hazing as a, 81
    male, 131
    N'Gol ritual, 81–82

S

Savanna principle, 269, 270
Selection, types/levels of, 3
    among organism, xiii, 6, 47
    emotional, 167
    group, 3–4, 85, 90, 94, 212, 215
    kin, see Kin selection
    Lamarckian, 168
    natural, xiii, 2, 3–4, 166, 168, 212
    runaway, 167
    sexual, 2, 85, 87, 165, 185, 215
    universal selectionism, xiii–xiv, 37
    within organism, xiii, 6, 35, 47
Selectivity hypothesis, 66, 138
    in financial decision making, 78–79
    and the savanna principle, 270
Self-deception
    evolution of, 172–173
    Machiavellian intent, 172
    on *Seinfeld*, *American Idol*, and *WB Super-
        stars USA*, 173
Self-help books
    Atkins diet, 202
    Carnegie, Dale, 203
    codependency syndrome in, 251
    Darwinian modules/themes in, 202–204,
        206
    Dr. Spock/parenting, 202–203
    feminist outlook on, 206–210
    government control via, 205–206
    intimacy and mutuality in, 209
    mating preferences in, 207, 208, 209, 210
    and menopause, 204–205
    and mental health therapy, 206
    Robbins, Anthony, 203
    and the SSSM, 206, 208
    therapeutic value of, 204
    unsubstantiated claims in, 204, 206
Self schema theory, 138
Semantic schizophrenia, 135
Senescence, 205, 225
Sex differences
    in advertised products, 149
    in aggregate consumption patterns, 69–70
    in attitudes toward money, 79
    in attitudes toward paternity testing, 44
    in compulsive buying, 256–257
    in cosmetic and plastic surgeries, 71–72
    in criminality, 214, 226
    in delay gratification, 78
    in eating disorders, 236, 241
    in the encoding, recognition, and recall of
        beautiful people, 43
    in erotomania, 223
    in ethical behavior, 79